GCC 6.1 GNAT Reference Manual

A catalogue record for this book is available from the Hong Kong Public Libraries.

Published in Hong Kong by Samurai Media Limited.

Email: info@samuraimedia.org

ISBN 978-988-8406-37-1

Table of Contents

1 About This Guide 2

1.1 What This Reference Manual Contains 2
1.2 Conventions 3
1.3 Related Information 3

2 Implementation Defined Pragmas 5

2.1 Pragma Abort_Defer 5
2.2 Pragma Abstract_State 5
2.3 Pragma Ada_83 6
2.4 Pragma Ada_95 6
2.5 Pragma Ada_05 7
2.6 Pragma Ada_2005 7
2.7 Pragma Ada_12 7
2.8 Pragma Ada_2012 7
2.9 Pragma Allow_Integer_Address 8
2.10 Pragma Annotate 8
2.11 Pragma Assert 9
2.12 Pragma Assert_And_Cut 10
2.13 Pragma Assertion_Policy 10
2.14 Pragma Assume 11
2.15 Pragma Assume_No_Invalid_Values 12
2.16 Pragma Async_Readers 12
2.17 Pragma Async_Writers 13
2.18 Pragma Attribute_Definition 13
2.19 Pragma C_Pass_By_Copy 13
2.20 Pragma Check 13
2.21 Pragma Check_Float_Overflow 14
2.22 Pragma Check_Name 15
2.23 Pragma Check_Policy 15
2.24 Pragma Comment 16
2.25 Pragma Common_Object 16
2.26 Pragma Compile_Time_Error 17
2.27 Pragma Compile_Time_Warning 17
2.28 Pragma Compiler_Unit 17
2.29 Pragma Compiler_Unit_Warning 18
2.30 Pragma Complete_Representation 18
2.31 Pragma Complex_Representation 18
2.32 Pragma Component_Alignment 18
2.33 Pragma Constant_After_Elaboration 19
2.34 Pragma Contract_Cases 19
2.35 Pragma Convention_Identifier 21
2.36 Pragma CPP_Class 21
2.37 Pragma CPP_Constructor 21

2.38 Pragma CPP_Virtual 22
2.39 Pragma CPP_Vtable 22
2.40 Pragma CPU 22
2.41 Pragma Default_Initial_Condition 23
2.42 Pragma Debug 23
2.43 Pragma Debug_Policy 23
2.44 Pragma Default_Scalar_Storage_Order 23
2.45 Pragma Default_Storage_Pool 24
2.46 Pragma Depends 25
2.47 Pragma Detect_Blocking 25
2.48 Pragma Disable_Atomic_Synchronization 25
2.49 Pragma Dispatching_Domain 26
2.50 Pragma Effective_Reads 26
2.51 Pragma Effective_Writes 26
2.52 Pragma Elaboration_Checks 26
2.53 Pragma Eliminate 26
2.54 Pragma Enable_Atomic_Synchronization 27
2.55 Pragma Export_Function 28
2.56 Pragma Export_Object 29
2.57 Pragma Export_Procedure 29
2.58 Pragma Export_Value 30
2.59 Pragma Export_Valued_Procedure 30
2.60 Pragma Extend_System 31
2.61 Pragma Extensions_Allowed 32
2.62 Pragma Extensions_Visible 32
2.63 Pragma External 32
2.64 Pragma External_Name_Casing 33
2.65 Pragma Fast_Math 34
2.66 Pragma Favor_Top_Level 34
2.67 Pragma Finalize_Storage_Only 34
2.68 Pragma Float_Representation 34
2.69 Pragma Ghost 35
2.70 Pragma Global 35
2.71 Pragma Ident 35
2.72 Pragma Ignore_Pragma 35
2.73 Pragma Implementation_Defined 36
2.74 Pragma Implemented 36
2.75 Pragma Implicit_Packing 37
2.76 Pragma Import_Function 37
2.77 Pragma Import_Object 38
2.78 Pragma Import_Procedure 39
2.79 Pragma Import_Valued_Procedure 39
2.80 Pragma Independent 40
2.81 Pragma Independent_Components 41
2.82 Pragma Initial_Condition 41
2.83 Pragma Initialize_Scalars 41
2.84 Pragma Initializes 42
2.85 Pragma Inline_Always 42

2.86 Pragma Inline_Generic 42
2.87 Pragma Interface 43
2.88 Pragma Interface_Name 43
2.89 Pragma Interrupt_Handler 43
2.90 Pragma Interrupt_State 43
2.91 Pragma Invariant 45
2.92 Pragma Keep_Names 45
2.93 Pragma License 45
2.94 Pragma Link_With 47
2.95 Pragma Linker_Alias 47
2.96 Pragma Linker_Constructor 47
2.97 Pragma Linker_Destructor 48
2.98 Pragma Linker_Section 48
2.99 Pragma Lock_Free 49
2.100 Pragma Loop_Invariant 49
2.101 Pragma Loop_Optimize 50
2.102 Pragma Loop_Variant 50
2.103 Pragma Machine_Attribute 51
2.104 Pragma Main 51
2.105 Pragma Main_Storage 52
2.106 Pragma No_Body 52
2.107 Pragma No_Elaboration_Code_All 52
2.108 Pragma No_Inline 52
2.109 Pragma No_Return 53
2.110 Pragma No_Run_Time 53
2.111 Pragma No_Strict_Aliasing 53
2.112 Pragma No_Tagged_Streams 54
2.113 Pragma Normalize_Scalars 54
2.114 Pragma Obsolescent 55
2.115 Pragma Optimize_Alignment 57
2.116 Pragma Ordered 58
2.117 Pragma Overflow_Mode 59
2.118 Pragma Overriding_Renamings 60
2.119 Pragma Partition_Elaboration_Policy 60
2.120 Pragma Part_Of 60
2.121 Pragma Passive 60
2.122 Pragma Persistent_BSS 61
2.123 Pragma Polling 61
2.124 Pragma Post 62
2.125 Pragma Postcondition 62
2.126 Pragma Post_Class 64
2.127 Pragma Pre 64
2.128 Pragma Precondition 65
2.129 Pragma Predicate 65
2.130 Pragma Predicate_Failure 66
2.131 Pragma Preelaborable_Initialization 66
2.132 Pragma Prefix_Exception_Messages 66
2.133 Pragma Pre_Class 67

2.134 Pragma Priority_Specific_Dispatching 67
2.135 Pragma Profile 67
2.136 Pragma Profile_Warnings 70
2.137 Pragma Propagate_Exceptions 70
2.138 Pragma Provide_Shift_Operators 70
2.139 Pragma Psect_Object 71
2.140 Pragma Pure_Function 71
2.141 Pragma Rational 72
2.142 Pragma Ravenscar 72
2.143 Pragma Refined_Depends 72
2.144 Pragma Refined_Global 73
2.145 Pragma Refined_Post 73
2.146 Pragma Refined_State 73
2.147 Pragma Relative_Deadline 74
2.148 Pragma Remote_Access_Type 74
2.149 Pragma Restricted_Run_Time 74
2.150 Pragma Restriction_Warnings 74
2.151 Pragma Reviewable 75
2.152 Pragma Share_Generic 76
2.153 Pragma Shared 76
2.154 Pragma Short_Circuit_And_Or 76
2.155 Pragma Short_Descriptors 76
2.156 Pragma Simple_Storage_Pool_Type 76
2.157 Pragma Source_File_Name 77
2.158 Pragma Source_File_Name_Project 79
2.159 Pragma Source_Reference 79
2.160 Pragma SPARK_Mode 79
2.161 Pragma Static_Elaboration_Desired 80
2.162 Pragma Stream_Convert 81
2.163 Pragma Style_Checks 82
2.164 Pragma Subtitle 83
2.165 Pragma Suppress 83
2.166 Pragma Suppress_All 84
2.167 Pragma Suppress_Debug_Info 84
2.168 Pragma Suppress_Exception_Locations 84
2.169 Pragma Suppress_Initialization 84
2.170 Pragma Task_Name 85
2.171 Pragma Task_Storage 86
2.172 Pragma Test_Case 86
2.173 Pragma Thread_Local_Storage 87
2.174 Pragma Time_Slice 87
2.175 Pragma Title 87
2.176 Pragma Type_Invariant 88
2.177 Pragma Type_Invariant_Class 88
2.178 Pragma Unchecked_Union 88
2.179 Pragma Unevaluated_Use_Of_Old 88
2.180 Pragma Unimplemented_Unit 89
2.181 Pragma Universal_Aliasing 89

2.182 Pragma Universal_Data 90
2.183 Pragma Unmodified 90
2.184 Pragma Unreferenced 90
2.185 Pragma Unreferenced_Objects 91
2.186 Pragma Unreserve_All_Interrupts 91
2.187 Pragma Unsuppress 92
2.188 Pragma Use_VADS_Size 92
2.189 Pragma Validity_Checks 92
2.190 Pragma Volatile 93
2.191 Pragma Volatile_Full_Access 93
2.192 Pragma Volatile_Function 94
2.193 Pragma Warning_As_Error 94
2.194 Pragma Warnings 95
2.195 Pragma Weak_External 97
2.196 Pragma Wide_Character_Encoding 98

3 Implementation Defined Aspects 99

3.1 Aspect Abstract_State 99
3.2 Annotate 99
3.3 Aspect Async_Readers 100
3.4 Aspect Async_Writers 100
3.5 Aspect Constant_After_Elaboration 100
3.6 Aspect Contract_Cases 100
3.7 Aspect Depends 100
3.8 Aspect Default_Initial_Condition 100
3.9 Aspect Dimension 100
3.10 Aspect Dimension_System 101
3.11 Aspect Disable_Controlled 101
3.12 Aspect Effective_Reads 102
3.13 Aspect Effective_Writes 102
3.14 Aspect Extensions_Visible 102
3.15 Aspect Favor_Top_Level 102
3.16 Aspect Ghost 102
3.17 Aspect Global 102
3.18 Aspect Initial_Condition 102
3.19 Aspect Initializes 102
3.20 Aspect Inline_Always 102
3.21 Aspect Invariant 102
3.22 Aspect Invariant'Class 102
3.23 Aspect Iterable 102
3.24 Aspect Linker_Section 103
3.25 Aspect Lock_Free 103
3.26 Aspect No_Elaboration_Code_All 103
3.27 Aspect No_Tagged_Streams 103
3.28 Aspect Object_Size 103
3.29 Aspect Obsolescent 104
3.30 Aspect Part_Of 104
3.31 Aspect Persistent_BSS 104

3.32 Aspect Predicate 104
3.33 Aspect Pure_Function 104
3.34 Aspect Refined_Depends 104
3.35 Aspect Refined_Global 104
3.36 Aspect Refined_Post 104
3.37 Aspect Refined_State 104
3.38 Aspect Remote_Access_Type 104
3.39 Aspect Scalar_Storage_Order 104
3.40 Aspect Shared 104
3.41 Aspect Simple_Storage_Pool 105
3.42 Aspect Simple_Storage_Pool_Type 105
3.43 Aspect SPARK_Mode 105
3.44 Aspect Suppress_Debug_Info 105
3.45 Aspect Suppress_Initialization 105
3.46 Aspect Test_Case 105
3.47 Aspect Thread_Local_Storage 105
3.48 Aspect Universal_Aliasing 105
3.49 Aspect Universal_Data 105
3.50 Aspect Unmodified 105
3.51 Aspect Unreferenced 105
3.52 Aspect Unreferenced_Objects 105
3.53 Aspect Value_Size 105
3.54 Aspect Volatile_Full_Access 106
3.55 Aspect Volatile_Function 106
3.56 Aspect Warnings 106

4 Implementation Defined Attributes 107

4.1 Attribute Abort_Signal 107
4.2 Attribute Address_Size 107
4.3 Attribute Asm_Input 107
4.4 Attribute Asm_Output 107
4.5 Attribute Atomic_Always_Lock_Free 108
4.6 Attribute Bit 108
4.7 Attribute Bit_Position 108
4.8 Attribute Code_Address 108
4.9 Attribute Compiler_Version 109
4.10 Attribute Constrained 109
4.11 Attribute Default_Bit_Order 109
4.12 Attribute Default_Scalar_Storage_Order 109
4.13 Attribute Deref 109
4.14 Attribute Descriptor_Size 109
4.15 Attribute Elaborated 110
4.16 Attribute Elab_Body 110
4.17 Attribute Elab_Spec 110
4.18 Attribute Elab_Subp_Body 110
4.19 Attribute Emax 110
4.20 Attribute Enabled 110
4.21 Attribute Enum_Rep 111

4.22 Attribute Enum_Val 111
4.23 Attribute Epsilon 111
4.24 Attribute Fast_Math 111
4.25 Attribute Fixed_Value 112
4.26 Attribute From_Any 112
4.27 Attribute Has_Access_Values 112
4.28 Attribute Has_Discriminants 112
4.29 Attribute Img 112
4.30 Attribute Integer_Value 113
4.31 Attribute Invalid_Value 113
4.32 Attribute Iterable 113
4.33 Attribute Large 113
4.34 Attribute Library_Level 113
4.35 Attribute Lock_Free 113
4.36 Attribute Loop_Entry 114
4.37 Attribute Machine_Size 114
4.38 Attribute Mantissa 114
4.39 Attribute Maximum_Alignment 114
4.40 Attribute Mechanism_Code 114
4.41 Attribute Null_Parameter 114
4.42 Attribute Object_Size 115
4.43 Attribute Old 116
4.44 Attribute Passed_By_Reference 116
4.45 Attribute Pool_Address 116
4.46 Attribute Range_Length 116
4.47 Attribute Restriction_Set 116
4.48 Attribute Result 117
4.49 Attribute Safe_Emax 117
4.50 Attribute Safe_Large 117
4.51 Attribute Safe_Small 118
4.52 Attribute Scalar_Storage_Order 118
4.53 Attribute Simple_Storage_Pool 119
4.54 Attribute Small 120
4.55 Attribute Storage_Unit 120
4.56 Attribute Stub_Type 120
4.57 Attribute System_Allocator_Alignment 121
4.58 Attribute Target_Name 121
4.59 Attribute To_Address 121
4.60 Attribute To_Any 121
4.61 Attribute Type_Class 121
4.62 Attribute Type_Key 122
4.63 Attribute TypeCode 122
4.64 Attribute Unconstrained_Array 122
4.65 Attribute Universal_Literal_String 122
4.66 Attribute Unrestricted_Access 122
4.67 Attribute Update 125
4.68 Attribute Valid_Scalars 126
4.69 Attribute VADS_Size 127

4.70 Attribute Value_Size 127
4.71 Attribute Wchar_T_Size 127
4.72 Attribute Word_Size 127

5 Standard and Implementation Defined Restrictions 128

5.1 Partition-Wide Restrictions 128
5.1.1 Immediate_Reclamation 128
5.1.2 Max_Asynchronous_Select_Nesting 128
5.1.3 Max_Entry_Queue_Length 128
5.1.4 Max_Protected_Entries 128
5.1.5 Max_Select_Alternatives 128
5.1.6 Max_Storage_At_Blocking 129
5.1.7 Max_Task_Entries 129
5.1.8 Max_Tasks 129
5.1.9 No_Abort_Statements 129
5.1.10 No_Access_Parameter_Allocators 129
5.1.11 No_Access_Subprograms 129
5.1.12 No_Allocators 129
5.1.13 No_Anonymous_Allocators 129
5.1.14 No_Asynchronous_Control 129
5.1.15 No_Calendar 129
5.1.16 No_Coextensions 129
5.1.17 No_Default_Initialization 130
5.1.18 No_Delay 130
5.1.19 No_Dependence 130
5.1.20 No_Direct_Boolean_Operators 130
5.1.21 No_Dispatch 130
5.1.22 No_Dispatching_Calls 130
5.1.23 No_Dynamic_Attachment 131
5.1.24 No_Dynamic_Priorities 131
5.1.25 No_Entry_Calls_In_Elaboration_Code 131
5.1.26 No_Enumeration_Maps 132
5.1.27 No_Exception_Handlers 132
5.1.28 No_Exception_Propagation 132
5.1.29 No_Exception_Registration 132
5.1.30 No_Exceptions 132
5.1.31 No_Finalization 132
5.1.32 No_Fixed_Point 133
5.1.33 No_Floating_Point 133
5.1.34 No_Implicit_Conditionals 133
5.1.35 No_Implicit_Dynamic_Code 133
5.1.36 No_Implicit_Heap_Allocations 133
5.1.37 No_Implicit_Loops 134
5.1.38 No_Implicit_Protected_Object_Allocations 134
5.1.39 No_Implicit_Task_Allocations 134
5.1.40 No_Initialize_Scalars 134
5.1.41 No_IO 134

5.1.42 No_Local_Allocators ... 134
5.1.43 No_Local_Protected_Objects ... 134
5.1.44 No_Local_Timing_Events ... 134
5.1.45 No_Long_Long_Integers ... 134
5.1.46 No_Multiple_Elaboration ... 134
5.1.47 No_Nested_Finalization ... 135
5.1.48 No_Protected_Type_Allocators ... 135
5.1.49 No_Protected_Types ... 135
5.1.50 No_Recursion ... 135
5.1.51 No_Reentrancy ... 135
5.1.52 No_Relative_Delay ... 135
5.1.53 No_Requeue_Statements ... 135
5.1.54 No_Secondary_Stack ... 135
5.1.55 No_Select_Statements ... 135
5.1.56 No_Specific_Termination_Handlers ... 136
5.1.57 No_Specification_of_Aspect ... 136
5.1.58 No_Standard_Allocators_After_Elaboration ... 136
5.1.59 No_Standard_Storage_Pools ... 136
5.1.60 No_Stream_Optimizations ... 136
5.1.61 No_Streams ... 136
5.1.62 No_Task_Allocators ... 136
5.1.63 No_Task_At_Interrupt_Priority ... 136
5.1.64 No_Task_Attributes_Package ... 136
5.1.65 No_Task_Hierarchy ... 137
5.1.66 No_Task_Termination ... 137
5.1.67 No_Tasking ... 137
5.1.68 No_Terminate_Alternatives ... 137
5.1.69 No_Unchecked_Access ... 137
5.1.70 No_Unchecked_Conversion ... 137
5.1.71 No_Unchecked_Deallocation ... 137
5.1.72 No_Use_Of_Entity ... 137
5.1.73 Pure_Barriers ... 137
5.1.74 Simple_Barriers ... 138
5.1.75 Static_Priorities ... 138
5.1.76 Static_Storage_Size ... 138
5.2 Program Unit Level Restrictions ... 138
5.2.1 No_Elaboration_Code ... 138
5.2.2 No_Dynamic_Sized_Objects ... 139
5.2.3 No_Entry_Queue ... 139
5.2.4 No_Implementation_Aspect_Specifications ... 139
5.2.5 No_Implementation_Attributes ... 139
5.2.6 No_Implementation_Identifiers ... 140
5.2.7 No_Implementation_Pragmas ... 140
5.2.8 No_Implementation_Restrictions ... 140
5.2.9 No_Implementation_Units ... 140
5.2.10 No_Implicit_Aliasing ... 140
5.2.11 No_Obsolescent_Features ... 140
5.2.12 No_Wide_Characters ... 140

5.2.13 SPARK_05 140

6 Implementation Advice 145

6.1 RM 1.1.3(20): Error Detection 145
6.2 RM 1.1.3(31): Child Units 145
6.3 RM 1.1.5(12): Bounded Errors 145
6.4 RM 2.8(16): Pragmas 145
6.5 RM 2.8(17-19): Pragmas 146
6.6 RM 3.5.2(5): Alternative Character Sets 146
6.7 RM 3.5.4(28): Integer Types 147
6.8 RM 3.5.4(29): Integer Types 147
6.9 RM 3.5.5(8): Enumeration Values 147
6.10 RM 3.5.7(17): Float Types 147
6.11 RM 3.6.2(11): Multidimensional Arrays 148
6.12 RM 9.6(30-31): Duration'Small 148
6.13 RM 10.2.1(12): Consistent Representation 148
6.14 RM 11.4.1(19): Exception Information 148
6.15 RM 11.5(28): Suppression of Checks 149
6.16 RM 13.1 (21-24): Representation Clauses 149
6.17 RM 13.2(6-8): Packed Types 149
6.18 RM 13.3(14-19): Address Clauses 150
6.19 RM 13.3(29-35): Alignment Clauses 150
6.20 RM 13.3(42-43): Size Clauses 151
6.21 RM 13.3(50-56): Size Clauses 151
6.22 RM 13.3(71-73): Component Size Clauses 152
6.23 RM 13.4(9-10): Enumeration Representation Clauses 152
6.24 RM 13.5.1(17-22): Record Representation Clauses 152
6.25 RM 13.5.2(5): Storage Place Attributes 153
6.26 RM 13.5.3(7-8): Bit Ordering 153
6.27 RM 13.7(37): Address as Private 153
6.28 RM 13.7.1(16): Address Operations 153
6.29 RM 13.9(14-17): Unchecked Conversion 153
6.30 RM 13.11(23-25): Implicit Heap Usage 154
6.31 RM 13.11.2(17): Unchecked Deallocation 154
6.32 RM 13.13.2(17): Stream Oriented Attributes 154
6.33 RM A.1(52): Names of Predefined Numeric Types 155
6.34 RM A.3.2(49): *Ada.Characters.Handling* 155
6.35 RM A.4.4(106): Bounded-Length String Handling 155
6.36 RM A.5.2(46-47): Random Number Generation 155
6.37 RM A.10.7(23): *Get_Immediate* 156
6.38 RM B.1(39-41): Pragma *Export* 156
6.39 RM B.2(12-13): Package *Interfaces* 156
6.40 RM B.3(63-71): Interfacing with C 157
6.41 RM B.4(95-98): Interfacing with COBOL 158
6.42 RM B.5(22-26): Interfacing with Fortran 158
6.43 RM C.1(3-5): Access to Machine Operations 159
6.44 RM C.1(10-16): Access to Machine Operations 159
6.45 RM C.3(28): Interrupt Support 160

6.46 RM C.3.1(20-21): Protected Procedure Handlers 160
6.47 RM C.3.2(25): Package *Interrupts* 160
6.48 RM C.4(14): Pre-elaboration Requirements 160
6.49 RM C.5(8): Pragma *Discard_Names* 160
6.50 RM C.7.2(30): The Package Task_Attributes 160
6.51 RM D.3(17): Locking Policies 161
6.52 RM D.4(16): Entry Queuing Policies 161
6.53 RM D.6(9-10): Preemptive Abort 161
6.54 RM D.7(21): Tasking Restrictions 161
6.55 RM D.8(47-49): Monotonic Time 161
6.56 RM E.5(28-29): Partition Communication Subsystem 162
6.57 RM F(7): COBOL Support 162
6.58 RM F.1(2): Decimal Radix Support 162
6.59 RM G: Numerics 162
6.60 RM G.1.1(56-58): Complex Types 162
6.61 RM G.1.2(49): Complex Elementary Functions 163
6.62 RM G.2.4(19): Accuracy Requirements 164
6.63 RM G.2.6(15): Complex Arithmetic Accuracy 164
6.64 RM H.6(15/2): Pragma Partition_Elaboration_Policy 164

7 Implementation Defined Characteristics ... 165

8 Intrinsic Subprograms 182

8.1 Intrinsic Operators 182
8.2 Compilation_Date 182
8.3 Compilation_Time 182
8.4 Enclosing_Entity 183
8.5 Exception_Information 183
8.6 Exception_Message 183
8.7 Exception_Name 183
8.8 File 183
8.9 Line 183
8.10 Shifts and Rotates 183
8.11 Source_Location 184

9 Representation Clauses and Pragmas 185

9.1 Alignment Clauses 185
9.2 Size Clauses 186
9.3 Storage_Size Clauses 187
9.4 Size of Variant Record Objects 188
9.5 Biased Representation 190
9.6 Value_Size and Object_Size Clauses 190
9.7 Component_Size Clauses 193
9.8 Bit_Order Clauses 194
9.9 Effect of Bit_Order on Byte Ordering 195
9.10 Pragma Pack for Arrays 199
9.11 Pragma Pack for Records 201

9.12 Record Representation Clauses 202
9.13 Handling of Records with Holes 203
9.14 Enumeration Clauses 204
9.15 Address Clauses 205
9.16 Use of Address Clauses for Memory-Mapped I/O 209
9.17 Effect of Convention on Representation 210
9.18 Conventions and Anonymous Access Types 211
9.19 Determining the Representations chosen by GNAT 212

10 Standard Library Routines 216

11 The Implementation of Standard I/O 227

11.1 Standard I/O Packages 227
11.2 FORM Strings 228
11.3 Direct_IO 228
11.4 Sequential_IO 228
11.5 Text_IO 229
11.5.1 Stream Pointer Positioning 230
11.5.2 Reading and Writing Non-Regular Files 230
11.5.3 Get_Immediate 231
11.5.4 Treating Text_IO Files as Streams 231
11.5.5 Text_IO Extensions 231
11.5.6 Text_IO Facilities for Unbounded Strings 231
11.6 Wide_Text_IO 232
11.6.1 Stream Pointer Positioning 234
11.6.2 Reading and Writing Non-Regular Files 234
11.7 Wide_Wide_Text_IO 235
11.7.1 Stream Pointer Positioning 236
11.7.2 Reading and Writing Non-Regular Files 236
11.8 Stream_IO 236
11.9 Text Translation 237
11.10 Shared Files 237
11.11 Filenames encoding 238
11.12 File content encoding 238
11.13 Open Modes 239
11.14 Operations on C Streams 239
11.15 Interfacing to C Streams 242

12 The GNAT Library 245

12.1 *Ada.Characters.Latin_9* (a-chlat9.ads) 245
12.2 *Ada.Characters.Wide_Latin_1* (a-cwila1.ads) 245
12.3 *Ada.Characters.Wide_Latin_9* (a-cwila1.ads) 245
12.4 *Ada.Characters.Wide_Wide_Latin_1* (a-chzla1.ads) 246
12.5 *Ada.Characters.Wide_Wide_Latin_9* (a-chzla9.ads) 246
12.6 *Ada.Containers.Formal_Doubly_Linked_Lists* (a-cfdlli.ads) 246
12.7 *Ada.Containers.Formal_Hashed_Maps* (a-cfhama.ads) 246
12.8 *Ada.Containers.Formal_Hashed_Sets* (a-cfhase.ads) 246
12.9 *Ada.Containers.Formal_Ordered_Maps* (a-cforma.ads) 247
12.10 *Ada.Containers.Formal_Ordered_Sets* (a-cforse.ads) 247
12.11 *Ada.Containers.Formal_Vectors* (a-cofove.ads) 247
12.12 *Ada.Containers.Formal_Indefinite_Vectors* (a-cfinve.ads) 247
12.13 *Ada.Containers.Bounded_Holders* (a-coboho.ads) 247
12.14 *Ada.Command_Line.Environment* (a-colien.ads) 248
12.15 *Ada.Command_Line.Remove* (a-colire.ads) 248
12.16 *Ada.Command_Line.Response_File* (a-clrefi.ads) 248
12.17 *Ada.Direct_IO.C_Streams* (a-diocst.ads) 248
12.18 *Ada.Exceptions.Is_Null_Occurrence* (a-einuoc.ads) 248
12.19 *Ada.Exceptions.Last_Chance_Handler* (a-elchha.ads) 248
12.20 *Ada.Exceptions.Traceback* (a-exctra.ads) 248
12.21 *Ada.Sequential_IO.C_Streams* (a-siocst.ads) 248
12.22 *Ada.Streams.Stream_IO.C_Streams* (a-ssicst.ads) 248
12.23 *Ada.Strings.Unbounded.Text_IO* (a-suteio.ads) 249
12.24 *Ada.Strings.Wide_Unbounded.Wide_Text_IO* (a-swuwti.ads) 249
12.25 *Ada.Strings.Wide_Wide_Unbounded.Wide_Wide_Text_IO* (a-szuzti.ads) 249
12.26 *Ada.Text_IO.C_Streams* (a-tiocst.ads) 249
12.27 *Ada.Text_IO.Reset_Standard_Files* (a-tirsfi.ads) 249
12.28 *Ada.Wide_Characters.Unicode* (a-wichun.ads) 249
12.29 *Ada.Wide_Text_IO.C_Streams* (a-wtcstr.ads) 249
12.30 *Ada.Wide_Text_IO.Reset_Standard_Files* (a-wrstfi.ads) .. 249
12.31 *Ada.Wide_Wide_Characters.Unicode* (a-zchuni.ads) 250
12.32 *Ada.Wide_Wide_Text_IO.C_Streams* (a-ztcstr.ads) 250
12.33 *Ada.Wide_Wide_Text_IO.Reset_Standard_Files* (a-zrstfi.ads) 250
12.34 *GNAT.Altivec* (g-altive.ads) 250
12.35 *GNAT.Altivec.Conversions* (g-altcon.ads) 250
12.36 *GNAT.Altivec.Vector_Operations* (g-alveop.ads) 250
12.37 *GNAT.Altivec.Vector_Types* (g-alvety.ads) 250
12.38 *GNAT.Altivec.Vector_Views* (g-alvevi.ads) 250
12.39 *GNAT.Array_Split* (g-arrspl.ads) 250
12.40 *GNAT.AWK* (g-awk.ads) 251
12.41 *GNAT.Bind_Environment* (g-binenv.ads) 251
12.42 *GNAT.Bounded_Buffers* (g-boubuf.ads) 251

12.43 GNAT.Bounded_Mailboxes (g-boumai.ads) 251
12.44 GNAT.Bubble_Sort (g-bubsor.ads) 251
12.45 GNAT.Bubble_Sort_A (g-busora.ads) 251
12.46 GNAT.Bubble_Sort_G (g-busorg.ads) 251
12.47 GNAT.Byte_Order_Mark (g-byorma.ads) 251
12.48 GNAT.Byte_Swapping (g-bytswa.ads) 251
12.49 GNAT.Calendar (g-calend.ads) 252
12.50 GNAT.Calendar.Time_IO (g-catiio.ads) 252
12.51 GNAT.CRC32 (g-crc32.ads) 252
12.52 GNAT.Case_Util (g-casuti.ads) 252
12.53 GNAT.CGI (g-cgi.ads) 252
12.54 GNAT.CGI.Cookie (g-cgicoo.ads) 252
12.55 GNAT.CGI.Debug (g-cgideb.ads) 252
12.56 GNAT.Command_Line (g-comlin.ads) 252
12.57 GNAT.Compiler_Version (g-comver.ads) 252
12.58 GNAT.Ctrl_C (g-ctrl_c.ads) 253
12.59 GNAT.Current_Exception (g-curexc.ads) 253
12.60 GNAT.Debug_Pools (g-debpoo.ads) 253
12.61 GNAT.Debug_Utilities (g-debuti.ads) 253
12.62 GNAT.Decode_String (g-decstr.ads) 253
12.63 GNAT.Decode_UTF8_String (g-deutst.ads) 253
12.64 GNAT.Directory_Operations (g-dirope.ads) 253
12.65 GNAT.Directory_Operations.Iteration (g-diopit.ads) 253
12.66 GNAT.Dynamic_HTables (g-dynhta.ads) 253
12.67 GNAT.Dynamic_Tables (g-dyntab.ads) 254
12.68 GNAT.Encode_String (g-encstr.ads) 254
12.69 GNAT.Encode_UTF8_String (g-enutst.ads) 254
12.70 GNAT.Exception_Actions (g-excact.ads) 254
12.71 GNAT.Exception_Traces (g-exctra.ads) 254
12.72 GNAT.Exceptions (g-expect.ads) 254
12.73 GNAT.Expect (g-expect.ads) 254
12.74 GNAT.Expect.TTY (g-exptty.ads) 254
12.75 GNAT.Float_Control (g-flocon.ads) 255
12.76 GNAT.Formatted_String (g-forstr.ads) 255
12.77 GNAT.Heap_Sort (g-heasor.ads) 255
12.78 GNAT.Heap_Sort_A (g-hesora.ads) 255
12.79 GNAT.Heap_Sort_G (g-hesorg.ads) 255
12.80 GNAT.HTable (g-htable.ads) 255
12.81 GNAT.IO (g-io.ads) 255
12.82 GNAT.IO_Aux (g-io_aux.ads) 255
12.83 GNAT.Lock_Files (g-locfil.ads) 256
12.84 GNAT.MBBS_Discrete_Random (g-mbdira.ads) 256
12.85 GNAT.MBBS_Float_Random (g-mbflra.ads) 256
12.86 GNAT.MD5 (g-md5.ads) 256
12.87 GNAT.Memory_Dump (g-memdum.ads) 256
12.88 GNAT.Most_Recent_Exception (g-moreex.ads) 256
12.89 GNAT.OS_Lib (g-os_lib.ads) 256
12.90 GNAT.Perfect_Hash_Generators (g-pehage.ads) 256

12.91 *GNAT.Random_Numbers* (g-rannum.ads) 256
12.92 *GNAT.Regexp* (g-regexp.ads) 257
12.93 *GNAT.Registry* (g-regist.ads) 257
12.94 *GNAT.Regpat* (g-regpat.ads) 257
12.95 *GNAT.Rewrite_Data* (g-rewdat.ads) 257
12.96 *GNAT.Secondary_Stack_Info* (g-sestin.ads) 257
12.97 *GNAT.Semaphores* (g-semaph.ads) 257
12.98 *GNAT.Serial_Communications* (g-sercom.ads) 257
12.99 *GNAT.SHA1* (g-sha1.ads) 257
12.100 *GNAT.SHA224* (g-sha224.ads) 257
12.101 *GNAT.SHA256* (g-sha256.ads) 258
12.102 *GNAT.SHA384* (g-sha384.ads) 258
12.103 *GNAT.SHA512* (g-sha512.ads) 258
12.104 *GNAT.Signals* (g-signal.ads) 258
12.105 *GNAT.Sockets* (g-socket.ads) 258
12.106 *GNAT.Source_Info* (g-souinf.ads) 258
12.107 *GNAT.Spelling_Checker* (g-speche.ads) 258
12.108 *GNAT.Spelling_Checker_Generic* (g-spchge.ads) 258
12.109 *GNAT.Spitbol.Patterns* (g-spipat.ads) 258
12.110 *GNAT.Spitbol* (g-spitbo.ads) 259
12.111 *GNAT.Spitbol.Table_Boolean* (g-sptabo.ads) 259
12.112 *GNAT.Spitbol.Table_Integer* (g-sptain.ads) 259
12.113 *GNAT.Spitbol.Table_VString* (g-sptavs.ads) 259
12.114 *GNAT.SSE* (g-sse.ads) 259
12.115 *GNAT.SSE.Vector_Types* (g-ssvety.ads) 259
12.116 *GNAT.Strings* (g-string.ads) 259
12.117 *GNAT.String_Split* (g-strspl.ads) 259
12.118 *GNAT.Table* (g-table.ads) 259
12.119 *GNAT.Task_Lock* (g-tasloc.ads) 260
12.120 *GNAT.Time_Stamp* (g-timsta.ads) 260
12.121 *GNAT.Threads* (g-thread.ads) 260
12.122 *GNAT.Traceback* (g-traceb.ads) 260
12.123 *GNAT.Traceback.Symbolic* (g-trasym.ads) 260
12.124 *GNAT.UTF_32* (g-table.ads) 260
12.125 *GNAT.Wide_Spelling_Checker* (g-u3spch.ads) 260
12.126 *GNAT.Wide_Spelling_Checker* (g-wispch.ads) 260
12.127 *GNAT.Wide_String_Split* (g-wistsp.ads) 260
12.128 *GNAT.Wide_Wide_Spelling_Checker* (g-zspche.ads) 261
12.129 *GNAT.Wide_Wide_String_Split* (g-zistsp.ads) 261
12.130 *Interfaces.C.Extensions* (i-cexten.ads) 261
12.131 *Interfaces.C.Streams* (i-cstrea.ads) 261
12.132 *Interfaces.Packed_Decimal* (i-pacdec.ads) 261
12.133 *Interfaces.VxWorks* (i-vxwork.ads) 261
12.134 *Interfaces.VxWorks.IO* (i-vxwoio.ads) 261
12.135 *System.Address_Image* (s-addima.ads) 261
12.136 *System.Assertions* (s-assert.ads) 261
12.137 *System.Atomic_Counters* (s-atocou.ads) 261
12.138 *System.Memory* (s-memory.ads) 262

12.139 *System.Multiprocessors* (`s-multip.ads`) 262
12.140 *System.Multiprocessors.Dispatching_Domains* (`s-mudido.ads`) 262
12.141 *System.Partition_Interface* (`s-parint.ads`) 262
12.142 *System.Pool_Global* (`s-pooglo.ads`) 262
12.143 *System.Pool_Local* (`s-pooloc.ads`) 262
12.144 *System.Restrictions* (`s-restri.ads`) 262
12.145 *System.Rident* (`s-rident.ads`) 262
12.146 *System.Strings.Stream_Ops* (`s-ststop.ads`) 263
12.147 *System.Unsigned_Types* (`s-unstyp.ads`) 263
12.148 *System.Wch_Cnv* (`s-wchcnv.ads`) 263
12.149 *System.Wch_Con* (`s-wchcon.ads`) 263

13 Interfacing to Other Languages 264

13.1 Interfacing to C 264
13.2 Interfacing to C++ 265
13.3 Interfacing to COBOL 265
13.4 Interfacing to Fortran 266
13.5 Interfacing to non-GNAT Ada code 266

14 Specialized Needs Annexes 267

15 Implementation of Specific Ada Features 268

15.1 Machine Code Insertions 268
15.2 GNAT Implementation of Tasking 270
15.2.1 Mapping Ada Tasks onto the Underlying Kernel Threads 270
15.2.2 Ensuring Compliance with the Real-Time Annex 271
15.3 GNAT Implementation of Shared Passive Packages 271
15.4 Code Generation for Array Aggregates 273
15.4.1 Static constant aggregates with static bounds 273
15.4.2 Constant aggregates with unconstrained nominal types .. 273
15.4.3 Aggregates with static bounds 274
15.4.4 Aggregates with nonstatic bounds 274
15.4.5 Aggregates in assignment statements 274
15.5 The Size of Discriminated Records with Default Discriminants 275
15.6 Strict Conformance to the Ada Reference Manual 276

16 Implementation of Ada 2012 Features 277

17 Obsolescent Features 294
17.1 pragma No_Run_Time 294
17.2 pragma Ravenscar 294
17.3 pragma Restricted_Run_Time 294
17.4 pragma Task_Info 294
17.5 package System.Task_Info (`s-tasinf.ads`) 294

18 Compatibility and Porting Guide 295
18.1 Writing Portable Fixed-Point Declarations 295
18.2 Compatibility with Ada 83 296
18.2.1 Legal Ada 83 programs that are illegal in Ada 95 296
18.2.2 More deterministic semantics 298
18.2.3 Changed semantics 298
18.2.4 Other language compatibility issues 298
18.3 Compatibility between Ada 95 and Ada 2005 299
18.4 Implementation-dependent characteristics 300
18.4.1 Implementation-defined pragmas 300
18.4.2 Implementation-defined attributes 300
18.4.3 Libraries 300
18.4.4 Elaboration order 300
18.4.5 Target-specific aspects 301
18.5 Compatibility with Other Ada Systems 301
18.6 Representation Clauses 302
18.7 Compatibility with HP Ada 83 303

19 GNU Free Documentation License 304

Index 311

GNAT, The GNU Ada Development Environment

GCC version 6.1.0
AdaCore

1 About This Guide

This manual contains useful information in writing programs using the GNAT compiler. It includes information on implementation dependent characteristics of GNAT, including all the information required by Annex M of the Ada language standard.

GNAT implements Ada 95, Ada 2005 and Ada 2012, and it may also be invoked in Ada 83 compatibility mode. By default, GNAT assumes Ada 2012, but you can override with a compiler switch to explicitly specify the language version. (Please refer to the *GNAT User's Guide* for details on these switches.) Throughout this manual, references to 'Ada' without a year suffix apply to all the Ada versions of the language.

Ada is designed to be highly portable. In general, a program will have the same effect even when compiled by different compilers on different platforms. However, since Ada is designed to be used in a wide variety of applications, it also contains a number of system dependent features to be used in interfacing to the external world.

Note: Any program that makes use of implementation-dependent features may be non-portable. You should follow good programming practice and isolate and clearly document any sections of your program that make use of these features in a non-portable manner.

1.1 What This Reference Manual Contains

This reference manual contains the following chapters:

* [Implementation Defined Pragmas], page 4, lists GNAT implementation-dependent pragmas, which can be used to extend and enhance the functionality of the compiler.
* [Implementation Defined Attributes], page 106, lists GNAT implementation-dependent attributes, which can be used to extend and enhance the functionality of the compiler.
* [Standard and Implementation Defined Restrictions], page 127, lists GNAT implementation-dependent restrictions, which can be used to extend and enhance the functionality of the compiler.
* [Implementation Advice], page 144, provides information on generally desirable behavior which are not requirements that all compilers must follow since it cannot be provided on all systems, or which may be undesirable on some systems.
* [Implementation Defined Characteristics], page 164, provides a guide to minimizing implementation dependent features.
* [Intrinsic Subprograms], page 181, describes the intrinsic subprograms implemented by GNAT, and how they can be imported into user application programs.
* [Representation Clauses and Pragmas], page 184, describes in detail the way that GNAT represents data, and in particular the exact set of representation clauses and pragmas that is accepted.
* [Standard Library Routines], page 215, provides a listing of packages and a brief description of the functionality that is provided by Ada's extensive set of standard library routines as implemented by GNAT.
* [The Implementation of Standard I/O], page 226, details how the GNAT implementation of the input-output facilities.
* [The GNAT Library], page 244, is a catalog of packages that complement the Ada predefined library.

* [Interfacing to Other Languages], page 263, describes how programs written in Ada using GNAT can be interfaced to other programming languages.
* [Specialized Needs Annexes], page 266, describes the GNAT implementation of all of the specialized needs annexes.
* [Implementation of Specific Ada Features], page 267, discusses issues related to GNAT's implementation of machine code insertions, tasking, and several other features.
* [Implementation of Ada 2012 Features], page 276, describes the status of the GNAT implementation of the Ada 2012 language standard.
* [Obsolescent Features], page 293 documents implementation dependent features, including pragmas and attributes, which are considered obsolescent, since there are other preferred ways of achieving the same results. These obsolescent forms are retained for backwards compatibility.
* [Compatibility and Porting Guide], page 294 presents some guidelines for developing portable Ada code, describes the compatibility issues that may arise between GNAT and other Ada compilation systems (including those for Ada 83), and shows how GNAT can expedite porting applications developed in other Ada environments.
* [GNU Free Documentation License], page 303 contains the license for this document.

This reference manual assumes a basic familiarity with the Ada 95 language, as described in the *International Standard ANSI/ISO/IEC-8652:1995*. It does not require knowledge of the new features introduced by Ada 2005 or Ada 2012. All three reference manuals are included in the GNAT documentation package.

1.2 Conventions

Following are examples of the typographical and graphic conventions used in this guide:

* *Functions*, *utility program names*, *standard names*, and *classes*.
* *Option flags*
* `File names`
* *Variables*
* *Emphasis*
* [optional information or parameters]
* Examples are described by text

  ```
  and then shown this way.
  ```
* Commands that are entered by the user are shown as preceded by a prompt string comprising the `$` character followed by a space.

1.3 Related Information

See the following documents for further information on GNAT:

* *GNAT User's Guide for Native Platforms*, which provides information on how to use the GNAT development environment.
* *Ada 95 Reference Manual*, the Ada 95 programming language standard.

* *Ada 95 Annotated Reference Manual*, which is an annotated version of the Ada 95 standard. The annotations describe detailed aspects of the design decision, and in particular contain useful sections on Ada 83 compatibility.
* *Ada 2005 Reference Manual*, the Ada 2005 programming language standard.
* *Ada 2005 Annotated Reference Manual*, which is an annotated version of the Ada 2005 standard. The annotations describe detailed aspects of the design decision.
* *Ada 2012 Reference Manual*, the Ada 2012 programming language standard.
* *DEC Ada, Technical Overview and Comparison on DIGITAL Platforms*, which contains specific information on compatibility between GNAT and DEC Ada 83 systems.
* *DEC Ada, Language Reference Manual*, part number AA-PYZAB-TK, which describes in detail the pragmas and attributes provided by the DEC Ada 83 compiler system.

2 Implementation Defined Pragmas

Ada defines a set of pragmas that can be used to supply additional information to the compiler. These language defined pragmas are implemented in GNAT and work as described in the Ada Reference Manual.

In addition, Ada allows implementations to define additional pragmas whose meaning is defined by the implementation. GNAT provides a number of these implementation-defined pragmas, which can be used to extend and enhance the functionality of the compiler. This section of the GNAT Reference Manual describes these additional pragmas.

Note that any program using these pragmas might not be portable to other compilers (although GNAT implements this set of pragmas on all platforms). Therefore if portability to other compilers is an important consideration, the use of these pragmas should be minimized.

2.1 Pragma Abort_Defer

Syntax:

```
pragma Abort_Defer;
```

This pragma must appear at the start of the statement sequence of a handled sequence of statements (right after the *begin*). It has the effect of deferring aborts for the sequence of statements (but not for the declarations or handlers, if any, associated with this statement sequence).

2.2 Pragma Abstract_State

Syntax:

```
pragma Abstract_State (ABSTRACT_STATE_LIST);

ABSTRACT_STATE_LIST ::=
     null
  |  STATE_NAME_WITH_OPTIONS
  | (STATE_NAME_WITH_OPTIONS {, STATE_NAME_WITH_OPTIONS} )

STATE_NAME_WITH_OPTIONS ::=
     STATE_NAME
  | (STATE_NAME with OPTION_LIST)

OPTION_LIST ::= OPTION {, OPTION}

OPTION ::=
    SIMPLE_OPTION
  | NAME_VALUE_OPTION

SIMPLE_OPTION ::= Ghost | Synchronous

NAME_VALUE_OPTION ::=
```

```
          Part_Of => ABSTRACT_STATE
        | External [=> EXTERNAL_PROPERTY_LIST]

      EXTERNAL_PROPERTY_LIST ::=
           EXTERNAL_PROPERTY
        | (EXTERNAL_PROPERTY {, EXTERNAL_PROPERTY} )

      EXTERNAL_PROPERTY ::=
          Async_Readers     [=> boolean_EXPRESSION]
        | Async_Writers     [=> boolean_EXPRESSION]
        | Effective_Reads   [=> boolean_EXPRESSION]
        | Effective_Writes  [=> boolean_EXPRESSION]
          others             => boolean_EXPRESSION

      STATE_NAME ::= defining_identifier

      ABSTRACT_STATE ::= name
```

For the semantics of this pragma, see the entry for aspect *Abstract_State* in the SPARK 2014 Reference Manual, section 7.1.4.

2.3 Pragma Ada_83

Syntax:

```
pragma Ada_83;
```

A configuration pragma that establishes Ada 83 mode for the unit to which it applies, regardless of the mode set by the command line switches. In Ada 83 mode, GNAT attempts to be as compatible with the syntax and semantics of Ada 83, as defined in the original Ada 83 Reference Manual as possible. In particular, the keywords added by Ada 95 and Ada 2005 are not recognized, optional package bodies are allowed, and generics may name types with unknown discriminants without using the *(<>)* notation. In addition, some but not all of the additional restrictions of Ada 83 are enforced.

Ada 83 mode is intended for two purposes. Firstly, it allows existing Ada 83 code to be compiled and adapted to GNAT with less effort. Secondly, it aids in keeping code backwards compatible with Ada 83. However, there is no guarantee that code that is processed correctly by GNAT in Ada 83 mode will in fact compile and execute with an Ada 83 compiler, since GNAT does not enforce all the additional checks required by Ada 83.

2.4 Pragma Ada_95

Syntax:

```
pragma Ada_95;
```

A configuration pragma that establishes Ada 95 mode for the unit to which it applies, regardless of the mode set by the command line switches. This mode is set automatically for the *Ada* and *System* packages and their children, so you need not specify it in these contexts. This pragma is useful when writing a reusable component that itself uses Ada 95 features, but which is intended to be usable from either Ada 83 or Ada 95 programs.

2.5 Pragma Ada_05

Syntax:

```
pragma Ada_05;
pragma Ada_05 (local_NAME);
```

A configuration pragma that establishes Ada 2005 mode for the unit to which it applies, regardless of the mode set by the command line switches. This pragma is useful when writing a reusable component that itself uses Ada 2005 features, but which is intended to be usable from either Ada 83 or Ada 95 programs.

The one argument form (which is not a configuration pragma) is used for managing the transition from Ada 95 to Ada 2005 in the run-time library. If an entity is marked as Ada_2005 only, then referencing the entity in Ada_83 or Ada_95 mode will generate a warning. In addition, in Ada_83 or Ada_95 mode, a preference rule is established which does not choose such an entity unless it is unambiguously specified. This avoids extra subprograms marked this way from generating ambiguities in otherwise legal pre-Ada_2005 programs. The one argument form is intended for exclusive use in the GNAT run-time library.

2.6 Pragma Ada_2005

Syntax:

```
pragma Ada_2005;
```

This configuration pragma is a synonym for pragma Ada_05 and has the same syntax and effect.

2.7 Pragma Ada_12

Syntax:

```
pragma Ada_12;
pragma Ada_12 (local_NAME);
```

A configuration pragma that establishes Ada 2012 mode for the unit to which it applies, regardless of the mode set by the command line switches. This mode is set automatically for the *Ada* and *System* packages and their children, so you need not specify it in these contexts. This pragma is useful when writing a reusable component that itself uses Ada 2012 features, but which is intended to be usable from Ada 83, Ada 95, or Ada 2005 programs.

The one argument form, which is not a configuration pragma, is used for managing the transition from Ada 2005 to Ada 2012 in the run-time library. If an entity is marked as Ada_201 only, then referencing the entity in any pre-Ada_2012 mode will generate a warning. In addition, in any pre-Ada_2012 mode, a preference rule is established which does not choose such an entity unless it is unambiguously specified. This avoids extra subprograms marked this way from generating ambiguities in otherwise legal pre-Ada_2012 programs. The one argument form is intended for exclusive use in the GNAT run-time library.

2.8 Pragma Ada_2012

Syntax:

```
pragma Ada_2012;
```

This configuration pragma is a synonym for pragma Ada_12 and has the same syntax and effect.

2.9 Pragma Allow_Integer_Address

Syntax:

```
pragma Allow_Integer_Address;
```

In almost all versions of GNAT, *System.Address* is a private type in accordance with the implementation advice in the RM. This means that integer values, in particular integer literals, are not allowed as address values. If the configuration pragma *Allow_Integer_Address* is given, then integer expressions may be used anywhere a value of type *System.Address* is required. The effect is to introduce an implicit unchecked conversion from the integer value to type *System.Address*. The reverse case of using an address where an integer type is required is handled analogously. The following example compiles without errors:

```
pragma Allow_Integer_Address;
with System; use System;
package AddrAsInt is
   X : Integer;
   Y : Integer;
   for X'Address use 16#1240#;
   for Y use at 16#3230#;
   m : Address := 16#4000#;
   n : constant Address := 4000;
   p : constant Address := Address (X + Y);
   v : Integer := y'Address;
   w : constant Integer := Integer (Y'Address);
   type R is new integer;
   RR : R := 1000;
   Z : Integer;
   for Z'Address use RR;
end AddrAsInt;
```

Note that pragma *Allow_Integer_Address* is ignored if *System.Address* is not a private type. In implementations of *GNAT* where System.Address is a visible integer type, this pragma serves no purpose but is ignored rather than rejected to allow common sets of sources to be used in the two situations.

2.10 Pragma Annotate

Syntax:

```
pragma Annotate (IDENTIFIER [, IDENTIFIER {, ARG}] [, entity => local_NAME]);

ARG ::= NAME | EXPRESSION
```

This pragma is used to annotate programs. *identifier* identifies the type of annotation. GNAT verifies that it is an identifier, but does not otherwise analyze it. The second optional identifier is also left unanalyzed, and by convention is used to control the action of the tool to which the annotation is addressed. The remaining *arg* arguments can be either string literals or more generally expressions. String literals are assumed to be either of type *Standard.String* or else *Wide_String* or *Wide_Wide_String* depending on the character literals they contain. All other kinds of arguments are analyzed as expressions, and must be unambiguous. The last argument if present must have the identifier *Entity* and GNAT verifies that a local name is given.

The analyzed pragma is retained in the tree, but not otherwise processed by any part of the GNAT compiler, except to generate corresponding note lines in the generated ALI file. For the format of these note lines, see the compiler source file lib-writ.ads. This pragma is intended for use by external tools, including ASIS. The use of pragma Annotate does not affect the compilation process in any way. This pragma may be used as a configuration pragma.

2.11 Pragma Assert

Syntax:

```
pragma Assert (
  boolean_EXPRESSION
  [, string_EXPRESSION]);
```

The effect of this pragma depends on whether the corresponding command line switch is set to activate assertions. The pragma expands into code equivalent to the following:

```
if assertions-enabled then
   if not boolean_EXPRESSION then
      System.Assertions.Raise_Assert_Failure
        (string_EXPRESSION);
   end if;
end if;
```

The string argument, if given, is the message that will be associated with the exception occurrence if the exception is raised. If no second argument is given, the default message is *file:nnn*, where *file* is the name of the source file containing the assert, and *nnn* is the line number of the assert.

Note that, as with the *if* statement to which it is equivalent, the type of the expression is either *Standard.Boolean*, or any type derived from this standard type.

Assert checks can be either checked or ignored. By default they are ignored. They will be checked if either the command line switch *-gnata* is used, or if an *Assertion_Policy* or *Check_Policy* pragma is used to enable *Assert_Checks*.

If assertions are ignored, then there is no run-time effect (and in particular, any side effects from the expression will not occur at run time). (The expression is still analyzed at compile time, and may cause types to be frozen if they are mentioned here for the first time).

If assertions are checked, then the given expression is tested, and if it is *False* then *System.Assertions.Raise_Assert_Failure* is called which results in the raising of *Assert_Failure* with the given message.

You should generally avoid side effects in the expression arguments of this pragma, because these side effects will turn on and off with the setting of the assertions mode, resulting in assertions that have an effect on the program. However, the expressions are analyzed for semantic correctness whether or not assertions are enabled, so turning assertions on and off cannot affect the legality of a program.

Note that the implementation defined policy *DISABLE*, given in a pragma *Assertion_Policy*, can be used to suppress this semantic analysis.

Note: this is a standard language-defined pragma in versions of Ada from 2005 on. In GNAT, it is implemented in all versions of Ada, and the DISABLE policy is an implementation-defined addition.

2.12 Pragma Assert_And_Cut

Syntax:

```
pragma Assert_And_Cut (
  boolean_EXPRESSION
  [, string_EXPRESSION]);
```

The effect of this pragma is identical to that of pragma *Assert*, except that in an *Assertion_Policy* pragma, the identifier *Assert_And_Cut* is used to control whether it is ignored or checked (or disabled).

The intention is that this be used within a subprogram when the given test expresion sums up all the work done so far in the subprogram, so that the rest of the subprogram can be verified (informally or formally) using only the entry preconditions, and the expression in this pragma. This allows dividing up a subprogram into sections for the purposes of testing or formal verification. The pragma also serves as useful documentation.

2.13 Pragma Assertion_Policy

Syntax:

```
pragma Assertion_Policy (CHECK | DISABLE | IGNORE);

pragma Assertion_Policy (
    ASSERTION_KIND => POLICY_IDENTIFIER
 {, ASSERTION_KIND => POLICY_IDENTIFIER});

ASSERTION_KIND ::= RM_ASSERTION_KIND | ID_ASSERTION_KIND

RM_ASSERTION_KIND ::= Assert               |
                      Static_Predicate     |
                      Dynamic_Predicate    |
                      Pre                  |
                      Pre'Class            |
                      Post                 |
                      Post'Class           |
                      Type_Invariant       |
                      Type_Invariant'Class

ID_ASSERTION_KIND ::= Assertions           |
                      Assert_And_Cut       |
```

```
                      Assume                 |
                      Contract_Cases         |
                      Debug                  |
                      Invariant              |
                      Invariant'Class        |
                      Loop_Invariant         |
                      Loop_Variant           |
                      Postcondition          |
                      Precondition           |
                      Predicate              |
                      Refined_Post           |
                      Statement_Assertions

POLICY_IDENTIFIER ::= Check | Disable | Ignore
```

This is a standard Ada 2012 pragma that is available as an implementation-defined pragma in earlier versions of Ada. The assertion kinds *RM_ASSERTION_KIND* are those defined in the Ada standard. The assertion kinds *ID_ASSERTION_KIND* are implementation defined additions recognized by the GNAT compiler.

The pragma applies in both cases to pragmas and aspects with matching names, e.g. *Pre* applies to the Pre aspect, and *Precondition* applies to both the *Precondition* pragma and the aspect *Precondition*. Note that the identifiers for pragmas Pre_Class and Post_Class are Pre'Class and Post'Class (not Pre_Class and Post_Class), since these pragmas are intended to be identical to the corresponding aspects).

If the policy is *CHECK*, then assertions are enabled, i.e. the corresponding pragma or aspect is activated. If the policy is *IGNORE*, then assertions are ignored, i.e. the corresponding pragma or aspect is deactivated. This pragma overrides the effect of the *-gnata* switch on the command line.

The implementation defined policy *DISABLE* is like *IGNORE* except that it completely disables semantic checking of the corresponding pragma or aspect. This is useful when the pragma or aspect argument references subprograms in a with'ed package which is replaced by a dummy package for the final build.

The implementation defined assertion kind *Assertions* applies to all assertion kinds. The form with no assertion kind given implies this choice, so it applies to all assertion kinds (RM defined, and implementation defined).

The implementation defined assertion kind *Statement_Assertions* applies to *Assert*, *Assert_And_Cut*, *Assume*, *Loop_Invariant*, and *Loop_Variant*.

2.14 Pragma Assume

Syntax:

```
pragma Assume (
  boolean_EXPRESSION
  [, string_EXPRESSION]);
```

The effect of this pragma is identical to that of pragma *Assert*, except that in an *Assertion_Policy* pragma, the identifier *Assume* is used to control whether it is ignored or checked (or disabled).

The intention is that this be used for assumptions about the external environment. So you cannot expect to verify formally or informally that the condition is met, this must be established by examining things outside the program itself. For example, we may have code that depends on the size of *Long_Long_Integer* being at least 64. So we could write:

```
pragma Assume (Long_Long_Integer'Size >= 64);
```

This assumption cannot be proved from the program itself, but it acts as a useful run-time check that the assumption is met, and documents the need to ensure that it is met by reference to information outside the program.

2.15 Pragma Assume_No_Invalid_Values

Syntax:

```
pragma Assume_No_Invalid_Values (On | Off);
```

This is a configuration pragma that controls the assumptions made by the compiler about the occurrence of invalid representations (invalid values) in the code.

The default behavior (corresponding to an Off argument for this pragma), is to assume that values may in general be invalid unless the compiler can prove they are valid. Consider the following example:

```
V1 : Integer range 1 .. 10;
V2 : Integer range 11 .. 20;
...
for J in V2 .. V1 loop
   ...
end loop;
```

if V1 and V2 have valid values, then the loop is known at compile time not to execute since the lower bound must be greater than the upper bound. However in default mode, no such assumption is made, and the loop may execute. If *Assume_No_Invalid_Values (On)* is given, the compiler will assume that any occurrence of a variable other than in an explicit *'Valid* test always has a valid value, and the loop above will be optimized away.

The use of *Assume_No_Invalid_Values (On)* is appropriate if you know your code is free of uninitialized variables and other possible sources of invalid representations, and may result in more efficient code. A program that accesses an invalid representation with this pragma in effect is erroneous, so no guarantees can be made about its behavior.

It is peculiar though permissible to use this pragma in conjunction with validity checking (-gnatVa). In such cases, accessing invalid values will generally give an exception, though formally the program is erroneous so there are no guarantees that this will always be the case, and it is recommended that these two options not be used together.

2.16 Pragma Async_Readers

Syntax:

```
pragma Asynch_Readers   [ (boolean_EXPRESSION) ];
```

For the semantics of this pragma, see the entry for aspect *Async_Readers* in the SPARK 2014 Reference Manual, section 7.1.2.

2.17 Pragma Async_Writers

Syntax:

```
pragma Asynch_Writers    [ (boolean_EXPRESSION) ];
```

For the semantics of this pragma, see the entry for aspect *Async_Writers* in the SPARK 2014 Reference Manual, section 7.1.2.

2.18 Pragma Attribute_Definition

Syntax:

```
pragma Attribute_Definition
  ([Attribute  =>] ATTRIBUTE_DESIGNATOR,
   [Entity     =>] LOCAL_NAME,
   [Expression =>] EXPRESSION | NAME);
```

If *Attribute* is a known attribute name, this pragma is equivalent to the attribute definition clause:

```
for Entity'Attribute use Expression;
```

If *Attribute* is not a recognized attribute name, the pragma is ignored, and a warning is emitted. This allows source code to be written that takes advantage of some new attribute, while remaining compilable with earlier compilers.

2.19 Pragma C_Pass_By_Copy

Syntax:

```
pragma C_Pass_By_Copy
  ([Max_Size =>] static_integer_EXPRESSION);
```

Normally the default mechanism for passing C convention records to C convention subprograms is to pass them by reference, as suggested by RM B.3(69). Use the configuration pragma *C_Pass_By_Copy* to change this default, by requiring that record formal parameters be passed by copy if all of the following conditions are met:

* The size of the record type does not exceed the value specified for *Max_Size*.
* The record type has *Convention C*.
* The formal parameter has this record type, and the subprogram has a foreign (non-Ada) convention.

If these conditions are met the argument is passed by copy; i.e., in a manner consistent with what C expects if the corresponding formal in the C prototype is a struct (rather than a pointer to a struct).

You can also pass records by copy by specifying the convention *C_Pass_By_Copy* for the record type, or by using the extended *Import* and *Export* pragmas, which allow specification of passing mechanisms on a parameter by parameter basis.

2.20 Pragma Check

Syntax:

```
pragma Check (
     [Name    =>] CHECK_KIND,
     [Check   =>] Boolean_EXPRESSION
  [, [Message =>] string_EXPRESSION] );

CHECK_KIND ::= IDENTIFIER            |
               Pre'Class             |
               Post'Class            |
               Type_Invariant'Class  |
               Invariant'Class
```

This pragma is similar to the predefined pragma *Assert* except that an extra identifier argument is present. In conjunction with pragma *Check_Policy*, this can be used to define groups of assertions that can be independently controlled. The identifier *Assertion* is special, it refers to the normal set of pragma *Assert* statements.

Checks introduced by this pragma are normally deactivated by default. They can be activated either by the command line option *-gnata*, which turns on all checks, or individually controlled using pragma *Check_Policy*.

The identifiers *Assertions* and *Statement_Assertions* are not permitted as check kinds, since this would cause confusion with the use of these identifiers in *Assertion_Policy* and *Check_Policy* pragmas, where they are used to refer to sets of assertions.

2.21 Pragma Check_Float_Overflow

Syntax:

```
pragma Check_Float_Overflow;
```

In Ada, the predefined floating-point types (*Short_Float*, *Float*, *Long_Float*, *Long_Long_Float*) are defined to be *unconstrained*. This means that even though each has a well-defined base range, an operation that delivers a result outside this base range is not required to raise an exception. This implementation permission accommodates the notion of infinities in IEEE floating-point, and corresponds to the efficient execution mode on most machines. GNAT will not raise overflow exceptions on these machines; instead it will generate infinities and NaN's as defined in the IEEE standard.

Generating infinities, although efficient, is not always desirable. Often the preferable approach is to check for overflow, even at the (perhaps considerable) expense of run-time performance. This can be accomplished by defining your own constrained floating-point subtypes – i.e., by supplying explicit range constraints – and indeed such a subtype can have the same base range as its base type. For example:

```
subtype My_Float is Float range Float'Range;
```

Here *My_Float* has the same range as *Float* but is constrained, so operations on *My_Float* values will be checked for overflow against this range.

This style will achieve the desired goal, but it is often more convenient to be able to simply use the standard predefined floating-point types as long as overflow checking could be guaranteed. The *Check_Float_Overflow* configuration pragma achieves this effect. If a unit is compiled subject to this configuration pragma, then all operations on predefined floating-point types including operations on base types of these floating-point types will be treated as though those types were constrained, and overflow checks will be generated. The *Constraint_Error* exception is raised if the result is out of range.

This mode can also be set by use of the compiler switch *-gnateF*.

2.22 Pragma Check_Name

Syntax:

```
pragma Check_Name (check_name_IDENTIFIER);
```

This is a configuration pragma that defines a new implementation defined check name (unless IDENTIFIER matches one of the predefined check names, in which case the pragma has no effect). Check names are global to a partition, so if two or more configuration pragmas are present in a partition mentioning the same name, only one new check name is introduced.

An implementation defined check name introduced with this pragma may be used in only three contexts: *pragma Suppress*, *pragma Unsuppress*, and as the prefix of a *Check_Name'Enabled* attribute reference. For any of these three cases, the check name must be visible. A check name is visible if it is in the configuration pragmas applying to the current unit, or if it appears at the start of any unit that is part of the dependency set of the current unit (e.g., units that are mentioned in *with* clauses).

Check names introduced by this pragma are subject to control by compiler switches (in particular -gnatp) in the usual manner.

2.23 Pragma Check_Policy

Syntax:

```
pragma Check_Policy
 ([Name   =>] CHECK_KIND,
  [Policy =>] POLICY_IDENTIFIER);

pragma Check_Policy (
    CHECK_KIND => POLICY_IDENTIFIER
 {, CHECK_KIND => POLICY_IDENTIFIER});

ASSERTION_KIND ::= RM_ASSERTION_KIND | ID_ASSERTION_KIND

CHECK_KIND ::= IDENTIFIER             |
               Pre'Class              |
               Post'Class             |
               Type_Invariant'Class   |
               Invariant'Class

The identifiers Name and Policy are not allowed as CHECK_KIND values. This
avoids confusion between the two possible syntax forms for this pragma.

POLICY_IDENTIFIER ::= ON | OFF | CHECK | DISABLE | IGNORE
```

This pragma is used to set the checking policy for assertions (specified by aspects or pragmas), the *Debug* pragma, or additional checks to be checked using the *Check* pragma. It may appear either as a configuration pragma, or within a declarative part of package. In the latter case, it applies from the point where it appears to the end of the declarative region (like pragma *Suppress*).

The *Check_Policy* pragma is similar to the predefined *Assertion_Policy* pragma, and if the check kind corresponds to one of the assertion kinds that are allowed by *Assertion_Policy*, then the effect is identical.

If the first argument is Debug, then the policy applies to Debug pragmas, disabling their effect if the policy is *OFF*, *DISABLE*, or *IGNORE*, and allowing them to execute with normal semantics if the policy is *ON* or *CHECK*. In addition if the policy is *DISABLE*, then the procedure call in *Debug* pragmas will be totally ignored and not analyzed semantically.

Finally the first argument may be some other identifier than the above possibilities, in which case it controls a set of named assertions that can be checked using pragma *Check*. For example, if the pragma:

```
pragma Check_Policy (Critical_Error, OFF);
```

is given, then subsequent *Check* pragmas whose first argument is also *Critical_Error* will be disabled.

The check policy is *OFF* to turn off corresponding checks, and *ON* to turn on corresponding checks. The default for a set of checks for which no *Check_Policy* is given is *OFF* unless the compiler switch *-gnata* is given, which turns on all checks by default.

The check policy settings *CHECK* and *IGNORE* are recognized as synonyms for *ON* and *OFF*. These synonyms are provided for compatibility with the standard *Assertion_Policy* pragma. The check policy setting *DISABLE* causes the second argument of a corresponding *Check* pragma to be completely ignored and not analyzed.

2.24 Pragma Comment

Syntax:

```
pragma Comment (static_string_EXPRESSION);
```

This is almost identical in effect to pragma *Ident*. It allows the placement of a comment into the object file and hence into the executable file if the operating system permits such usage. The difference is that *Comment*, unlike *Ident*, has no limitations on placement of the pragma (it can be placed anywhere in the main source unit), and if more than one pragma is used, all comments are retained.

2.25 Pragma Common_Object

Syntax:

```
pragma Common_Object (
     [Internal =>] LOCAL_NAME
  [, [External =>] EXTERNAL_SYMBOL]
  [, [Size     =>] EXTERNAL_SYMBOL] );

EXTERNAL_SYMBOL ::=
  IDENTIFIER
| static_string_EXPRESSION
```

This pragma enables the shared use of variables stored in overlaid linker areas corresponding to the use of *COMMON* in Fortran. The single object *LOCAL_NAME* is assigned to the area designated by the *External* argument. You may define a record to correspond to a series of fields. The *Size* argument is syntax checked in GNAT, but otherwise ignored.

Common_Object is not supported on all platforms. If no support is available, then the code generator will issue a message indicating that the necessary attribute for implementation of this pragma is not available.

2.26 Pragma Compile_Time_Error

Syntax:

```
pragma Compile_Time_Error
         (boolean_EXPRESSION, static_string_EXPRESSION);
```

This pragma can be used to generate additional compile time error messages. It is particularly useful in generics, where errors can be issued for specific problematic instantiations. The first parameter is a boolean expression. The pragma is effective only if the value of this expression is known at compile time, and has the value True. The set of expressions whose values are known at compile time includes all static boolean expressions, and also other values which the compiler can determine at compile time (e.g., the size of a record type set by an explicit size representation clause, or the value of a variable which was initialized to a constant and is known not to have been modified). If these conditions are met, an error message is generated using the value given as the second argument. This string value may contain embedded ASCII.LF characters to break the message into multiple lines.

2.27 Pragma Compile_Time_Warning

Syntax:

```
pragma Compile_Time_Warning
         (boolean_EXPRESSION, static_string_EXPRESSION);
```

Same as pragma Compile_Time_Error, except a warning is issued instead of an error message. Note that if this pragma is used in a package that is with'ed by a client, the client will get the warning even though it is issued by a with'ed package (normally warnings in with'ed units are suppressed, but this is a special exception to that rule).

One typical use is within a generic where compile time known characteristics of formal parameters are tested, and warnings given appropriately. Another use with a first parameter of True is to warn a client about use of a package, for example that it is not fully implemented.

2.28 Pragma Compiler_Unit

Syntax:

```
pragma Compiler_Unit;
```

This pragma is obsolete. It is equivalent to Compiler_Unit_Warning. It is retained so that old versions of the GNAT run-time that use this pragma can be compiled with newer versions of the compiler.

2.29 Pragma Compiler_Unit_Warning

Syntax:

```
pragma Compiler_Unit_Warning;
```

This pragma is intended only for internal use in the GNAT run-time library. It indicates that the unit is used as part of the compiler build. The effect is to generate warnings for the use of constructs (for example, conditional expressions) that would cause trouble when bootstrapping using an older version of GNAT. For the exact list of restrictions, see the compiler sources and references to Check_Compiler_Unit.

2.30 Pragma Complete_Representation

Syntax:

```
pragma Complete_Representation;
```

This pragma must appear immediately within a record representation clause. Typical placements are before the first component clause or after the last component clause. The effect is to give an error message if any component is missing a component clause. This pragma may be used to ensure that a record representation clause is complete, and that this invariant is maintained if fields are added to the record in the future.

2.31 Pragma Complex_Representation

Syntax:

```
pragma Complex_Representation
        ([Entity =>] LOCAL_NAME);
```

The *Entity* argument must be the name of a record type which has two fields of the same floating-point type. The effect of this pragma is to force gcc to use the special internal complex representation form for this record, which may be more efficient. Note that this may result in the code for this type not conforming to standard ABI (application binary interface) requirements for the handling of record types. For example, in some environments, there is a requirement for passing records by pointer, and the use of this pragma may result in passing this type in floating-point registers.

2.32 Pragma Component_Alignment

Syntax:

```
pragma Component_Alignment (
     [Form =>] ALIGNMENT_CHOICE
  [, [Name =>] type_LOCAL_NAME]);

ALIGNMENT_CHOICE ::=
  Component_Size
| Component_Size_4
| Storage_Unit
| Default
```

Specifies the alignment of components in array or record types. The meaning of the *Form* argument is as follows:

Component_Size
Aligns scalar components and subcomponents of the array or record type on boundaries appropriate to their inherent size (naturally aligned). For example, 1-byte components are aligned on byte boundaries, 2-byte integer components are aligned on 2-byte boundaries, 4-byte integer components are aligned on 4-byte boundaries and so on. These alignment rules correspond to the normal rules for C compilers on all machines except the VAX.

Component_Size_4
Naturally aligns components with a size of four or fewer bytes. Components that are larger than 4 bytes are placed on the next 4-byte boundary.

Storage_Unit
Specifies that array or record components are byte aligned, i.e., aligned on boundaries determined by the value of the constant *System.Storage_Unit*.

Default
Specifies that array or record components are aligned on default boundaries, appropriate to the underlying hardware or operating system or both. The *Default* choice is the same as *Component_Size* (natural alignment).

If the *Name* parameter is present, *type_LOCAL_NAME* must refer to a local record or array type, and the specified alignment choice applies to the specified type. The use of *Component_Alignment* together with a pragma *Pack* causes the *Component_Alignment* pragma to be ignored. The use of *Component_Alignment* together with a record representation clause is only effective for fields not specified by the representation clause.

If the *Name* parameter is absent, the pragma can be used as either a configuration pragma, in which case it applies to one or more units in accordance with the normal rules for configuration pragmas, or it can be used within a declarative part, in which case it applies to types that are declared within this declarative part, or within any nested scope within this declarative part. In either case it specifies the alignment to be applied to any record or array type which has otherwise standard representation.

If the alignment for a record or array type is not specified (using pragma *Pack*, pragma *Component_Alignment*, or a record rep clause), the GNAT uses the default alignment as described previously.

2.33 Pragma Constant_After_Elaboration

Syntax:

```
pragma Constant_After_Elaboration [ (boolean_EXPRESSION) ];
```

For the semantics of this pragma, see the entry for aspect *Constant_After_Elaboration* in the SPARK 2014 Reference Manual, section 3.3.1.

2.34 Pragma Contract_Cases

Syntax:

```
pragma Contract_Cases ((CONTRACT_CASE {, CONTRACT_CASE));

CONTRACT_CASE ::= CASE_GUARD => CONSEQUENCE
```

```
CASE_GUARD ::= boolean_EXPRESSION | others

CONSEQUENCE ::= boolean_EXPRESSION
```

The *Contract_Cases* pragma allows defining fine-grain specifications that can complement or replace the contract given by a precondition and a postcondition. Additionally, the *Contract_Cases* pragma can be used by testing and formal verification tools. The compiler checks its validity and, depending on the assertion policy at the point of declaration of the pragma, it may insert a check in the executable. For code generation, the contract cases

```
pragma Contract_Cases (
  Cond1 => Pred1,
  Cond2 => Pred2);
```

are equivalent to

```
C1 : constant Boolean := Cond1;  -- evaluated at subprogram entry
C2 : constant Boolean := Cond2;  -- evaluated at subprogram entry
pragma Precondition ((C1 and not C2) or (C2 and not C1));
pragma Postcondition (if C1 then Pred1);
pragma Postcondition (if C2 then Pred2);
```

The precondition ensures that one and only one of the conditions is satisfied on entry to the subprogram. The postcondition ensures that for the condition that was True on entry, the corrresponding consequence is True on exit. Other consequence expressions are not evaluated.

A precondition P and postcondition Q can also be expressed as contract cases:

```
pragma Contract_Cases (P => Q);
```

The placement and visibility rules for *Contract_Cases* pragmas are identical to those described for preconditions and postconditions.

The compiler checks that boolean expressions given in conditions and consequences are valid, where the rules for conditions are the same as the rule for an expression in *Precondition* and the rules for consequences are the same as the rule for an expression in *Postcondition*. In particular, attributes *'Old* and *'Result* can only be used within consequence expressions. The condition for the last contract case may be *others*, to denote any case not captured by the previous cases. The following is an example of use within a package spec:

```
package Math_Functions is
   ...
   function Sqrt (Arg : Float) return Float;
   pragma Contract_Cases ((Arg in 0 .. 99) => Sqrt'Result < 10,
                          Arg >= 100       => Sqrt'Result >= 10,
                          others           => Sqrt'Result = 0);
   ...
end Math_Functions;
```

The meaning of contract cases is that only one case should apply at each call, as determined by the corresponding condition evaluating to True, and that the consequence for this case should hold when the subprogram returns.

2.35 Pragma Convention_Identifier

Syntax:

```
pragma Convention_Identifier (
         [Name =>]       IDENTIFIER,
         [Convention =>] convention_IDENTIFIER);
```

This pragma provides a mechanism for supplying synonyms for existing convention identifiers. The *Name* identifier can subsequently be used as a synonym for the given convention in other pragmas (including for example pragma *Import* or another *Convention_Identifier* pragma). As an example of the use of this, suppose you had legacy code which used Fortran77 as the identifier for Fortran. Then the pragma:

```
pragma Convention_Identifier (Fortran77, Fortran);
```

would allow the use of the convention identifier *Fortran77* in subsequent code, avoiding the need to modify the sources. As another example, you could use this to parameterize convention requirements according to systems. Suppose you needed to use *Stdcall* on windows systems, and *C* on some other system, then you could define a convention identifier *Library* and use a single *Convention_Identifier* pragma to specify which convention would be used system-wide.

2.36 Pragma CPP_Class

Syntax:

```
pragma CPP_Class ([Entity =>] LOCAL_NAME);
```

The argument denotes an entity in the current declarative region that is declared as a record type. It indicates that the type corresponds to an externally declared C++ class type, and is to be laid out the same way that C++ would lay out the type. If the C++ class has virtual primitives then the record must be declared as a tagged record type.

Types for which *CPP_Class* is specified do not have assignment or equality operators defined (such operations can be imported or declared as subprograms as required). Initialization is allowed only by constructor functions (see pragma *CPP_Constructor*). Such types are implicitly limited if not explicitly declared as limited or derived from a limited type, and an error is issued in that case.

See [Interfacing to C++], page 265 for related information.

Note: Pragma *CPP_Class* is currently obsolete. It is supported for backward compatibility but its functionality is available using pragma *Import* with *Convention* = *CPP*.

2.37 Pragma CPP_Constructor

Syntax:

```
pragma CPP_Constructor ([Entity =>] LOCAL_NAME
  [, [External_Name =>] static_string_EXPRESSION ]
  [, [Link_Name     =>] static_string_EXPRESSION ]);
```

This pragma identifies an imported function (imported in the usual way with pragma *Import*) as corresponding to a C++ constructor. If *External_Name* and *Link_Name* are not specified then the *Entity* argument is a name that must have been previously mentioned in a pragma *Import* with *Convention* = *CPP*. Such name must be of one of the following forms:

* **function** *Fname* **return** T'
* **function** *Fname* **return** T'Class
* **function** *Fname* (...) **return** T'
* **function** *Fname* (...) **return** T'Class

where *T* is a limited record type imported from C++ with pragma *Import* and *Convention* = *CPP*.

The first two forms import the default constructor, used when an object of type *T* is created on the Ada side with no explicit constructor. The latter two forms cover all the non-default constructors of the type. See the GNAT User's Guide for details.

If no constructors are imported, it is impossible to create any objects on the Ada side and the type is implicitly declared abstract.

Pragma *CPP_Constructor* is intended primarily for automatic generation using an automatic binding generator tool (such as the *-fdump-ada-spec* GCC switch). See [Interfacing to C++], page 265 for more related information.

Note: The use of functions returning class-wide types for constructors is currently obsolete. They are supported for backward compatibility. The use of functions returning the type T leave the Ada sources more clear because the imported C++ constructors always return an object of type T; that is, they never return an object whose type is a descendant of type T.

2.38 Pragma CPP_Virtual

This pragma is now obsolete and, other than generating a warning if warnings on obsolescent features are enabled, is completely ignored. It is retained for compatibility purposes. It used to be required to ensure compoatibility with C++, but is no longer required for that purpose because GNAT generates the same object layout as the G++ compiler by default.

See [Interfacing to C++], page 265 for related information.

2.39 Pragma CPP_Vtable

This pragma is now obsolete and, other than generating a warning if warnings on obsolescent features are enabled, is completely ignored. It used to be required to ensure compatibility with C++, but is no longer required for that purpose because GNAT generates the same object layout as the G++ compiler by default.

See [Interfacing to C++], page 265 for related information.

2.40 Pragma CPU

Syntax:

```
pragma CPU (EXPRESSION);
```

This pragma is standard in Ada 2012, but is available in all earlier versions of Ada as an implementation-defined pragma. See Ada 2012 Reference Manual for details.

2.41 Pragma Default_Initial_Condition

Syntax:

```
pragma Default_Initial_Condition [ (null | boolean_EXPRESSION) ];
```

For the semantics of this pragma, see the entry for aspect *Default_Initial_Condition* in the SPARK 2014 Reference Manual, section 7.3.3.

2.42 Pragma Debug

Syntax:

```
pragma Debug ([CONDITION, ]PROCEDURE_CALL_WITHOUT_SEMICOLON);

PROCEDURE_CALL_WITHOUT_SEMICOLON ::=
  PROCEDURE_NAME
| PROCEDURE_PREFIX ACTUAL_PARAMETER_PART
```

The procedure call argument has the syntactic form of an expression, meeting the syntactic requirements for pragmas.

If debug pragmas are not enabled or if the condition is present and evaluates to False, this pragma has no effect. If debug pragmas are enabled, the semantics of the pragma is exactly equivalent to the procedure call statement corresponding to the argument with a terminating semicolon. Pragmas are permitted in sequences of declarations, so you can use pragma *Debug* to intersperse calls to debug procedures in the middle of declarations. Debug pragmas can be enabled either by use of the command line switch *-gnata* or by use of the pragma *Check_Policy* with a first argument of *Debug*.

2.43 Pragma Debug_Policy

Syntax:

```
pragma Debug_Policy (CHECK | DISABLE | IGNORE | ON | OFF);
```

This pragma is equivalent to a corresponding *Check_Policy* pragma with a first argument of *Debug*. It is retained for historical compatibility reasons.

2.44 Pragma Default_Scalar_Storage_Order

Syntax:

```
pragma Default_Scalar_Storage_Order (High_Order_First | Low_Order_First);
```

Normally if no explicit *Scalar_Storage_Order* is given for a record type or array type, then the scalar storage order defaults to the ordinary default for the target. But this default may be overridden using this pragma. The pragma may appear as a configuration pragma, or locally within a package spec or declarative part. In the latter case, it applies to all subsequent types declared within that package spec or declarative part.

The following example shows the use of this pragma:

```
pragma Default_Scalar_Storage_Order (High_Order_First);
with System; use System;
package DSSO1 is
   type H1 is record
```

```
      a : Integer;
   end record;

   type L2 is record
      a : Integer;
   end record;
   for L2'Scalar_Storage_Order use Low_Order_First;

   type L2a is new L2;

   package Inner is
      type H3 is record
         a : Integer;
      end record;

      pragma Default_Scalar_Storage_Order (Low_Order_First);

      type L4 is record
         a : Integer;
      end record;
   end Inner;

   type H4a is new Inner.L4;

   type H5 is record
      a : Integer;
   end record;
end DSSO1;
```

In this example record types L.. have *Low_Order_First* scalar storage order, and record types H.. have *High_Order_First*. Note that in the case of *H4a*, the order is not inherited from the parent type. Only an explicitly set *Scalar_Storage_Order* gets inherited on type derivation.

If this pragma is used as a configuration pragma which appears within a configuration pragma file (as opposed to appearing explicitly at the start of a single unit), then the binder will require that all units in a partition be compiled in a similar manner, other than run-time units, which are not affected by this pragma. Note that the use of this form is discouraged because it may significantly degrade the run-time performance of the software, instead the default scalar storage order ought to be changed only on a local basis.

2.45 Pragma Default_Storage_Pool

Syntax:

```
pragma Default_Storage_Pool (storage_pool_NAME | null);
```

This pragma is standard in Ada 2012, but is available in all earlier versions of Ada as an implementation-defined pragma. See Ada 2012 Reference Manual for details.

2.46 Pragma Depends

Syntax:

```
pragma Depends (DEPENDENCY_RELATION);

DEPENDENCY_RELATION ::=
     null
  | (DEPENDENCY_CLAUSE {, DEPENDENCY_CLAUSE})

DEPENDENCY_CLAUSE ::=
    OUTPUT_LIST =>[+] INPUT_LIST
  | NULL_DEPENDENCY_CLAUSE

NULL_DEPENDENCY_CLAUSE ::= null => INPUT_LIST

OUTPUT_LIST ::= OUTPUT | (OUTPUT {, OUTPUT})

INPUT_LIST ::= null | INPUT | (INPUT {, INPUT})

OUTPUT ::= NAME | FUNCTION_RESULT
INPUT  ::= NAME

where FUNCTION_RESULT is a function Result attribute_reference
```

For the semantics of this pragma, see the entry for aspect *Depends* in the SPARK 2014 Reference Manual, section 6.1.5.

2.47 Pragma Detect_Blocking

Syntax:

```
pragma Detect_Blocking;
```

This is a standard pragma in Ada 2005, that is available in all earlier versions of Ada as an implementation-defined pragma.

This is a configuration pragma that forces the detection of potentially blocking operations within a protected operation, and to raise Program_Error if that happens.

2.48 Pragma Disable_Atomic_Synchronization

Syntax:

```
pragma Disable_Atomic_Synchronization [(Entity)];
```

Ada requires that accesses (reads or writes) of an atomic variable be regarded as synchronization points in the case of multiple tasks. Particularly in the case of multi-processors this may require special handling, e.g. the generation of memory barriers. This capability may be turned off using this pragma in cases where it is known not to be required.

The placement and scope rules for this pragma are the same as those for *pragma Suppress*. In particular it can be used as a configuration pragma, or in a declaration sequence where it applies till the end of the scope. If an *Entity* argument is present, the action applies only to that entity.

2.49 Pragma Dispatching_Domain

Syntax:

```
pragma Dispatching_Domain (EXPRESSION);
```

This pragma is standard in Ada 2012, but is available in all earlier versions of Ada as an implementation-defined pragma. See Ada 2012 Reference Manual for details.

2.50 Pragma Effective_Reads

Syntax:

```
pragma Effective_Reads  [ (boolean_EXPRESSION) ];
```

For the semantics of this pragma, see the entry for aspect *Effective_Reads* in the SPARK 2014 Reference Manual, section 7.1.2.

2.51 Pragma Effective_Writes

Syntax:

```
pragma Effective_Writes [ (boolean_EXPRESSION) ];
```

For the semantics of this pragma, see the entry for aspect *Effective_Writes* in the SPARK 2014 Reference Manual, section 7.1.2.

2.52 Pragma Elaboration_Checks

Syntax:

```
pragma Elaboration_Checks (Dynamic | Static);
```

This is a configuration pragma that provides control over the elaboration model used by the compilation affected by the pragma. If the parameter is *Dynamic*, then the dynamic elaboration model described in the Ada Reference Manual is used, as though the *-gnatE* switch had been specified on the command line. If the parameter is *Static*, then the default GNAT static model is used. This configuration pragma overrides the setting of the command line. For full details on the elaboration models used by the GNAT compiler, see the chapter on elaboration order handling in the *GNAT User's Guide*.

2.53 Pragma Eliminate

Syntax:

```
pragma Eliminate ([Entity          =>] DEFINING_DESIGNATOR,
                  [Source_Location =>] STRING_LITERAL);
```

The string literal given for the source location is a string which specifies the line number of the occurrence of the entity, using the syntax for SOURCE_TRACE given below:

```
SOURCE_TRACE     ::= SOURCE_REFERENCE [LBRACKET SOURCE_TRACE RBRACKET]

LBRACKET         ::= [
RBRACKET         ::= ]

SOURCE_REFERENCE ::= FILE_NAME : LINE_NUMBER
```

```
LINE_NUMBER      ::= DIGIT {DIGIT}
```

Spaces around the colon in a *Source_Reference* are optional.

The *DEFINING_DESIGNATOR* matches the defining designator used in an explicit subprogram declaration, where the *entity* name in this designator appears on the source line specified by the source location.

The source trace that is given as the *Source_Location* shall obey the following rules. The *FILE_NAME* is the short name (with no directory information) of an Ada source file, given using exactly the required syntax for the underlying file system (e.g. case is important if the underlying operating system is case sensitive). *LINE_NUMBER* gives the line number of the occurrence of the *entity* as a decimal literal without an exponent or point. If an *entity* is not declared in a generic instantiation (this includes generic subprogram instances), the source trace includes only one source reference. If an entity is declared inside a generic instantiation, its source trace (when parsing from left to right) starts with the source location of the declaration of the entity in the generic unit and ends with the source location of the instantiation (it is given in square brackets). This approach is recursively used in case of nested instantiations: the rightmost (nested most deeply in square brackets) element of the source trace is the location of the outermost instantiation, the next to left element is the location of the next (first nested) instantiation in the code of the corresponding generic unit, and so on, and the leftmost element (that is out of any square brackets) is the location of the declaration of the entity to eliminate in a generic unit.

Note that the *Source_Location* argument specifies which of a set of similarly named entities is being eliminated, dealing both with overloading, and also appearance of the same entity name in different scopes.

This pragma indicates that the given entity is not used in the program to be compiled and built. The effect of the pragma is to allow the compiler to eliminate the code or data associated with the named entity. Any reference to an eliminated entity causes a compile-time or link-time error.

The intention of pragma *Eliminate* is to allow a program to be compiled in a system-independent manner, with unused entities eliminated, without needing to modify the source text. Normally the required set of *Eliminate* pragmas is constructed automatically using the gnatelim tool.

Any source file change that removes, splits, or adds lines may make the set of Eliminate pragmas invalid because their *Source_Location* argument values may get out of date.

Pragma *Eliminate* may be used where the referenced entity is a dispatching operation. In this case all the subprograms to which the given operation can dispatch are considered to be unused (are never called as a result of a direct or a dispatching call).

2.54 Pragma Enable_Atomic_Synchronization

Syntax:

```
pragma Enable_Atomic_Synchronization [(Entity)];
```

Ada requires that accesses (reads or writes) of an atomic variable be regarded as synchronization points in the case of multiple tasks. Particularly in the case of multi-processors this may require special handling, e.g. the generation of memory barriers. This synchronization is performed by default, but can be turned off using *pragma Disable_Atomic_Synchronization*. The *Enable_Atomic_Synchronization* pragma can be used to turn it back on.

The placement and scope rules for this pragma are the same as those for *pragma Unsuppress*. In particular it can be used as a configuration pragma, or in a declaration sequence where it applies till the end of the scope. If an *Entity* argument is present, the action applies only to that entity.

2.55 Pragma Export_Function

Syntax:

```
pragma Export_Function (
     [Internal         =>] LOCAL_NAME
  [, [External         =>] EXTERNAL_SYMBOL]
  [, [Parameter_Types  =>] PARAMETER_TYPES]
  [, [Result_Type      =>] result_SUBTYPE_MARK]
  [, [Mechanism        =>] MECHANISM]
  [, [Result_Mechanism =>] MECHANISM_NAME]);

EXTERNAL_SYMBOL ::=
  IDENTIFIER
| static_string_EXPRESSION
| ""

PARAMETER_TYPES ::=
  null
| TYPE_DESIGNATOR {, TYPE_DESIGNATOR}

TYPE_DESIGNATOR ::=
  subtype_NAME
| subtype_Name ' Access

MECHANISM ::=
  MECHANISM_NAME
| (MECHANISM_ASSOCIATION {, MECHANISM_ASSOCIATION})

MECHANISM_ASSOCIATION ::=
  [formal_parameter_NAME =>] MECHANISM_NAME

MECHANISM_NAME ::= Value | Reference
```

Use this pragma to make a function externally callable and optionally provide information on mechanisms to be used for passing parameter and result values. We recommend, for the purposes of improving portability, this pragma always be used in conjunction with a separate pragma *Export*, which must precede the pragma *Export_Function*. GNAT does not require a separate pragma *Export*, but if none is present, *Convention Ada* is assumed, which is usually not what is wanted, so it is usually appropriate to use this pragma in conjunction with a *Export* or *Convention* pragma that specifies the desired foreign convention. Pragma

Export_Function (and *Export*, if present) must appear in the same declarative region as the function to which they apply.

internal_name must uniquely designate the function to which the pragma applies. If more than one function name exists of this name in the declarative part you must use the *Parameter_Types* and *Result_Type* parameters is mandatory to achieve the required unique designation. *subtype_mark's in these parameters must exactly match the subtypes in the corresponding function specification, using positional notation to match parameters with subtype marks. The form with an ''Access* attribute can be used to match an anonymous access parameter.

Special treatment is given if the EXTERNAL is an explicit null string or a static string expressions that evaluates to the null string. In this case, no external name is generated. This form still allows the specification of parameter mechanisms.

2.56 Pragma Export_Object

Syntax:

```
pragma Export_Object
      [Internal =>] LOCAL_NAME
   [, [External =>] EXTERNAL_SYMBOL]
   [, [Size     =>] EXTERNAL_SYMBOL]

EXTERNAL_SYMBOL ::=
  IDENTIFIER
| static_string_EXPRESSION
```

This pragma designates an object as exported, and apart from the extended rules for external symbols, is identical in effect to the use of the normal *Export* pragma applied to an object. You may use a separate Export pragma (and you probably should from the point of view of portability), but it is not required. *Size* is syntax checked, but otherwise ignored by GNAT.

2.57 Pragma Export_Procedure

Syntax:

```
pragma Export_Procedure (
     [Internal        =>] LOCAL_NAME
  [, [External        =>] EXTERNAL_SYMBOL]
  [, [Parameter_Types =>] PARAMETER_TYPES]
  [, [Mechanism       =>] MECHANISM]);

EXTERNAL_SYMBOL ::=
  IDENTIFIER
| static_string_EXPRESSION
| ""

PARAMETER_TYPES ::=
  null
| TYPE_DESIGNATOR {, TYPE_DESIGNATOR}
```

```
TYPE_DESIGNATOR ::=
  subtype_NAME
| subtype_Name ' Access

MECHANISM ::=
  MECHANISM_NAME
| (MECHANISM_ASSOCIATION {, MECHANISM_ASSOCIATION})

MECHANISM_ASSOCIATION ::=
  [formal_parameter_NAME =>] MECHANISM_NAME

MECHANISM_NAME ::= Value | Reference
```

This pragma is identical to *Export_Function* except that it applies to a procedure rather than a function and the parameters *Result_Type* and *Result_Mechanism* are not permitted. GNAT does not require a separate pragma *Export*, but if none is present, *Convention Ada* is assumed, which is usually not what is wanted, so it is usually appropriate to use this pragma in conjunction with a *Export* or *Convention* pragma that specifies the desired foreign convention.

Special treatment is given if the EXTERNAL is an explicit null string or a static string expressions that evaluates to the null string. In this case, no external name is generated. This form still allows the specification of parameter mechanisms.

2.58 Pragma Export_Value

Syntax:

```
pragma Export_Value (
  [Value     =>] static_integer_EXPRESSION,
  [Link_Name =>] static_string_EXPRESSION);
```

This pragma serves to export a static integer value for external use. The first argument specifies the value to be exported. The Link_Name argument specifies the symbolic name to be associated with the integer value. This pragma is useful for defining a named static value in Ada that can be referenced in assembly language units to be linked with the application. This pragma is currently supported only for the AAMP target and is ignored for other targets.

2.59 Pragma Export_Valued_Procedure

Syntax:

```
pragma Export_Valued_Procedure (
     [Internal        =>] LOCAL_NAME
  [, [External        =>] EXTERNAL_SYMBOL]
  [, [Parameter_Types =>] PARAMETER_TYPES]
  [, [Mechanism       =>] MECHANISM]);

EXTERNAL_SYMBOL ::=
  IDENTIFIER
```

```
  | static_string_EXPRESSION
  | ""

PARAMETER_TYPES ::=
    null
  | TYPE_DESIGNATOR {, TYPE_DESIGNATOR}

TYPE_DESIGNATOR ::=
    subtype_NAME
  | subtype_Name ' Access

MECHANISM ::=
    MECHANISM_NAME
  | (MECHANISM_ASSOCIATION {, MECHANISM_ASSOCIATION})

MECHANISM_ASSOCIATION ::=
    [formal_parameter_NAME =>] MECHANISM_NAME

MECHANISM_NAME ::= Value | Reference
```

This pragma is identical to *Export_Procedure* except that the first parameter of *LOCAL_NAME*, which must be present, must be of mode *OUT*, and externally the subprogram is treated as a function with this parameter as the result of the function. GNAT provides for this capability to allow the use of *OUT* and *IN OUT* parameters in interfacing to external functions (which are not permitted in Ada functions). GNAT does not require a separate pragma *Export*, but if none is present, *Convention Ada* is assumed, which is almost certainly not what is wanted since the whole point of this pragma is to interface with foreign language functions, so it is usually appropriate to use this pragma in conjunction with a *Export* or *Convention* pragma that specifies the desired foreign convention.

Special treatment is given if the EXTERNAL is an explicit null string or a static string expressions that evaluates to the null string. In this case, no external name is generated. This form still allows the specification of parameter mechanisms.

2.60 Pragma Extend_System

Syntax:

```
pragma Extend_System ([Name =>] IDENTIFIER);
```

This pragma is used to provide backwards compatibility with other implementations that extend the facilities of package *System*. In GNAT, *System* contains only the definitions that are present in the Ada RM. However, other implementations, notably the DEC Ada 83 implementation, provide many extensions to package *System*.

For each such implementation accommodated by this pragma, GNAT provides a package *Aux_*'xxx', e.g., *Aux_DEC* for the DEC Ada 83 implementation, which provides the required additional definitions. You can use this package in two ways. You can *with* it in the normal way and access entities either by selection or using a *use* clause. In this case no special processing is required.

However, if existing code contains references such as *System.'xxx'* where *xxx* is an entity in the extended definitions provided in package *System*, you may use this pragma to extend visibility in *System* in a non-standard way that provides greater compatibility with the existing code. Pragma *Extend_System* is a configuration pragma whose single argument is the name of the package containing the extended definition (e.g., *Aux_DEC* for the DEC Ada case). A unit compiled under control of this pragma will be processed using special visibility processing that looks in package *System.Aux_'xxx'* where *Aux_'xxx'* is the pragma argument for any entity referenced in package *System*, but not found in package *System*.

You can use this pragma either to access a predefined *System* extension supplied with the compiler, for example *Aux_DEC* or you can construct your own extension unit following the above definition. Note that such a package is a child of *System* and thus is considered part of the implementation. To compile it you will have to use the *-gnatg* switch for compiling System units, as explained in the GNAT User's Guide.

2.61 Pragma Extensions_Allowed

Syntax:

```
pragma Extensions_Allowed (On | Off);
```

This configuration pragma enables or disables the implementation extension mode (the use of Off as a parameter cancels the effect of the *-gnatX* command switch).

In extension mode, the latest version of the Ada language is implemented (currently Ada 2012), and in addition a small number of GNAT specific extensions are recognized as follows:

Constrained attribute for generic objects
: The *Constrained* attribute is permitted for objects of generic types. The result indicates if the corresponding actual is constrained.

2.62 Pragma Extensions_Visible

Syntax:

```
pragma Extensions_Visible [ (boolean_EXPRESSION) ];
```

For the semantics of this pragma, see the entry for aspect *Extensions_Visible* in the SPARK 2014 Reference Manual, section 6.1.7.

2.63 Pragma External

Syntax:

```
pragma External (
  [   Convention    =>] convention_IDENTIFIER,
  [   Entity        =>] LOCAL_NAME
  [, [External_Name =>] static_string_EXPRESSION ]
  [, [Link_Name     =>] static_string_EXPRESSION ]);
```

This pragma is identical in syntax and semantics to pragma *Export* as defined in the Ada Reference Manual. It is provided for compatibility with some Ada 83 compilers that used this pragma for exactly the same purposes as pragma *Export* before the latter was standardized.

2.64 Pragma External_Name_Casing

Syntax:

```
pragma External_Name_Casing (
  Uppercase | Lowercase
  [, Uppercase | Lowercase | As_Is]);
```

This pragma provides control over the casing of external names associated with Import and Export pragmas. There are two cases to consider:

* Implicit external names

  Implicit external names are derived from identifiers. The most common case arises when a standard Ada Import or Export pragma is used with only two arguments, as in:

  ```
  pragma Import (C, C_Routine);
  ```

  Since Ada is a case-insensitive language, the spelling of the identifier in the Ada source program does not provide any information on the desired casing of the external name, and so a convention is needed. In GNAT the default treatment is that such names are converted to all lower case letters. This corresponds to the normal C style in many environments. The first argument of pragma *External_Name_Casing* can be used to control this treatment. If *Uppercase* is specified, then the name will be forced to all uppercase letters. If *Lowercase* is specified, then the normal default of all lower case letters will be used.

  This same implicit treatment is also used in the case of extended DEC Ada 83 compatible Import and Export pragmas where an external name is explicitly specified using an identifier rather than a string.

* Explicit external names

  Explicit external names are given as string literals. The most common case arises when a standard Ada Import or Export pragma is used with three arguments, as in:

  ```
  pragma Import (C, C_Routine, "C_routine");
  ```

  In this case, the string literal normally provides the exact casing required for the external name. The second argument of pragma *External_Name_Casing* may be used to modify this behavior. If *Uppercase* is specified, then the name will be forced to all uppercase letters. If *Lowercase* is specified, then the name will be forced to all lowercase letters. A specification of *As_Is* provides the normal default behavior in which the casing is taken from the string provided.

This pragma may appear anywhere that a pragma is valid. In particular, it can be used as a configuration pragma in the `gnat.adc` file, in which case it applies to all subsequent compilations, or it can be used as a program unit pragma, in which case it only applies to the current unit, or it can be used more locally to control individual Import/Export pragmas.

It was primarily intended for use with OpenVMS systems, where many compilers convert all symbols to upper case by default. For interfacing to such compilers (e.g., the DEC C compiler), it may be convenient to use the pragma:

```
pragma External_Name_Casing (Uppercase, Uppercase);
```

to enforce the upper casing of all external symbols.

2.65 Pragma Fast_Math

Syntax:

```
pragma Fast_Math;
```

This is a configuration pragma which activates a mode in which speed is considered more important for floating-point operations than absolutely accurate adherence to the requirements of the standard. Currently the following operations are affected:

Complex Multiplication
: The normal simple formula for complex multiplication can result in intermediate overflows for numbers near the end of the range. The Ada standard requires that this situation be detected and corrected by scaling, but in Fast_Math mode such cases will simply result in overflow. Note that to take advantage of this you must instantiate your own version of *Ada.Numerics.Generic_Complex_Types* under control of the pragma, rather than use the preinstantiated versions.

2.66 Pragma Favor_Top_Level

Syntax:

```
pragma Favor_Top_Level (type_NAME);
```

The named type must be an access-to-subprogram type. This pragma is an efficiency hint to the compiler, regarding the use of 'Access or 'Unrestricted_Access on nested (non-library-level) subprograms. The pragma means that nested subprograms are not used with this type, or are rare, so that the generated code should be efficient in the top-level case. When this pragma is used, dynamically generated trampolines may be used on some targets for nested subprograms. See also the No_Implicit_Dynamic_Code restriction.

2.67 Pragma Finalize_Storage_Only

Syntax:

```
pragma Finalize_Storage_Only (first_subtype_LOCAL_NAME);
```

This pragma allows the compiler not to emit a Finalize call for objects defined at the library level. This is mostly useful for types where finalization is only used to deal with storage reclamation since in most environments it is not necessary to reclaim memory just before terminating execution, hence the name.

2.68 Pragma Float_Representation

Syntax:

```
pragma Float_Representation (FLOAT_REP[, float_type_LOCAL_NAME]);

FLOAT_REP ::= VAX_Float | IEEE_Float
```

In the one argument form, this pragma is a configuration pragma which allows control over the internal representation chosen for the predefined floating point types declared in the packages *Standard* and *System*. This pragma is only provided for compatibility and has no effect.

The two argument form specifies the representation to be used for the specified floating-point type. The argument must be *IEEE_Float* to specify the use of IEEE format, as follows:

* For a digits value of 6, 32-bit IEEE short format will be used.
* For a digits value of 15, 64-bit IEEE long format will be used.
* No other value of digits is permitted.

2.69 Pragma Ghost

Syntax:

```
pragma Ghost [ (boolean_EXPRESSION) ];
```

For the semantics of this pragma, see the entry for aspect *Ghost* in the SPARK 2014 Reference Manual, section 6.9.

2.70 Pragma Global

Syntax:

```
pragma Global (GLOBAL_SPECIFICATION);

GLOBAL_SPECIFICATION ::=
     null
  | (GLOBAL_LIST)
  | (MODED_GLOBAL_LIST {, MODED_GLOBAL_LIST})

MODED_GLOBAL_LIST ::= MODE_SELECTOR => GLOBAL_LIST

MODE_SELECTOR ::= In_Out | Input | Output | Proof_In
GLOBAL_LIST   ::= GLOBAL_ITEM | (GLOBAL_ITEM {, GLOBAL_ITEM})
GLOBAL_ITEM   ::= NAME
```

For the semantics of this pragma, see the entry for aspect *Global* in the SPARK 2014 Reference Manual, section 6.1.4.

2.71 Pragma Ident

Syntax:

```
pragma Ident (static_string_EXPRESSION);
```

This pragma is identical in effect to pragma *Comment*. It is provided for compatibility with other Ada compilers providing this pragma.

2.72 Pragma Ignore_Pragma

Syntax:

```
pragma Ignore_Pragma (pragma_IDENTIFIER);
```

This is a configuration pragma that takes a single argument that is a simple identifier. Any subsequent use of a pragma whose pragma identifier matches this argument will be silently ignored. This may be useful when legacy code or code intended for compilation with some other compiler contains pragmas that match the name, but not the exact implementation, of a *GNAT* pragma. The use of this pragma allows such pragmas to be ignored, which may be useful in *CodePeer* mode, or during porting of legacy code.

2.73 Pragma Implementation_Defined

Syntax:

```
pragma Implementation_Defined (local_NAME);
```

This pragma marks a previously declared entioty as implementation-defined. For an overloaded entity, applies to the most recent homonym.

```
pragma Implementation_Defined;
```

The form with no arguments appears anywhere within a scope, most typically a package spec, and indicates that all entities that are defined within the package spec are Implementation_Defined.

This pragma is used within the GNAT runtime library to identify implementation-defined entities introduced in language-defined units, for the purpose of implementing the No_Implementation_Identifiers restriction.

2.74 Pragma Implemented

Syntax:

```
pragma Implemented (procedure_LOCAL_NAME, implementation_kind);

implementation_kind ::= By_Entry | By_Protected_Procedure | By_Any
```

This is an Ada 2012 representation pragma which applies to protected, task and synchronized interface primitives. The use of pragma Implemented provides a way to impose a static requirement on the overriding operation by adhering to one of the three implementation kinds: entry, protected procedure or any of the above. This pragma is available in all earlier versions of Ada as an implementation-defined pragma.

```
type Synch_Iface is synchronized interface;
procedure Prim_Op (Obj : in out Iface) is abstract;
pragma Implemented (Prim_Op, By_Protected_Procedure);

protected type Prot_1 is new Synch_Iface with
   procedure Prim_Op;  --  Legal
end Prot_1;

protected type Prot_2 is new Synch_Iface with
   entry Prim_Op;      --  Illegal
end Prot_2;

task type Task_Typ is new Synch_Iface with
   entry Prim_Op;      --  Illegal
end Task_Typ;
```

When applied to the procedure_or_entry_NAME of a requeue statement, pragma Implemented determines the runtime behavior of the requeue. Implementation kind By_Entry guarantees that the action of requeueing will proceed from an entry to another entry. Implementation kind By_Protected_Procedure transforms the requeue into a dispatching call, thus eliminating the chance of blocking. Kind By_Any shares the behavior of By_Entry and By_Protected_Procedure depending on the target's overriding subprogram kind.

2.75 Pragma Implicit_Packing

Syntax:

```
pragma Implicit_Packing;
```

This is a configuration pragma that requests implicit packing for packed arrays for which a size clause is given but no explicit pragma Pack or specification of Component_Size is present. It also applies to records where no record representation clause is present. Consider this example:

```
type R is array (0 .. 7) of Boolean;
for R'Size use 8;
```

In accordance with the recommendation in the RM (RM 13.3(53)), a Size clause does not change the layout of a composite object. So the Size clause in the above example is normally rejected, since the default layout of the array uses 8-bit components, and thus the array requires a minimum of 64 bits.

If this declaration is compiled in a region of code covered by an occurrence of the configuration pragma Implicit_Packing, then the Size clause in this and similar examples will cause implicit packing and thus be accepted. For this implicit packing to occur, the type in question must be an array of small components whose size is known at compile time, and the Size clause must specify the exact size that corresponds to the number of elements in the array multiplied by the size in bits of the component type (both single and multi-dimensioned arrays can be controlled with this pragma).

Similarly, the following example shows the use in the record case

```
type r is record
   a, b, c, d, e, f, g, h : boolean;
   chr                    : character;
end record;
for r'size use 16;
```

Without a pragma Pack, each Boolean field requires 8 bits, so the minimum size is 72 bits, but with a pragma Pack, 16 bits would be sufficient. The use of pragma Implicit_Packing allows this record declaration to compile without an explicit pragma Pack.

2.76 Pragma Import_Function

Syntax:

```
pragma Import_Function (
     [Internal                 =>] LOCAL_NAME,
  [, [External                 =>] EXTERNAL_SYMBOL]
  [, [Parameter_Types          =>] PARAMETER_TYPES]
  [, [Result_Type              =>] SUBTYPE_MARK]
  [, [Mechanism                =>] MECHANISM]
  [, [Result_Mechanism         =>] MECHANISM_NAME]);
```

```
EXTERNAL_SYMBOL ::=
  IDENTIFIER
| static_string_EXPRESSION

PARAMETER_TYPES ::=
  null
| TYPE_DESIGNATOR {, TYPE_DESIGNATOR}

TYPE_DESIGNATOR ::=
  subtype_NAME
| subtype_Name ' Access

MECHANISM ::=
  MECHANISM_NAME
| (MECHANISM_ASSOCIATION {, MECHANISM_ASSOCIATION})

MECHANISM_ASSOCIATION ::=
  [formal_parameter_NAME =>] MECHANISM_NAME

MECHANISM_NAME ::=
  Value
| Reference
```

This pragma is used in conjunction with a pragma *Import* to specify additional information for an imported function. The pragma *Import* (or equivalent pragma *Interface*) must precede the *Import_Function* pragma and both must appear in the same declarative part as the function specification.

The *Internal* argument must uniquely designate the function to which the pragma applies. If more than one function name exists of this name in the declarative part you must use the *Parameter_Types* and *Result_Type* parameters to achieve the required unique designation. Subtype marks in these parameters must exactly match the subtypes in the corresponding function specification, using positional notation to match parameters with subtype marks. The form with an *'Access* attribute can be used to match an anonymous access parameter.

You may optionally use the *Mechanism* and *Result_Mechanism* parameters to specify passing mechanisms for the parameters and result. If you specify a single mechanism name, it applies to all parameters. Otherwise you may specify a mechanism on a parameter by parameter basis using either positional or named notation. If the mechanism is not specified, the default mechanism is used.

2.77 Pragma Import_Object

Syntax:

```
pragma Import_Object
     [Internal =>] LOCAL_NAME
  [, [External =>] EXTERNAL_SYMBOL]
  [, [Size     =>] EXTERNAL_SYMBOL]);
```

```
EXTERNAL_SYMBOL ::=
  IDENTIFIER
| static_string_EXPRESSION
```

This pragma designates an object as imported, and apart from the extended rules for external symbols, is identical in effect to the use of the normal *Import* pragma applied to an object. Unlike the subprogram case, you need not use a separate *Import* pragma, although you may do so (and probably should do so from a portability point of view). *size* is syntax checked, but otherwise ignored by GNAT.

2.78 Pragma Import_Procedure

Syntax:

```
pragma Import_Procedure (
     [Internal                 =>] LOCAL_NAME
  [, [External                 =>] EXTERNAL_SYMBOL]
  [, [Parameter_Types          =>] PARAMETER_TYPES]
  [, [Mechanism                =>] MECHANISM]);

EXTERNAL_SYMBOL ::=
  IDENTIFIER
| static_string_EXPRESSION

PARAMETER_TYPES ::=
  null
| TYPE_DESIGNATOR {, TYPE_DESIGNATOR}

TYPE_DESIGNATOR ::=
  subtype_NAME
| subtype_Name ' Access

MECHANISM ::=
  MECHANISM_NAME
| (MECHANISM_ASSOCIATION {, MECHANISM_ASSOCIATION})

MECHANISM_ASSOCIATION ::=
  [formal_parameter_NAME =>] MECHANISM_NAME

MECHANISM_NAME ::= Value | Reference
```

This pragma is identical to *Import_Function* except that it applies to a procedure rather than a function and the parameters *Result_Type* and *Result_Mechanism* are not permitted.

2.79 Pragma Import_Valued_Procedure

Syntax:

```
pragma Import_Valued_Procedure (
     [Internal                 =>] LOCAL_NAME
```

```
  [, [External                   =>] EXTERNAL_SYMBOL]
  [, [Parameter_Types            =>] PARAMETER_TYPES]
  [, [Mechanism                  =>] MECHANISM]);

EXTERNAL_SYMBOL ::=
  IDENTIFIER
| static_string_EXPRESSION

PARAMETER_TYPES ::=
  null
| TYPE_DESIGNATOR {, TYPE_DESIGNATOR}

TYPE_DESIGNATOR ::=
  subtype_NAME
| subtype_Name ' Access

MECHANISM ::=
  MECHANISM_NAME
| (MECHANISM_ASSOCIATION {, MECHANISM_ASSOCIATION})

MECHANISM_ASSOCIATION ::=
  [formal_parameter_NAME =>] MECHANISM_NAME

MECHANISM_NAME ::= Value | Reference
```

This pragma is identical to *Import_Procedure* except that the first parameter of *LOCAL_NAME*, which must be present, must be of mode *OUT*, and externally the subprogram is treated as a function with this parameter as the result of the function. The purpose of this capability is to allow the use of *OUT* and *IN OUT* parameters in interfacing to external functions (which are not permitted in Ada functions). You may optionally use the *Mechanism* parameters to specify passing mechanisms for the parameters. If you specify a single mechanism name, it applies to all parameters. Otherwise you may specify a mechanism on a parameter by parameter basis using either positional or named notation. If the mechanism is not specified, the default mechanism is used.

Note that it is important to use this pragma in conjunction with a separate pragma Import that specifies the desired convention, since otherwise the default convention is Ada, which is almost certainly not what is required.

2.80 Pragma Independent

Syntax:

```
pragma Independent (Local_NAME);
```

This pragma is standard in Ada 2012 mode (which also provides an aspect of the same name). It is also available as an implementation-defined pragma in all earlier versions. It specifies that the designated object or all objects of the designated type must be independently addressable. This means that separate tasks can safely manipulate such objects. For example, if two components of a record are independent, then two separate tasks may access these two components. This may place constraints on the representation of the object (for instance prohibiting tight packing).

2.81 Pragma Independent_Components

Syntax:

```
pragma Independent_Components (Local_NAME);
```

This pragma is standard in Ada 2012 mode (which also provides an aspect of the same name). It is also available as an implementation-defined pragma in all earlier versions. It specifies that the components of the designated object, or the components of each object of the designated type, must be independently addressable. This means that separate tasks can safely manipulate separate components in the composite object. This may place constraints on the representation of the object (for instance prohibiting tight packing).

2.82 Pragma Initial_Condition

Syntax:

```
pragma Initial_Condition (boolean_EXPRESSION);
```

For the semantics of this pragma, see the entry for aspect *Initial_Condition* in the SPARK 2014 Reference Manual, section 7.1.6.

2.83 Pragma Initialize_Scalars

Syntax:

```
pragma Initialize_Scalars;
```

This pragma is similar to *Normalize_Scalars* conceptually but has two important differences. First, there is no requirement for the pragma to be used uniformly in all units of a partition, in particular, it is fine to use this just for some or all of the application units of a partition, without needing to recompile the run-time library.

In the case where some units are compiled with the pragma, and some without, then a declaration of a variable where the type is defined in package Standard or is locally declared will always be subject to initialization, as will any declaration of a scalar variable. For composite variables, whether the variable is initialized may also depend on whether the package in which the type of the variable is declared is compiled with the pragma.

The other important difference is that you can control the value used for initializing scalar objects. At bind time, you can select several options for initialization. You can initialize with invalid values (similar to Normalize_Scalars, though for Initialize_Scalars it is not always possible to determine the invalid values in complex cases like signed component fields with non-standard sizes). You can also initialize with high or low values, or with a specified bit pattern. See the GNAT User's Guide for binder options for specifying these cases.

This means that you can compile a program, and then without having to recompile the program, you can run it with different values being used for initializing otherwise uninitialized values, to test if your program behavior depends on the choice. Of course the behavior should not change, and if it does, then most likely you have an incorrect reference to an uninitialized value.

It is even possible to change the value at execution time eliminating even the need to rebind with a different switch using an environment variable. See the GNAT User's Guide for details.

Note that pragma *Initialize_Scalars* is particularly useful in conjunction with the enhanced validity checking that is now provided in GNAT, which checks for invalid values under more conditions. Using this feature (see description of the *-gnatV* flag in the GNAT User's Guide) in conjunction with pragma *Initialize_Scalars* provides a powerful new tool to assist in the detection of problems caused by uninitialized variables.

Note: the use of *Initialize_Scalars* has a fairly extensive effect on the generated code. This may cause your code to be substantially larger. It may also cause an increase in the amount of stack required, so it is probably a good idea to turn on stack checking (see description of stack checking in the GNAT User's Guide) when using this pragma.

2.84 Pragma Initializes

Syntax:

```
pragma Initializes (INITIALIZATION_LIST);

INITIALIZATION_LIST ::=
     null
  | (INITIALIZATION_ITEM {, INITIALIZATION_ITEM})

INITIALIZATION_ITEM ::= name [=> INPUT_LIST]

INPUT_LIST ::=
     null
  |  INPUT
  | (INPUT {, INPUT})

INPUT ::= name
```

For the semantics of this pragma, see the entry for aspect *Initializes* in the SPARK 2014 Reference Manual, section 7.1.5.

2.85 Pragma Inline_Always

Syntax:

```
pragma Inline_Always (NAME [, NAME]);
```

Similar to pragma *Inline* except that inlining is not subject to the use of option *-gnatn* or *-gnatN* and the inlining happens regardless of whether these options are used.

2.86 Pragma Inline_Generic

Syntax:

```
pragma Inline_Generic (GNAME {, GNAME});

GNAME ::= generic_unit_NAME | generic_instance_NAME
```

This pragma is provided for compatibility with Dec Ada 83. It has no effect in *GNAT* (which always inlines generics), other than to check that the given names are all names of generic units or generic instances.

2.87 Pragma Interface

Syntax:

```
pragma Interface (
     [Convention    =>] convention_identifier,
     [Entity        =>] local_NAME
  [, [External_Name =>] static_string_expression]
  [, [Link_Name     =>] static_string_expression]);
```

This pragma is identical in syntax and semantics to the standard Ada pragma *Import*. It is provided for compatibility with Ada 83. The definition is upwards compatible both with pragma *Interface* as defined in the Ada 83 Reference Manual, and also with some extended implementations of this pragma in certain Ada 83 implementations. The only difference between pragma *Interface* and pragma *Import* is that there is special circuitry to allow both pragmas to appear for the same subprogram entity (normally it is illegal to have multiple *Import* pragmas. This is useful in maintaining Ada 83/Ada 95 compatibility and is compatible with other Ada 83 compilers.

2.88 Pragma Interface_Name

Syntax:

```
pragma Interface_Name (
     [Entity        =>] LOCAL_NAME
  [, [External_Name =>] static_string_EXPRESSION]
  [, [Link_Name     =>] static_string_EXPRESSION]);
```

This pragma provides an alternative way of specifying the interface name for an interfaced subprogram, and is provided for compatibility with Ada 83 compilers that use the pragma for this purpose. You must provide at least one of *External_Name* or *Link_Name*.

2.89 Pragma Interrupt_Handler

Syntax:

```
pragma Interrupt_Handler (procedure_LOCAL_NAME);
```

This program unit pragma is supported for parameterless protected procedures as described in Annex C of the Ada Reference Manual. On the AAMP target the pragma can also be specified for nonprotected parameterless procedures that are declared at the library level (which includes procedures declared at the top level of a library package). In the case of AAMP, when this pragma is applied to a nonprotected procedure, the instruction *IERET* is generated for returns from the procedure, enabling maskable interrupts, in place of the normal return instruction.

2.90 Pragma Interrupt_State

Syntax:

```
pragma Interrupt_State
 ([Name  =>] value,
  [State =>] SYSTEM | RUNTIME | USER);
```

Normally certain interrupts are reserved to the implementation. Any attempt to attach an interrupt causes Program_Error to be raised, as described in RM C.3.2(22). A typical example is the *SIGINT* interrupt used in many systems for an `Ctrl-C` interrupt. Normally this interrupt is reserved to the implementation, so that `Ctrl-C` can be used to interrupt execution. Additionally, signals such as *SIGSEGV*, *SIGABRT*, *SIGFPE* and *SIGILL* are often mapped to specific Ada exceptions, or used to implement run-time functions such as the *abort* statement and stack overflow checking.

Pragma *Interrupt_State* provides a general mechanism for overriding such uses of interrupts. It subsumes the functionality of pragma *Unreserve_All_Interrupts*. Pragma *Interrupt_State* is not available on Windows or VMS. On all other platforms than VxWorks, it applies to signals; on VxWorks, it applies to vectored hardware interrupts and may be used to mark interrupts required by the board support package as reserved.

Interrupts can be in one of three states:

* System

  The interrupt is reserved (no Ada handler can be installed), and the Ada run-time may not install a handler. As a result you are guaranteed standard system default action if this interrupt is raised.

* Runtime

  The interrupt is reserved (no Ada handler can be installed). The run time is allowed to install a handler for internal control purposes, but is not required to do so.

* User

  The interrupt is unreserved. The user may install a handler to provide some other action.

These states are the allowed values of the *State* parameter of the pragma. The *Name* parameter is a value of the type *Ada.Interrupts.Interrupt_ID*. Typically, it is a name declared in *Ada.Interrupts.Names*.

This is a configuration pragma, and the binder will check that there are no inconsistencies between different units in a partition in how a given interrupt is specified. It may appear anywhere a pragma is legal.

The effect is to move the interrupt to the specified state.

By declaring interrupts to be SYSTEM, you guarantee the standard system action, such as a core dump.

By declaring interrupts to be USER, you guarantee that you can install a handler.

Note that certain signals on many operating systems cannot be caught and handled by applications. In such cases, the pragma is ignored. See the operating system documentation, or the value of the array *Reserved* declared in the spec of package *System.OS_Interface*.

Overriding the default state of signals used by the Ada runtime may interfere with an application's runtime behavior in the cases of the synchronous signals, and in the case of the signal used to implement the *abort* statement.

2.91 Pragma Invariant

Syntax:

```
pragma Invariant
  ([Entity =>]    private_type_LOCAL_NAME,
   [Check  =>]    EXPRESSION
   [,[Message =>] String_Expression]);
```

This pragma provides exactly the same capabilities as the Type_Invariant aspect defined in AI05-0146-1, and in the Ada 2012 Reference Manual. The Type_Invariant aspect is fully implemented in Ada 2012 mode, but since it requires the use of the aspect syntax, which is not available except in 2012 mode, it is not possible to use the Type_Invariant aspect in earlier versions of Ada. However the Invariant pragma may be used in any version of Ada. Also note that the aspect Invariant is a synonym in GNAT for the aspect Type_Invariant, but there is no pragma Type_Invariant.

The pragma must appear within the visible part of the package specification, after the type to which its Entity argument appears. As with the Invariant aspect, the Check expression is not analyzed until the end of the visible part of the package, so it may contain forward references. The Message argument, if present, provides the exception message used if the invariant is violated. If no Message parameter is provided, a default message that identifies the line on which the pragma appears is used.

It is permissible to have multiple Invariants for the same type entity, in which case they are and'ed together. It is permissible to use this pragma in Ada 2012 mode, but you cannot have both an invariant aspect and an invariant pragma for the same entity.

For further details on the use of this pragma, see the Ada 2012 documentation of the Type_Invariant aspect.

2.92 Pragma Keep_Names

Syntax:

```
pragma Keep_Names ([On =>] enumeration_first_subtype_LOCAL_NAME);
```

The *LOCAL_NAME* argument must refer to an enumeration first subtype in the current declarative part. The effect is to retain the enumeration literal names for use by *Image* and *Value* even if a global *Discard_Names* pragma applies. This is useful when you want to generally suppress enumeration literal names and for example you therefore use a *Discard_Names* pragma in the `gnat.adc` file, but you want to retain the names for specific enumeration types.

2.93 Pragma License

Syntax:

```
pragma License (Unrestricted | GPL | Modified_GPL | Restricted);
```

This pragma is provided to allow automated checking for appropriate license conditions with respect to the standard and modified GPL. A pragma *License*, which is a configuration pragma that typically appears at the start of a source file or in a separate `gnat.adc` file, specifies the licensing conditions of a unit as follows:

* Unrestricted This is used for a unit that can be freely used with no license restrictions. Examples of such units are public domain units, and units from the Ada Reference Manual.
* GPL This is used for a unit that is licensed under the unmodified GPL, and which therefore cannot be *with*'ed by a restricted unit.
* Modified_GPL This is used for a unit licensed under the GNAT modified GPL that includes a special exception paragraph that specifically permits the inclusion of the unit in programs without requiring the entire program to be released under the GPL.
* Restricted This is used for a unit that is restricted in that it is not permitted to depend on units that are licensed under the GPL. Typical examples are proprietary code that is to be released under more restrictive license conditions. Note that restricted units are permitted to *with* units which are licensed under the modified GPL (this is the whole point of the modified GPL).

Normally a unit with no *License* pragma is considered to have an unknown license, and no checking is done. However, standard GNAT headers are recognized, and license information is derived from them as follows.

A GNAT license header starts with a line containing 78 hyphens. The following comment text is searched for the appearance of any of the following strings.

If the string 'GNU General Public License' is found, then the unit is assumed to have GPL license, unless the string 'As a special exception' follows, in which case the license is assumed to be modified GPL.

If one of the strings 'This specification is adapted from the Ada Semantic Interface' or 'This specification is derived from the Ada Reference Manual' is found then the unit is assumed to be unrestricted.

These default actions means that a program with a restricted license pragma will automatically get warnings if a GPL unit is inappropriately *with*'ed. For example, the program:

```
with Sem_Ch3;
with GNAT.Sockets;
procedure Secret_Stuff is
  ...
end Secret_Stuff
```

if compiled with pragma *License* (*Restricted*) in a `gnat.adc` file will generate the warning:

```
1.  with Sem_Ch3;
            |
   >>> license of withed unit "Sem_Ch3" is incompatible

2.  with GNAT.Sockets;
3.  procedure Secret_Stuff is
```

Here we get a warning on *Sem_Ch3* since it is part of the GNAT compiler and is licensed under the GPL, but no warning for *GNAT.Sockets* which is part of the GNAT run time, and is therefore licensed under the modified GPL.

2.94 Pragma Link_With

Syntax:

```
pragma Link_With (static_string_EXPRESSION {,static_string_EXPRESSION});
```

This pragma is provided for compatibility with certain Ada 83 compilers. It has exactly the same effect as pragma *Linker_Options* except that spaces occurring within one of the string expressions are treated as separators. For example, in the following case:

```
pragma Link_With ("-labc -ldef");
```

results in passing the strings *-labc* and *-ldef* as two separate arguments to the linker. In addition pragma Link_With allows multiple arguments, with the same effect as successive pragmas.

2.95 Pragma Linker_Alias

Syntax:

```
pragma Linker_Alias (
  [Entity =>] LOCAL_NAME,
  [Target =>] static_string_EXPRESSION);
```

LOCAL_NAME must refer to an object that is declared at the library level. This pragma establishes the given entity as a linker alias for the given target. It is equivalent to *__attribute__((alias))* in GNU C and causes *LOCAL_NAME* to be emitted as an alias for the symbol *static_string_EXPRESSION* in the object file, that is to say no space is reserved for *LOCAL_NAME* by the assembler and it will be resolved to the same address as *static_string_EXPRESSION* by the linker.

The actual linker name for the target must be used (e.g., the fully encoded name with qualification in Ada, or the mangled name in C++), or it must be declared using the C convention with *pragma Import* or *pragma Export*.

Not all target machines support this pragma. On some of them it is accepted only if *pragma Weak_External* has been applied to *LOCAL_NAME*.

```
--  Example of the use of pragma Linker_Alias

package p is
  i : Integer := 1;
  pragma Export (C, i);

  new_name_for_i : Integer;
  pragma Linker_Alias (new_name_for_i, "i");
end p;
```

2.96 Pragma Linker_Constructor

Syntax:

```
pragma Linker_Constructor (procedure_LOCAL_NAME);
```

procedure_LOCAL_NAME must refer to a parameterless procedure that is declared at the library level. A procedure to which this pragma is applied will be treated as an initialization routine by the linker. It is equivalent to *__attribute__((constructor))* in GNU C and causes *procedure_LOCAL_NAME* to be invoked before the entry point of the executable is called (or immediately after the shared library is loaded if the procedure is linked in a shared library), in particular before the Ada run-time environment is set up.

Because of these specific contexts, the set of operations such a procedure can perform is very limited and the type of objects it can manipulate is essentially restricted to the elementary types. In particular, it must only contain code to which pragma Restrictions (No_Elaboration_Code) applies.

This pragma is used by GNAT to implement auto-initialization of shared Stand Alone Libraries, which provides a related capability without the restrictions listed above. Where possible, the use of Stand Alone Libraries is preferable to the use of this pragma.

2.97 Pragma Linker_Destructor

Syntax:

```
pragma Linker_Destructor (procedure_LOCAL_NAME);
```

procedure_LOCAL_NAME must refer to a parameterless procedure that is declared at the library level. A procedure to which this pragma is applied will be treated as a finalization routine by the linker. It is equivalent to *__attribute__((destructor))* in GNU C and causes *procedure_LOCAL_NAME* to be invoked after the entry point of the executable has exited (or immediately before the shared library is unloaded if the procedure is linked in a shared library), in particular after the Ada run-time environment is shut down.

See *pragma Linker_Constructor* for the set of restrictions that apply because of these specific contexts.

2.98 Pragma Linker_Section

Syntax:

```
pragma Linker_Section (
  [Entity  =>] LOCAL_NAME,
  [Section =>] static_string_EXPRESSION);
```

LOCAL_NAME must refer to an object, type, or subprogram that is declared at the library level. This pragma specifies the name of the linker section for the given entity. It is equivalent to *__attribute__((section))* in GNU C and causes *LOCAL_NAME* to be placed in the *static_string_EXPRESSION* section of the executable (assuming the linker doesn't rename the section). GNAT also provides an implementation defined aspect of the same name.

In the case of specifying this aspect for a type, the effect is to specify the corresponding for all library level objects of the type which do not have an explicit linker section set. Note that this only applies to whole objects, not to components of composite objects.

In the case of a subprogram, the linker section applies to all previously declared matching overloaded subprograms in the current declarative part which do not already have a linker section assigned. The linker section aspect is useful in this case for specifying different linker sections for different elements of such an overloaded set.

Note that an empty string specifies that no linker section is specified. This is not quite the same as omitting the pragma or aspect, since it can be used to specify that one element of an overloaded set of subprograms has the default linker section, or that one object of a type for which a linker section is specified should has the default linker section.

The compiler normally places library-level entities in standard sections depending on the class: procedures and functions generally go in the *.text* section, initialized variables in the *.data* section and uninitialized variables in the *.bss* section.

Other, special sections may exist on given target machines to map special hardware, for example I/O ports or flash memory. This pragma is a means to defer the final layout of the executable to the linker, thus fully working at the symbolic level with the compiler.

Some file formats do not support arbitrary sections so not all target machines support this pragma. The use of this pragma may cause a program execution to be erroneous if it is used to place an entity into an inappropriate section (e.g., a modified variable into the *.text* section). See also *pragma Persistent_BSS*.

```
--  Example of the use of pragma Linker_Section

package IO_Card is
  Port_A : Integer;
  pragma Volatile (Port_A);
  pragma Linker_Section (Port_A, ".bss.port_a");

  Port_B : Integer;
  pragma Volatile (Port_B);
  pragma Linker_Section (Port_B, ".bss.port_b");

  type Port_Type is new Integer with Linker_Section => ".bss";
  PA : Port_Type with Linker_Section => ".bss.PA";
  PB : Port_Type; --  ends up in linker section ".bss"

  procedure Q with Linker_Section => "Qsection";
end IO_Card;
```

2.99 Pragma Lock_Free

Syntax: This pragma may be specified for protected types or objects. It specifies that the implementation of protected operations must be implemented without locks. Compilation fails if the compiler cannot generate lock-free code for the operations.

2.100 Pragma Loop_Invariant

Syntax:

```
pragma Loop_Invariant ( boolean_EXPRESSION );
```

The effect of this pragma is similar to that of pragma *Assert*, except that in an *Assertion_Policy* pragma, the identifier *Loop_Invariant* is used to control whether it is ignored or checked (or disabled).

Loop_Invariant can only appear as one of the items in the sequence of statements of a loop body, or nested inside block statements that appear in the sequence of statements of a loop body. The intention is that it be used to represent a "loop invariant" assertion, i.e.

something that is true each time through the loop, and which can be used to show that the loop is achieving its purpose.

Multiple *Loop_Invariant* and *Loop_Variant* pragmas that apply to the same loop should be grouped in the same sequence of statements.

To aid in writing such invariants, the special attribute *Loop_Entry* may be used to refer to the value of an expression on entry to the loop. This attribute can only be used within the expression of a *Loop_Invariant* pragma. For full details, see documentation of attribute *Loop_Entry*.

2.101 Pragma Loop_Optimize

Syntax:

```
pragma Loop_Optimize (OPTIMIZATION_HINT {, OPTIMIZATION_HINT});

OPTIMIZATION_HINT ::= Ivdep | No_Unroll | Unroll | No_Vector | Vector
```

This pragma must appear immediately within a loop statement. It allows the programmer to specify optimization hints for the enclosing loop. The hints are not mutually exclusive and can be freely mixed, but not all combinations will yield a sensible outcome.

There are five supported optimization hints for a loop:

* Ivdep

  The programmer asserts that there are no loop-carried dependencies which would prevent consecutive iterations of the loop from being executed simultaneously.

* No_Unroll

  The loop must not be unrolled. This is a strong hint: the compiler will not unroll a loop marked with this hint.

* Unroll

  The loop should be unrolled. This is a weak hint: the compiler will try to apply unrolling to this loop preferably to other optimizations, notably vectorization, but there is no guarantee that the loop will be unrolled.

* No_Vector

  The loop must not be vectorized. This is a strong hint: the compiler will not vectorize a loop marked with this hint.

* Vector

  The loop should be vectorized. This is a weak hint: the compiler will try to apply vectorization to this loop preferably to other optimizations, notably unrolling, but there is no guarantee that the loop will be vectorized.

These hints do not remove the need to pass the appropriate switches to the compiler in order to enable the relevant optimizations, that is to say *-funroll-loops* for unrolling and *-ftree-vectorize* for vectorization.

2.102 Pragma Loop_Variant

Syntax:

```
pragma Loop_Variant ( LOOP_VARIANT_ITEM {, LOOP_VARIANT_ITEM } );
LOOP_VARIANT_ITEM ::= CHANGE_DIRECTION => discrete_EXPRESSION
CHANGE_DIRECTION ::= Increases | Decreases
```

Loop_Variant can only appear as one of the items in the sequence of statements of a loop body, or nested inside block statements that appear in the sequence of statements of a loop body. It allows the specification of quantities which must always decrease or increase in successive iterations of the loop. In its simplest form, just one expression is specified, whose value must increase or decrease on each iteration of the loop.

In a more complex form, multiple arguments can be given which are intepreted in a nesting lexicographic manner. For example:

```
pragma Loop_Variant (Increases => X, Decreases => Y);
```

specifies that each time through the loop either X increases, or X stays the same and Y decreases. A *Loop_Variant* pragma ensures that the loop is making progress. It can be useful in helping to show informally or prove formally that the loop always terminates.

Loop_Variant is an assertion whose effect can be controlled using an *Assertion_Policy* with a check name of *Loop_Variant*. The policy can be *Check* to enable the loop variant check, *Ignore* to ignore the check (in which case the pragma has no effect on the program), or *Disable* in which case the pragma is not even checked for correct syntax.

Multiple *Loop_Invariant* and *Loop_Variant* pragmas that apply to the same loop should be grouped in the same sequence of statements.

The *Loop_Entry* attribute may be used within the expressions of the *Loop_Variant* pragma to refer to values on entry to the loop.

2.103 Pragma Machine_Attribute

Syntax:

```
pragma Machine_Attribute (
     [Entity         =>] LOCAL_NAME,
     [Attribute_Name =>] static_string_EXPRESSION
  [, [Info           =>] static_EXPRESSION] );
```

Machine-dependent attributes can be specified for types and/or declarations. This pragma is semantically equivalent to *__attribute__((‘attribute_name))‘* (if *info* is not specified) or *__attribute__((‘attribute_name‘(‘info)))* in GNU C, where `attribute_name` is recognized by the compiler middle-end or the *TARGET_ATTRIBUTE_TABLE* machine specific macro. A string literal for the optional parameter *info* is transformed into an identifier, which may make this pragma unusable for some attributes. For further information see *GNU Compiler Collection (GCC) Internals.*

2.104 Pragma Main

Syntax:

```
pragma Main
 (MAIN_OPTION [, MAIN_OPTION]);

MAIN_OPTION ::=
```

```
     [Stack_Size              =>] static_integer_EXPRESSION
   | [Task_Stack_Size_Default =>] static_integer_EXPRESSION
   | [Time_Slicing_Enabled    =>] static_boolean_EXPRESSION
```

This pragma is provided for compatibility with OpenVMS VAX Systems. It has no effect in GNAT, other than being syntax checked.

2.105 Pragma Main_Storage

Syntax:

```
pragma Main_Storage
  (MAIN_STORAGE_OPTION [, MAIN_STORAGE_OPTION]);

MAIN_STORAGE_OPTION ::=
  [WORKING_STORAGE =>] static_SIMPLE_EXPRESSION
| [TOP_GUARD       =>] static_SIMPLE_EXPRESSION
```

This pragma is provided for compatibility with OpenVMS VAX Systems. It has no effect in GNAT, other than being syntax checked.

2.106 Pragma No_Body

Syntax:

```
pragma No_Body;
```

There are a number of cases in which a package spec does not require a body, and in fact a body is not permitted. GNAT will not permit the spec to be compiled if there is a body around. The pragma No_Body allows you to provide a body file, even in a case where no body is allowed. The body file must contain only comments and a single No_Body pragma. This is recognized by the compiler as indicating that no body is logically present.

This is particularly useful during maintenance when a package is modified in such a way that a body needed before is no longer needed. The provision of a dummy body with a No_Body pragma ensures that there is no interference from earlier versions of the package body.

2.107 Pragma No_Elaboration_Code_All

Syntax:

```
pragma No_Elaboration_Code_All [(program_unit_NAME)];
```

This is a program unit pragma (there is also an equivalent aspect of the same name) that establishes the restriction *No_Elaboration_Code* for the current unit and any extended main source units (body and subunits. It also has has the effect of enforcing a transitive application of this aspect, so that if any unit is implicitly or explicitly WITH'ed by the current unit, it must also have the No_Elaboration_Code_All aspect set. It may be applied to package or subprogram specs or their generic versions.

2.108 Pragma No_Inline

Syntax:

```
pragma No_Inline (NAME {, NAME});
```

This pragma suppresses inlining for the callable entity or the instances of the generic subprogram designated by *NAME*, including inlining that results from the use of pragma *Inline*. This pragma is always active, in particular it is not subject to the use of option *-gnatn* or *-gnatN*. It is illegal to specify both pragma *No_Inline* and pragma *Inline_Always* for the same *NAME*.

2.109 Pragma No_Return

Syntax:

```
pragma No_Return (procedure_LOCAL_NAME {, procedure_LOCAL_NAME});
```

Each *procedure_LOCAL_NAME* argument must refer to one or more procedure declarations in the current declarative part. A procedure to which this pragma is applied may not contain any explicit *return* statements. In addition, if the procedure contains any implicit returns from falling off the end of a statement sequence, then execution of that implicit return will cause Program_Error to be raised.

One use of this pragma is to identify procedures whose only purpose is to raise an exception. Another use of this pragma is to suppress incorrect warnings about missing returns in functions, where the last statement of a function statement sequence is a call to such a procedure.

Note that in Ada 2005 mode, this pragma is part of the language. It is available in all earlier versions of Ada as an implementation-defined pragma.

2.110 Pragma No_Run_Time

Syntax:

```
pragma No_Run_Time;
```

This is an obsolete configuration pragma that historically was used to set up a runtime library with no object code. It is now used only for internal testing. The pragma has been superseded by the reconfigurable runtime capability of *GNAT*.

2.111 Pragma No_Strict_Aliasing

Syntax:

```
pragma No_Strict_Aliasing [([Entity =>] type_LOCAL_NAME)];
```

type_LOCAL_NAME must refer to an access type declaration in the current declarative part. The effect is to inhibit strict aliasing optimization for the given type. The form with no arguments is a configuration pragma which applies to all access types declared in units to which the pragma applies. For a detailed description of the strict aliasing optimization, and the situations in which it must be suppressed, see the section on Optimization and Strict Aliasing in the *GNAT User's Guide*.

This pragma currently has no effects on access to unconstrained array types.

2.112 Pragma No_Tagged_Streams

Syntax:

```
pragma No_Tagged_Streams;
pragma No_Tagged_Streams [([Entity =>] tagged_type_LOCAL_NAME)];
```

Normally when a tagged type is introduced using a full type declaration, part of the processing includes generating stream access routines to be used by stream attributes referencing the type (or one of its subtypes or derived types). This can involve the generation of significant amounts of code which is wasted space if stream routines are not needed for the type in question.

The *No_Tagged_Streams* pragma causes the generation of these stream routines to be skipped, and any attempt to use stream operations on types subject to this pragma will be statically rejected as illegal.

There are two forms of the pragma. The form with no arguments must appear in a declarative sequence or in the declarations of a package spec. This pragma affects all subsequent root tagged types declared in the declaration sequence, and specifies that no stream routines be generated. The form with an argument (for which there is also a corresponding aspect) specifies a single root tagged type for which stream routines are not to be generated.

Once the pragma has been given for a particular root tagged type, all subtypes and derived types of this type inherit the pragma automatically, so the effect applies to a complete hierarchy (this is necessary to deal with the class-wide dispatching versions of the stream routines).

2.113 Pragma Normalize_Scalars

Syntax:

```
pragma Normalize_Scalars;
```

This is a language defined pragma which is fully implemented in GNAT. The effect is to cause all scalar objects that are not otherwise initialized to be initialized. The initial values are implementation dependent and are as follows:

Standard.Character
: Objects whose root type is Standard.Character are initialized to Character'Last unless the subtype range excludes NUL (in which case NUL is used). This choice will always generate an invalid value if one exists.

Standard.Wide_Character
: Objects whose root type is Standard.Wide_Character are initialized to Wide_Character'Last unless the subtype range excludes NUL (in which case NUL is used). This choice will always generate an invalid value if one exists.

Standard.Wide_Wide_Character
: Objects whose root type is Standard.Wide_Wide_Character are initialized to the invalid value 16#FFFF_FFFF# unless the subtype range excludes NUL (in which case NUL is used). This choice will always generate an invalid value if one exists.

Integer types

Objects of an integer type are treated differently depending on whether negative values are present in the subtype. If no negative values are present, then all one bits is used as the initial value except in the special case where zero is excluded from the subtype, in which case all zero bits are used. This choice will always generate an invalid value if one exists.

For subtypes with negative values present, the largest negative number is used, except in the unusual case where this largest negative number is in the subtype, and the largest positive number is not, in which case the largest positive value is used. This choice will always generate an invalid value if one exists.

Floating-Point Types

Objects of all floating-point types are initialized to all 1-bits. For standard IEEE format, this corresponds to a NaN (not a number) which is indeed an invalid value.

Fixed-Point Types

Objects of all fixed-point types are treated as described above for integers, with the rules applying to the underlying integer value used to represent the fixed-point value.

Modular types

Objects of a modular type are initialized to all one bits, except in the special case where zero is excluded from the subtype, in which case all zero bits are used. This choice will always generate an invalid value if one exists.

Enumeration types

Objects of an enumeration type are initialized to all one-bits, i.e., to the value *2 ** typ'Size - 1* unless the subtype excludes the literal whose Pos value is zero, in which case a code of zero is used. This choice will always generate an invalid value if one exists.

2.114 Pragma Obsolescent

Syntax:

```
pragma Obsolescent;

pragma Obsolescent (
  [Message =>] static_string_EXPRESSION
[,[Version =>] Ada_05]]);

pragma Obsolescent (
  [Entity  =>] NAME
[,[Message =>] static_string_EXPRESSION
[,[Version =>] Ada_05]] );
```

This pragma can occur immediately following a declaration of an entity, including the case of a record component. If no Entity argument is present, then this declaration is the one to which the pragma applies. If an Entity parameter is present, it must either match the name of the entity in this declaration, or alternatively, the pragma can immediately follow an enumeration type declaration, where the Entity argument names one of the enumeration literals.

This pragma is used to indicate that the named entity is considered obsolescent and should not be used. Typically this is used when an API must be modified by eventually removing or modifying existing subprograms or other entities. The pragma can be used at an intermediate stage when the entity is still present, but will be removed later.

The effect of this pragma is to output a warning message on a reference to an entity thus marked that the subprogram is obsolescent if the appropriate warning option in the compiler is activated. If the Message parameter is present, then a second warning message is given containing this text. In addition, a reference to the entity is considered to be a violation of pragma Restrictions (No_Obsolescent_Features).

This pragma can also be used as a program unit pragma for a package, in which case the entity name is the name of the package, and the pragma indicates that the entire package is considered obsolescent. In this case a client *with*'ing such a package violates the restriction, and the *with* statement is flagged with warnings if the warning option is set.

If the Version parameter is present (which must be exactly the identifier Ada_05, no other argument is allowed), then the indication of obsolescence applies only when compiling in Ada 2005 mode. This is primarily intended for dealing with the situations in the predefined library where subprograms or packages have become defined as obsolescent in Ada 2005 (e.g., in Ada.Characters.Handling), but may be used anywhere.

The following examples show typical uses of this pragma:

```
package p is
   pragma Obsolescent (p, Message => "use pp instead of p");
end p;

package q is
   procedure q2;
   pragma Obsolescent ("use q2new instead");

   type R is new integer;
   pragma Obsolescent
     (Entity  => R,
      Message => "use RR in Ada 2005",
      Version => Ada_05);

   type M is record
      F1 : Integer;
      F2 : Integer;
      pragma Obsolescent;
      F3 : Integer;
   end record;

   type E is (a, bc, 'd', quack);
   pragma Obsolescent (Entity => bc)
   pragma Obsolescent (Entity => 'd')
```

```
      function "+"
        (a, b : character) return character;
      pragma Obsolescent (Entity => "+");
   end;
```

Note that, as for all pragmas, if you use a pragma argument identifier, then all subsequent parameters must also use a pragma argument identifier. So if you specify "Entity =>" for the Entity argument, and a Message argument is present, it must be preceded by "Message =>".

2.115 Pragma Optimize_Alignment

Syntax:

```
pragma Optimize_Alignment (TIME | SPACE | OFF);
```

This is a configuration pragma which affects the choice of default alignments for types and objects where no alignment is explicitly specified. There is a time/space trade-off in the selection of these values. Large alignments result in more efficient code, at the expense of larger data space, since sizes have to be increased to match these alignments. Smaller alignments save space, but the access code is slower. The normal choice of default alignments for types and individual alignment promotions for objects (which is what you get if you do not use this pragma, or if you use an argument of OFF), tries to balance these two requirements.

Specifying SPACE causes smaller default alignments to be chosen in two cases. First any packed record is given an alignment of 1. Second, if a size is given for the type, then the alignment is chosen to avoid increasing this size. For example, consider:

```
type R is record
   X : Integer;
   Y : Character;
end record;

for R'Size use 5*8;
```

In the default mode, this type gets an alignment of 4, so that access to the Integer field X are efficient. But this means that objects of the type end up with a size of 8 bytes. This is a valid choice, since sizes of objects are allowed to be bigger than the size of the type, but it can waste space if for example fields of type R appear in an enclosing record. If the above type is compiled in *Optimize_Alignment (Space)* mode, the alignment is set to 1.

However, there is one case in which SPACE is ignored. If a variable length record (that is a discriminated record with a component which is an array whose length depends on a discriminant), has a pragma Pack, then it is not in general possible to set the alignment of such a record to one, so the pragma is ignored in this case (with a warning).

Specifying SPACE also disables alignment promotions for standalone objects, which occur when the compiler increases the alignment of a specific object without changing the alignment of its type.

Specifying TIME causes larger default alignments to be chosen in the case of small types with sizes that are not a power of 2. For example, consider:

```
type R is record
   A : Character;
   B : Character;
   C : Boolean;
end record;

pragma Pack (R);
for R'Size use 17;
```

The default alignment for this record is normally 1, but if this type is compiled in *Optimize_Alignment (Time)* mode, then the alignment is set to 4, which wastes space for objects of the type, since they are now 4 bytes long, but results in more efficient access when the whole record is referenced.

As noted above, this is a configuration pragma, and there is a requirement that all units in a partition be compiled with a consistent setting of the optimization setting. This would normally be achieved by use of a configuration pragma file containing the appropriate setting. The exception to this rule is that units with an explicit configuration pragma in the same file as the source unit are excluded from the consistency check, as are all predefined units. The latter are compiled by default in pragma Optimize_Alignment (Off) mode if no pragma appears at the start of the file.

2.116 Pragma Ordered

Syntax:

```
pragma Ordered (enumeration_first_subtype_LOCAL_NAME);
```

Most enumeration types are from a conceptual point of view unordered. For example, consider:

```
type Color is (Red, Blue, Green, Yellow);
```

By Ada semantics *Blue* > *Red* and *Green* > *Blue*, but really these relations make no sense; the enumeration type merely specifies a set of possible colors, and the order is unimportant.

For unordered enumeration types, it is generally a good idea if clients avoid comparisons (other than equality or inequality) and explicit ranges. (A *client* is a unit where the type is referenced, other than the unit where the type is declared, its body, and its subunits.) For example, if code buried in some client says:

```
if Current_Color < Yellow then ...
if Current_Color in Blue .. Green then ...
```

then the client code is relying on the order, which is undesirable. It makes the code hard to read and creates maintenance difficulties if entries have to be added to the enumeration type. Instead, the code in the client should list the possibilities, or an appropriate subtype should be declared in the unit that declares the original enumeration type. E.g., the following subtype could be declared along with the type *Color*:

```
subtype RBG is Color range Red .. Green;
```

and then the client could write:

```
if Current_Color in RBG then ...
if Current_Color = Blue or Current_Color = Green then ...
```

However, some enumeration types are legitimately ordered from a conceptual point of view. For example, if you declare:

```
type Day is (Mon, Tue, Wed, Thu, Fri, Sat, Sun);
```

then the ordering imposed by the language is reasonable, and clients can depend on it, writing for example:

```
if D in Mon .. Fri then ...
if D < Wed then ...
```

The pragma *Ordered* is provided to mark enumeration types that are conceptually ordered, alerting the reader that clients may depend on the ordering. GNAT provides a pragma to mark enumerations as ordered rather than one to mark them as unordered, since in our experience, the great majority of enumeration types are conceptually unordered.

The types *Boolean*, *Character*, *Wide_Character*, and *Wide_Wide_Character* are considered to be ordered types, so each is declared with a pragma *Ordered* in package *Standard*.

Normally pragma *Ordered* serves only as documentation and a guide for coding standards, but GNAT provides a warning switch *-gnatw.u* that requests warnings for inappropriate uses (comparisons and explicit subranges) for unordered types. If this switch is used, then any enumeration type not marked with pragma *Ordered* will be considered as unordered, and will generate warnings for inappropriate uses.

Note that generic types are not considered ordered or unordered (since the template can be instantiated for both cases), so we never generate warnings for the case of generic enumerated types.

For additional information please refer to the description of the *-gnatw.u* switch in the GNAT User's Guide.

2.117 Pragma Overflow_Mode

Syntax:

```
pragma Overflow_Mode
 (  [General     =>] MODE
  [,[Assertions =>] MODE]);

MODE ::= STRICT | MINIMIZED | ELIMINATED
```

This pragma sets the current overflow mode to the given setting. For details of the meaning of these modes, please refer to the 'Overflow Check Handling in GNAT' appendix in the GNAT User's Guide. If only the *General* parameter is present, the given mode applies to all expressions. If both parameters are present, the *General* mode applies to expressions outside assertions, and the *Eliminated* mode applies to expressions within assertions.

The case of the *MODE* parameter is ignored, so *MINIMIZED*, *Minimized* and *minimized* all have the same effect.

The *Overflow_Mode* pragma has the same scoping and placement rules as pragma *Suppress*, so it can occur either as a configuration pragma, specifying a default for the whole program, or in a declarative scope, where it applies to the remaining declarations and statements in that scope.

The pragma *Suppress (Overflow_Check)* suppresses overflow checking, but does not affect the overflow mode.

The pragma *Unsuppress (Overflow_Check)* unsuppresses (enables) overflow checking, but does not affect the overflow mode.

2.118 Pragma Overriding_Renamings

Syntax:

```
pragma Overriding_Renamings;
```

This is a GNAT configuration pragma to simplify porting legacy code accepted by the Rational Ada compiler. In the presence of this pragma, a renaming declaration that renames an inherited operation declared in the same scope is legal if selected notation is used as in:

```
pragma Overriding_Renamings;
...
package R is
  function F (..);
  ...
  function F (..) renames R.F;
end R;
```

even though RM 8.3 (15) stipulates that an overridden operation is not visible within the declaration of the overriding operation.

2.119 Pragma Partition_Elaboration_Policy

Syntax:

```
pragma Partition_Elaboration_Policy (POLICY_IDENTIFIER);

POLICY_IDENTIFIER ::= Concurrent | Sequential
```

This pragma is standard in Ada 2005, but is available in all earlier versions of Ada as an implementation-defined pragma. See Ada 2012 Reference Manual for details.

2.120 Pragma Part_Of

Syntax:

```
pragma Part_Of (ABSTRACT_STATE);

ABSTRACT_STATE ::= NAME
```

For the semantics of this pragma, see the entry for aspect *Part_Of* in the SPARK 2014 Reference Manual, section 7.2.6.

2.121 Pragma Passive

Syntax:

```
pragma Passive [(Semaphore | No)];
```

Syntax checked, but otherwise ignored by GNAT. This is recognized for compatibility with DEC Ada 83 implementations, where it is used within a task definition to request that a task be made passive. If the argument *Semaphore* is present, or the argument is omitted, then DEC Ada 83 treats the pragma as an assertion that the containing task is passive and that optimization of context switch with this task is permitted and desired. If the argument *No* is present, the task must not be optimized. GNAT does not attempt to optimize any tasks in this manner (since protected objects are available in place of passive tasks).

For more information on the subject of passive tasks, see the section 'Passive Task Optimization' in the GNAT Users Guide.

2.122 Pragma Persistent_BSS

Syntax:

```
pragma Persistent_BSS [(LOCAL_NAME)]
```

This pragma allows selected objects to be placed in the *.persistent_bss* section. On some targets the linker and loader provide for special treatment of this section, allowing a program to be reloaded without affecting the contents of this data (hence the name persistent).

There are two forms of usage. If an argument is given, it must be the local name of a library level object, with no explicit initialization and whose type is potentially persistent. If no argument is given, then the pragma is a configuration pragma, and applies to all library level objects with no explicit initialization of potentially persistent types.

A potentially persistent type is a scalar type, or an untagged, non-discriminated record, all of whose components have no explicit initialization and are themselves of a potentially persistent type, or an array, all of whose constraints are static, and whose component type is potentially persistent.

If this pragma is used on a target where this feature is not supported, then the pragma will be ignored. See also *pragma Linker_Section*.

2.123 Pragma Polling

Syntax:

```
pragma Polling (ON | OFF);
```

This pragma controls the generation of polling code. This is normally off. If *pragma Polling (ON)* is used then periodic calls are generated to the routine *Ada.Exceptions.Poll*. This routine is a separate unit in the runtime library, and can be found in file `a-excpol.adb`.

Pragma *Polling* can appear as a configuration pragma (for example it can be placed in the `gnat.adc` file) to enable polling globally, or it can be used in the statement or declaration sequence to control polling more locally.

A call to the polling routine is generated at the start of every loop and at the start of every subprogram call. This guarantees that the *Poll* routine is called frequently, and places an upper bound (determined by the complexity of the code) on the period between two *Poll* calls.

The primary purpose of the polling interface is to enable asynchronous aborts on targets that cannot otherwise support it (for example Windows NT), but it may be used for any other purpose requiring periodic polling. The standard version is null, and can be replaced by a user program. This will require re-compilation of the *Ada.Exceptions* package that can be found in files `a-except.ads` and `a-except.adb`.

A standard alternative unit (in file `4wexcpol.adb` in the standard GNAT distribution) is used to enable the asynchronous abort capability on targets that do not normally support the capability. The version of *Poll* in this file makes a call to the appropriate runtime routine to test for an abort condition.

Note that polling can also be enabled by use of the *-gnatP* switch. See the section on switches for gcc in the *GNAT User's Guide*.

2.124 Pragma Post

Syntax:

```
pragma Post (Boolean_Expression);
```

The *Post* pragma is intended to be an exact replacement for the language-defined *Post* aspect, and shares its restrictions and semantics. It must appear either immediately following the corresponding subprogram declaration (only other pragmas may intervene), or if there is no separate subprogram declaration, then it can appear at the start of the declarations in a subprogram body (preceded only by other pragmas).

2.125 Pragma Postcondition

Syntax:

```
pragma Postcondition (
   [Check   =>] Boolean_Expression
 [,[Message =>] String_Expression]);
```

The *Postcondition* pragma allows specification of automatic postcondition checks for subprograms. These checks are similar to assertions, but are automatically inserted just prior to the return statements of the subprogram with which they are associated (including implicit returns at the end of procedure bodies and associated exception handlers).

In addition, the boolean expression which is the condition which must be true may contain references to function'Result in the case of a function to refer to the returned value.

Postcondition pragmas may appear either immediately following the (separate) declaration of a subprogram, or at the start of the declarations of a subprogram body. Only other pragmas may intervene (that is appear between the subprogram declaration and its postconditions, or appear before the postcondition in the declaration sequence in a subprogram body). In the case of a postcondition appearing after a subprogram declaration, the formal arguments of the subprogram are visible, and can be referenced in the postcondition expressions.

The postconditions are collected and automatically tested just before any return (implicit or explicit) in the subprogram body. A postcondition is only recognized if postconditions are active at the time the pragma is encountered. The compiler switch *gnata* turns on all postconditions by default, and pragma *Check_Policy* with an identifier of *Postcondition* can also be used to control whether postconditions are active.

The general approach is that postconditions are placed in the spec if they represent functional aspects which make sense to the client. For example we might have:

```
function Direction return Integer;
pragma Postcondition
 (Direction'Result = +1
    or else
```

```
          Direction'Result = -1);
```

which serves to document that the result must be +1 or -1, and will test that this is the case at run time if postcondition checking is active.

Postconditions within the subprogram body can be used to check that some internal aspect of the implementation, not visible to the client, is operating as expected. For instance if a square root routine keeps an internal counter of the number of times it is called, then we might have the following postcondition:

```
Sqrt_Calls : Natural := 0;

function Sqrt (Arg : Float) return Float is
  pragma Postcondition
    (Sqrt_Calls = Sqrt_Calls'Old + 1);
  ...
end Sqrt
```

As this example, shows, the use of the *Old* attribute is often useful in postconditions to refer to the state on entry to the subprogram.

Note that postconditions are only checked on normal returns from the subprogram. If an abnormal return results from raising an exception, then the postconditions are not checked.

If a postcondition fails, then the exception *System.Assertions.Assert_Failure* is raised. If a message argument was supplied, then the given string will be used as the exception message. If no message argument was supplied, then the default message has the form "Postcondition failed at file_name:line". The exception is raised in the context of the subprogram body, so it is possible to catch postcondition failures within the subprogram body itself.

Within a package spec, normal visibility rules in Ada would prevent forward references within a postcondition pragma to functions defined later in the same package. This would introduce undesirable ordering constraints. To avoid this problem, all postcondition pragmas are analyzed at the end of the package spec, allowing forward references.

The following example shows that this even allows mutually recursive postconditions as in:

```
package Parity_Functions is
   function Odd  (X : Natural) return Boolean;
   pragma Postcondition
     (Odd'Result =
        (x = 1
          or else
        (x /= 0 and then Even (X - 1))));

   function Even (X : Natural) return Boolean;
   pragma Postcondition
     (Even'Result =
        (x = 0
          or else
        (x /= 1 and then Odd (X - 1))));

end Parity_Functions;
```

There are no restrictions on the complexity or form of conditions used within *Postcondition* pragmas. The following example shows that it is even possible to verify performance behavior.

```
package Sort is

   Performance : constant Float;
   --  Performance constant set by implementation
   --  to match target architecture behavior.

   procedure Treesort (Arg : String);
   --  Sorts characters of argument using N*logN sort
   pragma Postcondition
     (Float (Clock - Clock'Old) <=
        Float (Arg'Length) *
        log (Float (Arg'Length)) *
        Performance);
end Sort;
```

Note: postcondition pragmas associated with subprograms that are marked as Inline_Always, or those marked as Inline with front-end inlining (-gnatN option set) are accepted and legality-checked by the compiler, but are ignored at run-time even if postcondition checking is enabled.

Note that pragma *Postcondition* differs from the language-defined *Post* aspect (and corresponding *Post* pragma) in allowing multiple occurrences, allowing occurences in the body even if there is a separate spec, and allowing a second string parameter, and the use of the pragma identifier *Check*. Historically, pragma *Postcondition* was implemented prior to the development of Ada 2012, and has been retained in its original form for compatibility purposes.

2.126 Pragma Post_Class

Syntax:

```
pragma Post_Class (Boolean_Expression);
```

The *Post_Class* pragma is intended to be an exact replacement for the language-defined *Post'Class* aspect, and shares its restrictions and semantics. It must appear either immediately following the corresponding subprogram declaration (only other pragmas may intervene), or if there is no separate subprogram declaration, then it can appear at the start of the declarations in a subprogram body (preceded only by other pragmas).

Note: This pragma is called *Post_Class* rather than *Post'Class* because the latter would not be strictly conforming to the allowed syntax for pragmas. The motivation for provinding pragmas equivalent to the aspects is to allow a program to be written using the pragmas, and then compiled if necessary using an Ada compiler that does not recognize the pragmas or aspects, but is prepared to ignore the pragmas. The assertion policy that controls this pragma is *Post'Class*, not *Post_Class*.

2.127 Pragma Pre

Syntax:

```
pragma Pre (Boolean_Expression);
```

The *Pre* pragma is intended to be an exact replacement for the language-defined *Pre* aspect, and shares its restrictions and semantics. It must appear either immediately following the corresponding subprogram declaration (only other pragmas may intervene), or if there is no separate subprogram declaration, then it can appear at the start of the declarations in a subprogram body (preceded only by other pragmas).

2.128 Pragma Precondition

Syntax:

```
pragma Precondition (
   [Check   =>] Boolean_Expression
 [,[Message =>] String_Expression]);
```

The *Precondition* pragma is similar to *Postcondition* except that the corresponding checks take place immediately upon entry to the subprogram, and if a precondition fails, the exception is raised in the context of the caller, and the attribute 'Result cannot be used within the precondition expression.

Otherwise, the placement and visibility rules are identical to those described for postconditions. The following is an example of use within a package spec:

```
package Math_Functions is
   ...
   function Sqrt (Arg : Float) return Float;
   pragma Precondition (Arg >= 0.0)
   ...
end Math_Functions;
```

Precondition pragmas may appear either immediately following the (separate) declaration of a subprogram, or at the start of the declarations of a subprogram body. Only other pragmas may intervene (that is appear between the subprogram declaration and its postconditions, or appear before the postcondition in the declaration sequence in a subprogram body).

Note: precondition pragmas associated with subprograms that are marked as Inline_Always, or those marked as Inline with front-end inlining (-gnatN option set) are accepted and legality-checked by the compiler, but are ignored at run-time even if precondition checking is enabled.

Note that pragma *Precondition* differs from the language-defined *Pre* aspect (and corresponding *Pre* pragma) in allowing multiple occurrences, allowing occurences in the body even if there is a separate spec, and allowing a second string parameter, and the use of the pragma identifier *Check*. Historically, pragma *Precondition* was implemented prior to the development of Ada 2012, and has been retained in its original form for compatibility purposes.

2.129 Pragma Predicate

Syntax:

```
pragma Predicate
  ([Entity =>] type_LOCAL_NAME,
   [Check  =>] EXPRESSION);
```

This pragma (available in all versions of Ada in GNAT) encompasses both the *Static_Predicate* and *Dynamic_Predicate* aspects in Ada 2012. A predicate is regarded as static if it has an allowed form for *Static_Predicate* and is otherwise treated as a *Dynamic_Predicate*. Otherwise, predicates specified by this pragma behave exactly as described in the Ada 2012 reference manual. For example, if we have

```
type R is range 1 .. 10;
subtype S is R;
pragma Predicate (Entity => S, Check => S not in 4 .. 6);
subtype Q is R
pragma Predicate (Entity => Q, Check => F(Q) or G(Q));
```

the effect is identical to the following Ada 2012 code:

```
type R is range 1 .. 10;
subtype S is R with
  Static_Predicate => S not in 4 .. 6;
subtype Q is R with
  Dynamic_Predicate => F(Q) or G(Q);
```

Note that there are no pragmas *Dynamic_Predicate* or *Static_Predicate*. That is because these pragmas would affect legality and semantics of the program and thus do not have a neutral effect if ignored. The motivation behind providing pragmas equivalent to corresponding aspects is to allow a program to be written using the pragmas, and then compiled with a compiler that will ignore the pragmas. That doesn't work in the case of static and dynamic predicates, since if the corresponding pragmas are ignored, then the behavior of the program is fundamentally changed (for example a membership test *A in B* would not take into account a predicate defined for subtype B). When following this approach, the use of predicates should be avoided.

2.130 Pragma Predicate_Failure

Syntax:

```
pragma Predicate_Failure
  ([Entity  =>] type_LOCAL_NAME,
   [Message =>] String_Expression);
```

The *Predicate_Failure* pragma is intended to be an exact replacement for the language-defined *Predicate_Failure* aspect, and shares its restrictions and semantics.

2.131 Pragma Preelaborable_Initialization

Syntax:

```
pragma Preelaborable_Initialization (DIRECT_NAME);
```

This pragma is standard in Ada 2005, but is available in all earlier versions of Ada as an implementation-defined pragma. See Ada 2012 Reference Manual for details.

2.132 Pragma Prefix_Exception_Messages

Syntax:

```
pragma Prefix_Exception_Messages;
```

This is an implementation-defined configuration pragma that affects the behavior of raise statements with a message given as a static string constant (typically a string literal). In such cases, the string will be automatically prefixed by the name of the enclosing entity (giving the package and subprogram containing the raise statement). This helps to identify where messages are coming from, and this mode is automatic for the run-time library.

The pragma has no effect if the message is computed with an expression other than a static string constant, since the assumption in this case is that the program computes exactly the string it wants. If you still want the prefixing in this case, you can always call *GNAT.Source_Info.Enclosing_Entity* and prepend the string manually.

2.133 Pragma Pre_Class

Syntax:

```
pragma Pre_Class (Boolean_Expression);
```

The *Pre_Class* pragma is intended to be an exact replacement for the language-defined *Pre'Class* aspect, and shares its restrictions and semantics. It must appear either immediately following the corresponding subprogram declaration (only other pragmas may intervene), or if there is no separate subprogram declaration, then it can appear at the start of the declarations in a subprogram body (preceded only by other pragmas).

Note: This pragma is called *Pre_Class* rather than *Pre'Class* because the latter would not be strictly conforming to the allowed syntax for pragmas. The motivation for providing pragmas equivalent to the aspects is to allow a program to be written using the pragmas, and then compiled if necessary using an Ada compiler that does not recognize the pragmas or aspects, but is prepared to ignore the pragmas. The assertion policy that controls this pragma is *Pre'Class*, not *Pre_Class*.

2.134 Pragma Priority_Specific_Dispatching

Syntax:

```
pragma Priority_Specific_Dispatching (
   POLICY_IDENTIFIER,
   first_priority_EXPRESSION,
   last_priority_EXPRESSION)

POLICY_IDENTIFIER ::=
   EDF_Across_Priorities              |
   FIFO_Within_Priorities             |
   Non_Preemptive_Within_Priorities |
   Round_Robin_Within_Priorities
```

This pragma is standard in Ada 2005, but is available in all earlier versions of Ada as an implementation-defined pragma. See Ada 2012 Reference Manual for details.

2.135 Pragma Profile

Syntax:

```
pragma Profile (Ravenscar | Restricted | Rational | GNAT_Extended_Ravenscar);
```

This pragma is standard in Ada 2005, but is available in all earlier versions of Ada as an implementation-defined pragma. This is a configuration pragma that establishes a set of configuration pragmas that depend on the argument. *Ravenscar* is standard in Ada 2005. The other possibilities (*Restricted*, *Rational*, *GNAT_Extended_Ravenscar*) are implementation-defined. The set of configuration pragmas is defined in the following sections.

* Pragma Profile (Ravenscar)

  The *Ravenscar* profile is standard in Ada 2005, but is available in all earlier versions of Ada as an implementation-defined pragma. This profile establishes the following set of configuration pragmas:

  * `Task_Dispatching_Policy (FIFO_Within_Priorities)`

    [RM D.2.2] Tasks are dispatched following a preemptive priority-ordered scheduling policy.

  * `Locking_Policy (Ceiling_Locking)`

    [RM D.3] While tasks and interrupts execute a protected action, they inherit the ceiling priority of the corresponding protected object.

  * `Detect_Blocking`

    This pragma forces the detection of potentially blocking operations within a protected operation, and to raise Program_Error if that happens.

  plus the following set of restrictions:

  * `Max_Entry_Queue_Length => 1`

    No task can be queued on a protected entry.

  * `Max_Protected_Entries => 1`
  * `Max_Task_Entries => 0`

    No rendezvous statements are allowed.

  * `No_Abort_Statements`
  * `No_Dynamic_Attachment`
  * `No_Dynamic_Priorities`
  * `No_Implicit_Heap_Allocations`
  * `No_Local_Protected_Objects`
  * `No_Local_Timing_Events`
  * `No_Protected_Type_Allocators`
  * `No_Relative_Delay`
  * `No_Requeue_Statements`
  * `No_Select_Statements`
  * `No_Specific_Termination_Handlers`
  * `No_Task_Allocators`
  * `No_Task_Hierarchy`
  * `No_Task_Termination`

* `Simple_Barriers`

The Ravenscar profile also includes the following restrictions that specify that there are no semantic dependences on the corresponding predefined packages:

* `No_Dependence => Ada.Asynchronous_Task_Control`
* `No_Dependence => Ada.Calendar`
* `No_Dependence => Ada.Execution_Time.Group_Budget`
* `No_Dependence => Ada.Execution_Time.Timers`
* `No_Dependence => Ada.Task_Attributes`
* `No_Dependence => System.Multiprocessors.Dispatching_Domains`

This set of configuration pragmas and restrictions correspond to the definition of the 'Ravenscar Profile' for limited tasking, devised and published by the *International Real-Time Ada Workshop, 1997*. A description is also available at `http://www-users.cs.york.ac.uk/~burns/ravenscar.ps`.

The original definition of the profile was revised at subsequent IRTAW meetings. It has been included in the ISO *Guide for the Use of the Ada Programming Language in High Integrity Systems*, and was made part of the Ada 2005 standard. The formal definition given by the Ada Rapporteur Group (ARG) can be found in two Ada Issues (AI-249 and AI-305) available at `http://www.ada-auth.org/cgi-bin/cvsweb.cgi/ais/ai-00249.txt` and `http://www.ada-auth.org/cgi-bin/cvsweb.cgi/ais/ai-00305.txt`.

The above set is a superset of the restrictions provided by pragma `Profile (Restricted)`, it includes six additional restrictions (`Simple_Barriers`, `No_Select_Statements`, `No_Calendar`, `No_Implicit_Heap_Allocations`, `No_Relative_Delay` and `No_Task_Termination`). This means that pragma `Profile (Ravenscar)`, like the pragma `Profile (Restricted)`, automatically causes the use of a simplified, more efficient version of the tasking run-time library.

* Pragma Profile (GNAT_Extended_Ravenscar)

  This profile corresponds to a GNAT specific extension of the Ravenscar profile. The profile may change in the future although only in a compatible way: some restrictions may be removed or relaxed. It is defined as a variation of the Ravenscar profile.

  The `No_Implicit_Heap_Allocations` restriction has been replaced by `No_Implicit_Task_Allocations` and `No_Implicit_Protected_Object_Allocations`.

  The `Simple_Barriers` restriction has been replaced by `Pure_Barriers`.

* Pragma Profile (Restricted)

  This profile corresponds to the GNAT restricted run time. It establishes the following set of restrictions:

  * `No_Abort_Statements`
  * `No_Entry_Queue`
  * `No_Task_Hierarchy`
  * `No_Task_Allocators`
  * `No_Dynamic_Priorities`
  * `No_Terminate_Alternatives`

   * No_Dynamic_Attachment
   * No_Protected_Type_Allocators
   * No_Local_Protected_Objects
   * No_Requeue_Statements
   * No_Task_Attributes_Package
   * Max_Asynchronous_Select_Nesting = 0
   * Max_Task_Entries = 0
   * Max_Protected_Entries = 1
   * Max_Select_Alternatives = 0

  This set of restrictions causes the automatic selection of a simplified version of the run time that provides improved performance for the limited set of tasking functionality permitted by this set of restrictions.

* Pragma Profile (Rational)

  The Rational profile is intended to facilitate porting legacy code that compiles with the Rational APEX compiler, even when the code includes non- conforming Ada constructs. The profile enables the following three pragmas:

   * pragma Implicit_Packing
   * pragma Overriding_Renamings
   * pragma Use_VADS_Size

2.136 Pragma Profile_Warnings

Syntax:

```
pragma Profile_Warnings (Ravenscar | Restricted | Rational);
```

This is an implementation-defined pragma that is similar in effect to *pragma Profile* except that instead of generating *Restrictions* pragmas, it generates *Restriction_Warnings* pragmas. The result is that violations of the profile generate warning messages instead of error messages.

2.137 Pragma Propagate_Exceptions

Syntax:

```
pragma Propagate_Exceptions;
```

This pragma is now obsolete and, other than generating a warning if warnings on obsolescent features are enabled, is ignored. It is retained for compatibility purposes. It used to be used in connection with optimization of a now-obsolete mechanism for implementation of exceptions.

2.138 Pragma Provide_Shift_Operators

Syntax:

```
pragma Provide_Shift_Operators (integer_first_subtype_LOCAL_NAME);
```

This pragma can be applied to a first subtype local name that specifies either an unsigned or signed type. It has the effect of providing the five shift operators (Shift_Left, Shift_Right,

Shift_Right_Arithmetic, Rotate_Left and Rotate_Right) for the given type. It is similar to including the function declarations for these five operators, together with the pragma Import (Intrinsic, ...) statements.

2.139 Pragma Psect_Object

Syntax:

```
pragma Psect_Object (
     [Internal =>] LOCAL_NAME,
  [, [External =>] EXTERNAL_SYMBOL]
  [, [Size     =>] EXTERNAL_SYMBOL]);

EXTERNAL_SYMBOL ::=
  IDENTIFIER
| static_string_EXPRESSION
```

This pragma is identical in effect to pragma *Common_Object*.

2.140 Pragma Pure_Function

Syntax:

```
pragma Pure_Function ([Entity =>] function_LOCAL_NAME);
```

This pragma appears in the same declarative part as a function declaration (or a set of function declarations if more than one overloaded declaration exists, in which case the pragma applies to all entities). It specifies that the function *Entity* is to be considered pure for the purposes of code generation. This means that the compiler can assume that there are no side effects, and in particular that two calls with identical arguments produce the same result. It also means that the function can be used in an address clause.

Note that, quite deliberately, there are no static checks to try to ensure that this promise is met, so *Pure_Function* can be used with functions that are conceptually pure, even if they do modify global variables. For example, a square root function that is instrumented to count the number of times it is called is still conceptually pure, and can still be optimized, even though it modifies a global variable (the count). Memo functions are another example (where a table of previous calls is kept and consulted to avoid re-computation).

Note also that the normal rules excluding optimization of subprograms in pure units (when parameter types are descended from System.Address, or when the full view of a parameter type is limited), do not apply for the Pure_Function case. If you explicitly specify Pure_Function, the compiler may optimize away calls with identical arguments, and if that results in unexpected behavior, the proper action is not to use the pragma for subprograms that are not (conceptually) pure.

Note: Most functions in a *Pure* package are automatically pure, and there is no need to use pragma *Pure_Function* for such functions. One exception is any function that has at least one formal of type *System.Address* or a type derived from it. Such functions are not considered pure by default, since the compiler assumes that the *Address* parameter may be functioning as a pointer and that the referenced data may change even if the address value does not. Similarly, imported functions are not considered to be pure by default, since there is no way of checking that they are in fact pure. The use of pragma *Pure_Function* for such a function will override these default assumption, and cause the compiler to treat a designated subprogram as pure in these cases.

Note: If pragma *Pure_Function* is applied to a renamed function, it applies to the underlying renamed function. This can be used to disambiguate cases of overloading where some but not all functions in a set of overloaded functions are to be designated as pure.

If pragma *Pure_Function* is applied to a library level function, the function is also considered pure from an optimization point of view, but the unit is not a Pure unit in the categorization sense. So for example, a function thus marked is free to *with* non-pure units.

2.141 Pragma Rational

Syntax:

```
pragma Rational;
```

This pragma is considered obsolescent, but is retained for compatibility purposes. It is equivalent to:

```
pragma Profile (Rational);
```

2.142 Pragma Ravenscar

Syntax:

```
pragma Ravenscar;
```

This pragma is considered obsolescent, but is retained for compatibility purposes. It is equivalent to:

```
pragma Profile (Ravenscar);
```

which is the preferred method of setting the *Ravenscar* profile.

2.143 Pragma Refined_Depends

Syntax:

```
pragma Refined_Depends (DEPENDENCY_RELATION);

DEPENDENCY_RELATION ::=
     null
  | (DEPENDENCY_CLAUSE {, DEPENDENCY_CLAUSE})

DEPENDENCY_CLAUSE ::=
    OUTPUT_LIST =>[+] INPUT_LIST
  | NULL_DEPENDENCY_CLAUSE

NULL_DEPENDENCY_CLAUSE ::= null => INPUT_LIST

OUTPUT_LIST ::= OUTPUT | (OUTPUT {, OUTPUT})

INPUT_LIST ::= null | INPUT | (INPUT {, INPUT})

OUTPUT ::= NAME | FUNCTION_RESULT
```

```
INPUT  ::= NAME

where FUNCTION_RESULT is a function Result attribute_reference
```

For the semantics of this pragma, see the entry for aspect *Refined_Depends* in the SPARK 2014 Reference Manual, section 6.1.5.

2.144 Pragma Refined_Global

Syntax:

```
pragma Refined_Global (GLOBAL_SPECIFICATION);

GLOBAL_SPECIFICATION ::=
     null
  | (GLOBAL_LIST)
  | (MODED_GLOBAL_LIST {, MODED_GLOBAL_LIST})

MODED_GLOBAL_LIST ::= MODE_SELECTOR => GLOBAL_LIST

MODE_SELECTOR ::= In_Out | Input | Output | Proof_In
GLOBAL_LIST   ::= GLOBAL_ITEM | (GLOBAL_ITEM {, GLOBAL_ITEM})
GLOBAL_ITEM   ::= NAME
```

For the semantics of this pragma, see the entry for aspect *Refined_Global* in the SPARK 2014 Reference Manual, section 6.1.4.

2.145 Pragma Refined_Post

Syntax:

```
pragma Refined_Post (boolean_EXPRESSION);
```

For the semantics of this pragma, see the entry for aspect *Refined_Post* in the SPARK 2014 Reference Manual, section 7.2.7.

2.146 Pragma Refined_State

Syntax:

```
pragma Refined_State (REFINEMENT_LIST);

REFINEMENT_LIST ::=
  (REFINEMENT_CLAUSE {, REFINEMENT_CLAUSE})

REFINEMENT_CLAUSE ::= state_NAME => CONSTITUENT_LIST

CONSTITUENT_LIST ::=
     null
  |  CONSTITUENT
  | (CONSTITUENT {, CONSTITUENT})

CONSTITUENT ::= object_NAME | state_NAME
```

For the semantics of this pragma, see the entry for aspect *Refined_State* in the SPARK 2014 Reference Manual, section 7.2.2.

2.147 Pragma Relative_Deadline

Syntax:

```
pragma Relative_Deadline (time_span_EXPRESSION);
```

This pragma is standard in Ada 2005, but is available in all earlier versions of Ada as an implementation-defined pragma. See Ada 2012 Reference Manual for details.

2.148 Pragma Remote_Access_Type

Syntax:

```
pragma Remote_Access_Type ([Entity =>] formal_access_type_LOCAL_NAME);
```

This pragma appears in the formal part of a generic declaration. It specifies an exception to the RM rule from E.2.2(17/2), which forbids the use of a remote access to class-wide type as actual for a formal access type.

When this pragma applies to a formal access type *Entity*, that type is treated as a remote access to class-wide type in the generic. It must be a formal general access type, and its designated type must be the class-wide type of a formal tagged limited private type from the same generic declaration.

In the generic unit, the formal type is subject to all restrictions pertaining to remote access to class-wide types. At instantiation, the actual type must be a remote access to class-wide type.

2.149 Pragma Restricted_Run_Time

Syntax:

```
pragma Restricted_Run_Time;
```

This pragma is considered obsolescent, but is retained for compatibility purposes. It is equivalent to:

```
pragma Profile (Restricted);
```

which is the preferred method of setting the restricted run time profile.

2.150 Pragma Restriction_Warnings

Syntax:

```
pragma Restriction_Warnings
  (restriction_IDENTIFIER {, restriction_IDENTIFIER});
```

This pragma allows a series of restriction identifiers to be specified (the list of allowed identifiers is the same as for pragma *Restrictions*). For each of these identifiers the compiler checks for violations of the restriction, but generates a warning message rather than an error message if the restriction is violated.

One use of this is in situations where you want to know about violations of a restriction, but you want to ignore some of these violations. Consider this example, where you want to set Ada_95 mode and enable style checks, but you want to know about any other use of implementation pragmas:

```
pragma Restriction_Warnings (No_Implementation_Pragmas);
pragma Warnings (Off, "violation of No_Implementation_Pragmas");
pragma Ada_95;
pragma Style_Checks ("2bfhkM160");
pragma Warnings (On, "violation of No_Implementation_Pragmas");
```

By including the above lines in a configuration pragmas file, the Ada_95 and Style_Checks pragmas are accepted without generating a warning, but any other use of implementation defined pragmas will cause a warning to be generated.

2.151 Pragma Reviewable

Syntax:

```
pragma Reviewable;
```

This pragma is an RM-defined standard pragma, but has no effect on the program being compiled, or on the code generated for the program.

To obtain the required output specified in RM H.3.1, the compiler must be run with various special switches as follows:

* *Where compiler-generated run-time checks remain*

  The switch *-gnatGL* may be used to list the expanded code in pseudo-Ada form. Run-time checks show up in the listing either as explicit checks or operators marked with {} to indicate a check is present.

* *An identification of known exceptions at compile time*

  If the program is compiled with *-gnatwa*, the compiler warning messages will indicate all cases where the compiler detects that an exception is certain to occur at run time.

* *Possible reads of uninitialized variables*

  The compiler warns of many such cases, but its output is incomplete.

A supplemental static analysis tool may be used to obtain a comprehensive list of all possible points at which uninitialized data may be read.

* *Where run-time support routines are implicitly invoked*

  In the output from *-gnatGL*, run-time calls are explicitly listed as calls to the relevant run-time routine.

* *Object code listing*

  This may be obtained either by using the *-S* switch, or the objdump utility.

* *Constructs known to be erroneous at compile time*

  These are identified by warnings issued by the compiler (use *-gnatwa*).

* *Stack usage information*

  Static stack usage data (maximum per-subprogram) can be obtained via the *-fstack-usage* switch to the compiler. Dynamic stack usage data (per task) can be obtained via the *-u* switch to gnatbind

* *Object code listing of entire partition*

  This can be obtained by compiling the partition with *-S*, or by applying objdump to all the object files that are part of the partition.

* *A description of the run-time model*

  The full sources of the run-time are available, and the documentation of these routines describes how these run-time routines interface to the underlying operating system facilities.

* *Control and data-flow information*

A supplemental static analysis tool may be used to obtain complete control and data-flow information, as well as comprehensive messages identifying possible problems based on this information.

2.152 Pragma Share_Generic

Syntax:

```
pragma Share_Generic (GNAME {, GNAME});

GNAME ::= generic_unit_NAME | generic_instance_NAME
```

This pragma is provided for compatibility with Dec Ada 83. It has no effect in *GNAT* (which does not implement shared generics), other than to check that the given names are all names of generic units or generic instances.

2.153 Pragma Shared

This pragma is provided for compatibility with Ada 83. The syntax and semantics are identical to pragma Atomic.

2.154 Pragma Short_Circuit_And_Or

Syntax:

```
pragma Short_Circuit_And_Or;
```

This configuration pragma causes any occurrence of the AND operator applied to operands of type Standard.Boolean to be short-circuited (i.e. the AND operator is treated as if it were AND THEN). Or is similarly treated as OR ELSE. This may be useful in the context of certification protocols requiring the use of short-circuited logical operators. If this configuration pragma occurs locally within the file being compiled, it applies only to the file being compiled. There is no requirement that all units in a partition use this option.

2.155 Pragma Short_Descriptors

Syntax:

```
pragma Short_Descriptors
```

This pragma is provided for compatibility with other Ada implementations. It is recognized but ignored by all current versions of GNAT.

2.156 Pragma Simple_Storage_Pool_Type

Syntax:

```
pragma Simple_Storage_Pool_Type (type_LOCAL_NAME);
```

A type can be established as a 'simple storage pool type' by applying the representation pragma *Simple_Storage_Pool_Type* to the type. A type named in the pragma must be a library-level immutably limited record type or limited tagged type declared immediately within a package declaration. The type can also be a limited private type whose full type is allowed as a simple storage pool type.

For a simple storage pool type *SSP*, nonabstract primitive subprograms *Allocate*, *Deallocate*, and *Storage_Size* can be declared that are subtype conformant with the following subprogram declarations:

```
procedure Allocate
  (Pool                     : in out SSP;
   Storage_Address          : out System.Address;
   Size_In_Storage_Elements : System.Storage_Elements.Storage_Count;
   Alignment                : System.Storage_Elements.Storage_Count);

procedure Deallocate
  (Pool : in out SSP;
   Storage_Address          : System.Address;
   Size_In_Storage_Elements : System.Storage_Elements.Storage_Count;
   Alignment                : System.Storage_Elements.Storage_Count);

function Storage_Size (Pool : SSP)
  return System.Storage_Elements.Storage_Count;
```

Procedure *Allocate* must be declared, whereas *Deallocate* and *Storage_Size* are optional. If *Deallocate* is not declared, then applying an unchecked deallocation has no effect other than to set its actual parameter to null. If *Storage_Size* is not declared, then the *Storage_Size* attribute applied to an access type associated with a pool object of type SSP returns zero. Additional operations can be declared for a simple storage pool type (such as for supporting a mark/release storage-management discipline).

An object of a simple storage pool type can be associated with an access type by specifying the attribute [Simple_Storage_Pool], page 119. For example:

```
My_Pool : My_Simple_Storage_Pool_Type;

type Acc is access My_Data_Type;

for Acc'Simple_Storage_Pool use My_Pool;
```

See attribute [Simple_Storage_Pool], page 119 for further details.

2.157 Pragma Source_File_Name

Syntax:

```
pragma Source_File_Name (
  [Unit_Name   =>] unit_NAME,
  Spec_File_Name =>  STRING_LITERAL,
  [Index => INTEGER_LITERAL]);
```

```
pragma Source_File_Name (
  [Unit_Name   =>] unit_NAME,
  Body_File_Name =>  STRING_LITERAL,
  [Index => INTEGER_LITERAL]);
```

Use this to override the normal naming convention. It is a configuration pragma, and so has the usual applicability of configuration pragmas (i.e., it applies to either an entire partition, or to all units in a compilation, or to a single unit, depending on how it is used. *unit_name* is mapped to *file_name_literal*. The identifier for the second argument is required, and indicates whether this is the file name for the spec or for the body.

The optional Index argument should be used when a file contains multiple units, and when you do not want to use *gnatchop* to separate then into multiple files (which is the recommended procedure to limit the number of recompilations that are needed when some sources change). For instance, if the source file `source.ada` contains

```
package B is
...
end B;

with B;
procedure A is
begin
   ..
end A;
```

you could use the following configuration pragmas:

```
pragma Source_File_Name
  (B, Spec_File_Name => "source.ada", Index => 1);
pragma Source_File_Name
  (A, Body_File_Name => "source.ada", Index => 2);
```

Note that the *gnatname* utility can also be used to generate those configuration pragmas.

Another form of the *Source_File_Name* pragma allows the specification of patterns defining alternative file naming schemes to apply to all files.

```
pragma Source_File_Name
  (  [Spec_File_Name  =>] STRING_LITERAL
   [,[Casing          =>] CASING_SPEC]
   [,[Dot_Replacement =>] STRING_LITERAL]);

pragma Source_File_Name
  (  [Body_File_Name  =>] STRING_LITERAL
   [,[Casing          =>] CASING_SPEC]
   [,[Dot_Replacement =>] STRING_LITERAL]);

pragma Source_File_Name
  (  [Subunit_File_Name =>] STRING_LITERAL
   [,[Casing            =>] CASING_SPEC]
   [,[Dot_Replacement   =>] STRING_LITERAL]);
```

```
CASING_SPEC ::= Lowercase | Uppercase | Mixedcase
```

The first argument is a pattern that contains a single asterisk indicating the point at which the unit name is to be inserted in the pattern string to form the file name. The second argument is optional. If present it specifies the casing of the unit name in the resulting file name string. The default is lower case. Finally the third argument allows for systematic replacement of any dots in the unit name by the specified string literal.

Note that Source_File_Name pragmas should not be used if you are using project files. The reason for this rule is that the project manager is not aware of these pragmas, and so other tools that use the projet file would not be aware of the intended naming conventions. If you are using project files, file naming is controlled by Source_File_Name_Project pragmas, which are usually supplied automatically by the project manager. A pragma Source_File_Name cannot appear after a [Pragma Source_File_Name_Project], page 79.

For more details on the use of the *Source_File_Name* pragma, see the sections on *Using Other File Names* and *Alternative File Naming Schemes' in the :title:'GNAT User's Guide.*

2.158 Pragma Source_File_Name_Project

This pragma has the same syntax and semantics as pragma Source_File_Name. It is only allowed as a stand-alone configuration pragma. It cannot appear after a [Pragma Source_File_Name], page 77, and most importantly, once pragma Source_File_Name_Project appears, no further Source_File_Name pragmas are allowed.

The intention is that Source_File_Name_Project pragmas are always generated by the Project Manager in a manner consistent with the naming specified in a project file, and when naming is controlled in this manner, it is not permissible to attempt to modify this naming scheme using Source_File_Name or Source_File_Name_Project pragmas (which would not be known to the project manager).

2.159 Pragma Source_Reference

Syntax:

```
pragma Source_Reference (INTEGER_LITERAL, STRING_LITERAL);
```

This pragma must appear as the first line of a source file. *integer_literal* is the logical line number of the line following the pragma line (for use in error messages and debugging information). *string_literal* is a static string constant that specifies the file name to be used in error messages and debugging information. This is most notably used for the output of *gnatchop* with the *-r* switch, to make sure that the original unchopped source file is the one referred to.

The second argument must be a string literal, it cannot be a static string expression other than a string literal. This is because its value is needed for error messages issued by all phases of the compiler.

2.160 Pragma SPARK_Mode

Syntax:

```
pragma SPARK_Mode [(On | Off)] ;
```

In general a program can have some parts that are in SPARK 2014 (and follow all the rules in the SPARK Reference Manual), and some parts that are full Ada 2012.

The SPARK_Mode pragma is used to identify which parts are in SPARK 2014 (by default programs are in full Ada). The SPARK_Mode pragma can be used in the following places:

* As a configuration pragma, in which case it sets the default mode for all units compiled with this pragma.
* Immediately following a library-level subprogram spec
* Immediately within a library-level package body
* Immediately following the *private* keyword of a library-level package spec
* Immediately following the *begin* keyword of a library-level package body
* Immediately within a library-level subprogram body

Normally a subprogram or package spec/body inherits the current mode that is active at the point it is declared. But this can be overridden by pragma within the spec or body as above.

The basic consistency rule is that you can't turn SPARK_Mode back *On*, once you have explicitly (with a pragma) turned if *Off*. So the following rules apply:

If a subprogram spec has SPARK_Mode *Off*, then the body must also have SPARK_Mode *Off*.

For a package, we have four parts:

* the package public declarations
* the package private part
* the body of the package
* the elaboration code after *begin*

For a package, the rule is that if you explicitly turn SPARK_Mode *Off* for any part, then all the following parts must have SPARK_Mode *Off*. Note that this may require repeating a pragma SPARK_Mode (*Off*) in the body. For example, if we have a configuration pragma SPARK_Mode (*On*) that turns the mode on by default everywhere, and one particular package spec has pragma SPARK_Mode (*Off*), then that pragma will need to be repeated in the package body.

2.161 Pragma Static_Elaboration_Desired

Syntax:

```
pragma Static_Elaboration_Desired;
```

This pragma is used to indicate that the compiler should attempt to initialize statically the objects declared in the library unit to which the pragma applies, when these objects are initialized (explicitly or implicitly) by an aggregate. In the absence of this pragma, aggregates in object declarations are expanded into assignments and loops, even when the aggregate components are static constants. When the aggregate is present the compiler builds a static expression that requires no run-time code, so that the initialized object can be placed in read-only data space. If the components are not static, or the aggregate has more that 100 components, the compiler emits a warning that the pragma cannot be obeyed. (See also the restriction No_Implicit_Loops, which supports static construction of larger aggregates with static components that include an others choice.)

2.162 Pragma Stream_Convert

Syntax:

```
pragma Stream_Convert (
  [Entity =>] type_LOCAL_NAME,
  [Read   =>] function_NAME,
  [Write  =>] function_NAME);
```

This pragma provides an efficient way of providing user-defined stream attributes. Not only is it simpler to use than specifying the attributes directly, but more importantly, it allows the specification to be made in such a way that the predefined unit Ada.Streams is not loaded unless it is actually needed (i.e. unless the stream attributes are actually used); the use of the Stream_Convert pragma adds no overhead at all, unless the stream attributes are actually used on the designated type.

The first argument specifies the type for which stream functions are provided. The second parameter provides a function used to read values of this type. It must name a function whose argument type may be any subtype, and whose returned type must be the type given as the first argument to the pragma.

The meaning of the *Read* parameter is that if a stream attribute directly or indirectly specifies reading of the type given as the first parameter, then a value of the type given as the argument to the Read function is read from the stream, and then the Read function is used to convert this to the required target type.

Similarly the *Write* parameter specifies how to treat write attributes that directly or indirectly apply to the type given as the first parameter. It must have an input parameter of the type specified by the first parameter, and the return type must be the same as the input type of the Read function. The effect is to first call the Write function to convert to the given stream type, and then write the result type to the stream.

The Read and Write functions must not be overloaded subprograms. If necessary renamings can be supplied to meet this requirement. The usage of this attribute is best illustrated by a simple example, taken from the GNAT implementation of package Ada.Strings.Unbounded:

```
function To_Unbounded (S : String) return Unbounded_String
  renames To_Unbounded_String;

pragma Stream_Convert
  (Unbounded_String, To_Unbounded, To_String);
```

The specifications of the referenced functions, as given in the Ada Reference Manual are:

```
function To_Unbounded_String (Source : String)
  return Unbounded_String;

function To_String (Source : Unbounded_String)
  return String;
```

The effect is that if the value of an unbounded string is written to a stream, then the representation of the item in the stream is in the same format that would be used for *Standard.String'Output*, and this same representation is expected when a value of this type is read from the stream. Note that the value written always includes the bounds, even for Unbounded_String'Write, since Unbounded_String is not an array type.

Note that the *Stream_Convert* pragma is not effective in the case of a derived type of a non-limited tagged type. If such a type is specified then the pragma is silently ignored, and the default implementation of the stream attributes is used instead.

2.163 Pragma Style_Checks

Syntax:

```
pragma Style_Checks (string_LITERAL | ALL_CHECKS |
                     On | Off [, LOCAL_NAME]);
```

This pragma is used in conjunction with compiler switches to control the built in style checking provided by GNAT. The compiler switches, if set, provide an initial setting for the switches, and this pragma may be used to modify these settings, or the settings may be provided entirely by the use of the pragma. This pragma can be used anywhere that a pragma is legal, including use as a configuration pragma (including use in the `gnat.adc` file).

The form with a string literal specifies which style options are to be activated. These are additive, so they apply in addition to any previously set style check options. The codes for the options are the same as those used in the *-gnaty* switch to *gcc* or *gnatmake*. For example the following two methods can be used to enable layout checking:

*

```
pragma Style_Checks ("l");
```

*

```
gcc -c -gnatyl ...
```

The form ALL_CHECKS activates all standard checks (its use is equivalent to the use of the *gnaty* switch with no options. See the *GNAT User's Guide* for details.)

Note: the behavior is slightly different in GNAT mode (*-gnatg* used). In this case, ALL_CHECKS implies the standard set of GNAT mode style check options (i.e. equivalent to *-gnatyg*).

The forms with *Off* and *On* can be used to temporarily disable style checks as shown in the following example:

```
pragma Style_Checks ("k"); -- requires keywords in lower case
pragma Style_Checks (Off); -- turn off style checks
NULL;                      -- this will not generate an error message
pragma Style_Checks (On);  -- turn style checks back on
NULL;                      -- this will generate an error message
```

Finally the two argument form is allowed only if the first argument is *On* or *Off*. The effect is to turn of semantic style checks for the specified entity, as shown in the following example:

```
pragma Style_Checks ("r"); -- require consistency of identifier casing
Arg : Integer;
Rf1 : Integer := ARG;      -- incorrect, wrong case
pragma Style_Checks (Off, Arg);
Rf2 : Integer := ARG;      -- OK, no error
```

2.164 Pragma Subtitle

Syntax:

```
pragma Subtitle ([Subtitle =>] STRING_LITERAL);
```

This pragma is recognized for compatibility with other Ada compilers but is ignored by GNAT.

2.165 Pragma Suppress

Syntax:

```
pragma Suppress (Identifier [, [On =>] Name]);
```

This is a standard pragma, and supports all the check names required in the RM. It is included here because GNAT recognizes some additional check names that are implementation defined (as permitted by the RM):

* *Alignment_Check* can be used to suppress alignment checks on addresses used in address clauses. Such checks can also be suppressed by suppressing range checks, but the specific use of *Alignment_Check* allows suppression of alignment checks without suppressing other range checks. Note that *Alignment_Check* is suppressed by default on machines (such as the x86) with non-strict alignment.
* *Atomic_Synchronization* can be used to suppress the special memory synchronization instructions that are normally generated for access to *Atomic* variables to ensure correct synchronization between tasks that use such variables for synchronization purposes.
* *Duplicated_Tag_Check* Can be used to suppress the check that is generated for a duplicated tag value when a tagged type is declared.
* *Container_Checks* Can be used to suppress all checks within Ada.Containers and instances of its children, including Tampering_Check.
* *Tampering_Check* Can be used to suppress tampering check in the containers.
* *Predicate_Check* can be used to control whether predicate checks are active. It is applicable only to predicates for which the policy is *Check*. Unlike *Assertion_Policy*, which determines if a given predicate is ignored or checked for the whole program, the use of *Suppress* and *Unsuppress* with this check name allows a given predicate to be turned on and off at specific points in the program.
* *Validity_Check* can be used specifically to control validity checks. If *Suppress* is used to suppress validity checks, then no validity checks are performed, including those specified by the appropriate compiler switch or the *Validity_Checks* pragma.
* Additional check names previously introduced by use of the *Check_Name* pragma are also allowed.

Note that pragma Suppress gives the compiler permission to omit checks, but does not require the compiler to omit checks. The compiler will generate checks if they are essentially free, even when they are suppressed. In particular, if the compiler can prove that a certain check will necessarily fail, it will generate code to do an unconditional 'raise', even if checks are suppressed. The compiler warns in this case.

Of course, run-time checks are omitted whenever the compiler can prove that they will not fail, whether or not checks are suppressed.

2.166 Pragma Suppress_All

Syntax:

```
pragma Suppress_All;
```

This pragma can appear anywhere within a unit. The effect is to apply *Suppress (All_Checks)* to the unit in which it appears. This pragma is implemented for compatibility with DEC Ada 83 usage where it appears at the end of a unit, and for compatibility with Rational Ada, where it appears as a program unit pragma. The use of the standard Ada pragma *Suppress (All_Checks)* as a normal configuration pragma is the preferred usage in GNAT.

2.167 Pragma Suppress_Debug_Info

Syntax:

```
pragma Suppress_Debug_Info ([Entity =>] LOCAL_NAME);
```

This pragma can be used to suppress generation of debug information for the specified entity. It is intended primarily for use in debugging the debugger, and navigating around debugger problems.

2.168 Pragma Suppress_Exception_Locations

Syntax:

```
pragma Suppress_Exception_Locations;
```

In normal mode, a raise statement for an exception by default generates an exception message giving the file name and line number for the location of the raise. This is useful for debugging and logging purposes, but this entails extra space for the strings for the messages. The configuration pragma *Suppress_Exception_Locations* can be used to suppress the generation of these strings, with the result that space is saved, but the exception message for such raises is null. This configuration pragma may appear in a global configuration pragma file, or in a specific unit as usual. It is not required that this pragma be used consistently within a partition, so it is fine to have some units within a partition compiled with this pragma and others compiled in normal mode without it.

2.169 Pragma Suppress_Initialization

Syntax:

```
pragma Suppress_Initialization ([Entity =>] variable_or_subtype_Name);
```

Here variable_or_subtype_Name is the name introduced by a type declaration or subtype declaration or the name of a variable introduced by an object declaration.

In the case of a type or subtype this pragma suppresses any implicit or explicit initialization for all variables of the given type or subtype, including initialization resulting from the use of pragmas Normalize_Scalars or Initialize_Scalars.

This is considered a representation item, so it cannot be given after the type is frozen. It applies to all subsequent object declarations, and also any allocator that creates objects of the type.

If the pragma is given for the first subtype, then it is considered to apply to the base type and all its subtypes. If the pragma is given for other than a first subtype, then it applies only to the given subtype. The pragma may not be given after the type is frozen.

Note that this includes eliminating initialization of discriminants for discriminated types, and tags for tagged types. In these cases, you will have to use some non-portable mechanism (e.g. address overlays or unchecked conversion) to achieve required initialization of these fields before accessing any object of the corresponding type.

For the variable case, implicit initialization for the named variable is suppressed, just as though its subtype had been given in a pragma Suppress_Initialization, as described above.

2.170 Pragma Task_Name

Syntax

```
pragma Task_Name (string_EXPRESSION);
```

This pragma appears within a task definition (like pragma *Priority*) and applies to the task in which it appears. The argument must be of type String, and provides a name to be used for the task instance when the task is created. Note that this expression is not required to be static, and in particular, it can contain references to task discriminants. This facility can be used to provide different names for different tasks as they are created, as illustrated in the example below.

The task name is recorded internally in the run-time structures and is accessible to tools like the debugger. In addition the routine *Ada.Task_Identification.Image* will return this string, with a unique task address appended.

```
--  Example of the use of pragma Task_Name

with Ada.Task_Identification;
use Ada.Task_Identification;
with Text_IO; use Text_IO;
procedure t3 is

   type Astring is access String;

   task type Task_Typ (Name : access String) is
      pragma Task_Name (Name.all);
   end Task_Typ;

   task body Task_Typ is
      Nam : constant String := Image (Current_Task);
   begin
      Put_Line ("-->" & Nam (1 .. 14) & "<--");
   end Task_Typ;

   type Ptr_Task is access Task_Typ;
   Task_Var : Ptr_Task;

begin
```

```
   Task_Var :=
     new Task_Typ (new String'("This is task 1"));
   Task_Var :=
     new Task_Typ (new String'("This is task 2"));
end;
```

2.171 Pragma Task_Storage

Syntax:

```
pragma Task_Storage (
  [Task_Type =>] LOCAL_NAME,
  [Top_Guard =>] static_integer_EXPRESSION);
```

This pragma specifies the length of the guard area for tasks. The guard area is an additional storage area allocated to a task. A value of zero means that either no guard area is created or a minimal guard area is created, depending on the target. This pragma can appear anywhere a *Storage_Size* attribute definition clause is allowed for a task type.

2.172 Pragma Test_Case

Syntax:

```
pragma Test_Case (
   [Name     =>] static_string_Expression
  ,[Mode     =>] (Nominal | Robustness)
 [, Requires =>  Boolean_Expression]
 [, Ensures  =>  Boolean_Expression]);
```

The *Test_Case* pragma allows defining fine-grain specifications for use by testing tools. The compiler checks the validity of the *Test_Case* pragma, but its presence does not lead to any modification of the code generated by the compiler.

Test_Case pragmas may only appear immediately following the (separate) declaration of a subprogram in a package declaration, inside a package spec unit. Only other pragmas may intervene (that is appear between the subprogram declaration and a test case).

The compiler checks that boolean expressions given in *Requires* and *Ensures* are valid, where the rules for *Requires* are the same as the rule for an expression in *Precondition* and the rules for *Ensures* are the same as the rule for an expression in *Postcondition*. In particular, attributes *'Old* and *'Result* can only be used within the *Ensures* expression. The following is an example of use within a package spec:

```
package Math_Functions is
   ...
   function Sqrt (Arg : Float) return Float;
   pragma Test_Case (Name     => "Test 1",
                     Mode     => Nominal,
                     Requires => Arg < 10000,
                     Ensures  => Sqrt'Result < 10);
   ...
end Math_Functions;
```

The meaning of a test case is that there is at least one context where *Requires* holds such that, if the associated subprogram is executed in that context, then *Ensures* holds when the subprogram returns. Mode *Nominal* indicates that the input context should also satisfy the precondition of the subprogram, and the output context should also satisfy its postcondition. Mode *Robustness* indicates that the precondition and postcondition of the subprogram should be ignored for this test case.

2.173 Pragma Thread_Local_Storage

Syntax:

```
pragma Thread_Local_Storage ([Entity =>] LOCAL_NAME);
```

This pragma specifies that the specified entity, which must be a variable declared in a library level package, is to be marked as "Thread Local Storage" (*TLS*). On systems supporting this (which include Windows, Solaris, GNU/Linux and VxWorks 6), this causes each thread (and hence each Ada task) to see a distinct copy of the variable.

The variable may not have default initialization, and if there is an explicit initialization, it must be either *null* for an access variable, or a static expression for a scalar variable. This provides a low level mechanism similar to that provided by the *Ada.Task_Attributes* package, but much more efficient and is also useful in writing interface code that will interact with foreign threads.

If this pragma is used on a system where *TLS* is not supported, then an error message will be generated and the program will be rejected.

2.174 Pragma Time_Slice

Syntax:

```
pragma Time_Slice (static_duration_EXPRESSION);
```

For implementations of GNAT on operating systems where it is possible to supply a time slice value, this pragma may be used for this purpose. It is ignored if it is used in a system that does not allow this control, or if it appears in other than the main program unit.

2.175 Pragma Title

Syntax:

```
pragma Title (TITLING_OPTION [, TITLING OPTION]);

TITLING_OPTION ::=
  [Title    =>] STRING_LITERAL,
| [Subtitle =>] STRING_LITERAL
```

Syntax checked but otherwise ignored by GNAT. This is a listing control pragma used in DEC Ada 83 implementations to provide a title and/or subtitle for the program listing. The program listing generated by GNAT does not have titles or subtitles.

Unlike other pragmas, the full flexibility of named notation is allowed for this pragma, i.e., the parameters may be given in any order if named notation is used, and named and positional notation can be mixed following the normal rules for procedure calls in Ada.

2.176 Pragma Type_Invariant

Syntax:

```
pragma Type_Invariant
  ([Entity =>] type_LOCAL_NAME,
   [Check  =>] EXPRESSION);
```

The *Type_Invariant* pragma is intended to be an exact replacement for the language-defined *Type_Invariant* aspect, and shares its restrictions and semantics. It differs from the language defined *Invariant* pragma in that it does not permit a string parameter, and it is controlled by the assertion identifier *Type_Invariant* rather than *Invariant*.

2.177 Pragma Type_Invariant_Class

Syntax:

```
pragma Type_Invariant_Class
  ([Entity =>] type_LOCAL_NAME,
   [Check  =>] EXPRESSION);
```

The *Type_Invariant_Class* pragma is intended to be an exact replacement for the language-defined *Type_Invariant'Class* aspect, and shares its restrictions and semantics.

Note: This pragma is called *Type_Invariant_Class* rather than *Type_Invariant'Class* because the latter would not be strictly conforming to the allowed syntax for pragmas. The motivation for providing pragmas equivalent to the aspects is to allow a program to be written using the pragmas, and then compiled if necessary using an Ada compiler that does not recognize the pragmas or aspects, but is prepared to ignore the pragmas. The assertion policy that controls this pragma is *Type_Invariant'Class*, not *Type_Invariant_Class*.

2.178 Pragma Unchecked_Union

Syntax:

```
pragma Unchecked_Union (first_subtype_LOCAL_NAME);
```

This pragma is used to specify a representation of a record type that is equivalent to a C union. It was introduced as a GNAT implementation defined pragma in the GNAT Ada 95 mode. Ada 2005 includes an extended version of this pragma, making it language defined, and GNAT fully implements this extended version in all language modes (Ada 83, Ada 95, and Ada 2005). For full details, consult the Ada 2012 Reference Manual, section B.3.3.

2.179 Pragma Unevaluated_Use_Of_Old

Syntax:

```
pragma Unevaluated_Use_Of_Old (Error | Warn | Allow);
```

This pragma controls the processing of attributes Old and Loop_Entry. If either of these attributes is used in a potentially unevaluated expression (e.g. the then or else parts of an if expression), then normally this usage is considered illegal if the prefix of the attribute is other than an entity name. The language requires this behavior for Old, and GNAT copies the same rule for Loop_Entry.

The reason for this rule is that otherwise, we can have a situation where we save the Old value, and this results in an exception, even though we might not evaluate the attribute. Consider this example:

```
package UnevalOld is
   K : Character;
   procedure U (A : String; C : Boolean)  -- ERROR
     with Post => (if C then A(1)'Old = K else True);
end;
```

If procedure U is called with a string with a lower bound of 2, and C false, then an exception would be raised trying to evaluate A(1) on entry even though the value would not be actually used.

Although the rule guarantees against this possibility, it is sometimes too restrictive. For example if we know that the string has a lower bound of 1, then we will never raise an exception. The pragma *Unevaluated_Use_Of_Old* can be used to modify this behavior. If the argument is *Error* then an error is given (this is the default RM behavior). If the argument is *Warn* then the usage is allowed as legal but with a warning that an exception might be raised. If the argument is *Allow* then the usage is allowed as legal without generating a warning.

This pragma may appear as a configuration pragma, or in a declarative part or package specification. In the latter case it applies to uses up to the end of the corresponding statement sequence or sequence of package declarations.

2.180 Pragma Unimplemented_Unit

Syntax:

```
pragma Unimplemented_Unit;
```

If this pragma occurs in a unit that is processed by the compiler, GNAT aborts with the message `xxx not implemented`, where *xxx* is the name of the current compilation unit. This pragma is intended to allow the compiler to handle unimplemented library units in a clean manner.

The abort only happens if code is being generated. Thus you can use specs of unimplemented packages in syntax or semantic checking mode.

2.181 Pragma Universal_Aliasing

Syntax:

```
pragma Universal_Aliasing [([Entity =>] type_LOCAL_NAME)];
```

type_LOCAL_NAME must refer to a type declaration in the current declarative part. The effect is to inhibit strict type-based aliasing optimization for the given type. In other words, the effect is as though access types designating this type were subject to pragma No_Strict_Aliasing. For a detailed description of the strict aliasing optimization, and the situations in which it must be suppressed, see the section on *Optimization and Strict Aliasing* in the *GNAT User's Guide*.

2.182 Pragma Universal_Data

Syntax:

```
pragma Universal_Data [(library_unit_Name)];
```

This pragma is supported only for the AAMP target and is ignored for other targets. The pragma specifies that all library-level objects (Counter 0 data) associated with the library unit are to be accessed and updated using universal addressing (24-bit addresses for AAMP5) rather than the default of 16-bit Data Environment (DENV) addressing. Use of this pragma will generally result in less efficient code for references to global data associated with the library unit, but allows such data to be located anywhere in memory. This pragma is a library unit pragma, but can also be used as a configuration pragma (including use in the `gnat.adc` file). The functionality of this pragma is also available by applying the -univ switch on the compilations of units where universal addressing of the data is desired.

2.183 Pragma Unmodified

Syntax:

```
pragma Unmodified (LOCAL_NAME {, LOCAL_NAME});
```

This pragma signals that the assignable entities (variables, *out* parameters, *in out* parameters) whose names are listed are deliberately not assigned in the current source unit. This suppresses warnings about the entities being referenced but not assigned, and in addition a warning will be generated if one of these entities is in fact assigned in the same unit as the pragma (or in the corresponding body, or one of its subunits).

This is particularly useful for clearly signaling that a particular parameter is not modified, even though the spec suggests that it might be.

For the variable case, warnings are never given for unreferenced variables whose name contains one of the substrings *DISCARD, DUMMY, IGNORE, JUNK, UNUSED* in any casing. Such names are typically to be used in cases where such warnings are expected. Thus it is never necessary to use *pragma Unmodified* for such variables, though it is harmless to do so.

2.184 Pragma Unreferenced

Syntax:

```
pragma Unreferenced (LOCAL_NAME {, LOCAL_NAME});
pragma Unreferenced (library_unit_NAME {, library_unit_NAME});
```

This pragma signals that the entities whose names are listed are deliberately not referenced in the current source unit after the occurrence of the pragma. This suppresses warnings about the entities being unreferenced, and in addition a warning will be generated if one of these entities is in fact subsequently referenced in the same unit as the pragma (or in the corresponding body, or one of its subunits).

This is particularly useful for clearly signaling that a particular parameter is not referenced in some particular subprogram implementation and that this is deliberate. It can also be useful in the case of objects declared only for their initialization or finalization side effects.

If *LOCAL_NAME* identifies more than one matching homonym in the current scope, then the entity most recently declared is the one to which the pragma applies. Note that in the case of accept formals, the pragma Unreferenced may appear immediately after the keyword *do* which allows the indication of whether or not accept formals are referenced or not to be given individually for each accept statement.

The left hand side of an assignment does not count as a reference for the purpose of this pragma. Thus it is fine to assign to an entity for which pragma Unreferenced is given.

Note that if a warning is desired for all calls to a given subprogram, regardless of whether they occur in the same unit as the subprogram declaration, then this pragma should not be used (calls from another unit would not be flagged); pragma Obsolescent can be used instead for this purpose, see [Pragma Obsolescent], page 55.

The second form of pragma *Unreferenced* is used within a context clause. In this case the arguments must be unit names of units previously mentioned in *with* clauses (similar to the usage of pragma *Elaborate_All*. The effect is to suppress warnings about unreferenced units and unreferenced entities within these units.

For the variable case, warnings are never given for unreferenced variables whose name contains one of the substrings *DISCARD, DUMMY, IGNORE, JUNK, UNUSED* in any casing. Such names are typically to be used in cases where such warnings are expected. Thus it is never necessary to use *pragma Unreferenced* for such variables, though it is harmless to do so.

2.185 Pragma Unreferenced_Objects

Syntax:

```
pragma Unreferenced_Objects (local_subtype_NAME {, local_subtype_NAME});
```

This pragma signals that for the types or subtypes whose names are listed, objects which are declared with one of these types or subtypes may not be referenced, and if no references appear, no warnings are given.

This is particularly useful for objects which are declared solely for their initialization and finalization effect. Such variables are sometimes referred to as RAII variables (Resource Acquisition Is Initialization). Using this pragma on the relevant type (most typically a limited controlled type), the compiler will automatically suppress unwanted warnings about these variables not being referenced.

2.186 Pragma Unreserve_All_Interrupts

Syntax:

```
pragma Unreserve_All_Interrupts;
```

Normally certain interrupts are reserved to the implementation. Any attempt to attach an interrupt causes Program_Error to be raised, as described in RM C.3.2(22). A typical example is the *SIGINT* interrupt used in many systems for a `Ctrl-C` interrupt. Normally this interrupt is reserved to the implementation, so that `Ctrl-C` can be used to interrupt execution.

If the pragma *Unreserve_All_Interrupts* appears anywhere in any unit in a program, then all such interrupts are unreserved. This allows the program to handle these interrupts, but disables their standard functions. For example, if this pragma is used, then pressing `Ctrl-C` will not automatically interrupt execution. However, a program can then handle the *SIGINT* interrupt as it chooses.

For a full list of the interrupts handled in a specific implementation, see the source code for the spec of *Ada.Interrupts.Names* in file `a-intnam.ads`. This is a target dependent file that contains the list of interrupts recognized for a given target. The documentation in this file also specifies what interrupts are affected by the use of the *Unreserve_All_Interrupts* pragma.

For a more general facility for controlling what interrupts can be handled, see pragma *Interrupt_State*, which subsumes the functionality of the *Unreserve_All_Interrupts* pragma.

2.187 Pragma Unsuppress

Syntax:

```
pragma Unsuppress (IDENTIFIER [, [On =>] NAME]);
```

This pragma undoes the effect of a previous pragma *Suppress*. If there is no corresponding pragma *Suppress* in effect, it has no effect. The range of the effect is the same as for pragma *Suppress*. The meaning of the arguments is identical to that used in pragma *Suppress*.

One important application is to ensure that checks are on in cases where code depends on the checks for its correct functioning, so that the code will compile correctly even if the compiler switches are set to suppress checks. For example, in a program that depends on external names of tagged types and wants to ensure that the duplicated tag check occurs even if all run-time checks are suppressed by a compiler switch, the following configuration pragma will ensure this test is not suppressed:

```
pragma Unsuppress (Duplicated_Tag_Check);
```

This pragma is standard in Ada 2005. It is available in all earlier versions of Ada as an implementation-defined pragma.

Note that in addition to the checks defined in the Ada RM, GNAT recogizes a number of implementation-defined check names. See the description of pragma *Suppress* for full details.

2.188 Pragma Use_VADS_Size

Syntax:

```
pragma Use_VADS_Size;
```

This is a configuration pragma. In a unit to which it applies, any use of the 'Size attribute is automatically interpreted as a use of the 'VADS_Size attribute. Note that this may result in incorrect semantic processing of valid Ada 95 or Ada 2005 programs. This is intended to aid in the handling of existing code which depends on the interpretation of Size as implemented in the VADS compiler. See description of the VADS_Size attribute for further details.

2.189 Pragma Validity_Checks

Syntax:

```
pragma Validity_Checks (string_LITERAL | ALL_CHECKS | On | Off);
```

This pragma is used in conjunction with compiler switches to control the built-in validity checking provided by GNAT. The compiler switches, if set provide an initial setting for the switches, and this pragma may be used to modify these settings, or the settings may be provided entirely by the use of the pragma. This pragma can be used anywhere that a pragma is legal, including use as a configuration pragma (including use in the `gnat.adc` file).

The form with a string literal specifies which validity options are to be activated. The validity checks are first set to include only the default reference manual settings, and then a string of letters in the string specifies the exact set of options required. The form of this string is exactly as described for the *-gnatVx* compiler switch (see the GNAT User's Guide for details). For example the following two methods can be used to enable validity checking for mode *in* and *in out* subprogram parameters:

*

```
pragma Validity_Checks ("im");
```

*

```
$ gcc -c -gnatVim ...
```

The form ALL_CHECKS activates all standard checks (its use is equivalent to the use of the *gnatva* switch.

The forms with *Off* and *On* can be used to temporarily disable validity checks as shown in the following example:

```
pragma Validity_Checks ("c"); -- validity checks for copies
pragma Validity_Checks (Off); -- turn off validity checks
A := B;                       -- B will not be validity checked
pragma Validity_Checks (On);  -- turn validity checks back on
A := C;                       -- C will be validity checked
```

2.190 Pragma Volatile

Syntax:

```
pragma Volatile (LOCAL_NAME);
```

This pragma is defined by the Ada Reference Manual, and the GNAT implementation is fully conformant with this definition. The reason it is mentioned in this section is that a pragma of the same name was supplied in some Ada 83 compilers, including DEC Ada 83. The Ada 95 / Ada 2005 implementation of pragma Volatile is upwards compatible with the implementation in DEC Ada 83.

2.191 Pragma Volatile_Full_Access

Syntax:

```
pragma Volatile_Full_Access (LOCAL_NAME);
```

This is similar in effect to pragma Volatile, except that any reference to the object is guaranteed to be done only with instructions that read or write all the bits of the object. Furthermore, if the object is of a composite type, then any reference to a component of the object is guaranteed to read and/or write all the bits of the object.

The intention is that this be suitable for use with memory-mapped I/O devices on some machines. Note that there are two important respects in which this is different from *pragma Atomic*. First a reference to a *Volatile_Full_Access* object is not a sequential action in the RM 9.10 sense and, therefore, does not create a synchronization point. Second, in the case of *pragma Atomic*, there is no guarantee that all the bits will be accessed if the reference is not to the whole object; the compiler is allowed (and generally will) access only part of the object in this case.

It is not permissible to specify *Atomic* and *Volatile_Full_Access* for the same object.

It is not permissible to specify *Volatile_Full_Access* for a composite (record or array) type or object that has at least one *Aliased* component.

2.192 Pragma Volatile_Function

Syntax:

```
pragma Volatile_Function [ (boolean_EXPRESSION) ];
```

For the semantics of this pragma, see the entry for aspect *Volatile_Function* in the SPARK 2014 Reference Manual, section 7.1.2.

2.193 Pragma Warning_As_Error

Syntax:

```
pragma Warning_As_Error (static_string_EXPRESSION);
```

This configuration pragma allows the programmer to specify a set of warnings that will be treated as errors. Any warning which matches the pattern given by the pragma argument will be treated as an error. This gives much more precise control that -gnatwe which treats all warnings as errors.

The pattern may contain asterisks, which match zero or more characters in the message. For example, you can use *pragma Warning_As_Error ("bits of*unused")* to treat the warning message *warning: 960 bits of "a" unused* as an error. No other regular expression notations are permitted. All characters other than asterisk in these three specific cases are treated as literal characters in the match. The match is case insensitive, for example XYZ matches xyz.

Note that the pattern matches if it occurs anywhere within the warning message string (it is not necessary to put an asterisk at the start and the end of the message, since this is implied).

Another possibility for the static_string_EXPRESSION which works whether or not error tags are enabled (*-gnatw.d*) is to use the *-gnatw* tag string, enclosed in brackets, as shown in the example below, to treat a class of warnings as errors.

The above use of patterns to match the message applies only to warning messages generated by the front end. This pragma can also be applied to warnings provided by the back end and mentioned in [Pragma Warnings], page 95. By using a single full *-Wxxx* switch in the pragma, such warnings can also be treated as errors.

The pragma can appear either in a global configuration pragma file (e.g. `gnat.adc`), or at the start of a file. Given a global configuration pragma file containing:

```
pragma Warning_As_Error ("[-gnatwj]");
```

which will treat all obsolescent feature warnings as errors, the following program compiles as shown (compile options here are *-gnatwa.d -gnatl -gnatj55*).

```
1. pragma Warning_As_Error ("*never assigned*");
2. function Warnerr return String is
3.    X : Integer;
```

```
             |
          >>> error: variable "X" is never read and
              never assigned [-gnatwv] [warning-as-error]

     4.      Y : Integer;
             |
          >>> warning: variable "Y" is assigned but
              never read [-gnatwu]

     5. begin
     6.      Y := 0;
     7.      return %ABC%;
                    |
          >>> error: use of "%" is an obsolescent
              feature (RM J.2(4)), use """ instead
              [-gnatwj] [warning-as-error]

     8. end;

 8 lines: No errors, 3 warnings (2 treated as errors)
```

Note that this pragma does not affect the set of warnings issued in any way, it merely changes the effect of a matching warning if one is produced as a result of other warnings options. As shown in this example, if the pragma results in a warning being treated as an error, the tag is changed from "warning:" to "error:" and the string "[warning-as-error]" is appended to the end of the message.

2.194 Pragma Warnings

Syntax:

```
pragma Warnings ([TOOL_NAME,] DETAILS [, REASON]);

DETAILS ::= On | Off
DETAILS ::= On | Off, local_NAME
DETAILS ::= static_string_EXPRESSION
DETAILS ::= On | Off, static_string_EXPRESSION

TOOL_NAME ::= GNAT | GNATProve

REASON ::= Reason => STRING_LITERAL {& STRING_LITERAL}
```

Note: in Ada 83 mode, a string literal may be used in place of a static string expression (which does not exist in Ada 83).

Note if the second argument of *DETAILS* is a *local_NAME* then the second form is always understood. If the intention is to use the fourth form, then you can write *NAME &* "" to force the intepretation as a *static_string_EXPRESSION*.

Note: if the first argument is a valid *TOOL_NAME*, it will be interpreted that way. The use of the *TOOL_NAME* argument is relevant only to users of SPARK and GNATprove, see last part of this section for details.

Normally warnings are enabled, with the output being controlled by the command line switch. Warnings (*Off*) turns off generation of warnings until a Warnings (*On*) is encountered or the end of the current unit. If generation of warnings is turned off using this pragma, then some or all of the warning messages are suppressed, regardless of the setting of the command line switches.

The *Reason* parameter may optionally appear as the last argument in any of the forms of this pragma. It is intended purely for the purposes of documenting the reason for the *Warnings* pragma. The compiler will check that the argument is a static string but otherwise ignore this argument. Other tools may provide specialized processing for this string.

The form with a single argument (or two arguments if Reason present), where the first argument is *ON* or *OFF* may be used as a configuration pragma.

If the *LOCAL_NAME* parameter is present, warnings are suppressed for the specified entity. This suppression is effective from the point where it occurs till the end of the extended scope of the variable (similar to the scope of *Suppress*). This form cannot be used as a configuration pragma.

In the case where the first argument is other than *ON* or *OFF*, the third form with a single static_string_EXPRESSION argument (and possible reason) provides more precise control over which warnings are active. The string is a list of letters specifying which warnings are to be activated and which deactivated. The code for these letters is the same as the string used in the command line switch controlling warnings. For a brief summary, use the gnatmake command with no arguments, which will generate usage information containing the list of warnings switches supported. For full details see the section on *Warning Message Control* in the *GNAT User's Guide*. This form can also be used as a configuration pragma.

The warnings controlled by the *-gnatw* switch are generated by the front end of the compiler. The GCC back end can provide additional warnings and they are controlled by the *-W* switch. Such warnings can be identified by the appearance of a string of the form *[-Wxxx]* in the message which designates the *-Wxxx* switch that controls the message. The form with a single static_string_EXPRESSION argument also works for these warnings, but the string must be a single full *-Wxxx* switch in this case. The above reference lists a few examples of these additional warnings.

The specified warnings will be in effect until the end of the program or another pragma Warnings is encountered. The effect of the pragma is cumulative. Initially the set of warnings is the standard default set as possibly modified by compiler switches. Then each pragma Warning modifies this set of warnings as specified. This form of the pragma may also be used as a configuration pragma.

The fourth form, with an *On|Off* parameter and a string, is used to control individual messages, based on their text. The string argument is a pattern that is used to match against the text of individual warning messages (not including the initial "warning: " tag).

The pattern may contain asterisks, which match zero or more characters in the message. For example, you can use *pragma Warnings (Off, "bits of*unused")* to suppress the warning message *warning: 960 bits of "a" unused*. No other regular expression notations are permitted. All characters other than asterisk in these three specific cases are treated as literal characters in the match. The match is case insensitive, for example XYZ matches xyz.

Note that the pattern matches if it occurs anywhere within the warning message string (it is not necessary to put an asterisk at the start and the end of the message, since this is implied).

The above use of patterns to match the message applies only to warning messages generated by the front end. This form of the pragma with a string argument can also be used to control warnings provided by the back end and mentioned above. By using a single full *-Wxxx* switch in the pragma, such warnings can be turned on and off.

There are two ways to use the pragma in this form. The OFF form can be used as a configuration pragma. The effect is to suppress all warnings (if any) that match the pattern string throughout the compilation (or match the -W switch in the back end case).

The second usage is to suppress a warning locally, and in this case, two pragmas must appear in sequence:

```
pragma Warnings (Off, Pattern);
... code where given warning is to be suppressed
pragma Warnings (On, Pattern);
```

In this usage, the pattern string must match in the Off and On pragmas, and (if *-gnatw.w* is given) at least one matching warning must be suppressed.

Note: to write a string that will match any warning, use the string `"***"`. It will not work to use a single asterisk or two asterisks since this looks like an operator name. This form with three asterisks is similar in effect to specifying *pragma Warnings (Off)* except (if *-gnatw.w* is given) that a matching *pragma Warnings (On,* `"***"`*)* will be required. This can be helpful in avoiding forgetting to turn warnings back on.

Note: the debug flag -gnatd.i (*/NOWARNINGS_PRAGMAS* in VMS) can be used to cause the compiler to entirely ignore all WARNINGS pragmas. This can be useful in checking whether obsolete pragmas in existing programs are hiding real problems.

Note: pragma Warnings does not affect the processing of style messages. See separate entry for pragma Style_Checks for control of style messages.

Users of the formal verification tool GNATprove for the SPARK subset of Ada may use the version of the pragma with a *TOOL_NAME* parameter.

If present, *TOOL_NAME* is the name of a tool, currently either *GNAT* for the compiler or *GNATprove* for the formal verification tool. A given tool only takes into account pragma Warnings that do not specify a tool name, or that specify the matching tool name. This makes it possible to disable warnings selectively for each tool, and as a consequence to detect useless pragma Warnings with switch *-gnatw.w*.

2.195 Pragma Weak_External

Syntax:

```
pragma Weak_External ([Entity =>] LOCAL_NAME);
```

LOCAL_NAME must refer to an object that is declared at the library level. This pragma specifies that the given entity should be marked as a weak symbol for the linker. It is equivalent to *__attribute__((weak))* in GNU C and causes *LOCAL_NAME* to be emitted as a weak symbol instead of a regular symbol, that is to say a symbol that does not have to be resolved by the linker if used in conjunction with a pragma Import.

When a weak symbol is not resolved by the linker, its address is set to zero. This is useful in writing interfaces to external modules that may or may not be linked in the final executable, for example depending on configuration settings.

If a program references at run time an entity to which this pragma has been applied, and the corresponding symbol was not resolved at link time, then the execution of the program is erroneous. It is not erroneous to take the Address of such an entity, for example to guard potential references, as shown in the example below.

Some file formats do not support weak symbols so not all target machines support this pragma.

```
--  Example of the use of pragma Weak_External

package External_Module is
  key : Integer;
  pragma Import (C, key);
  pragma Weak_External (key);
  function Present return boolean;
end External_Module;

with System; use System;
package body External_Module is
  function Present return boolean is
  begin
    return key'Address /= System.Null_Address;
  end Present;
end External_Module;
```

2.196 Pragma Wide_Character_Encoding

Syntax:

```
pragma Wide_Character_Encoding (IDENTIFIER | CHARACTER_LITERAL);
```

This pragma specifies the wide character encoding to be used in program source text appearing subsequently. It is a configuration pragma, but may also be used at any point that a pragma is allowed, and it is permissible to have more than one such pragma in a file, allowing multiple encodings to appear within the same file.

The argument can be an identifier or a character literal. In the identifier case, it is one of *HEX*, *UPPER*, *SHIFT_JIS*, *EUC*, *UTF8*, or *BRACKETS*. In the character literal case it is correspondingly one of the characters `h`, `u`, `s`, `e`, `8`, or `b`.

Note that when the pragma is used within a file, it affects only the encoding within that file, and does not affect withed units, specs, or subunits.

3 Implementation Defined Aspects

Ada defines (throughout the Ada 2012 reference manual, summarized in Annex K) a set of aspects that can be specified for certain entities. These language defined aspects are implemented in GNAT in Ada 2012 mode and work as described in the Ada 2012 Reference Manual.

In addition, Ada 2012 allows implementations to define additional aspects whose meaning is defined by the implementation. GNAT provides a number of these implementation-defined aspects which can be used to extend and enhance the functionality of the compiler. This section of the GNAT reference manual describes these additional aspects.

Note that any program using these aspects may not be portable to other compilers (although GNAT implements this set of aspects on all platforms). Therefore if portability to other compilers is an important consideration, you should minimize the use of these aspects.

Note that for many of these aspects, the effect is essentially similar to the use of a pragma or attribute specification with the same name applied to the entity. For example, if we write:

```
type R is range 1 .. 100
  with Value_Size => 10;
```

then the effect is the same as:

```
type R is range 1 .. 100;
for R'Value_Size use 10;
```

and if we write:

```
type R is new Integer
  with Shared => True;
```

then the effect is the same as:

```
type R is new Integer;
pragma Shared (R);
```

In the documentation below, such cases are simply marked as being boolean aspects equivalent to the corresponding pragma or attribute definition clause.

3.1 Aspect Abstract_State

This aspect is equivalent to pragma *Abstract_State*.

3.2 Annotate

There are three forms of this aspect (where ID is an identifier, and ARG is a general expression).

Annotate => ID
: Equivalent to *pragma Annotate (ID, Entity => Name);*

Annotate => (ID)
: Equivalent to *pragma Annotate (ID, Entity => Name);*

Annotate => (ID ,ID {, ARG})
: Equivalent to *pragma Annotate (ID, ID {, ARG}, Entity => Name);*

3.3 Aspect Async_Readers

This boolean aspect is equivalent to pragma *Async_Readers*.

3.4 Aspect Async_Writers

This boolean aspect is equivalent to pragma *Async_Writers*.

3.5 Aspect Constant_After_Elaboration

This aspect is equivalent to pragma *Constant_After_Elaboration*.

3.6 Aspect Contract_Cases

This aspect is equivalent to pragma *Contract_Cases*, the sequence of clauses being enclosed in parentheses so that syntactically it is an aggregate.

3.7 Aspect Depends

This aspect is equivalent to pragma *Depends*.

3.8 Aspect Default_Initial_Condition

This aspect is equivalent to pragma *Default_Initial_Condition*.

3.9 Aspect Dimension

The *Dimension* aspect is used to specify the dimensions of a given subtype of a dimensioned numeric type. The aspect also specifies a symbol used when doing formatted output of dimensioned quantities. The syntax is:

```
with Dimension =>
  ([Symbol =>] SYMBOL, DIMENSION_VALUE {, DIMENSION_Value})

SYMBOL ::= STRING_LITERAL | CHARACTER_LITERAL

DIMENSION_VALUE ::=
  RATIONAL
| others                 => RATIONAL
| DISCRETE_CHOICE_LIST => RATIONAL

RATIONAL ::= [-] NUMERIC_LITERAL [/ NUMERIC_LITERAL]
```

This aspect can only be applied to a subtype whose parent type has a *Dimension_Systen* aspect. The aspect must specify values for all dimensions of the system. The rational values are the powers of the corresponding dimensions that are used by the compiler to verify that physical (numeric) computations are dimensionally consistent. For example, the computation of a force must result in dimensions (L => 1, M => 1, T => -2). For further examples of the usage of this aspect, see package *System.Dim.Mks*. Note that when the dimensioned type is an integer type, then any dimension value must be an integer literal.

3.10 Aspect Dimension_System

The *Dimension_System* aspect is used to define a system of dimensions that will be used in subsequent subtype declarations with *Dimension* aspects that reference this system. The syntax is:

```
with Dimension_System => (DIMENSION {, DIMENSION});

DIMENSION ::= ([Unit_Name   =>] IDENTIFIER,
               [Unit_Symbol =>] SYMBOL,
               [Dim_Symbol  =>] SYMBOL)

SYMBOL ::= CHARACTER_LITERAL | STRING_LITERAL
```

This aspect is applied to a type, which must be a numeric derived type (typically a floating-point type), that will represent values within the dimension system. Each *DIMENSION* corresponds to one particular dimension. A maximum of 7 dimensions may be specified. *Unit_Name* is the name of the dimension (for example *Meter*). *Unit_Symbol* is the shorthand used for quantities of this dimension (for example *m* for *Meter*). *Dim_Symbol* gives the identification within the dimension system (typically this is a single letter, e.g. *L* standing for length for unit name *Meter*). The *Unit_Symbol* is used in formatted output of dimensioned quantities. The *Dim_Symbol* is used in error messages when numeric operations have inconsistent dimensions.

GNAT provides the standard definition of the International MKS system in the run-time package *System.Dim.Mks*. You can easily define similar packages for cgs units or British units, and define conversion factors between values in different systems. The MKS system is characterized by the following aspect:

```
type Mks_Type is new Long_Long_Float with
  Dimension_System => (
    (Unit_Name => Meter,    Unit_Symbol => 'm',   Dim_Symbol => 'L'),
    (Unit_Name => Kilogram, Unit_Symbol => "kg",  Dim_Symbol => 'M'),
    (Unit_Name => Second,   Unit_Symbol => 's',   Dim_Symbol => 'T'),
    (Unit_Name => Ampere,   Unit_Symbol => 'A',   Dim_Symbol => 'I'),
    (Unit_Name => Kelvin,   Unit_Symbol => 'K',   Dim_Symbol => '@'),
    (Unit_Name => Mole,     Unit_Symbol => "mol", Dim_Symbol => 'N'),
    (Unit_Name => Candela,  Unit_Symbol => "cd",  Dim_Symbol => 'J'));
```

Note that in the above type definition, we use the *at* symbol (`@`) to represent a theta character (avoiding the use of extended Latin-1 characters in this context).

See section 'Performing Dimensionality Analysis in GNAT' in the GNAT Users Guide for detailed examples of use of the dimension system.

3.11 Aspect Disable_Controlled

The aspect *Disable_Controlled* is defined for controlled record types. If active, this aspect causes suppression of all related calls to *Initialize*, *Adjust*, and *Finalize*. The intended use is for conditional compilation, where for example you might want a record to be controlled or not depending on whether some run-time check is enabled or suppressed.

3.12 Aspect Effective_Reads

This aspect is equivalent to pragma *Effective_Reads*.

3.13 Aspect Effective_Writes

This aspect is equivalent to pragma *Effective_Writes*.

3.14 Aspect Extensions_Visible

This aspect is equivalent to pragma *Extensions_Visible*.

3.15 Aspect Favor_Top_Level

This boolean aspect is equivalent to pragma *Favor_Top_Level*.

3.16 Aspect Ghost

This aspect is equivalent to pragma *Ghost*.

3.17 Aspect Global

This aspect is equivalent to pragma *Global*.

3.18 Aspect Initial_Condition

This aspect is equivalent to pragma *Initial_Condition*.

3.19 Aspect Initializes

This aspect is equivalent to pragma *Initializes*.

3.20 Aspect Inline_Always

This boolean aspect is equivalent to pragma *Inline_Always*.

3.21 Aspect Invariant

This aspect is equivalent to pragma *Invariant*. It is a synonym for the language defined aspect *Type_Invariant* except that it is separately controllable using pragma *Assertion_Policy*.

3.22 Aspect Invariant'Class

This aspect is equivalent to pragma *Type_Invariant_Class*. It is a synonym for the language defined aspect *Type_Invariant'Class* except that it is separately controllable using pragma *Assertion_Policy*.

3.23 Aspect Iterable

This aspect provides a light-weight mechanism for loops and quantified expressions over container types, without the overhead imposed by the tampering checks of standard Ada 2012 iterators. The value of the aspect is an aggregate with four named components: *First*,

Next, *Has_Element*, and *Element* (the last one being optional). When only 3 components are specified, only the *for .. in* form of iteration over cursors is available. When all 4 components are specified, both this form and the *for .. of* form of iteration over elements are available. The following is a typical example of use:

```
type List is private with
    Iterable => (First       => First_Cursor,
                 Next        => Advance,
                 Has_Element => Cursor_Has_Element,
                [Element     => Get_Element]);
```

* The value denoted by *First* must denote a primitive operation of the container type that returns a *Cursor*, which must a be a type declared in the container package or visible from it. For example:

```
function First_Cursor (Cont : Container) return Cursor;
```

* The value of *Next* is a primitive operation of the container type that takes both a container and a cursor and yields a cursor. For example:

```
function Advance (Cont : Container; Position : Cursor) return Cursor;
```

* The value of *Has_Element* is a primitive operation of the container type that takes both a container and a cursor and yields a boolean. For example:

```
function Cursor_Has_Element (Cont : Container; Position : Cursor) return Boolea
```

* The value of *Element* is a primitive operation of the container type that takes both a container and a cursor and yields an *Element_Type*, which must be a type declared in the container package or visible from it. For example:

```
function Get_Element (Cont : Container; Position : Cursor) return Element_Type;
```

This aspect is used in the GNAT-defined formal container packages.

3.24 Aspect Linker_Section

This aspect is equivalent to an *Linker_Section* pragma.

3.25 Aspect Lock_Free

This boolean aspect is equivalent to pragma *Lock_Free*.

3.26 Aspect No_Elaboration_Code_All

This aspect is equivalent to a *pragma No_Elaboration_Code_All* statement for a program unit.

3.27 Aspect No_Tagged_Streams

This aspect is equivalent to a *pragma No_Tagged_Streams* with an argument specifying a root tagged type (thus this aspect can only be applied to such a type).

3.28 Aspect Object_Size

This aspect is equivalent to an *Object_Size* attribute definition clause.

3.29 Aspect Obsolescent

This aspect is equivalent to an *Obsolescent* pragma. Note that the evaluation of this aspect happens at the point of occurrence, it is not delayed until the freeze point.

3.30 Aspect Part_Of

This aspect is equivalent to pragma *Part_Of.*

3.31 Aspect Persistent_BSS

This boolean aspect is equivalent to pragma *Persistent_BSS.*

3.32 Aspect Predicate

This aspect is equivalent to pragma *Predicate.* It is thus similar to the language defined aspects *Dynamic_Predicate* and *Static_Predicate* except that whether the resulting predicate is static or dynamic is controlled by the form of the expression. It is also separately controllable using pragma *Assertion_Policy.*

3.33 Aspect Pure_Function

This boolean aspect is equivalent to pragma *Pure_Function.*

3.34 Aspect Refined_Depends

This aspect is equivalent to pragma *Refined_Depends.*

3.35 Aspect Refined_Global

This aspect is equivalent to pragma *Refined_Global.*

3.36 Aspect Refined_Post

This aspect is equivalent to pragma *Refined_Post.*

3.37 Aspect Refined_State

This aspect is equivalent to pragma *Refined_State.*

3.38 Aspect Remote_Access_Type

This aspect is equivalent to pragma *Remote_Access_Type.*

3.39 Aspect Scalar_Storage_Order

This aspect is equivalent to a *Scalar_Storage_Order* attribute definition clause.

3.40 Aspect Shared

This boolean aspect is equivalent to pragma *Shared,* and is thus a synonym for aspect *Atomic.*

3.41 Aspect Simple_Storage_Pool

This aspect is equivalent to a *Simple_Storage_Pool* attribute definition clause.

3.42 Aspect Simple_Storage_Pool_Type

This boolean aspect is equivalent to pragma *Simple_Storage_Pool_Type*.

3.43 Aspect SPARK_Mode

This aspect is equivalent to pragma *SPARK_Mode* and may be specified for either or both of the specification and body of a subprogram or package.

3.44 Aspect Suppress_Debug_Info

This boolean aspect is equivalent to pragma *Suppress_Debug_Info*.

3.45 Aspect Suppress_Initialization

This boolean aspect is equivalent to pragma *Suppress_Initialization*.

3.46 Aspect Test_Case

This aspect is equivalent to pragma *Test_Case*.

3.47 Aspect Thread_Local_Storage

This boolean aspect is equivalent to pragma *Thread_Local_Storage*.

3.48 Aspect Universal_Aliasing

This boolean aspect is equivalent to pragma *Universal_Aliasing*.

3.49 Aspect Universal_Data

This aspect is equivalent to pragma *Universal_Data*.

3.50 Aspect Unmodified

This boolean aspect is equivalent to pragma *Unmodified*.

3.51 Aspect Unreferenced

This boolean aspect is equivalent to pragma *Unreferenced*. Note that in the case of formal parameters, it is not permitted to have aspects for a formal parameter, so in this case the pragma form must be used.

3.52 Aspect Unreferenced_Objects

This boolean aspect is equivalent to pragma *Unreferenced_Objects*.

3.53 Aspect Value_Size

This aspect is equivalent to a *Value_Size* attribute definition clause.

3.54 Aspect Volatile_Full_Access

This boolean aspect is equivalent to pragma *Volatile_Full_Access*.

3.55 Aspect Volatile_Function

This boolean aspect is equivalent to pragma *Volatile_Function*.

3.56 Aspect Warnings

This aspect is equivalent to the two argument form of pragma *Warnings*, where the first argument is *ON* or *OFF* and the second argument is the entity.

4 Implementation Defined Attributes

Ada defines (throughout the Ada reference manual, summarized in Annex K), a set of attributes that provide useful additional functionality in all areas of the language. These language defined attributes are implemented in GNAT and work as described in the Ada Reference Manual.

In addition, Ada allows implementations to define additional attributes whose meaning is defined by the implementation. GNAT provides a number of these implementation-dependent attributes which can be used to extend and enhance the functionality of the compiler. This section of the GNAT reference manual describes these additional attributes. It also describes additional implementation-dependent features of standard language-defined attributes.

Note that any program using these attributes may not be portable to other compilers (although GNAT implements this set of attributes on all platforms). Therefore if portability to other compilers is an important consideration, you should minimize the use of these attributes.

4.1 Attribute Abort_Signal

Standard'Abort_Signal (*Standard* is the only allowed prefix) provides the entity for the special exception used to signal task abort or asynchronous transfer of control. Normally this attribute should only be used in the tasking runtime (it is highly peculiar, and completely outside the normal semantics of Ada, for a user program to intercept the abort exception).

4.2 Attribute Address_Size

Standard'Address_Size (*Standard* is the only allowed prefix) is a static constant giving the number of bits in an *Address*. It is the same value as System.Address'Size, but has the advantage of being static, while a direct reference to System.Address'Size is nonstatic because Address is a private type.

4.3 Attribute Asm_Input

The *Asm_Input* attribute denotes a function that takes two parameters. The first is a string, the second is an expression of the type designated by the prefix. The first (string) argument is required to be a static expression, and is the constraint for the parameter, (e.g., what kind of register is required). The second argument is the value to be used as the input argument. The possible values for the constant are the same as those used in the RTL, and are dependent on the configuration file used to built the GCC back end. [Machine Code Insertions], page 268

4.4 Attribute Asm_Output

The *Asm_Output* attribute denotes a function that takes two parameters. The first is a string, the second is the name of a variable of the type designated by the attribute prefix. The first (string) argument is required to be a static expression and designates the constraint for the parameter (e.g., what kind of register is required). The second argument is the variable to be updated with the result. The possible values for constraint are the same as those used in the RTL, and are dependent on the configuration file used to build the GCC back end. If there are no output operands, then this argument may either be omitted, or explicitly given as *No_Output_Operands*. [Machine Code Insertions], page 268

4.5 Attribute Atomic_Always_Lock_Free

The prefix of the *Atomic_Always_Lock_Free* attribute is a type. The result is a Boolean value which is True if the type has discriminants, and False otherwise. The result indicate whether atomic operations are supported by the target for the given type.

4.6 Attribute Bit

`obj'Bit`, where *obj* is any object, yields the bit offset within the storage unit (byte) that contains the first bit of storage allocated for the object. The value of this attribute is of the type *Universal_Integer*, and is always a non-negative number not exceeding the value of *System.Storage_Unit*.

For an object that is a variable or a constant allocated in a register, the value is zero. (The use of this attribute does not force the allocation of a variable to memory).

For an object that is a formal parameter, this attribute applies to either the matching actual parameter or to a copy of the matching actual parameter.

For an access object the value is zero. Note that `obj.all'Bit` is subject to an *Access_Check* for the designated object. Similarly for a record component `X.C'Bit` is subject to a discriminant check and `X(I).Bit` and `X(I1..I2)'Bit` are subject to index checks.

This attribute is designed to be compatible with the DEC Ada 83 definition and implementation of the *Bit* attribute.

4.7 Attribute Bit_Position

`R.C'Bit_Position`, where *R* is a record object and *C* is one of the fields of the record type, yields the bit offset within the record contains the first bit of storage allocated for the object. The value of this attribute is of the type *Universal_Integer*. The value depends only on the field *C* and is independent of the alignment of the containing record *R*.

4.8 Attribute Code_Address

The *'Address* attribute may be applied to subprograms in Ada 95 and Ada 2005, but the intended effect seems to be to provide an address value which can be used to call the subprogram by means of an address clause as in the following example:

```
procedure K is ...

procedure L;
for L'Address use K'Address;
pragma Import (Ada, L);
```

A call to *L* is then expected to result in a call to *K*. In Ada 83, where there were no access-to-subprogram values, this was a common work-around for getting the effect of an indirect call. GNAT implements the above use of *Address* and the technique illustrated by the example code works correctly.

However, for some purposes, it is useful to have the address of the start of the generated code for the subprogram. On some architectures, this is not necessarily the same as the *Address* value described above. For example, the *Address* value may reference a subprogram descriptor rather than the subprogram itself.

The *'Code_Address* attribute, which can only be applied to subprogram entities, always returns the address of the start of the generated code of the specified subprogram, which may or may not be the same value as is returned by the corresponding *'Address* attribute.

4.9 Attribute Compiler_Version

Standard'Compiler_Version (*Standard* is the only allowed prefix) yields a static string identifying the version of the compiler being used to compile the unit containing the attribute reference.

4.10 Attribute Constrained

In addition to the usage of this attribute in the Ada RM, *GNAT* also permits the use of the *'Constrained* attribute in a generic template for any type, including types without discriminants. The value of this attribute in the generic instance when applied to a scalar type or a record type without discriminants is always *True*. This usage is compatible with older Ada compilers, including notably DEC Ada.

4.11 Attribute Default_Bit_Order

Standard'Default_Bit_Order (*Standard* is the only permissible prefix), provides the value *System.Default_Bit_Order* as a *Pos* value (0 for *High_Order_First*, 1 for *Low_Order_First*). This is used to construct the definition of *Default_Bit_Order* in package *System*.

4.12 Attribute Default_Scalar_Storage_Order

Standard'Default_Scalar_Storage_Order (*Standard* is the only permissible prefix), provides the current value of the default scalar storage order (as specified using pragma *Default_Scalar_Storage_Order*, or equal to *Default_Bit_Order* if unspecified) as a *System.Bit_Order* value. This is a static attribute.

4.13 Attribute Deref

The attribute *typ'Deref(expr)* where *expr* is of type *System.Address* yields the variable of type *typ* that is located at the given address. It is similar to *(totyp (expr).all)*, where *totyp* is an unchecked conversion from address to a named access-to-*typ* type, except that it yields a variable, so it can be used on the left side of an assignment.

4.14 Attribute Descriptor_Size

Nonstatic attribute *Descriptor_Size* returns the size in bits of the descriptor allocated for a type. The result is non-zero only for unconstrained array types and the returned value is of type universal integer. In GNAT, an array descriptor contains bounds information and is located immediately before the first element of the array.

```
type Unconstr_Array is array (Positive range <>) of Boolean;
```

```
      Put_Line ("Descriptor size = " & Unconstr_Array'Descriptor_Size'Img);
```

The attribute takes into account any additional padding due to type alignment. In the example above, the descriptor contains two values of type *Positive* representing the low and high bound. Since *Positive* has a size of 31 bits and an alignment of 4, the descriptor size is *2 * Positive'Size + 2* or 64 bits.

4.15 Attribute Elaborated

The prefix of the *'Elaborated* attribute must be a unit name. The value is a Boolean which indicates whether or not the given unit has been elaborated. This attribute is primarily intended for internal use by the generated code for dynamic elaboration checking, but it can also be used in user programs. The value will always be True once elaboration of all units has been completed. An exception is for units which need no elaboration, the value is always False for such units.

4.16 Attribute Elab_Body

This attribute can only be applied to a program unit name. It returns the entity for the corresponding elaboration procedure for elaborating the body of the referenced unit. This is used in the main generated elaboration procedure by the binder and is not normally used in any other context. However, there may be specialized situations in which it is useful to be able to call this elaboration procedure from Ada code, e.g., if it is necessary to do selective re-elaboration to fix some error.

4.17 Attribute Elab_Spec

This attribute can only be applied to a program unit name. It returns the entity for the corresponding elaboration procedure for elaborating the spec of the referenced unit. This is used in the main generated elaboration procedure by the binder and is not normally used in any other context. However, there may be specialized situations in which it is useful to be able to call this elaboration procedure from Ada code, e.g., if it is necessary to do selective re-elaboration to fix some error.

4.18 Attribute Elab_Subp_Body

This attribute can only be applied to a library level subprogram name and is only allowed in CodePeer mode. It returns the entity for the corresponding elaboration procedure for elaborating the body of the referenced subprogram unit. This is used in the main generated elaboration procedure by the binder in CodePeer mode only and is unrecognized otherwise.

4.19 Attribute Emax

The *Emax* attribute is provided for compatibility with Ada 83. See the Ada 83 reference manual for an exact description of the semantics of this attribute.

4.20 Attribute Enabled

The *Enabled* attribute allows an application program to check at compile time to see if the designated check is currently enabled. The prefix is a simple identifier, referencing any predefined check name (other than *All_Checks*) or a check name introduced by pragma Check_Name. If no argument is given for the attribute, the check is for the general state of the check, if an argument is given, then it is an entity name, and the check indicates whether an *Suppress* or *Unsuppress* has been given naming the entity (if not, then the argument is ignored).

Note that instantiations inherit the check status at the point of the instantiation, so a useful idiom is to have a library package that introduces a check name with *pragma Check_Name*, and then contains generic packages or subprograms which use the *Enabled* attribute to see if the check is enabled. A user of this package can then issue a *pragma Suppress* or *pragma Unsuppress* before instantiating the package or subprogram, controlling whether the check will be present.

4.21 Attribute Enum_Rep

For every enumeration subtype *S*, `S'Enum_Rep` denotes a function with the following spec:

```
function S'Enum_Rep (Arg : S'Base) return <Universal_Integer>;
```

It is also allowable to apply *Enum_Rep* directly to an object of an enumeration type or to a non-overloaded enumeration literal. In this case `S'Enum_Rep` is equivalent to `typ'Enum_Rep(S)` where *typ* is the type of the enumeration literal or object.

The function returns the representation value for the given enumeration value. This will be equal to value of the *Pos* attribute in the absence of an enumeration representation clause. This is a static attribute (i.e.,:the result is static if the argument is static).

`S'Enum_Rep` can also be used with integer types and objects, in which case it simply returns the integer value. The reason for this is to allow it to be used for *(<>)* discrete formal arguments in a generic unit that can be instantiated with either enumeration types or integer types. Note that if *Enum_Rep* is used on a modular type whose upper bound exceeds the upper bound of the largest signed integer type, and the argument is a variable, so that the universal integer calculation is done at run time, then the call to *Enum_Rep* may raise *Constraint_Error*.

4.22 Attribute Enum_Val

For every enumeration subtype *S*, `S'Enum_Val` denotes a function with the following spec:

```
function S'Enum_Val (Arg : <Universal_Integer>) return S'Base;
```

The function returns the enumeration value whose representation matches the argument, or raises Constraint_Error if no enumeration literal of the type has the matching value. This will be equal to value of the *Val* attribute in the absence of an enumeration representation clause. This is a static attribute (i.e., the result is static if the argument is static).

4.23 Attribute Epsilon

The *Epsilon* attribute is provided for compatibility with Ada 83. See the Ada 83 reference manual for an exact description of the semantics of this attribute.

4.24 Attribute Fast_Math

Standard'Fast_Math (*Standard* is the only allowed prefix) yields a static Boolean value that is True if pragma *Fast_Math* is active, and False otherwise.

4.25 Attribute Fixed_Value

For every fixed-point type *S*, `S'Fixed_Value` denotes a function with the following specification:

```
function S'Fixed_Value (Arg : <Universal_Integer>) return S;
```

The value returned is the fixed-point value *V* such that:

```
V = Arg * S'Small
```

The effect is thus similar to first converting the argument to the integer type used to represent *S*, and then doing an unchecked conversion to the fixed-point type. The difference is that there are full range checks, to ensure that the result is in range. This attribute is primarily intended for use in implementation of the input-output functions for fixed-point values.

4.26 Attribute From_Any

This internal attribute is used for the generation of remote subprogram stubs in the context of the Distributed Systems Annex.

4.27 Attribute Has_Access_Values

The prefix of the *Has_Access_Values* attribute is a type. The result is a Boolean value which is True if the is an access type, or is a composite type with a component (at any nesting depth) that is an access type, and is False otherwise. The intended use of this attribute is in conjunction with generic definitions. If the attribute is applied to a generic private type, it indicates whether or not the corresponding actual type has access values.

4.28 Attribute Has_Discriminants

The prefix of the *Has_Discriminants* attribute is a type. The result is a Boolean value which is True if the type has discriminants, and False otherwise. The intended use of this attribute is in conjunction with generic definitions. If the attribute is applied to a generic private type, it indicates whether or not the corresponding actual type has discriminants.

4.29 Attribute Img

The *Img* attribute differs from *Image* in that it is applied directly to an object, and yields the same result as *Image* for the subtype of the object. This is convenient for debugging:

```
Put_Line ("X = " & X'Img);
```

has the same meaning as the more verbose:

```
Put_Line ("X = " & T'Image (X));
```

where *T* is the (sub)type of the object *X*.

Note that technically, in analogy to *Image*, *X'Img* returns a parameterless function that returns the appropriate string when called. This means that *X'Img* can be renamed as a function-returning-string, or used in an instantiation as a function parameter.

4.30 Attribute Integer_Value

For every integer type *S*, `S'Integer_Value` denotes a function with the following spec:

```
function S'Integer_Value (Arg : <Universal_Fixed>) return S;
```

The value returned is the integer value *V*, such that:

```
Arg = V * T'Small
```

where *T* is the type of *Arg*. The effect is thus similar to first doing an unchecked conversion from the fixed-point type to its corresponding implementation type, and then converting the result to the target integer type. The difference is that there are full range checks, to ensure that the result is in range. This attribute is primarily intended for use in implementation of the standard input-output functions for fixed-point values.

4.31 Attribute Invalid_Value

For every scalar type S, S'Invalid_Value returns an undefined value of the type. If possible this value is an invalid representation for the type. The value returned is identical to the value used to initialize an otherwise uninitialized value of the type if pragma Initialize_Scalars is used, including the ability to modify the value with the binder -Sxx flag and relevant environment variables at run time.

4.32 Attribute Iterable

Equivalent to Aspect Iterable.

4.33 Attribute Large

The *Large* attribute is provided for compatibility with Ada 83. See the Ada 83 reference manual for an exact description of the semantics of this attribute.

4.34 Attribute Library_Level

P'Library_Level, where P is an entity name, returns a Boolean value which is True if the entity is declared at the library level, and False otherwise. Note that within a generic instantition, the name of the generic unit denotes the instance, which means that this attribute can be used to test if a generic is instantiated at the library level, as shown in this example:

```
generic
  ...
package Gen is
  pragma Compile_Time_Error
    (not Gen'Library_Level,
     "Gen can only be instantiated at library level");
  ...
end Gen;
```

4.35 Attribute Lock_Free

P'Lock_Free, where P is a protected object, returns True if a pragma *Lock_Free* applies to P.

4.36 Attribute Loop_Entry

Syntax:

```
X'Loop_Entry [(loop_name)]
```

The *Loop_Entry* attribute is used to refer to the value that an expression had upon entry to a given loop in much the same way that the *Old* attribute in a subprogram postcondition can be used to refer to the value an expression had upon entry to the subprogram. The relevant loop is either identified by the given loop name, or it is the innermost enclosing loop when no loop name is given.

A *Loop_Entry* attribute can only occur within a *Loop_Variant* or *Loop_Invariant* pragma. A common use of *Loop_Entry* is to compare the current value of objects with their initial value at loop entry, in a *Loop_Invariant* pragma.

The effect of using *X'Loop_Entry* is the same as declaring a constant initialized with the initial value of *X* at loop entry. This copy is not performed if the loop is not entered, or if the corresponding pragmas are ignored or disabled.

4.37 Attribute Machine_Size

This attribute is identical to the *Object_Size* attribute. It is provided for compatibility with the DEC Ada 83 attribute of this name.

4.38 Attribute Mantissa

The *Mantissa* attribute is provided for compatibility with Ada 83. See the Ada 83 reference manual for an exact description of the semantics of this attribute.

4.39 Attribute Maximum_Alignment

Standard'Maximum_Alignment (*Standard* is the only permissible prefix) provides the maximum useful alignment value for the target. This is a static value that can be used to specify the alignment for an object, guaranteeing that it is properly aligned in all cases.

4.40 Attribute Mechanism_Code

`function'Mechanism_Code` yields an integer code for the mechanism used for the result of function, and `subprogram'Mechanism_Code (n)` yields the mechanism used for formal parameter number *n* (a static integer value with 1 meaning the first parameter) of *subprogram*. The code returned is:

1

by copy (value)

2

by reference

4.41 Attribute Null_Parameter

A reference `T'Null_Parameter` denotes an imaginary object of type or subtype *T* allocated at machine address zero. The attribute is allowed only as the default expression of a formal parameter, or as an actual expression of a subprogram call. In either case, the subprogram must be imported.

The identity of the object is represented by the address zero in the argument list, independent of the passing mechanism (explicit or default).

This capability is needed to specify that a zero address should be passed for a record or other composite object passed by reference. There is no way of indicating this without the *Null_Parameter* attribute.

4.42 Attribute Object_Size

The size of an object is not necessarily the same as the size of the type of an object. This is because by default object sizes are increased to be a multiple of the alignment of the object. For example, *Natural'Size* is 31, but by default objects of type *Natural* will have a size of 32 bits. Similarly, a record containing an integer and a character:

```
type Rec is record
   I : Integer;
   C : Character;
end record;
```

will have a size of 40 (that is *Rec'Size* will be 40). The alignment will be 4, because of the integer field, and so the default size of record objects for this type will be 64 (8 bytes).

If the alignment of the above record is specified to be 1, then the object size will be 40 (5 bytes). This is true by default, and also an object size of 40 can be explicitly specified in this case.

A consequence of this capability is that different object sizes can be given to subtypes that would otherwise be considered in Ada to be statically matching. But it makes no sense to consider such subtypes as statically matching. Consequently, in *GNAT* we add a rule to the static matching rules that requires object sizes to match. Consider this example:

```
 1. procedure BadAVConvert is
 2.    type R is new Integer;
 3.    subtype R1 is R range 1 .. 10;
 4.    subtype R2 is R range 1 .. 10;
 5.    for R1'Object_Size use 8;
 6.    for R2'Object_Size use 16;
 7.    type R1P is access all R1;
 8.    type R2P is access all R2;
 9.    R1PV : R1P := new R1'(4);
10.    R2PV : R2P;
11. begin
12.    R2PV := R2P (R1PV);
                 |
       >>> target designated subtype not compatible with
           type "R1" defined at line 3

13. end;
```

In the absence of lines 5 and 6, types *R1* and *R2* statically match and hence the conversion on line 12 is legal. But since lines 5 and 6 cause the object sizes to differ, *GNAT* considers that types *R1* and *R2* are not statically matching, and line 12 generates the diagnostic shown above.

Similar additional checks are performed in other contexts requiring statically matching subtypes.

4.43 Attribute Old

In addition to the usage of *Old* defined in the Ada 2012 RM (usage within *Post* aspect), GNAT also permits the use of this attribute in implementation defined pragmas *Postcondition*, *Contract_Cases* and *Test_Case*. Also usages of *Old* which would be illegal according to the Ada 2012 RM definition are allowed under control of implementation defined pragma *Unevaluated_Use_Of_Old*.

4.44 Attribute Passed_By_Reference

`type'Passed_By_Reference` for any subtype *type* returns a value of type *Boolean* value that is *True* if the type is normally passed by reference and *False* if the type is normally passed by copy in calls. For scalar types, the result is always *False* and is static. For non-scalar types, the result is nonstatic.

4.45 Attribute Pool_Address

`X'Pool_Address` for any object *X* returns the address of X within its storage pool. This is the same as `X'Address`, except that for an unconstrained array whose bounds are allocated just before the first component, `X'Pool_Address` returns the address of those bounds, whereas `X'Address` returns the address of the first component.

Here, we are interpreting 'storage pool' broadly to mean `wherever the object is allocated`, which could be a user-defined storage pool, the global heap, on the stack, or in a static memory area. For an object created by *new*, `Ptr.all'Pool_Address` is what is passed to *Allocate* and returned from *Deallocate*.

4.46 Attribute Range_Length

`type'Range_Length` for any discrete type *type* yields the number of values represented by the subtype (zero for a null range). The result is static for static subtypes. *Range_Length* applied to the index subtype of a one dimensional array always gives the same result as *Length* applied to the array itself.

4.47 Attribute Restriction_Set

This attribute allows compile time testing of restrictions that are currently in effect. It is primarily intended for specializing code in the run-time based on restrictions that are active (e.g. don't need to save fpt registers if restriction No_Floating_Point is known to be in effect), but can be used anywhere.

There are two forms:

```
System'Restriction_Set (partition_boolean_restriction_NAME)
System'Restriction_Set (No_Dependence => library_unit_NAME);
```

In the case of the first form, the only restriction names allowed are parameterless restrictions that are checked for consistency at bind time. For a complete list see the subtype *System.Rident.Partition_Boolean_Restrictions*.

The result returned is True if the restriction is known to be in effect, and False if the restriction is known not to be in effect. An important guarantee is that the value of a Restriction_Set attribute is known to be consistent throughout all the code of a partition.

This is trivially achieved if the entire partition is compiled with a consistent set of restriction pragmas. However, the compilation model does not require this. It is possible to compile one set of units with one set of pragmas, and another set of units with another set of pragmas. It is even possible to compile a spec with one set of pragmas, and then WITH the same spec with a different set of pragmas. Inconsistencies in the actual use of the restriction are checked at bind time.

In order to achieve the guarantee of consistency for the Restriction_Set pragma, we consider that a use of the pragma that yields False is equivalent to a violation of the restriction.

So for example if you write

```
if System'Restriction_Set (No_Floating_Point) then
   ...
else
   ...
end if;
```

And the result is False, so that the else branch is executed, you can assume that this restriction is not set for any unit in the partition. This is checked by considering this use of the restriction pragma to be a violation of the restriction No_Floating_Point. This means that no other unit can attempt to set this restriction (if some unit does attempt to set it, the binder will refuse to bind the partition).

Technical note: The restriction name and the unit name are intepreted entirely syntactically, as in the corresponding Restrictions pragma, they are not analyzed semantically, so they do not have a type.

4.48 Attribute Result

`function'Result` can only be used with in a Postcondition pragma for a function. The prefix must be the name of the corresponding function. This is used to refer to the result of the function in the postcondition expression. For a further discussion of the use of this attribute and examples of its use, see the description of pragma Postcondition.

4.49 Attribute Safe_Emax

The *Safe_Emax* attribute is provided for compatibility with Ada 83. See the Ada 83 reference manual for an exact description of the semantics of this attribute.

4.50 Attribute Safe_Large

The *Safe_Large* attribute is provided for compatibility with Ada 83. See the Ada 83 reference manual for an exact description of the semantics of this attribute.

4.51 Attribute Safe_Small

The *Safe_Small* attribute is provided for compatibility with Ada 83. See the Ada 83 reference manual for an exact description of the semantics of this attribute.

4.52 Attribute Scalar_Storage_Order

For every array or record type *S*, the representation attribute *Scalar_Storage_Order* denotes the order in which storage elements that make up scalar components are ordered within S. The value given must be a static expression of type System.Bit_Order. The following is an example of the use of this feature:

```
--  Component type definitions

subtype Yr_Type is Natural range 0 .. 127;
subtype Mo_Type is Natural range 1 .. 12;
subtype Da_Type is Natural range 1 .. 31;

--  Record declaration

type Date is record
   Years_Since_1980 : Yr_Type;
   Month            : Mo_Type;
   Day_Of_Month     : Da_Type;
end record;

--  Record representation clause

for Date use record
   Years_Since_1980 at 0 range 0  ..  6;
   Month            at 0 range 7  .. 10;
   Day_Of_Month     at 0 range 11 .. 15;
end record;

--  Attribute definition clauses

for Date'Bit_Order use System.High_Order_First;
for Date'Scalar_Storage_Order use System.High_Order_First;
--  If Scalar_Storage_Order is specified, it must be consistent with
--  Bit_Order, so it's best to always define the latter explicitly if
--  the former is used.
```

Other properties are as for standard representation attribute *Bit_Order*, as defined by Ada RM 13.5.3(4). The default is *System.Default_Bit_Order*.

For a record type *T*, if `T'Scalar_Storage_Order` is specified explicitly, it shall be equal to `T'Bit_Order`. Note: this means that if a *Scalar_Storage_Order* attribute definition clause is not confirming, then the type's *Bit_Order* shall be specified explicitly and set to the same value.

Derived types inherit an explicitly set scalar storage order from their parent types. This may be overridden for the derived type by giving an explicit scalar storage order for the derived type. For a record extension, the derived type must have the same scalar storage order as the parent type.

If a component of *T* is of a record or array type, then that type must also have a *Scalar_Storage_Order* attribute definition clause.

A component of a record or array type that is a packed array, or that does not start on a byte boundary, must have the same scalar storage order as the enclosing record or array type.

No component of a type that has an explicit *Scalar_Storage_Order* attribute definition may be aliased.

A confirming *Scalar_Storage_Order* attribute definition clause (i.e. with a value equal to *System.Default_Bit_Order*) has no effect.

If the opposite storage order is specified, then whenever the value of a scalar component of an object of type *S* is read, the storage elements of the enclosing machine scalar are first reversed (before retrieving the component value, possibly applying some shift and mask operatings on the enclosing machine scalar), and the opposite operation is done for writes.

In that case, the restrictions set forth in 13.5.1(10.3/2) for scalar components are relaxed. Instead, the following rules apply:

* the underlying storage elements are those at positions *(position + first_bit / storage_element_size) .. (position + (last_bit + storage_element_size - 1) / storage_element_size)*
* the sequence of underlying storage elements shall have a size no greater than the largest machine scalar
* the enclosing machine scalar is defined as the smallest machine scalar starting at a position no greater than *position + first_bit / storage_element_size* and covering storage elements at least up to *position + (last_bit + storage_element_size - 1) / storage_element_size*
* the position of the component is interpreted relative to that machine scalar.

If no scalar storage order is specified for a type (either directly, or by inheritance in the case of a derived type), then the default is normally the native ordering of the target, but this default can be overridden using pragma *Default_Scalar_Storage_Order*.

Note that the scalar storage order only affects the in-memory data representation. It has no effect on the representation used by stream attributes.

4.53 Attribute Simple_Storage_Pool

For every nonformal, nonderived access-to-object type *Acc*, the representation attribute *Simple_Storage_Pool* may be specified via an attribute_definition_clause (or by specifying the equivalent aspect):

```
My_Pool : My_Simple_Storage_Pool_Type;

type Acc is access My_Data_Type;
```

```
for Acc'Simple_Storage_Pool use My_Pool;
```

The name given in an attribute_definition_clause for the *Simple_Storage_Pool* attribute shall denote a variable of a 'simple storage pool type' (see pragma *Simple_Storage_Pool_Type*).

The use of this attribute is only allowed for a prefix denoting a type for which it has been specified. The type of the attribute is the type of the variable specified as the simple storage pool of the access type, and the attribute denotes that variable.

It is illegal to specify both *Storage_Pool* and *Simple_Storage_Pool* for the same access type.

If the *Simple_Storage_Pool* attribute has been specified for an access type, then applying the *Storage_Pool* attribute to the type is flagged with a warning and its evaluation raises the exception *Program_Error*.

If the Simple_Storage_Pool attribute has been specified for an access type *S*, then the evaluation of the attribute `S'Storage_Size` returns the result of calling `Storage_Size (S'Simple_Storage_Pool)`, which is intended to indicate the number of storage elements reserved for the simple storage pool. If the Storage_Size function has not been defined for the simple storage pool type, then this attribute returns zero.

If an access type *S* has a specified simple storage pool of type *SSP*, then the evaluation of an allocator for that access type calls the primitive *Allocate* procedure for type *SSP*, passing `S'Simple_Storage_Pool` as the pool parameter. The detailed semantics of such allocators is the same as those defined for allocators in section 13.11 of the *Ada Reference Manual*, with the term *simple storage pool* substituted for *storage pool*.

If an access type *S* has a specified simple storage pool of type *SSP*, then a call to an instance of the *Ada.Unchecked_Deallocation* for that access type invokes the primitive *Deallocate* procedure for type *SSP*, passing `S'Simple_Storage_Pool` as the pool parameter. The detailed semantics of such unchecked deallocations is the same as defined in section 13.11.2 of the Ada Reference Manual, except that the term 'simple storage pool' is substituted for 'storage pool'.

4.54 Attribute Small

The *Small* attribute is defined in Ada 95 (and Ada 2005) only for fixed-point types. GNAT also allows this attribute to be applied to floating-point types for compatibility with Ada 83. See the Ada 83 reference manual for an exact description of the semantics of this attribute when applied to floating-point types.

4.55 Attribute Storage_Unit

Standard'Storage_Unit (*Standard* is the only permissible prefix) provides the same value as *System.Storage_Unit*.

4.56 Attribute Stub_Type

The GNAT implementation of remote access-to-classwide types is organized as described in AARM section E.4 (20.t): a value of an RACW type (designating a remote object) is represented as a normal access value, pointing to a "stub" object which in turn contains the necessary information to contact the designated remote object. A call on any dispatching operation of such a stub object does the remote call, if necessary, using the information in the stub object to locate the target partition, etc.

For a prefix *T* that denotes a remote access-to-classwide type, *T'Stub_Type* denotes the type of the corresponding stub objects.

By construction, the layout of *T'Stub_Type* is identical to that of type *RACW_Stub_Type* declared in the internal implementation-defined unit *System.Partition_Interface*. Use of this attribute will create an implicit dependency on this unit.

4.57 Attribute System_Allocator_Alignment

Standard'System_Allocator_Alignment (*Standard* is the only permissible prefix) provides the observable guaranted to be honored by the system allocator (malloc). This is a static value that can be used in user storage pools based on malloc either to reject allocation with alignment too large or to enable a realignment circuitry if the alignment request is larger than this value.

4.58 Attribute Target_Name

Standard'Target_Name (*Standard* is the only permissible prefix) provides a static string value that identifies the target for the current compilation. For GCC implementations, this is the standard gcc target name without the terminating slash (for example, GNAT 5.0 on windows yields "i586-pc-mingw32msv").

4.59 Attribute To_Address

The *System'To_Address* (*System* is the only permissible prefix) denotes a function identical to *System.Storage_Elements.To_Address* except that it is a static attribute. This means that if its argument is a static expression, then the result of the attribute is a static expression. This means that such an expression can be used in contexts (e.g., preelaborable packages) which require a static expression and where the function call could not be used (since the function call is always nonstatic, even if its argument is static). The argument must be in the range -(2**(m-1) .. 2**m-1, where m is the memory size (typically 32 or 64). Negative values are intepreted in a modular manner (e.g., -1 means the same as 16#FFFF_FFFF# on a 32 bits machine).

4.60 Attribute To_Any

This internal attribute is used for the generation of remote subprogram stubs in the context of the Distributed Systems Annex.

4.61 Attribute Type_Class

`type'Type_Class` for any type or subtype *type* yields the value of the type class for the full type of *type*. If *type* is a generic formal type, the value is the value for the corresponding actual subtype. The value of this attribute is of type `System.Aux_DEC.Type_Class`, which has the following definition:

```
type Type_Class is
  (Type_Class_Enumeration,
   Type_Class_Integer,
   Type_Class_Fixed_Point,
   Type_Class_Floating_Point,
```

```
          Type_Class_Array,
          Type_Class_Record,
          Type_Class_Access,
          Type_Class_Task,
          Type_Class_Address);
```

Protected types yield the value *Type_Class_Task*, which thus applies to all concurrent types. This attribute is designed to be compatible with the DEC Ada 83 attribute of the same name.

4.62 Attribute Type_Key

The *Type_Key* attribute is applicable to a type or subtype and yields a value of type Standard.String containing encoded information about the type or subtype. This provides improved compatibility with other implementations that support this attribute.

4.63 Attribute TypeCode

This internal attribute is used for the generation of remote subprogram stubs in the context of the Distributed Systems Annex.

4.64 Attribute Unconstrained_Array

The *Unconstrained_Array* attribute can be used with a prefix that denotes any type or subtype. It is a static attribute that yields *True* if the prefix designates an unconstrained array, and *False* otherwise. In a generic instance, the result is still static, and yields the result of applying this test to the generic actual.

4.65 Attribute Universal_Literal_String

The prefix of *Universal_Literal_String* must be a named number. The static result is the string consisting of the characters of the number as defined in the original source. This allows the user program to access the actual text of named numbers without intermediate conversions and without the need to enclose the strings in quotes (which would preclude their use as numbers).

For example, the following program prints the first 50 digits of pi:

```
with Text_IO; use Text_IO;
with Ada.Numerics;
procedure Pi is
begin
   Put (Ada.Numerics.Pi'Universal_Literal_String);
end;
```

4.66 Attribute Unrestricted_Access

The *Unrestricted_Access* attribute is similar to *Access* except that all accessibility and aliased view checks are omitted. This is a user-beware attribute.

For objects, it is similar to *Address*, for which it is a desirable replacement where the value desired is an access type. In other words, its effect is similar to first applying the *Address* attribute and then doing an unchecked conversion to a desired access type.

For subprograms, *P'Unrestricted_Access* may be used where *P'Access* would be illegal, to construct a value of a less-nested named access type that designates a more-nested subprogram. This value may be used in indirect calls, so long as the more-nested subprogram still exists; once the subprogram containing it has returned, such calls are erroneous. For example:

```
package body P is

   type Less_Nested is not null access procedure;
   Global : Less_Nested;

   procedure P1 is
   begin
      Global.all;
   end P1;

   procedure P2 is
      Local_Var : Integer;

      procedure More_Nested is
      begin
         ... Local_Var ...
      end More_Nested;
   begin
      Global := More_Nested'Unrestricted_Access;
      P1;
   end P2;

end P;
```

When P1 is called from P2, the call via Global is OK, but if P1 were called after P2 returns, it would be an erroneous use of a dangling pointer.

For objects, it is possible to use *Unrestricted_Access* for any type. However, if the result is of an access-to-unconstrained array subtype, then the resulting pointer has the same scope as the context of the attribute, and must not be returned to some enclosing scope. For instance, if a function uses *Unrestricted_Access* to create an access-to-unconstrained-array and returns that value to the caller, the result will involve dangling pointers. In addition, it is only valid to create pointers to unconstrained arrays using this attribute if the pointer has the normal default 'fat' representation where a pointer has two components, one points to the array and one points to the bounds. If a size clause is used to force 'thin' representation for a pointer to unconstrained where there is only space for a single pointer, then the resulting pointer is not usable.

In the simple case where a direct use of Unrestricted_Access attempts to make a thin pointer for a non-aliased object, the compiler will reject the use as illegal, as shown in the following example:

```
with System; use System;
procedure SliceUA2 is
   type A is access all String;
```

```
   for A'Size use Standard'Address_Size;

   procedure P (Arg : A) is
   begin
      null;
   end P;

   X : String := "hello world!";
   X2 : aliased String := "hello world!";

   AV : A := X'Unrestricted_Access;    -- ERROR
             |
>>> illegal use of Unrestricted_Access attribute
>>> attempt to generate thin pointer to unaliased object

begin
   P (X'Unrestricted_Access);          -- ERROR
      |
>>> illegal use of Unrestricted_Access attribute
>>> attempt to generate thin pointer to unaliased object

   P (X(7 .. 12)'Unrestricted_Access); -- ERROR
      |
>>> illegal use of Unrestricted_Access attribute
>>> attempt to generate thin pointer to unaliased object

   P (X2'Unrestricted_Access);         -- OK
end;
```

but other cases cannot be detected by the compiler, and are considered to be erroneous. Consider the following example:

```
with System; use System;
with System; use System;
procedure SliceUA is
   type AF is access all String;

   type A is access all String;
   for A'Size use Standard'Address_Size;

   procedure P (Arg : A) is
   begin
      if Arg'Length /= 6 then
         raise Program_Error;
      end if;
   end P;

   X : String := "hello world!";
```

```
   Y : AF := X (7 .. 12)'Unrestricted_Access;

begin
   P (A (Y));
end;
```

A normal unconstrained array value or a constrained array object marked as aliased has the bounds in memory just before the array, so a thin pointer can retrieve both the data and the bounds. But in this case, the non-aliased object *X* does not have the bounds before the string. If the size clause for type *A* were not present, then the pointer would be a fat pointer, where one component is a pointer to the bounds, and all would be well. But with the size clause present, the conversion from fat pointer to thin pointer in the call loses the bounds, and so this is erroneous, and the program likely raises a *Program_Error* exception.

In general, it is advisable to completely avoid mixing the use of thin pointers and the use of *Unrestricted_Access* where the designated type is an unconstrained array. The use of thin pointers should be restricted to cases of porting legacy code that implicitly assumes the size of pointers, and such code should not in any case be using this attribute.

Another erroneous situation arises if the attribute is applied to a constant. The resulting pointer can be used to access the constant, but the effect of trying to modify a constant in this manner is not well-defined. Consider this example:

```
P : constant Integer := 4;
type R is access all Integer;
RV : R := P'Unrestricted_Access;
..
RV.all := 3;
```

Here we attempt to modify the constant P from 4 to 3, but the compiler may or may not notice this attempt, and subsequent references to P may yield either the value 3 or the value 4 or the assignment may blow up if the compiler decides to put P in read-only memory. One particular case where *Unrestricted_Access* can be used in this way is to modify the value of an *IN* parameter:

```
procedure K (S : in String) is
   type R is access all Character;
   RV : R := S (3)'Unrestricted_Access;
begin
   RV.all := 'a';
end;
```

In general this is a risky approach. It may appear to "work" but such uses of *Unrestricted_Access* are potentially non-portable, even from one version of *GNAT* to another, so are best avoided if possible.

4.67 Attribute Update

The *Update* attribute creates a copy of an array or record value with one or more modified components. The syntax is:

```
PREFIX'Update ( RECORD_COMPONENT_ASSOCIATION_LIST )
PREFIX'Update ( ARRAY_COMPONENT_ASSOCIATION {, ARRAY_COMPONENT_ASSOCIATION } )
```

```
PREFIX'Update ( MULTIDIMENSIONAL_ARRAY_COMPONENT_ASSOCIATION
               {, MULTIDIMENSIONAL_ARRAY_COMPONENT_ASSOCIATION } )

MULTIDIMENSIONAL_ARRAY_COMPONENT_ASSOCIATION ::= INDEX_EXPRESSION_LIST_LIST => EXPR
INDEX_EXPRESSION_LIST_LIST                   ::= INDEX_EXPRESSION_LIST {| INDEX_EXP
INDEX_EXPRESSION_LIST                        ::= ( EXPRESSION {, EXPRESSION } )
```

where *PREFIX* is the name of an array or record object, the association list in parentheses does not contain an *others* choice and the box symbol <> may not appear in any expression. The effect is to yield a copy of the array or record value which is unchanged apart from the components mentioned in the association list, which are changed to the indicated value. The original value of the array or record value is not affected. For example:

```
type Arr is Array (1 .. 5) of Integer;
...
Avar1 : Arr := (1,2,3,4,5);
Avar2 : Arr := Avar1'Update (2 => 10, 3 .. 4 => 20);
```

yields a value for *Avar2* of 1,10,20,20,5 with *Avar1* begin unmodified. Similarly:

```
type Rec is A, B, C : Integer;
...
Rvar1 : Rec := (A => 1, B => 2, C => 3);
Rvar2 : Rec := Rvar1'Update (B => 20);
```

yields a value for *Rvar2* of (A => 1, B => 20, C => 3), with *Rvar1* being unmodifed. Note that the value of the attribute reference is computed completely before it is used. This means that if you write:

```
Avar1 := Avar1'Update (1 => 10, 2 => Function_Call);
```

then the value of *Avar1* is not modified if *Function_Call* raises an exception, unlike the effect of a series of direct assignments to elements of *Avar1*. In general this requires that two extra complete copies of the object are required, which should be kept in mind when considering efficiency.

The *Update* attribute cannot be applied to prefixes of a limited type, and cannot reference discriminants in the case of a record type. The accessibility level of an Update attribute result object is defined as for an aggregate.

In the record case, no component can be mentioned more than once. In the array case, two overlapping ranges can appear in the association list, in which case the modifications are processed left to right.

Multi-dimensional arrays can be modified, as shown by this example:

```
A : array (1 .. 10, 1 .. 10) of Integer;
..
A := A'Update ((1, 2) => 20, (3, 4) => 30);
```

which changes element (1,2) to 20 and (3,4) to 30.

4.68 Attribute Valid_Scalars

The *'Valid_Scalars* attribute is intended to make it easier to check the validity of scalar subcomponents of composite objects. It is defined for any prefix *X* that denotes an object. The value of this attribute is of the predefined type Boolean. *X'Valid_Scalars* yields True if and only if evaluation of *P'Valid* yields True for every scalar part P of X or if X has no scalar parts. It is not specified in what order the scalar parts are checked, nor whether any more are checked after any one of them is determined to be invalid. If the prefix *X* is of a class-wide type *T'Class* (where *T* is the associated specific type), or if the prefix *X* is of a specific tagged type *T*, then only the scalar parts of components of *T* are traversed; in other words, components of extensions of *T* are not traversed even if *T'Class (X)'Tag /= T'Tag* . The compiler will issue a warning if it can be determined at compile time that the prefix of the attribute has no scalar parts (e.g., if the prefix is of an access type, an interface type, an undiscriminated task type, or an undiscriminated protected type).

For scalar types, *Valid_Scalars* is equivalent to *Valid*. The use of this attribute is not permitted for *Unchecked_Union* types for which in general it is not possible to determine the values of the discriminants.

Note: *Valid_Scalars* can generate a lot of code, especially in the case of a large variant record. If the attribute is called in many places in the same program applied to objects of the same type, it can reduce program size to write a function with a single use of the attribute, and then call that function from multiple places.

4.69 Attribute VADS_Size

The *'VADS_Size* attribute is intended to make it easier to port legacy code which relies on the semantics of *'Size* as implemented by the VADS Ada 83 compiler. GNAT makes a best effort at duplicating the same semantic interpretation. In particular, *'VADS_Size* applied to a predefined or other primitive type with no Size clause yields the Object_Size (for example, *Natural'Size* is 32 rather than 31 on typical machines). In addition *'VADS_Size* applied to an object gives the result that would be obtained by applying the attribute to the corresponding type.

4.70 Attribute Value_Size

`type'Value_Size` is the number of bits required to represent a value of the given subtype. It is the same as `type'Size`, but, unlike *Size*, may be set for non-first subtypes.

4.71 Attribute Wchar_T_Size

Standard'Wchar_T_Size (*Standard* is the only permissible prefix) provides the size in bits of the C *wchar_t* type primarily for constructing the definition of this type in package *Interfaces.C*. The result is a static constant.

4.72 Attribute Word_Size

Standard'Word_Size (*Standard* is the only permissible prefix) provides the value *System.Word_Size*. The result is a static constant.

5 Standard and Implementation Defined Restrictions

All Ada Reference Manual-defined Restriction identifiers are implemented:

* language-defined restrictions (see 13.12.1)
* tasking restrictions (see D.7)
* high integrity restrictions (see H.4)

GNAT implements additional restriction identifiers. All restrictions, whether language defined or GNAT-specific, are listed in the following.

5.1 Partition-Wide Restrictions

There are two separate lists of restriction identifiers. The first set requires consistency throughout a partition (in other words, if the restriction identifier is used for any compilation unit in the partition, then all compilation units in the partition must obey the restriction).

5.1.1 Immediate_Reclamation

[RM H.4] This restriction ensures that, except for storage occupied by objects created by allocators and not deallocated via unchecked deallocation, any storage reserved at run time for an object is immediately reclaimed when the object no longer exists.

5.1.2 Max_Asynchronous_Select_Nesting

[RM D.7] Specifies the maximum dynamic nesting level of asynchronous selects. Violations of this restriction with a value of zero are detected at compile time. Violations of this restriction with values other than zero cause Storage_Error to be raised.

5.1.3 Max_Entry_Queue_Length

[RM D.7] This restriction is a declaration that any protected entry compiled in the scope of the restriction has at most the specified number of tasks waiting on the entry at any one time, and so no queue is required. Note that this restriction is checked at run time. Violation of this restriction results in the raising of Program_Error exception at the point of the call.

The restriction *Max_Entry_Queue_Depth* is recognized as a synonym for *Max_Entry_Queue_Length*. This is retained for historical compatibility purposes (and a warning will be generated for its use if warnings on obsolescent features are activated).

5.1.4 Max_Protected_Entries

[RM D.7] Specifies the maximum number of entries per protected type. The bounds of every entry family of a protected unit shall be static, or shall be defined by a discriminant of a subtype whose corresponding bound is static.

5.1.5 Max_Select_Alternatives

[RM D.7] Specifies the maximum number of alternatives in a selective accept.

5.1.6 Max_Storage_At_Blocking

[RM D.7] Specifies the maximum portion (in storage elements) of a task's Storage_Size that can be retained by a blocked task. A violation of this restriction causes Storage_Error to be raised.

5.1.7 Max_Task_Entries

[RM D.7] Specifies the maximum number of entries per task. The bounds of every entry family of a task unit shall be static, or shall be defined by a discriminant of a subtype whose corresponding bound is static.

5.1.8 Max_Tasks

[RM D.7] Specifies the maximum number of task that may be created, not counting the creation of the environment task. Violations of this restriction with a value of zero are detected at compile time. Violations of this restriction with values other than zero cause Storage_Error to be raised.

5.1.9 No_Abort_Statements

[RM D.7] There are no abort_statements, and there are no calls to Task_Identification.Abort_Task.

5.1.10 No_Access_Parameter_Allocators

[RM H.4] This restriction ensures at compile time that there are no occurrences of an allocator as the actual parameter to an access parameter.

5.1.11 No_Access_Subprograms

[RM H.4] This restriction ensures at compile time that there are no declarations of access-to-subprogram types.

5.1.12 No_Allocators

[RM H.4] This restriction ensures at compile time that there are no occurrences of an allocator.

5.1.13 No_Anonymous_Allocators

[RM H.4] This restriction ensures at compile time that there are no occurrences of an allocator of anonymous access type.

5.1.14 No_Asynchronous_Control

[RM J.13] This restriction ensures at compile time that there are no semantic dependences on the predefined package Asynchronous_Task_Control.

5.1.15 No_Calendar

[GNAT] This restriction ensures at compile time that there are no semantic dependences on package Calendar.

5.1.16 No_Coextensions

[RM H.4] This restriction ensures at compile time that there are no coextensions. See 3.10.2.

5.1.17 No_Default_Initialization

[GNAT] This restriction prohibits any instance of default initialization of variables. The binder implements a consistency rule which prevents any unit compiled without the restriction from with'ing a unit with the restriction (this allows the generation of initialization procedures to be skipped, since you can be sure that no call is ever generated to an initialization procedure in a unit with the restriction active). If used in conjunction with Initialize_Scalars or Normalize_Scalars, the effect is to prohibit all cases of variables declared without a specific initializer (including the case of OUT scalar parameters).

5.1.18 No_Delay

[RM H.4] This restriction ensures at compile time that there are no delay statements and no semantic dependences on package Calendar.

5.1.19 No_Dependence

[RM 13.12.1] This restriction ensures at compile time that there are no dependences on a library unit.

5.1.20 No_Direct_Boolean_Operators

[GNAT] This restriction ensures that no logical operators (and/or/xor) are used on operands of type Boolean (or any type derived from Boolean). This is intended for use in safety critical programs where the certification protocol requires the use of short-circuit (and then, or else) forms for all composite boolean operations.

5.1.21 No_Dispatch

[RM H.4] This restriction ensures at compile time that there are no occurrences of *T'Class*, for any (tagged) subtype *T*.

5.1.22 No_Dispatching_Calls

[GNAT] This restriction ensures at compile time that the code generated by the compiler involves no dispatching calls. The use of this restriction allows the safe use of record extensions, classwide membership tests and other classwide features not involving implicit dispatching. This restriction ensures that the code contains no indirect calls through a dispatching mechanism. Note that this includes internally-generated calls created by the compiler, for example in the implementation of class-wide objects assignments. The membership test is allowed in the presence of this restriction, because its implementation requires no dispatching. This restriction is comparable to the official Ada restriction *No_Dispatch* except that it is a bit less restrictive in that it allows all classwide constructs that do not imply dispatching. The following example indicates constructs that violate this restriction.

```
package Pkg is
  type T is tagged record
    Data : Natural;
  end record;
  procedure P (X : T);

  type DT is new T with record
    More_Data : Natural;
```

```
     end record;
     procedure Q (X : DT);
   end Pkg;

   with Pkg; use Pkg;
   procedure Example is
     procedure Test (O : T'Class) is
       N : Natural  := O'Size;--  Error: Dispatching call
       C : T'Class := O;       --  Error: implicit Dispatching Call
     begin
       if O in DT'Class then   --  OK   : Membership test
          Q (DT (O));          --  OK   : Type conversion plus direct call
       else
          P (O);               --  Error: Dispatching call
       end if;
     end Test;

     Obj : DT;
   begin
     P (Obj);                  --  OK   : Direct call
     P (T (Obj));              --  OK   : Type conversion plus direct call
     P (T'Class (Obj));        --  Error: Dispatching call

     Test (Obj);               --  OK   : Type conversion

     if Obj in T'Class then    --  OK   : Membership test
        null;
     end if;
   end Example;
```

5.1.23 No_Dynamic_Attachment

[RM D.7] This restriction ensures that there is no call to any of the operations defined in package Ada.Interrupts (Is_Reserved, Is_Attached, Current_Handler, Attach_Handler, Exchange_Handler, Detach_Handler, and Reference).

The restriction *No_Dynamic_Interrupts* is recognized as a synonym for *No_Dynamic_Attachment*. This is retained for historical compatibility purposes (and a warning will be generated for its use if warnings on obsolescent features are activated).

5.1.24 No_Dynamic_Priorities

[RM D.7] There are no semantic dependencies on the package Dynamic_Priorities.

5.1.25 No_Entry_Calls_In_Elaboration_Code

[GNAT] This restriction ensures at compile time that no task or protected entry calls are made during elaboration code. As a result of the use of this restriction, the compiler can assume that no code past an accept statement in a task can be executed at elaboration time.

5.1.26 No_Enumeration_Maps

[GNAT] This restriction ensures at compile time that no operations requiring enumeration maps are used (that is Image and Value attributes applied to enumeration types).

5.1.27 No_Exception_Handlers

[GNAT] This restriction ensures at compile time that there are no explicit exception handlers. It also indicates that no exception propagation will be provided. In this mode, exceptions may be raised but will result in an immediate call to the last chance handler, a routine that the user must define with the following profile:

```
procedure Last_Chance_Handler
  (Source_Location : System.Address; Line : Integer);
pragma Export (C, Last_Chance_Handler,
               "__gnat_last_chance_handler");
```

The parameter is a C null-terminated string representing a message to be associated with the exception (typically the source location of the raise statement generated by the compiler). The Line parameter when nonzero represents the line number in the source program where the raise occurs.

5.1.28 No_Exception_Propagation

[GNAT] This restriction guarantees that exceptions are never propagated to an outer subprogram scope. The only case in which an exception may be raised is when the handler is statically in the same subprogram, so that the effect of a raise is essentially like a goto statement. Any other raise statement (implicit or explicit) will be considered unhandled. Exception handlers are allowed, but may not contain an exception occurrence identifier (exception choice). In addition, use of the package GNAT.Current_Exception is not permitted, and reraise statements (raise with no operand) are not permitted.

5.1.29 No_Exception_Registration

[GNAT] This restriction ensures at compile time that no stream operations for types Exception_Id or Exception_Occurrence are used. This also makes it impossible to pass exceptions to or from a partition with this restriction in a distributed environment. If this restriction is active, the generated code is simplified by omitting the otherwise-required global registration of exceptions when they are declared.

5.1.30 No_Exceptions

[RM H.4] This restriction ensures at compile time that there are no raise statements and no exception handlers.

5.1.31 No_Finalization

[GNAT] This restriction disables the language features described in chapter 7.6 of the Ada 2005 RM as well as all form of code generation performed by the compiler to support these features. The following types are no longer considered controlled when this restriction is in effect:

* *Ada.Finalization.Controlled*
* *Ada.Finalization.Limited_Controlled*
* Derivations from *Controlled* or *Limited_Controlled*
* Class-wide types
* Protected types
* Task types
* Array and record types with controlled components

The compiler no longer generates code to initialize, finalize or adjust an object or a nested component, either declared on the stack or on the heap. The deallocation of a controlled object no longer finalizes its contents.

5.1.32 No_Fixed_Point

[RM H.4] This restriction ensures at compile time that there are no occurrences of fixed point types and operations.

5.1.33 No_Floating_Point

[RM H.4] This restriction ensures at compile time that there are no occurrences of floating point types and operations.

5.1.34 No_Implicit_Conditionals

[GNAT] This restriction ensures that the generated code does not contain any implicit conditionals, either by modifying the generated code where possible, or by rejecting any construct that would otherwise generate an implicit conditional. Note that this check does not include run time constraint checks, which on some targets may generate implicit conditionals as well. To control the latter, constraint checks can be suppressed in the normal manner. Constructs generating implicit conditionals include comparisons of composite objects and the Max/Min attributes.

5.1.35 No_Implicit_Dynamic_Code

[GNAT] This restriction prevents the compiler from building 'trampolines'. This is a structure that is built on the stack and contains dynamic code to be executed at run time. On some targets, a trampoline is built for the following features: *Access*, *Unrestricted_Access*, or *Address* of a nested subprogram; nested task bodies; primitive operations of nested tagged types. Trampolines do not work on machines that prevent execution of stack data. For example, on windows systems, enabling DEP (data execution protection) will cause trampolines to raise an exception. Trampolines are also quite slow at run time.

On many targets, trampolines have been largely eliminated. Look at the version of system.ads for your target — if it has Always_Compatible_Rep equal to False, then trampolines are largely eliminated. In particular, a trampoline is built for the following features: *Address* of a nested subprogram; *Access* or *Unrestricted_Access* of a nested subprogram, but only if pragma Favor_Top_Level applies, or the access type has a foreign-language convention; primitive operations of nested tagged types.

5.1.36 No_Implicit_Heap_Allocations

[RM D.7] No constructs are allowed to cause implicit heap allocation.

5.1.37 No_Implicit_Loops

[GNAT] This restriction ensures that the generated code does not contain any implicit *for* loops, either by modifying the generated code where possible, or by rejecting any construct that would otherwise generate an implicit *for* loop. If this restriction is active, it is possible to build large array aggregates with all static components without generating an intermediate temporary, and without generating a loop to initialize individual components. Otherwise, a loop is created for arrays larger than about 5000 scalar components.

5.1.38 No_Implicit_Protected_Object_Allocations

[GNAT] No constructs are allowed to cause implicit heap allocation of a protected object.

5.1.39 No_Implicit_Task_Allocations

[GNAT] No constructs are allowed to cause implicit heap allocation of a task.

5.1.40 No_Initialize_Scalars

[GNAT] This restriction ensures that no unit in the partition is compiled with pragma Initialize_Scalars. This allows the generation of more efficient code, and in particular eliminates dummy null initialization routines that are otherwise generated for some record and array types.

5.1.41 No_IO

[RM H.4] This restriction ensures at compile time that there are no dependences on any of the library units Sequential_IO, Direct_IO, Text_IO, Wide_Text_IO, Wide_Wide_Text_IO, or Stream_IO.

5.1.42 No_Local_Allocators

[RM H.4] This restriction ensures at compile time that there are no occurrences of an allocator in subprograms, generic subprograms, tasks, and entry bodies.

5.1.43 No_Local_Protected_Objects

[RM D.7] This restriction ensures at compile time that protected objects are only declared at the library level.

5.1.44 No_Local_Timing_Events

[RM D.7] All objects of type Ada.Timing_Events.Timing_Event are declared at the library level.

5.1.45 No_Long_Long_Integers

[GNAT] This partition-wide restriction forbids any explicit reference to type Standard.Long_Long_Integer, and also forbids declaring range types whose implicit base type is Long_Long_Integer, and modular types whose size exceeds Long_Integer'Size.

5.1.46 No_Multiple_Elaboration

[GNAT] Normally each package contains a 16-bit counter used to check for access before elaboration, and to control multiple elaboration attempts. This counter is eliminated for units compiled with the static model of elaboration if restriction *No_Elaboration_Code* is active but because of the need to check for multiple elaboration in the general case, these counters cannot be eliminated if elaboration code may be present. The restriction *No_Multiple_Elaboration* allows suppression of these counters in static elaboration units even if they do have elaboration code. If this restriction is used, then the situations in which multiple elaboration is possible, including non-Ada main programs, and Stand Alone libraries, are not permitted, and will be diagnosed by the binder.

5.1.47 No_Nested_Finalization

[RM D.7] All objects requiring finalization are declared at the library level.

5.1.48 No_Protected_Type_Allocators

[RM D.7] This restriction ensures at compile time that there are no allocator expressions that attempt to allocate protected objects.

5.1.49 No_Protected_Types

[RM H.4] This restriction ensures at compile time that there are no declarations of protected types or protected objects.

5.1.50 No_Recursion

[RM H.4] A program execution is erroneous if a subprogram is invoked as part of its execution.

5.1.51 No_Reentrancy

[RM H.4] A program execution is erroneous if a subprogram is executed by two tasks at the same time.

5.1.52 No_Relative_Delay

[RM D.7] This restriction ensures at compile time that there are no delay relative statements and prevents expressions such as *delay 1.23;* from appearing in source code.

5.1.53 No_Requeue_Statements

[RM D.7] This restriction ensures at compile time that no requeue statements are permitted and prevents keyword *requeue* from being used in source code.

The restriction *No_Requeue* is recognized as a synonym for *No_Requeue_Statements*. This is retained for historical compatibility purposes (and a warning will be generated for its use if warnings on oNobsolescent features are activated).

5.1.54 No_Secondary_Stack

[GNAT] This restriction ensures at compile time that the generated code does not contain any reference to the secondary stack. The secondary stack is used to implement functions returning unconstrained objects (arrays or records) on some targets.

5.1.55 No_Select_Statements

[RM D.7] This restriction ensures at compile time no select statements of any kind are permitted, that is the keyword *select* may not appear.

5.1.56 No_Specific_Termination_Handlers

[RM D.7] There are no calls to Ada.Task_Termination.Set_Specific_Handler or to Ada.Task_Termination.Specific_Handler.

5.1.57 No_Specification_of_Aspect

[RM 13.12.1] This restriction checks at compile time that no aspect specification, attribute definition clause, or pragma is given for a given aspect.

5.1.58 No_Standard_Allocators_After_Elaboration

[RM D.7] Specifies that an allocator using a standard storage pool should never be evaluated at run time after the elaboration of the library items of the partition has completed. Otherwise, Storage_Error is raised.

5.1.59 No_Standard_Storage_Pools

[GNAT] This restriction ensures at compile time that no access types use the standard default storage pool. Any access type declared must have an explicit Storage_Pool attribute defined specifying a user-defined storage pool.

5.1.60 No_Stream_Optimizations

[GNAT] This restriction affects the performance of stream operations on types *String*, *Wide_String* and *Wide_Wide_String*. By default, the compiler uses block reads and writes when manipulating *String* objects due to their supperior performance. When this restriction is in effect, the compiler performs all IO operations on a per-character basis.

5.1.61 No_Streams

[GNAT] This restriction ensures at compile/bind time that there are no stream objects created and no use of stream attributes. This restriction does not forbid dependences on the package *Ada.Streams*. So it is permissible to with *Ada.Streams* (or another package that does so itself) as long as no actual stream objects are created and no stream attributes are used.

Note that the use of restriction allows optimization of tagged types, since they do not need to worry about dispatching stream operations. To take maximum advantage of this space-saving optimization, any unit declaring a tagged type should be compiled with the restriction, though this is not required.

5.1.62 No_Task_Allocators

[RM D.7] There are no allocators for task types or types containing task subcomponents.

5.1.63 No_Task_At_Interrupt_Priority

[GNAT] This restriction ensures at compile time that there is no Interrupt_Priority aspect or pragma for a task or a task type. As a consequence, the tasks are always created with a priority below that an interrupt priority.

5.1.64 No_Task_Attributes_Package

[GNAT] This restriction ensures at compile time that there are no implicit or explicit dependencies on the package *Ada.Task_Attributes*.

The restriction *No_Task_Attributes* is recognized as a synonym for *No_Task_Attributes_Package*. This is retained for historical compatibility purposes (and a warning will be generated for its use if warnings on obsolescent features are activated).

5.1.65 No_Task_Hierarchy

[RM D.7] All (non-environment) tasks depend directly on the environment task of the partition.

5.1.66 No_Task_Termination

[RM D.7] Tasks that terminate are erroneous.

5.1.67 No_Tasking

[GNAT] This restriction prevents the declaration of tasks or task types throughout the partition. It is similar in effect to the use of *Max_Tasks => 0* except that violations are caught at compile time and cause an error message to be output either by the compiler or binder.

5.1.68 No_Terminate_Alternatives

[RM D.7] There are no selective accepts with terminate alternatives.

5.1.69 No_Unchecked_Access

[RM H.4] This restriction ensures at compile time that there are no occurrences of the Unchecked_Access attribute.

5.1.70 No_Unchecked_Conversion

[RM J.13] This restriction ensures at compile time that there are no semantic dependences on the predefined generic function Unchecked_Conversion.

5.1.71 No_Unchecked_Deallocation

[RM J.13] This restriction ensures at compile time that there are no semantic dependences on the predefined generic procedure Unchecked_Deallocation.

5.1.72 No_Use_Of_Entity

[GNAT] This restriction ensures at compile time that there are no references to the entity given in the form

```
No_Use_Of_Entity => Name
```

where `Name` is the fully qualified entity, for example

```
No_Use_Of_Entity => Ada.Text_IO.Put_Line
```

5.1.73 Pure_Barriers

[GNAT] This restriction ensures at compile time that protected entry barriers are restricted to:

* simple variables defined in the private part of the protected type/object,
* constant declarations,

* named numbers,
* enumeration literals,
* integer literals,
* real literals,
* character literals,
* implicitly defined comparison operators,
* uses of the Standard."not" operator,
* short-circuit operator

This restriction is a relaxation of the Simple_Barriers restriction, but still ensures absence of side effects, exceptions, and recursion during the evaluation of the barriers.

5.1.74 Simple_Barriers

[RM D.7] This restriction ensures at compile time that barriers in entry declarations for protected types are restricted to either static boolean expressions or references to simple boolean variables defined in the private part of the protected type. No other form of entry barriers is permitted.

The restriction *Boolean_Entry_Barriers* is recognized as a synonym for *Simple_Barriers*. This is retained for historical compatibility purposes (and a warning will be generated for its use if warnings on obsolescent features are activated).

5.1.75 Static_Priorities

[GNAT] This restriction ensures at compile time that all priority expressions are static, and that there are no dependences on the package *Ada.Dynamic_Priorities*.

5.1.76 Static_Storage_Size

[GNAT] This restriction ensures at compile time that any expression appearing in a Storage_Size pragma or attribute definition clause is static.

5.2 Program Unit Level Restrictions

The second set of restriction identifiers does not require partition-wide consistency. The restriction may be enforced for a single compilation unit without any effect on any of the other compilation units in the partition.

5.2.1 No_Elaboration_Code

[GNAT] This restriction ensures at compile time that no elaboration code is generated. Note that this is not the same condition as is enforced by pragma *Preelaborate*. There are cases in which pragma *Preelaborate* still permits code to be generated (e.g., code to initialize a large array to all zeroes), and there are cases of units which do not meet the requirements for pragma *Preelaborate*, but for which no elaboration code is generated. Generally, it is the case that preelaborable units will meet the restrictions, with the exception of large aggregates initialized with an others_clause, and exception declarations (which generate calls to a run-time registry procedure). This restriction is enforced on a unit by unit basis, it need not be obeyed consistently throughout a partition.

In the case of aggregates with others, if the aggregate has a dynamic size, there is no way to eliminate the elaboration code (such dynamic bounds would be incompatible with *Preelaborate* in any case). If the bounds are static, then use of this restriction actually modifies the code choice of the compiler to avoid generating a loop, and instead generate the aggregate statically if possible, no matter how many times the data for the others clause must be repeatedly generated.

It is not possible to precisely document the constructs which are compatible with this restriction, since, unlike most other restrictions, this is not a restriction on the source code, but a restriction on the generated object code. For example, if the source contains a declaration:

```
Val : constant Integer := X;
```

where X is not a static constant, it may be possible, depending on complex optimization circuitry, for the compiler to figure out the value of X at compile time, in which case this initialization can be done by the loader, and requires no initialization code. It is not possible to document the precise conditions under which the optimizer can figure this out.

Note that this the implementation of this restriction requires full code generation. If it is used in conjunction with "semantics only" checking, then some cases of violations may be missed.

5.2.2 No_Dynamic_Sized_Objects

[GNAT] This restriction disallows certain constructs that might lead to the creation of dynamic-sized composite objects (or array or discriminated type). An array subtype indication is illegal if the bounds are not static or references to discriminants of an enclosing type. A discriminated subtype indication is illegal if the type has discriminant-dependent array components or a variant part, and the discriminants are not static. In addition, array and record aggregates are illegal in corresponding cases. Note that this restriction does not forbid access discriminants. It is often a good idea to combine this restriction with No_Secondary_Stack.

5.2.3 No_Entry_Queue

[GNAT] This restriction is a declaration that any protected entry compiled in the scope of the restriction has at most one task waiting on the entry at any one time, and so no queue is required. This restriction is not checked at compile time. A program execution is erroneous if an attempt is made to queue a second task on such an entry.

5.2.4 No_Implementation_Aspect_Specifications

[RM 13.12.1] This restriction checks at compile time that no GNAT-defined aspects are present. With this restriction, the only aspects that can be used are those defined in the Ada Reference Manual.

5.2.5 No_Implementation_Attributes

[RM 13.12.1] This restriction checks at compile time that no GNAT-defined attributes are present. With this restriction, the only attributes that can be used are those defined in the Ada Reference Manual.

5.2.6 No_Implementation_Identifiers

[RM 13.12.1] This restriction checks at compile time that no implementation-defined identifiers (marked with pragma Implementation_Defined) occur within language-defined packages.

5.2.7 No_Implementation_Pragmas

[RM 13.12.1] This restriction checks at compile time that no GNAT-defined pragmas are present. With this restriction, the only pragmas that can be used are those defined in the Ada Reference Manual.

5.2.8 No_Implementation_Restrictions

[GNAT] This restriction checks at compile time that no GNAT-defined restriction identifiers (other than *No_Implementation_Restrictions* itself) are present. With this restriction, the only other restriction identifiers that can be used are those defined in the Ada Reference Manual.

5.2.9 No_Implementation_Units

[RM 13.12.1] This restriction checks at compile time that there is no mention in the context clause of any implementation-defined descendants of packages Ada, Interfaces, or System.

5.2.10 No_Implicit_Aliasing

[GNAT] This restriction, which is not required to be partition-wide consistent, requires an explicit aliased keyword for an object to which 'Access, 'Unchecked_Access, or 'Address is applied, and forbids entirely the use of the 'Unrestricted_Access attribute for objects. Note: the reason that Unrestricted_Access is forbidden is that it would require the prefix to be aliased, and in such cases, it can always be replaced by the standard attribute Unchecked_Access which is preferable.

5.2.11 No_Obsolescent_Features

[RM 13.12.1] This restriction checks at compile time that no obsolescent features are used, as defined in Annex J of the Ada Reference Manual.

5.2.12 No_Wide_Characters

[GNAT] This restriction ensures at compile time that no uses of the types *Wide_Character* or *Wide_String* or corresponding wide wide types appear, and that no wide or wide wide string or character literals appear in the program (that is literals representing characters not in type *Character*).

5.2.13 SPARK_05

[GNAT] This restriction checks at compile time that some constructs forbidden in SPARK 2005 are not present. Error messages related to SPARK restriction have the form:

```
violation of restriction "SPARK_05" at <source-location>
 <error message>
```

The restriction *SPARK* is recognized as a synonym for *SPARK_05*. This is retained for historical compatibility purposes (and an unconditional warning will be generated for its use, advising replacement by *SPARK*).

This is not a replacement for the semantic checks performed by the SPARK Examiner tool, as the compiler currently only deals with code, not SPARK 2005 annotations, and does not guarantee catching all cases of constructs forbidden by SPARK 2005.

Thus it may well be the case that code which passes the compiler with the SPARK restriction is rejected by the SPARK Examiner, e.g. due to the different visibility rules of the Examiner based on SPARK 2005 *inherit* annotations.

This restriction can be useful in providing an initial filter for code developed using SPARK 2005, or in examining legacy code to see how far it is from meeting SPARK restrictions.

The list below summarizes the checks that are performed when this restriction is in force:

* No block statements
* No case statements with only an others clause
* Exit statements in loops must respect the SPARK 2005 language restrictions
* No goto statements
* Return can only appear as last statement in function
* Function must have return statement
* Loop parameter specification must include subtype mark
* Prefix of expanded name cannot be a loop statement
* Abstract subprogram not allowed
* User-defined operators not allowed
* Access type parameters not allowed
* Default expressions for parameters not allowed
* Default expressions for record fields not allowed
* No tasking constructs allowed
* Label needed at end of subprograms and packages
* No mixing of positional and named parameter association
* No access types as result type
* No unconstrained arrays as result types
* No null procedures
* Initial and later declarations must be in correct order (declaration can't come after body)
* No attributes on private types if full declaration not visible
* No package declaration within package specification
* No controlled types
* No discriminant types
* No overloading
* Selector name cannot be operator symbol (i.e. operator symbol cannot be prefixed)
* Access attribute not allowed
* Allocator not allowed
* Result of catenation must be String
* Operands of catenation must be string literal, static char or another catenation

* No conditional expressions
* No explicit dereference
* Quantified expression not allowed
* Slicing not allowed
* No exception renaming
* No generic renaming
* No object renaming
* No use clause
* Aggregates must be qualified
* Nonstatic choice in array aggregates not allowed
* The only view conversions which are allowed as in-out parameters are conversions of a tagged type to an ancestor type
* No mixing of positional and named association in aggregate, no multi choice
* AND, OR and XOR for arrays only allowed when operands have same static bounds
* Fixed point operands to * or / must be qualified or converted
* Comparison operators not allowed for Booleans or arrays (except strings)
* Equality not allowed for arrays with non-matching static bounds (except strings)
* Conversion / qualification not allowed for arrays with non-matching static bounds
* Subprogram declaration only allowed in package spec (unless followed by import)
* Access types not allowed
* Incomplete type declaration not allowed
* Object and subtype declarations must respect SPARK restrictions
* Digits or delta constraint not allowed
* Decimal fixed point type not allowed
* Aliasing of objects not allowed
* Modular type modulus must be power of 2
* Base not allowed on subtype mark
* Unary operators not allowed on modular types (except not)
* Untagged record cannot be null
* No class-wide operations
* Initialization expressions must respect SPARK restrictions
* Nonstatic ranges not allowed except in iteration schemes
* String subtypes must have lower bound of 1
* Subtype of Boolean cannot have constraint
* At most one tagged type or extension per package
* Interface is not allowed
* Character literal cannot be prefixed (selector name cannot be character literal)
* Record aggregate cannot contain 'others'
* Component association in record aggregate must contain a single choice

* Ancestor part cannot be a type mark
* Attributes 'Image, 'Width and 'Value not allowed
* Functions may not update globals
* Subprograms may not contain direct calls to themselves (prevents recursion within unit)
* Call to subprogram not allowed in same unit before body has been seen (prevents recursion within unit)

The following restrictions are enforced, but note that they are actually more strict that the latest SPARK 2005 language definition:

* No derived types other than tagged type extensions
* Subtype of unconstrained array must have constraint

This list summarises the main SPARK 2005 language rules that are not currently checked by the SPARK_05 restriction:

* SPARK annotations are treated as comments so are not checked at all
* Based real literals not allowed
* Objects cannot be initialized at declaration by calls to user-defined functions
* Objects cannot be initialized at declaration by assignments from variables
* Objects cannot be initialized at declaration by assignments from indexed/selected components
* Ranges shall not be null
* A fixed point delta expression must be a simple expression
* Restrictions on where renaming declarations may be placed
* Externals of mode 'out' cannot be referenced
* Externals of mode 'in' cannot be updated
* Loop with no iteration scheme or exits only allowed as last statement in main program or task
* Subprogram cannot have parent unit name
* SPARK 2005 inherited subprogram must be prefixed with overriding
* External variables (or functions that reference them) may not be passed as actual parameters
* Globals must be explicitly mentioned in contract
* Deferred constants cannot be completed by pragma Import
* Package initialization cannot read/write variables from other packages
* Prefix not allowed for entities that are directly visible
* Identifier declaration can't override inherited package name
* Cannot use Standard or other predefined packages as identifiers
* After renaming, cannot use the original name
* Subprograms can only be renamed to remove package prefix
* Pragma import must be immediately after entity it names

* No mutual recursion between multiple units (this can be checked with gnatcheck)

Note that if a unit is compiled in Ada 95 mode with the SPARK restriction, violations will be reported for constructs forbidden in SPARK 95, instead of SPARK 2005.

6 Implementation Advice

The main text of the Ada Reference Manual describes the required behavior of all Ada compilers, and the GNAT compiler conforms to these requirements.

In addition, there are sections throughout the Ada Reference Manual headed by the phrase 'Implementation advice'. These sections are not normative, i.e., they do not specify requirements that all compilers must follow. Rather they provide advice on generally desirable behavior. They are not requirements, because they describe behavior that cannot be provided on all systems, or may be undesirable on some systems.

As far as practical, GNAT follows the implementation advice in the Ada Reference Manual. Each such RM section corresponds to a section in this chapter whose title specifies the RM section number and paragraph number and the subject of the advice. The contents of each section consists of the RM text within quotation marks, followed by the GNAT interpretation of the advice. Most often, this simply says 'followed', which means that GNAT follows the advice. However, in a number of cases, GNAT deliberately deviates from this advice, in which case the text describes what GNAT does and why.

6.1 RM 1.1.3(20): Error Detection

> "If an implementation detects the use of an unsupported Specialized Needs Annex feature at run time, it should raise *Program_Error* if feasible."

Not relevant. All specialized needs annex features are either supported, or diagnosed at compile time.

6.2 RM 1.1.3(31): Child Units

> "If an implementation wishes to provide implementation-defined extensions to the functionality of a language-defined library unit, it should normally do so by adding children to the library unit."

Followed.

6.3 RM 1.1.5(12): Bounded Errors

> "If an implementation detects a bounded error or erroneous execution, it should raise *Program_Error*."

Followed in all cases in which the implementation detects a bounded error or erroneous execution. Not all such situations are detected at runtime.

6.4 RM 2.8(16): Pragmas

> "Normally, implementation-defined pragmas should have no semantic effect for error-free programs; that is, if the implementation-defined pragmas are removed from a working program, the program should still be legal, and should still have the same semantics."

The following implementation defined pragmas are exceptions to this rule:

Pragma	Explanation
Abort_Defer	Affects semantics
Ada_83	Affects legality
Assert	Affects semantics
CPP_Class	Affects semantics
CPP_Constructor	Affects semantics
Debug	Affects semantics
Interface_Name	Affects semantics
Machine_Attribute	Affects semantics
Unimplemented_Unit	Affects legality
Unchecked_Union	Affects semantics

In each of the above cases, it is essential to the purpose of the pragma that this advice not be followed. For details see [Implementation Defined Pragmas], page 4.

6.5 RM 2.8(17-19): Pragmas

> "Normally, an implementation should not define pragmas that can make an illegal program legal, except as follows:
>
> * A pragma used to complete a declaration, such as a pragma *Import*;
> * A pragma used to configure the environment by adding, removing, or replacing *library_items*."

See [RM 2.8(16); Pragmas], page 145.

6.6 RM 3.5.2(5): Alternative Character Sets

> "If an implementation supports a mode with alternative interpretations for *Character* and *Wide_Character*, the set of graphic characters of *Character* should nevertheless remain a proper subset of the set of graphic characters of *Wide_Character*. Any character set 'localizations' should be reflected in the results of the subprograms defined in the language-defined package *Characters.Handling* (see A.3) available in such a mode. In a mode with an alternative interpretation of *Character*, the implementation should also support a corresponding change in what is a legal *identifier_letter*."

Not all wide character modes follow this advice, in particular the JIS and IEC modes reflect standard usage in Japan, and in these encoding, the upper half of the Latin-1 set is not part of the wide-character subset, since the most significant bit is used for wide character encoding. However, this only applies to the external forms. Internally there is no such restriction.

6.7 RM 3.5.4(28): Integer Types

> "An implementation should support *Long_Integer* in addition to *Integer* if the target machine supports 32-bit (or longer) arithmetic. No other named integer subtypes are recommended for package *Standard.* Instead, appropriate named integer subtypes should be provided in the library package *Interfaces* (see B.2)."

Long_Integer is supported. Other standard integer types are supported so this advice is not fully followed. These types are supported for convenient interface to C, and so that all hardware types of the machine are easily available.

6.8 RM 3.5.4(29): Integer Types

> "An implementation for a two's complement machine should support modular types with a binary modulus up to `System.Max_Int*2+2`. An implementation should support a non-binary modules up to *Integer'Last.*"

Followed.

6.9 RM 3.5.5(8): Enumeration Values

> "For the evaluation of a call on `S'Pos` for an enumeration subtype, if the value of the operand does not correspond to the internal code for any enumeration literal of its type (perhaps due to an un-initialized variable), then the implementation should raise *Program_Error.* This is particularly important for enumeration types with noncontiguous internal codes specified by an enumeration_representation_clause."

Followed.

6.10 RM 3.5.7(17): Float Types

> "An implementation should support *Long_Float* in addition to *Float* if the target machine supports 11 or more digits of precision. No other named floating point subtypes are recommended for package *Standard.* Instead, appropriate named floating point subtypes should be provided in the library package *Interfaces* (see B.2)."

Short_Float and *Long_Long_Float* are also provided. The former provides improved compatibility with other implementations supporting this type. The latter corresponds to the highest precision floating-point type supported by the hardware. On most machines, this will be the same as *Long_Float,* but on some machines, it will correspond to the IEEE extended form. The notable case is all ia32 (x86) implementations, where *Long_Long_Float* corresponds to the 80-bit extended precision format supported in hardware on this processor. Note that the 128-bit format on SPARC is not supported, since this is a software rather than a hardware format.

6.11 RM 3.6.2(11): Multidimensional Arrays

> "An implementation should normally represent multidimensional arrays in row-major order, consistent with the notation used for multidimensional array aggregates (see 4.3.3). However, if a pragma *Convention* (*Fortran*, ...) applies to a multidimensional array type, then column-major order should be used instead (see B.5, *Interfacing with Fortran*)."

Followed.

6.12 RM 9.6(30-31): Duration'Small

> "Whenever possible in an implementation, the value of *Duration'Small* should be no greater than 100 microseconds."

Followed. (*Duration'Small* = 10**(-9)).

> "The time base for *delay_relative_statements* should be monotonic; it need not be the same time base as used for *Calendar.Clock*."

Followed.

6.13 RM 10.2.1(12): Consistent Representation

> "In an implementation, a type declared in a pre-elaborated package should have the same representation in every elaboration of a given version of the package, whether the elaborations occur in distinct executions of the same program, or in executions of distinct programs or partitions that include the given version."

Followed, except in the case of tagged types. Tagged types involve implicit pointers to a local copy of a dispatch table, and these pointers have representations which thus depend on a particular elaboration of the package. It is not easy to see how it would be possible to follow this advice without severely impacting efficiency of execution.

6.14 RM 11.4.1(19): Exception Information

> "*Exception_Message* by default and *Exception_Information* should produce information useful for debugging. *Exception_Message* should be short, about one line. *Exception_Information* can be long. *Exception_Message* should not include the *Exception_Name*. *Exception_Information* should include both the *Exception_Name* and the *Exception_Message*."

Followed. For each exception that doesn't have a specified *Exception_Message*, the compiler generates one containing the location of the raise statement. This location has the form 'file_name:line', where file_name is the short file name (without path information) and line is the line number in the file. Note that in the case of the Zero Cost Exception mechanism, these messages become redundant with the Exception_Information that contains a full backtrace of the calling sequence, so they are disabled. To disable explicitly the generation of the source location message, use the Pragma *Discard_Names*.

6.15 RM 11.5(28): Suppression of Checks

"The implementation should minimize the code executed for checks that have been suppressed."

Followed.

6.16 RM 13.1 (21-24): Representation Clauses

"The recommended level of support for all representation items is qualified as follows:

An implementation need not support representation items containing nonstatic expressions, except that an implementation should support a representation item for a given entity if each nonstatic expression in the representation item is a name that statically denotes a constant declared before the entity."

Followed. In fact, GNAT goes beyond the recommended level of support by allowing nonstatic expressions in some representation clauses even without the need to declare constants initialized with the values of such expressions. For example:

```
X : Integer;
Y : Float;
for Y'Address use X'Address;>>
```

```
"An implementation need not support a specification for the 'Size'
for a given composite subtype, nor the size or storage place for an
object (including a component) of a given composite subtype, unless the
constraints on the subtype and its composite subcomponents (if any) are
all static constraints."
```

Followed. Size Clauses are not permitted on nonstatic components, as described above.

"An aliased component, or a component whose type is by-reference, should always be allocated at an addressable location."

Followed.

6.17 RM 13.2(6-8): Packed Types

"If a type is packed, then the implementation should try to minimize storage allocated to objects of the type, possibly at the expense of speed of accessing components, subject to reasonable complexity in addressing calculations.

The recommended level of support pragma *Pack* is:

For a packed record type, the components should be packed as tightly as possible subject to the Sizes of the component subtypes, and subject to any *record_representation_clause* that applies to the type; the implementation may, but need not, reorder components or cross aligned word boundaries to improve the packing. A component whose *Size* is greater than the word size may be allocated an integral number of words."

Followed. Tight packing of arrays is supported for all component sizes up to 64-bits. If the array component size is 1 (that is to say, if the component is a boolean type or an enumeration type with two values) then values of the type are implicitly initialized to zero. This happens both for objects of the packed type, and for objects that have a subcomponent of the packed type.

> "An implementation should support Address clauses for imported subprograms."

Followed.

6.18 RM 13.3(14-19): Address Clauses

> "For an array *X*, `X'Address` should point at the first component of the array, and not at the array bounds."

Followed.

> "The recommended level of support for the *Address* attribute is:
>
> `X'Address` should produce a useful result if *X* is an object that is aliased or of a by-reference type, or is an entity whose *Address* has been specified."

Followed. A valid address will be produced even if none of those conditions have been met. If necessary, the object is forced into memory to ensure the address is valid.

> "An implementation should support *Address* clauses for imported subprograms."

Followed.

> "Objects (including subcomponents) that are aliased or of a by-reference type should be allocated on storage element boundaries."

Followed.

> "If the *Address* of an object is specified, or it is imported or exported, then the implementation should not perform optimizations based on assumptions of no aliases."

Followed.

6.19 RM 13.3(29-35): Alignment Clauses

> "The recommended level of support for the *Alignment* attribute for subtypes is:
>
> An implementation should support specified Alignments that are factors and multiples of the number of storage elements per word, subject to the following:"

Followed.

> "An implementation need not support specified Alignments for combinations of Sizes and Alignments that cannot be easily loaded and stored by available machine instructions."

Followed.

"An implementation need not support specified Alignments that are greater than the maximum *Alignment* the implementation ever returns by default."

Followed.

"The recommended level of support for the *Alignment* attribute for objects is:

Same as above, for subtypes, but in addition:"

Followed.

"For stand-alone library-level objects of statically constrained subtypes, the implementation should support all alignments supported by the target linker. For example, page alignment is likely to be supported for such objects, but not for subtypes."

Followed.

6.20 RM 13.3(42-43): Size Clauses

"The recommended level of support for the *Size* attribute of objects is:

A *Size* clause should be supported for an object if the specified *Size* is at least as large as its subtype's *Size*, and corresponds to a size in storage elements that is a multiple of the object's *Alignment* (if the *Alignment* is nonzero)."

Followed.

6.21 RM 13.3(50-56): Size Clauses

"If the *Size* of a subtype is specified, and allows for efficient independent addressability (see 9.10) on the target architecture, then the *Size* of the following objects of the subtype should equal the *Size* of the subtype:

Aliased objects (including components)."

Followed.

"*Size* clause on a composite subtype should not affect the internal layout of components."

Followed. But note that this can be overridden by use of the implementation pragma Implicit_Packing in the case of packed arrays.

"The recommended level of support for the *Size* attribute of subtypes is:

The *Size* (if not specified) of a static discrete or fixed point subtype should be the number of bits needed to represent each value belonging to the subtype using an unbiased representation, leaving space for a sign bit only if the subtype contains negative values. If such a subtype is a first subtype, then an implementation should support a specified *Size* for it that reflects this representation."

Followed.

"For a subtype implemented with levels of indirection, the *Size* should include the size of the pointers, but not the size of what they point at."

Followed.

6.22 RM 13.3(71-73): Component Size Clauses

"The recommended level of support for the *Component_Size* attribute is:

An implementation need not support specified *Component_Sizes* that are less than the *Size* of the component subtype."

Followed.

"An implementation should support specified Component_Sizes that are factors and multiples of the word size. For such Component_Sizes, the array should contain no gaps between components. For other Component_Sizes (if supported), the array should contain no gaps between components when packing is also specified; the implementation should forbid this combination in cases where it cannot support a no-gaps representation."

Followed.

6.23 RM 13.4(9-10): Enumeration Representation Clauses

"The recommended level of support for enumeration representation clauses is:

An implementation need not support enumeration representation clauses for boolean types, but should at minimum support the internal codes in the range *System.Min_Int .. System.Max_Int*."

Followed.

6.24 RM 13.5.1(17-22): Record Representation Clauses

"The recommended level of support for *record_representation_clauses* is:

An implementation should support storage places that can be extracted with a load, mask, shift sequence of machine code, and set with a load, shift, mask, store sequence, given the available machine instructions and run-time model."

Followed.

"A storage place should be supported if its size is equal to the *Size* of the component subtype, and it starts and ends on a boundary that obeys the *Alignment* of the component subtype."

Followed.

"If the default bit ordering applies to the declaration of a given type, then for a component whose subtype's *Size* is less than the word size, any storage place that does not cross an aligned word boundary should be supported."

Followed.

"An implementation may reserve a storage place for the tag field of a tagged type, and disallow other components from overlapping that place."

Followed. The storage place for the tag field is the beginning of the tagged record, and its size is Address'Size. GNAT will reject an explicit component clause for the tag field.

> "An implementation need not support a *component_clause* for a component of an extension part if the storage place is not after the storage places of all components of the parent type, whether or not those storage places had been specified."

Followed. The above advice on record representation clauses is followed, and all mentioned features are implemented.

6.25 RM 13.5.2(5): Storage Place Attributes

> "If a component is represented using some form of pointer (such as an offset) to the actual data of the component, and this data is contiguous with the rest of the object, then the storage place attributes should reflect the place of the actual data, not the pointer. If a component is allocated discontinuously from the rest of the object, then a warning should be generated upon reference to one of its storage place attributes."

Followed. There are no such components in GNAT.

6.26 RM 13.5.3(7-8): Bit Ordering

> "The recommended level of support for the non-default bit ordering is:
>
> If *Word_Size* = *Storage_Unit*, then the implementation should support the non-default bit ordering in addition to the default bit ordering."

Followed. Word size does not equal storage size in this implementation. Thus non-default bit ordering is not supported.

6.27 RM 13.7(37): Address as Private

> "*Address* should be of a private type."

Followed.

6.28 RM 13.7.1(16): Address Operations

> "Operations in *System* and its children should reflect the target environment semantics as closely as is reasonable. For example, on most machines, it makes sense for address arithmetic to 'wrap around'. Operations that do not make sense should raise *Program_Error*."

Followed. Address arithmetic is modular arithmetic that wraps around. No operation raises *Program_Error*, since all operations make sense.

6.29 RM 13.9(14-17): Unchecked Conversion

> "The *Size* of an array object should not include its bounds; hence, the bounds should not be part of the converted data."

Followed.

> "The implementation should not generate unnecessary run-time checks to ensure that the representation of *S* is a representation of the target type. It should take advantage of the permission to return by reference

> when possible. Restrictions on unchecked conversions should be avoided unless required by the target environment."

Followed. There are no restrictions on unchecked conversion. A warning is generated if the source and target types do not have the same size since the semantics in this case may be target dependent.

> "The recommended level of support for unchecked conversions is:
>
> Unchecked conversions should be supported and should be reversible in the cases where this clause defines the result. To enable meaningful use of unchecked conversion, a contiguous representation should be used for elementary subtypes, for statically constrained array subtypes whose component subtype is one of the subtypes described in this paragraph, and for record subtypes without discriminants whose component subtypes are described in this paragraph."

Followed.

6.30 RM 13.11(23-25): Implicit Heap Usage

> "An implementation should document any cases in which it dynamically allocates heap storage for a purpose other than the evaluation of an allocator."

Followed, the only other points at which heap storage is dynamically allocated are as follows:

* At initial elaboration time, to allocate dynamically sized global objects.
* To allocate space for a task when a task is created.
* To extend the secondary stack dynamically when needed. The secondary stack is used for returning variable length results.

> "A default (implementation-provided) storage pool for an access-to-constant type should not have overhead to support deallocation of individual objects."

Followed.

> "A storage pool for an anonymous access type should be created at the point of an allocator for the type, and be reclaimed when the designated object becomes inaccessible."

Followed.

6.31 RM 13.11.2(17): Unchecked Deallocation

> "For a standard storage pool, *Free* should actually reclaim the storage."

Followed.

6.32 RM 13.13.2(17): Stream Oriented Attributes

> "If a stream element is the same size as a storage element, then the normal in-memory representation should be used by *Read* and *Write* for scalar objects. Otherwise, *Read* and *Write* should use the smallest number of

> stream elements needed to represent all values in the base range of the scalar type."

Followed. By default, GNAT uses the interpretation suggested by AI-195, which specifies using the size of the first subtype. However, such an implementation is based on direct binary representations and is therefore target- and endianness-dependent. To address this issue, GNAT also supplies an alternate implementation of the stream attributes *Read* and *Write*, which uses the target-independent XDR standard representation for scalar types.

The XDR implementation is provided as an alternative body of the *System.Stream_Attributes* package, in the file `s-stratt-xdr.adb` in the GNAT library. There is no `s-stratt-xdr.ads` file. In order to install the XDR implementation, do the following:

* Replace the default implementation of the *System.Stream_Attributes* package with the XDR implementation. For example on a Unix platform issue the commands:

```
$ mv s-stratt.adb s-stratt-default.adb
$ mv s-stratt-xdr.adb s-stratt.adb
```

* Rebuild the GNAT run-time library as documented in the *GNAT and Libraries* section of the *GNAT User's Guide*.

6.33 RM A.1(52): Names of Predefined Numeric Types

> "If an implementation provides additional named predefined integer types, then the names should end with `Integer` as in `Long_Integer`. If an implementation provides additional named predefined floating point types, then the names should end with `Float` as in `Long_Float`."

Followed.

6.34 RM A.3.2(49): *Ada.Characters.Handling*

> "If an implementation provides a localized definition of *Character* or *Wide_Character*, then the effects of the subprograms in *Characters.Handling* should reflect the localizations. See also 3.5.2."

Followed. GNAT provides no such localized definitions.

6.35 RM A.4.4(106): Bounded-Length String Handling

> "Bounded string objects should not be implemented by implicit pointers and dynamic allocation."

Followed. No implicit pointers or dynamic allocation are used.

6.36 RM A.5.2(46-47): Random Number Generation

> "Any storage associated with an object of type *Generator* should be reclaimed on exit from the scope of the object."

Followed.

> "If the generator period is sufficiently long in relation to the number of distinct initiator values, then each possible value of *Initiator* passed to

> *Reset* should initiate a sequence of random numbers that does not, in a practical sense, overlap the sequence initiated by any other value. If this is not possible, then the mapping between initiator values and generator states should be a rapidly varying function of the initiator value."

Followed. The generator period is sufficiently long for the first condition here to hold true.

6.37 RM A.10.7(23): *Get_Immediate*

> "The *Get_Immediate* procedures should be implemented with unbuffered input. For a device such as a keyboard, input should be available if a key has already been typed, whereas for a disk file, input should always be available except at end of file. For a file associated with a keyboard-like device, any line-editing features of the underlying operating system should be disabled during the execution of *Get_Immediate*."

Followed on all targets except VxWorks. For VxWorks, there is no way to provide this functionality that does not result in the input buffer being flushed before the *Get_Immediate* call. A special unit *Interfaces.Vxworks.IO* is provided that contains routines to enable this functionality.

6.38 RM B.1(39-41): Pragma *Export*

> "If an implementation supports pragma *Export* to a given language, then it should also allow the main subprogram to be written in that language. It should support some mechanism for invoking the elaboration of the Ada library units included in the system, and for invoking the finalization of the environment task. On typical systems, the recommended mechanism is to provide two subprograms whose link names are *adainit* and *adafinal*. *adainit* should contain the elaboration code for library units. *adafinal* should contain the finalization code. These subprograms should have no effect the second and subsequent time they are called."

Followed.

> "Automatic elaboration of pre-elaborated packages should be provided when pragma *Export* is supported."

Followed when the main program is in Ada. If the main program is in a foreign language, then *adainit* must be called to elaborate pre-elaborated packages.

> "For each supported convention *L* other than *Intrinsic*, an implementation should support *Import* and *Export* pragmas for objects of *L*-compatible types and for subprograms, and pragma *Convention* for *L*-eligible types and for subprograms, presuming the other language has corresponding features. Pragma *Convention* need not be supported for scalar types."

Followed.

6.39 RM B.2(12-13): Package *Interfaces*

> "For each implementation-defined convention identifier, there should be a child package of package Interfaces with the corresponding name. This

package should contain any declarations that would be useful for interfacing to the language (implementation) represented by the convention. Any declarations useful for interfacing to any language on the given hardware architecture should be provided directly in *Interfaces*."

Followed.

"An implementation supporting an interface to C, COBOL, or Fortran should provide the corresponding package or packages described in the following clauses."

Followed. GNAT provides all the packages described in this section.

6.40 RM B.3(63-71): Interfacing with C

"An implementation should support the following interface correspondences between Ada and C."

Followed.

"An Ada procedure corresponds to a void-returning C function."

Followed.

"An Ada function corresponds to a non-void C function."

Followed.

"An Ada *in* scalar parameter is passed as a scalar argument to a C function."

Followed.

"An Ada *in* parameter of an access-to-object type with designated type *T* is passed as a `t*` argument to a C function, where `t` is the C type corresponding to the Ada type *T*."

Followed.

"An Ada access *T* parameter, or an Ada *out* or *in out* parameter of an elementary type *T*, is passed as a `t*` argument to a C function, where `t` is the C type corresponding to the Ada type *T*. In the case of an elementary *out* or *in out* parameter, a pointer to a temporary copy is used to preserve by-copy semantics."

Followed.

"An Ada parameter of a record type *T*, of any mode, is passed as a `t*` argument to a C function, where `t` is the C structure corresponding to the Ada type *T*."

Followed. This convention may be overridden by the use of the C_Pass_By_Copy pragma, or Convention, or by explicitly specifying the mechanism for a given call using an extended import or export pragma.

"An Ada parameter of an array type with component type *T*, of any mode, is passed as a `t*` argument to a C function, where `t` is the C type corresponding to the Ada type *T*."

Followed.

> "An Ada parameter of an access-to-subprogram type is passed as a pointer to a C function whose prototype corresponds to the designated subprogram's specification."

Followed.

6.41 RM B.4(95-98): Interfacing with COBOL

> "An Ada implementation should support the following interface correspondences between Ada and COBOL."

Followed.

> "An Ada access *T* parameter is passed as a `BY REFERENCE` data item of the COBOL type corresponding to *T*."

Followed.

> "An Ada in scalar parameter is passed as a `BY CONTENT` data item of the corresponding COBOL type."

Followed.

> "Any other Ada parameter is passed as a `BY REFERENCE` data item of the COBOL type corresponding to the Ada parameter type; for scalars, a local copy is used if necessary to ensure by-copy semantics."

Followed.

6.42 RM B.5(22-26): Interfacing with Fortran

> "An Ada implementation should support the following interface correspondences between Ada and Fortran:"

Followed.

> "An Ada procedure corresponds to a Fortran subroutine."

Followed.

> "An Ada function corresponds to a Fortran function."

Followed.

> "An Ada parameter of an elementary, array, or record type *T* is passed as a *T* argument to a Fortran procedure, where *T* is the Fortran type corresponding to the Ada type *T*, and where the INTENT attribute of the corresponding dummy argument matches the Ada formal parameter mode; the Fortran implementation's parameter passing conventions are used. For elementary types, a local copy is used if necessary to ensure by-copy semantics."

Followed.

> "An Ada parameter of an access-to-subprogram type is passed as a reference to a Fortran procedure whose interface corresponds to the designated subprogram's specification."

Followed.

6.43 RM C.1(3-5): Access to Machine Operations

> "The machine code or intrinsic support should allow access to all operations normally available to assembly language programmers for the target environment, including privileged instructions, if any."

Followed.

> "The interfacing pragmas (see Annex B) should support interface to assembler; the default assembler should be associated with the convention identifier *Assembler*."

Followed.

> "If an entity is exported to assembly language, then the implementation should allocate it at an addressable location, and should ensure that it is retained by the linking process, even if not otherwise referenced from the Ada code. The implementation should assume that any call to a machine code or assembler subprogram is allowed to read or update every object that is specified as exported."

Followed.

6.44 RM C.1(10-16): Access to Machine Operations

> "The implementation should ensure that little or no overhead is associated with calling intrinsic and machine-code subprograms."

Followed for both intrinsics and machine-code subprograms.

> "It is recommended that intrinsic subprograms be provided for convenient access to any machine operations that provide special capabilities or efficiency and that are not otherwise available through the language constructs."

Followed. A full set of machine operation intrinsic subprograms is provided.

> "Atomic read-modify-write operations—e.g., test and set, compare and swap, decrement and test, enqueue/dequeue."

Followed on any target supporting such operations.

> "Standard numeric functions—e.g.:, sin, log."

Followed on any target supporting such operations.

> "String manipulation operations—e.g.:, translate and test."

Followed on any target supporting such operations.

> "Vector operations—e.g.:, compare vector against thresholds."

Followed on any target supporting such operations.

> "Direct operations on I/O ports."

Followed on any target supporting such operations.

6.45 RM C.3(28): Interrupt Support

> "If the *Ceiling_Locking* policy is not in effect, the implementation should provide means for the application to specify which interrupts are to be blocked during protected actions, if the underlying system allows for a finer-grain control of interrupt blocking."

Followed. The underlying system does not allow for finer-grain control of interrupt blocking.

6.46 RM C.3.1(20-21): Protected Procedure Handlers

> "Whenever possible, the implementation should allow interrupt handlers to be called directly by the hardware."

Followed on any target where the underlying operating system permits such direct calls.

> "Whenever practical, violations of any implementation-defined restrictions should be detected before run time."

Followed. Compile time warnings are given when possible.

6.47 RM C.3.2(25): Package *Interrupts*

> "If implementation-defined forms of interrupt handler procedures are supported, such as protected procedures with parameters, then for each such form of a handler, a type analogous to *Parameterless_Handler* should be specified in a child package of *Interrupts*, with the same operations as in the predefined package Interrupts."

Followed.

6.48 RM C.4(14): Pre-elaboration Requirements

> "It is recommended that pre-elaborated packages be implemented in such a way that there should be little or no code executed at run time for the elaboration of entities not already covered by the Implementation Requirements."

Followed. Executable code is generated in some cases, e.g., loops to initialize large arrays.

6.49 RM C.5(8): Pragma *Discard_Names*

> "If the pragma applies to an entity, then the implementation should reduce the amount of storage used for storing names associated with that entity."

Followed.

6.50 RM C.7.2(30): The Package Task_Attributes

> "Some implementations are targeted to domains in which memory use at run time must be completely deterministic. For such implementations, it is recommended that the storage for task attributes will be pre-allocated statically and not from the heap. This can be accomplished by either placing restrictions on the number and the size of the task's attributes,

> or by using the pre-allocated storage for the first *N* attribute objects, and the heap for the others. In the latter case, *N* should be documented."

Not followed. This implementation is not targeted to such a domain.

6.51 RM D.3(17): Locking Policies

> "The implementation should use names that end with `_Locking` for locking policies defined by the implementation."

Followed. Two implementation-defined locking policies are defined, whose names (*Inheritance_Locking* and *Concurrent_Readers_Locking*) follow this suggestion.

6.52 RM D.4(16): Entry Queuing Policies

> "Names that end with `_Queuing` should be used for all implementation-defined queuing policies."

Followed. No such implementation-defined queuing policies exist.

6.53 RM D.6(9-10): Preemptive Abort

> "Even though the *abort_statement* is included in the list of potentially blocking operations (see 9.5.1), it is recommended that this statement be implemented in a way that never requires the task executing the *abort_statement* to block."

Followed.

> "On a multi-processor, the delay associated with aborting a task on another processor should be bounded; the implementation should use periodic polling, if necessary, to achieve this."

Followed.

6.54 RM D.7(21): Tasking Restrictions

> "When feasible, the implementation should take advantage of the specified restrictions to produce a more efficient implementation."

GNAT currently takes advantage of these restrictions by providing an optimized run time when the Ravenscar profile and the GNAT restricted run time set of restrictions are specified. See pragma *Profile (Ravenscar)* and pragma *Profile (Restricted)* for more details.

6.55 RM D.8(47-49): Monotonic Time

> "When appropriate, implementations should provide configuration mechanisms to change the value of *Tick*."

Such configuration mechanisms are not appropriate to this implementation and are thus not supported.

> "It is recommended that *Calendar.Clock* and *Real_Time.Clock* be implemented as transformations of the same time base."

Followed.

"It is recommended that the best time base which exists in the underlying system be available to the application through *Clock*. *Best* may mean highest accuracy or largest range."

Followed.

6.56 RM E.5(28-29): Partition Communication Subsystem

"Whenever possible, the PCS on the called partition should allow for multiple tasks to call the RPC-receiver with different messages and should allow them to block until the corresponding subprogram body returns."

Followed by GLADE, a separately supplied PCS that can be used with GNAT.

"The *Write* operation on a stream of type *Params_Stream_Type* should raise *Storage_Error* if it runs out of space trying to write the *Item* into the stream."

Followed by GLADE, a separately supplied PCS that can be used with GNAT.

6.57 RM F(7): COBOL Support

"If COBOL (respectively, C) is widely supported in the target environment, implementations supporting the Information Systems Annex should provide the child package *Interfaces.COBOL* (respectively, *Interfaces.C*) specified in Annex B and should support a *convention_identifier* of COBOL (respectively, C) in the interfacing pragmas (see Annex B), thus allowing Ada programs to interface with programs written in that language."

Followed.

6.58 RM F.1(2): Decimal Radix Support

"Packed decimal should be used as the internal representation for objects of subtype *S* when *S*'Machine_Radix = 10."

Not followed. GNAT ignores *S*'Machine_Radix and always uses binary representations.

6.59 RM G: Numerics

"If Fortran (respectively, C) is widely supported in the target environment, implementations supporting the Numerics Annex should provide the child package *Interfaces.Fortran* (respectively, *Interfaces.C*) specified in Annex B and should support a *convention_identifier* of Fortran (respectively, C) in the interfacing pragmas (see Annex B), thus allowing Ada programs to interface with programs written in that language."

Followed.

6.60 RM G.1.1(56-58): Complex Types

"Because the usual mathematical meaning of multiplication of a complex operand and a real operand is that of the scaling of both components of the former by the latter, an implementation should not perform this operation by first promoting the real operand to complex type and then performing a full complex multiplication. In systems that, in the future, support an Ada binding to IEC 559:1989, the latter technique will not generate the required result when one of the components of the complex operand is infinite. (Explicit multiplication of the infinite component by the zero component obtained during promotion yields a NaN that propagates into the final result.) Analogous advice applies in the case of multiplication of a complex operand and a pure-imaginary operand, and in the case of division of a complex operand by a real or pure-imaginary operand."

Not followed.

"Similarly, because the usual mathematical meaning of addition of a complex operand and a real operand is that the imaginary operand remains unchanged, an implementation should not perform this operation by first promoting the real operand to complex type and then performing a full complex addition. In implementations in which the *Signed_Zeros* attribute of the component type is *True* (and which therefore conform to IEC 559:1989 in regard to the handling of the sign of zero in predefined arithmetic operations), the latter technique will not generate the required result when the imaginary component of the complex operand is a negatively signed zero. (Explicit addition of the negative zero to the zero obtained during promotion yields a positive zero.) Analogous advice applies in the case of addition of a complex operand and a pure-imaginary operand, and in the case of subtraction of a complex operand and a real or pure-imaginary operand."

Not followed.

"Implementations in which *Real'Signed_Zeros* is *True* should attempt to provide a rational treatment of the signs of zero results and result components. As one example, the result of the *Argument* function should have the sign of the imaginary component of the parameter *X* when the point represented by that parameter lies on the positive real axis; as another, the sign of the imaginary component of the *Compose_From_Polar* function should be the same as (respectively, the opposite of) that of the *Argument* parameter when that parameter has a value of zero and the *Modulus* parameter has a nonnegative (respectively, negative) value."

Followed.

6.61 RM G.1.2(49): Complex Elementary Functions

"Implementations in which *Complex_Types.Real'Signed_Zeros* is *True* should attempt to provide a rational treatment of the signs of zero results and result components. For example, many of the complex elementary functions have components that are odd functions of one of the parameter components; in these cases, the result component should have the sign of the parameter component at the origin. Other complex elementary functions have zero components whose sign is opposite that of a parameter component at the origin, or is always positive or always negative."

Followed.

6.62 RM G.2.4(19): Accuracy Requirements

"The versions of the forward trigonometric functions without a *Cycle* parameter should not be implemented by calling the corresponding version with a *Cycle* parameter of *2.0*Numerics.Pi*, since this will not provide the required accuracy in some portions of the domain. For the same reason, the version of *Log* without a *Base* parameter should not be implemented by calling the corresponding version with a *Base* parameter of *Numerics.e*."

Followed.

6.63 RM G.2.6(15): Complex Arithmetic Accuracy

"The version of the *Compose_From_Polar* function without a *Cycle* parameter should not be implemented by calling the corresponding version with a *Cycle* parameter of *2.0*Numerics.Pi*, since this will not provide the required accuracy in some portions of the domain."

Followed.

6.64 RM H.6(15/2): Pragma Partition_Elaboration_Policy

"If the partition elaboration policy is *Sequential* and the Environment task becomes permanently blocked during elaboration then the partition is deadlocked and it is recommended that the partition be immediately terminated."

Not followed.

7 Implementation Defined Characteristics

In addition to the implementation dependent pragmas and attributes, and the implementation advice, there are a number of other Ada features that are potentially implementation dependent and are designated as implementation-defined. These are mentioned throughout the Ada Reference Manual, and are summarized in Annex M.

A requirement for conforming Ada compilers is that they provide documentation describing how the implementation deals with each of these issues. In this chapter you will find each point in Annex M listed, followed by a description of how GNAT handles the implementation dependence.

You can use this chapter as a guide to minimizing implementation dependent features in your programs if portability to other compilers and other operating systems is an important consideration. The numbers in each entry below correspond to the paragraph numbers in the Ada Reference Manual.

* "Whether or not each recommendation given in Implementation Advice is followed. See 1.1.2(37)."

See [Implementation Advice], page 144.

* "Capacity limitations of the implementation. See 1.1.3(3)."

The complexity of programs that can be processed is limited only by the total amount of available virtual memory, and disk space for the generated object files.

* "Variations from the standard that are impractical to avoid given the implementation's execution environment. See 1.1.3(6)."

There are no variations from the standard.

* "Which code_statements cause external interactions. See 1.1.3(10)."

Any *code_statement* can potentially cause external interactions.

* "The coded representation for the text of an Ada program. See 2.1(4)."

See separate section on source representation.

* "The control functions allowed in comments. See 2.1(14)."

See separate section on source representation.

* "The representation for an end of line. See 2.2(2)."

See separate section on source representation.

* "Maximum supported line length and lexical element length. See 2.2(15)."

The maximum line length is 255 characters and the maximum length of a lexical element is also 255 characters. This is the default setting if not overridden by the use of compiler switch *-gnaty* (which sets the maximum to 79) or *-gnatyMnn* which allows the maximum line length to be specified to be any value up to 32767. The maximum length of a lexical element is the same as the maximum line length.

* "Implementation defined pragmas. See 2.8(14)."

See [Implementation Defined Pragmas], page 4.

* "Effect of pragma *Optimize*. See 2.8(27)."

Pragma *Optimize*, if given with a *Time* or *Space* parameter, checks that the optimization flag is set, and aborts if it is not.

* "The sequence of characters of the value returned by `S'Image` when some of the graphic characters of `S'Wide_Image` are not defined in *Character*. See 3.5(37)."

The sequence of characters is as defined by the wide character encoding method used for the source. See section on source representation for further details.

* "The predefined integer types declared in *Standard*. See 3.5.4(25)."

Type	**Representation**
Short_Short_Integer	8 bit signed
Short_Integer	(Short) 16 bit signed
Integer	32 bit signed
Long_Integer	64 bit signed (on most 64 bit targets, depending on the C definition of long). 32 bit signed (all other targets)
Long_Long_Integer	64 bit signed

* "Any nonstandard integer types and the operators defined for them. See 3.5.4(26)."

There are no nonstandard integer types.

* "Any nonstandard real types and the operators defined for them. See 3.5.6(8)."

There are no nonstandard real types.

* "What combinations of requested decimal precision and range are supported for floating point types. See 3.5.7(7)."

The precision and range is as defined by the IEEE standard.

* "The predefined floating point types declared in *Standard*. See 3.5.7(16)."

Type	**Representation**
Short_Float	32 bit IEEE short
Float	(Short) 32 bit IEEE short
Long_Float	64 bit IEEE long
Long_Long_Float	64 bit IEEE long (80 bit IEEE long on x86 processors)

* "The small of an ordinary fixed point type. See 3.5.9(8)."

Fine_Delta is 2**(-63)

* "What combinations of small, range, and digits are supported for fixed point types. See 3.5.9(10)."

Any combinations are permitted that do not result in a small less than *Fine_Delta* and do not result in a mantissa larger than 63 bits. If the mantissa is larger than 53 bits on machines where Long_Long_Float is 64 bits (true of all architectures except ia32), then the output from Text_IO is accurate to only 53 bits, rather than the full mantissa. This is because floating-point conversions are used to convert fixed point.

* "The result of *Tags.Expanded_Name* for types declared within an unnamed *block_statement*. See 3.9(10)."

Block numbers of the form *B'nnn'*, where *nnn* is a decimal integer are allocated.

* "Implementation-defined attributes. See 4.1.4(12)."

See [Implementation Defined Attributes], page 106.

* "Any implementation-defined time types. See 9.6(6)."

There are no implementation-defined time types.

* "The time base associated with relative delays."

See 9.6(20). The time base used is that provided by the C library function *gettimeofday*.

* "The time base of the type *Calendar.Time*. See 9.6(23)."

The time base used is that provided by the C library function *gettimeofday*.

* "The time zone used for package *Calendar* operations. See 9.6(24)."

The time zone used by package *Calendar* is the current system time zone setting for local time, as accessed by the C library function *localtime*.

* "Any limit on *delay_until_statements* of *select_statements*. See 9.6(29)."

There are no such limits.

* "Whether or not two non-overlapping parts of a composite object are independently addressable, in the case where packing, record layout, or *Component_Size* is specified for the object. See 9.10(1)."

Separate components are independently addressable if they do not share overlapping storage units.

* "The representation for a compilation. See 10.1(2)."

A compilation is represented by a sequence of files presented to the compiler in a single invocation of the *gcc* command.

* "Any restrictions on compilations that contain multiple compilation_units. See 10.1(4)."

No single file can contain more than one compilation unit, but any sequence of files can be presented to the compiler as a single compilation.

* "The mechanisms for creating an environment and for adding and replacing compilation units. See 10.1.4(3)."

See separate section on compilation model.

* "The manner of explicitly assigning library units to a partition. See 10.2(2)."

If a unit contains an Ada main program, then the Ada units for the partition are determined by recursive application of the rules in the Ada Reference Manual section 10.2(2-6). In other words, the Ada units will be those that are needed by the main program, and then this definition of need is applied recursively to those units, and the partition contains the transitive closure determined by this relationship. In short, all the necessary units are included, with no need to explicitly specify the list. If additional units are required, e.g., by foreign language units, then all units must be mentioned in the context clause of one of the needed Ada units.

If the partition contains no main program, or if the main program is in a language other than Ada, then GNAT provides the binder options *-z* and *-n* respectively, and in this case a list of units can be explicitly supplied to the binder for inclusion in the partition (all units needed by these units will also be included automatically). For full details on the use of these options, refer to the *GNAT Make Program gnatmake* in the *GNAT User's Guide*.

* "The implementation-defined means, if any, of specifying which compilation units are needed by a given compilation unit. See 10.2(2)."

The units needed by a given compilation unit are as defined in the Ada Reference Manual section 10.2(2-6). There are no implementation-defined pragmas or other implementation-defined means for specifying needed units.

* "The manner of designating the main subprogram of a partition. See 10.2(7)."

The main program is designated by providing the name of the corresponding `ALI` file as the input parameter to the binder.

* "The order of elaboration of *library_items*. See 10.2(18)."

The first constraint on ordering is that it meets the requirements of Chapter 10 of the Ada Reference Manual. This still leaves some implementation dependent choices, which are resolved by first elaborating bodies as early as possible (i.e., in preference to specs where there is a choice), and second by evaluating the immediate with clauses of a unit to determine the probably best choice, and third by elaborating in alphabetical order of unit names where a choice still remains.

* "Parameter passing and function return for the main subprogram. See 10.2(21)."

The main program has no parameters. It may be a procedure, or a function returning an integer type. In the latter case, the returned integer value is the return code of the program (overriding any value that may have been set by a call to *Ada.Command_Line.Set_Exit_Status*).

* "The mechanisms for building and running partitions. See 10.2(24)."

GNAT itself supports programs with only a single partition. The GNATDIST tool provided with the GLADE package (which also includes an implementation of the PCS) provides a completely flexible method for building and running programs consisting of multiple partitions. See the separate GLADE manual for details.

* "The details of program execution, including program termination. See 10.2(25)."

See separate section on compilation model.

* "The semantics of any non-active partitions supported by the implementation. See 10.2(28)."

Passive partitions are supported on targets where shared memory is provided by the operating system. See the GLADE reference manual for further details.

* "The information returned by *Exception_Message*. See 11.4.1(10)."

Exception message returns the null string unless a specific message has been passed by the program.

* "The result of *Exceptions.Exception_Name* for types declared within an unnamed *block_statement*. See 11.4.1(12)."

Blocks have implementation defined names of the form *B'nnn'* where *nnn* is an integer.

* "The information returned by *Exception_Information*. See 11.4.1(13)."

Exception_Information returns a string in the following format:

```
*Exception_Name:* nnnnn
*Message:* mmmmm
*PID:* ppp
*Load address:* 0xhhhh
*Call stack traceback locations:*
0xhhhh 0xhhhh 0xhhhh ... 0xhhh
```

where

* *nnnn* is the fully qualified name of the exception in all upper case letters. This line is always present.
* *mmmm* is the message (this line present only if message is non-null)
* *ppp* is the Process Id value as a decimal integer (this line is present only if the Process Id is nonzero). Currently we are not making use of this field.
* The Load address line, the Call stack traceback locations line and the following values are present only if at least one traceback location was recorded. The Load address indicates the address at which the main executable was loaded; this line may not be present if operating system hasn't relocated the main executable. The values are given in C style format, with lower case letters for a-f, and only as many digits present as are necessary. The line terminator sequence at the end of each line, including the last line is a single *LF* character (*16#0A#*).

* "Implementation-defined check names. See 11.5(27)."

The implementation defined check names include Alignment_Check, Atomic_Synchronization, Duplicated_Tag_Check, Container_Checks, Tampering_Check, Predicate_Check, and Validity_Check. In addition, a user program can add implementation-defined check names by means of the pragma Check_Name. See the description of pragma *Suppress* for full details.

* "The interpretation of each aspect of representation. See 13.1(20)."

See separate section on data representations.

* "Any restrictions placed upon representation items. See 13.1(20)."

See separate section on data representations.

* "The meaning of *Size* for indefinite subtypes. See 13.3(48)."

Size for an indefinite subtype is the maximum possible size, except that for the case of a subprogram parameter, the size of the parameter object is the actual size.

* "The default external representation for a type tag. See 13.3(75)."

The default external representation for a type tag is the fully expanded name of the type in upper case letters.

* "What determines whether a compilation unit is the same in two different partitions. See 13.3(76)."

A compilation unit is the same in two different partitions if and only if it derives from the same source file.

* "Implementation-defined components. See 13.5.1(15)."

The only implementation defined component is the tag for a tagged type, which contains a pointer to the dispatching table.

* "If *Word_Size* = *Storage_Unit*, the default bit ordering. See 13.5.3(5)."

Word_Size (32) is not the same as *Storage_Unit* (8) for this implementation, so no non-default bit ordering is supported. The default bit ordering corresponds to the natural endianness of the target architecture.

* "The contents of the visible part of package *System* and its language-defined children. See 13.7(2)."

See the definition of these packages in files `system.ads` and `s-stoele.ads`. Note that two declarations are added to package System.

```
Max_Priority           : constant Positive := Priority'Last;
Max_Interrupt_Priority : constant Positive := Interrupt_Priority'Last;
```

* "The contents of the visible part of package *System.Machine_Code*, and the meaning of *code_statements*. See 13.8(7)."

See the definition and documentation in file `s-maccod.ads`.

* "The effect of unchecked conversion. See 13.9(11)."

Unchecked conversion between types of the same size results in an uninterpreted transmission of the bits from one type to the other. If the types are of unequal sizes, then in the case of discrete types, a shorter source is first zero or sign extended as necessary, and a shorter target is simply truncated on the left. For all non-discrete types, the source is first copied if necessary to ensure that the alignment requirements of the target are met, then a pointer is constructed to the source value, and the result is obtained by dereferencing this pointer after converting it to be a pointer to the target type. Unchecked conversions where the target subtype is an unconstrained array are not permitted. If the target alignment is greater than the source alignment, then a copy of the result is made with appropriate alignment

* "The semantics of operations on invalid representations. See 13.9.2(10-11)."

For assignments and other operations where the use of invalid values cannot result in erroneous behavior, the compiler ignores the possibility of invalid values. An exception is raised at the point where an invalid value would result in erroneous behavior. For example executing:

```
procedure invalidvals is
  X : Integer := -1;
  Y : Natural range 1 .. 10;
  for Y'Address use X'Address;
  Z : Natural range 1 .. 10;
  A : array (Natural range 1 .. 10) of Integer;
begin
  Z := Y;      -- no exception
  A (Z) := 3; -- exception raised;
end;
```

As indicated, an exception is raised on the array assignment, but not on the simple assignment of the invalid negative value from Y to Z.

* "The manner of choosing a storage pool for an access type when *Storage_Pool* is not specified for the type. See 13.11(17)."

There are 3 different standard pools used by the compiler when *Storage_Pool* is not specified depending whether the type is local to a subprogram or defined at the library level and whether *Storage_Size'is specified or not. See documentation in the runtime library units 'System.Pool_Global*, *System.Pool_Size* and *System.Pool_Local* in files `s-poosiz.ads`, `s-pooglo.ads` and `s-pooloc.ads` for full details on the default pools used.

* "Whether or not the implementation provides user-accessible names for the standard pool type(s). See 13.11(17)."

See documentation in the sources of the run time mentioned in the previous paragraph. All these pools are accessible by means of *with*'ing these units.

* "The meaning of *Storage_Size*. See 13.11(18)."

Storage_Size is measured in storage units, and refers to the total space available for an access type collection, or to the primary stack space for a task.

* "Implementation-defined aspects of storage pools. See 13.11(22)."

See documentation in the sources of the run time mentioned in the paragraph about standard storage pools above for details on GNAT-defined aspects of storage pools.

* "The set of restrictions allowed in a pragma *Restrictions*. See 13.12(7)."

See [Standard and Implementation Defined Restrictions], page 127.

* "The consequences of violating limitations on *Restrictions* pragmas. See 13.12(9)."

Restrictions that can be checked at compile time result in illegalities if violated. Currently there are no other consequences of violating restrictions.

* "The representation used by the *Read* and *Write* attributes of elementary types in terms of stream elements. See 13.13.2(9)."

The representation is the in-memory representation of the base type of the type, using the number of bits corresponding to the `type'Size` value, and the natural ordering of the machine.

* "The names and characteristics of the numeric subtypes declared in the visible part of package *Standard*. See A.1(3)."

See items describing the integer and floating-point types supported.

* "The string returned by *Character_Set_Version*. See A.3.5(3)."

Ada.Wide_Characters.Handling.Character_Set_Version returns the string "Unicode 4.0", referring to version 4.0 of the Unicode specification.

* "The accuracy actually achieved by the elementary functions. See A.5.1(1)."

The elementary functions correspond to the functions available in the C library. Only fast math mode is implemented.

* "The sign of a zero result from some of the operators or functions in *Numerics.Generic_Elementary_Functions*, when *Float_Type'Signed_Zeros* is *True*. See A.5.1(46)."

The sign of zeroes follows the requirements of the IEEE 754 standard on floating-point.

* "The value of *Numerics.Float_Random.Max_Image_Width*. See A.5.2(27)."

Maximum image width is 6864, see library file `s-rannum.ads`.

* "The value of *Numerics.Discrete_Random.Max_Image_Width*. See A.5.2(27)."

Maximum image width is 6864, see library file `s-rannum.ads`.

* "The algorithms for random number generation. See A.5.2(32)."

The algorithm is the Mersenne Twister, as documented in the source file `s-rannum.adb`. This version of the algorithm has a period of 2**19937-1.

* "The string representation of a random number generator's state. See A.5.2(38)."

The value returned by the Image function is the concatenation of the fixed-width decimal representations of the 624 32-bit integers of the state vector.

* "The minimum time interval between calls to the time-dependent Reset procedure that are guaranteed to initiate different random number sequences. See A.5.2(45)."

The minimum period between reset calls to guarantee distinct series of random numbers is one microsecond.

* "The values of the *Model_Mantissa*, *Model_Emin*, *Model_Epsilon*, *Model*, *Safe_First*, and *Safe_Last* attributes, if the Numerics Annex is not supported. See A.5.3(72)."

Run the compiler with *-gnatS* to produce a listing of package *Standard*, has the values of all numeric attributes.

* "Any implementation-defined characteristics of the input-output packages. See A.7(14)."

There are no special implementation defined characteristics for these packages.

* "The value of *Buffer_Size* in *Storage_IO*. See A.9(10)."

All type representations are contiguous, and the *Buffer_Size* is the value of `type'Size` rounded up to the next storage unit boundary.

* "External files for standard input, standard output, and standard error See A.10(5)."

These files are mapped onto the files provided by the C streams libraries. See source file `i-cstrea.ads` for further details.

* "The accuracy of the value produced by *Put*. See A.10.9(36)."

If more digits are requested in the output than are represented by the precision of the value, zeroes are output in the corresponding least significant digit positions.

* "The meaning of *Argument_Count*, *Argument*, and *Command_Name*. See A.15(1)."

These are mapped onto the *argv* and *argc* parameters of the main program in the natural manner.

* "The interpretation of the *Form* parameter in procedure *Create_Directory*. See A.16(56)."

The *Form* parameter is not used.

* "The interpretation of the *Form* parameter in procedure *Create_Path*. See A.16(60)."

The *Form* parameter is not used.

* "The interpretation of the *Form* parameter in procedure *Copy_File*. See A.16(68)."

The *Form* parameter is case-insensitive. Two fields are recognized in the *Form* parameter:

```
*preserve=<value>*
*mode=<value>*
```

<value> starts immediately after the character '=' and ends with the character immediately preceding the next comma (',') or with the last character of the parameter.

The only possible values for preserve= are:

Value	**Meaning**
no_attributes	Do not try to preserve any file attributes. This is the default if no pres found in Form.
all_attributes	Try to preserve all file attributes (timestamps, access rights).
timestamps	Preserve the timestamp of the copied file, but not the other file attributes

The only possible values for mode= are:

Value	**Meaning**
copy	Only do the copy if the destination file does not already exist. If it already exis
overwrite	Copy the file in all cases. Overwrite an already existing destination file.
append	Append the original file to the destination file. If the destination file does not ex file is a copy of the source file. When mode=append, the field preserve=, if it e into account.

If the Form parameter includes one or both of the fields and the value or values are incorrect, Copy_file fails with Use_Error.

Examples of correct Forms:

```
Form => "preserve=no_attributes,mode=overwrite" (the default)
Form => "mode=append"
Form => "mode=copy, preserve=all_attributes"
```

Examples of incorrect Forms:

```
Form => "preserve=junk"
Form => "mode=internal, preserve=timestamps"
```

* "The interpretation of the *Pattern* parameter, when not the null string, in the *Start_Search* and *Search* procedures. See A.16(104) and A.16(112)."

When the *Pattern* parameter is not the null string, it is interpreted according to the syntax of regular expressions as defined in the *GNAT.Regexp* package.

See [GNAT.Regexp (g-regexp.ads)], page 256.

* "Implementation-defined convention names. See B.1(11)."

The following convention names are supported

Convention Name	**Interpretation**
Ada	Ada
Ada_Pass_By_Copy	Allowed for any types except by-reference types such as limited records. vention Ada, but causes any parameters with this convention to be passed
Ada_Pass_By_Reference	Allowed for any types except by-copy types such as scalars. Compatible but causes any parameters with this convention to be passed by reference.
Assembler	Assembly language
Asm	Synonym for Assembler
Assembly	Synonym for Assembler
C	C
C_Pass_By_Copy	Allowed only for record types, like C, but also notes that record is to be than reference.
COBOL	COBOL
C_Plus_Plus (or CPP)	C++
Default	Treated the same as C
External	Treated the same as C
Fortran	Fortran

Intrinsic For support of pragma *Import* with convention Intrinsic, see separa programs.

Stdcall Stdcall (used for Windows implementations only). This convention (previously called Pascal convention) C/C++ convention under Win convention cleans the stack before exit. This pragma cannot be applie

DLL Synonym for Stdcall

Win32 Synonym for Stdcall

Stubbed Stubbed is a special convention used to indicate that the body of the ignored. Any call to the subprogram is converted into a raise of the *Pr* pragma *Import* specifies convention *stubbed* then no body need be pre is useful during development for the inclusion of subprograms whose bo In addition, all otherwise unrecognized convention names are also tr with convention C. In all implementations except for VMS, use of su warning. In VMS implementations, these names are accepted silently.

* "The meaning of link names. See B.1(36)."

Link names are the actual names used by the linker.

* "The manner of choosing link names when neither the link name nor the address of an imported or exported entity is specified. See B.1(36)."

The default linker name is that which would be assigned by the relevant external language, interpreting the Ada name as being in all lower case letters.

* "The effect of pragma *Linker_Options*. See B.1(37)."

The string passed to *Linker_Options* is presented uninterpreted as an argument to the link command, unless it contains ASCII.NUL characters. NUL characters if they appear act as argument separators, so for example

```
pragma Linker_Options ("-labc" & ASCII.NUL & "-ldef");
```

causes two separate arguments *-labc* and *-ldef* to be passed to the linker. The order of linker options is preserved for a given unit. The final list of options passed to the linker is in reverse order of the elaboration order. For example, linker options for a body always appear before the options from the corresponding package spec.

* "The contents of the visible part of package *Interfaces* and its language-defined descendants. See B.2(1)."

See files with prefix `i-` in the distributed library.

* "Implementation-defined children of package *Interfaces*. The contents of the visible part of package *Interfaces*. See B.2(11)."

See files with prefix `i-` in the distributed library.

* "The types *Floating*, *Long_Floating*, *Binary*, *Long_Binary*, *Decimal_ Element*, and *COBOL_Character*; and the initialization of the variables *Ada_To_COBOL* and *COBOL_To_Ada*, in *Interfaces.COBOL*. See B.4(50)."

COBOL	**Ada**
Floating	Float
Long_Floating	(Floating) Long_Float
Binary	Integer
Long_Binary	Long_Long_Integer
Decimal_Element	Character
COBOL_Character	Character

For initialization, see the file `i-cobol.ads` in the distributed library.

* "Support for access to machine instructions. See C.1(1)."

See documentation in file `s-maccod.ads` in the distributed library.

* "Implementation-defined aspects of access to machine operations. See C.1(9)."

See documentation in file `s-maccod.ads` in the distributed library.

* "Implementation-defined aspects of interrupts. See C.3(2)."

Interrupts are mapped to signals or conditions as appropriate. See definition of unit *Ada.Interrupt_Names* in source file `a-intnam.ads` for details on the interrupts supported on a particular target.

* "Implementation-defined aspects of pre-elaboration. See C.4(13)."

GNAT does not permit a partition to be restarted without reloading, except under control of the debugger.

* "The semantics of pragma *Discard_Names*. See C.5(7)."

Pragma *Discard_Names* causes names of enumeration literals to be suppressed. In the presence of this pragma, the Image attribute provides the image of the Pos of the literal, and Value accepts Pos values.

* "The result of the *Task_Identification.Image* attribute. See C.7.1(7)."

The result of this attribute is a string that identifies the object or component that denotes a given task. If a variable *Var* has a task type, the image for this task will have the form *Var_'XXXXXXXX'*, where the suffix is the hexadecimal representation of the virtual address of the corresponding task control block. If the variable is an array of tasks, the image of each task will have the form of an indexed component indicating the position of a given task in the array, e.g., *Group(5)_'XXXXXXX'*. If the task is a component of a record, the image of the task will have the form of a selected component. These rules are fully recursive, so that the image of a task that is a subcomponent of a composite object corresponds to the expression that designates this task.

If a task is created by an allocator, its image depends on the context. If the allocator is part of an object declaration, the rules described above are used to construct its image, and this image is not affected by subsequent assignments. If the allocator appears within an expression, the image includes only the name of the task type.

If the configuration pragma Discard_Names is present, or if the restriction No_Implicit_Heap_Allocation is in effect, the image reduces to the numeric suffix, that is to say the hexadecimal representation of the virtual address of the control block of the task.

* "The value of *Current_Task* when in a protected entry or interrupt handler. See C.7.1(17)."

Protected entries or interrupt handlers can be executed by any convenient thread, so the value of *Current_Task* is undefined.

* "The effect of calling *Current_Task* from an entry body or interrupt handler. See C.7.1(19)."

The effect of calling *Current_Task* from an entry body or interrupt handler is to return the identification of the task currently executing the code.

* "Implementation-defined aspects of *Task_Attributes*. See C.7.2(19)."

There are no implementation-defined aspects of *Task_Attributes*.

* "Values of all *Metrics*. See D(2)."

The metrics information for GNAT depends on the performance of the underlying operating system. The sources of the run-time for tasking implementation, together with the output from *-gnatG* can be used to determine the exact sequence of operating systems calls made to implement various tasking constructs. Together with appropriate information on the performance of the underlying operating system, on the exact target in use, this information can be used to determine the required metrics.

* "The declarations of *Any_Priority* and *Priority*. See D.1(11)."

See declarations in file `system.ads`.

* "Implementation-defined execution resources. See D.1(15)."

There are no implementation-defined execution resources.

* "Whether, on a multiprocessor, a task that is waiting for access to a protected object keeps its processor busy. See D.2.1(3)."

On a multi-processor, a task that is waiting for access to a protected object does not keep its processor busy.

* "The affect of implementation defined execution resources on task dispatching. See D.2.1(9)."

Tasks map to threads in the threads package used by GNAT. Where possible and appropriate, these threads correspond to native threads of the underlying operating system.

* "Implementation-defined *policy_identifiers* allowed in a pragma *Task_Dispatching_Policy*. See D.2.2(3)."

There are no implementation-defined policy-identifiers allowed in this pragma.

* "Implementation-defined aspects of priority inversion. See D.2.2(16)."

Execution of a task cannot be preempted by the implementation processing of delay expirations for lower priority tasks.

* "Implementation-defined task dispatching. See D.2.2(18)."

The policy is the same as that of the underlying threads implementation.

* "Implementation-defined *policy_identifiers* allowed in a pragma *Locking_Policy*. See D.3(4)."

The two implementation defined policies permitted in GNAT are *Inheritance_Locking* and *Conccurent_Readers_Locking*. On targets that support the *Inheritance_Locking* policy, locking is implemented by inheritance, i.e., the task owning the lock operates at a priority equal to the highest priority of any task currently requesting the lock. On targets that support the *Conccurent_Readers_Locking* policy, locking is implemented with a read/write lock allowing multiple propected object functions to enter concurrently.

* "Default ceiling priorities. See D.3(10)."

The ceiling priority of protected objects of the type *System.Interrupt_Priority'Last* as described in the Ada Reference Manual D.3(10),

* "The ceiling of any protected object used internally by the implementation. See D.3(16)."

The ceiling priority of internal protected objects is *System.Priority'Last*.

* "Implementation-defined queuing policies. See D.4(1)."

There are no implementation-defined queuing policies.

* "On a multiprocessor, any conditions that cause the completion of an aborted construct to be delayed later than what is specified for a single processor. See D.6(3)."

The semantics for abort on a multi-processor is the same as on a single processor, there are no further delays.

* "Any operations that implicitly require heap storage allocation. See D.7(8)."

The only operation that implicitly requires heap storage allocation is task creation.

* "What happens when a task terminates in the presence of pragma *No_Task_Termination*. See D.7(15)."

Execution is erroneous in that case.

* "Implementation-defined aspects of pragma *Restrictions*. See D.7(20)."

There are no such implementation-defined aspects.

* "Implementation-defined aspects of package *Real_Time*. See D.8(17)."

There are no implementation defined aspects of package *Real_Time*.

* "Implementation-defined aspects of *delay_statements*. See D.9(8)."

Any difference greater than one microsecond will cause the task to be delayed (see D.9(7)).

* "The upper bound on the duration of interrupt blocking caused by the implementation. See D.12(5)."

The upper bound is determined by the underlying operating system. In no cases is it more than 10 milliseconds.

* "The means for creating and executing distributed programs. See E(5)."

The GLADE package provides a utility GNATDIST for creating and executing distributed programs. See the GLADE reference manual for further details.

* "Any events that can result in a partition becoming inaccessible. See E.1(7)."

See the GLADE reference manual for full details on such events.

* "The scheduling policies, treatment of priorities, and management of shared resources between partitions in certain cases. See E.1(11)."

See the GLADE reference manual for full details on these aspects of multi-partition execution.

* "Events that cause the version of a compilation unit to change. See E.3(5)."

Editing the source file of a compilation unit, or the source files of any units on which it is dependent in a significant way cause the version to change. No other actions cause the version number to change. All changes are significant except those which affect only layout, capitalization or comments.

* "Whether the execution of the remote subprogram is immediately aborted as a result of cancellation. See E.4(13)."

See the GLADE reference manual for details on the effect of abort in a distributed application.

* "Implementation-defined aspects of the PCS. See E.5(25)."

See the GLADE reference manual for a full description of all implementation defined aspects of the PCS.

* "Implementation-defined interfaces in the PCS. See E.5(26)."

See the GLADE reference manual for a full description of all implementation defined interfaces.

* "The values of named numbers in the package *Decimal*. See F.2(7)."

Named Number	**Value**
Max_Scale	+18
Min_Scale	-18
Min_Delta	1.0E-18
Max_Delta	1.0E+18
Max_Decimal_Digits	18

* "The value of *Max_Picture_Length* in the package *Text_IO.Editing*. See F.3.3(16)."

64

* "The value of *Max_Picture_Length* in the package *Wide_Text_IO.Editing*. See F.3.4(5)."

64

* "The accuracy actually achieved by the complex elementary functions and by other complex arithmetic operations. See G.1(1)."

Standard library functions are used for the complex arithmetic operations. Only fast math mode is currently supported.

* "The sign of a zero result (or a component thereof) from any operator or function in *Numerics.Generic_Complex_Types*, when *Real'Signed_Zeros* is True. See G.1.1(53)."

The signs of zero values are as recommended by the relevant implementation advice.

* "The sign of a zero result (or a component thereof) from any operator or function in *Numerics.Generic_Complex_Elementary_Functions*, when *Real'Signed_Zeros* is *True*. See G.1.2(45)."

The signs of zero values are as recommended by the relevant implementation advice.

* "Whether the strict mode or the relaxed mode is the default. See G.2(2)."

The strict mode is the default. There is no separate relaxed mode. GNAT provides a highly efficient implementation of strict mode.

* "The result interval in certain cases of fixed-to-float conversion. See G.2.1(10)."

For cases where the result interval is implementation dependent, the accuracy is that provided by performing all operations in 64-bit IEEE floating-point format.

* "The result of a floating point arithmetic operation in overflow situations, when the *Machine_Overflows* attribute of the result type is *False*. See G.2.1(13)."

Infinite and NaN values are produced as dictated by the IEEE floating-point standard. Note that on machines that are not fully compliant with the IEEE floating-point standard, such as Alpha, the *-mieee* compiler flag must be used for achieving IEEE conforming behavior (although at the cost of a significant performance penalty), so infinite and NaN values are properly generated.

* "The result interval for division (or exponentiation by a negative exponent), when the floating point hardware implements division as multiplication by a reciprocal. See G.2.1(16)."

Not relevant, division is IEEE exact.

* "The definition of close result set, which determines the accuracy of certain fixed point multiplications and divisions. See G.2.3(5)."

Operations in the close result set are performed using IEEE long format floating-point arithmetic. The input operands are converted to floating-point, the operation is done in floating-point, and the result is converted to the target type.

* "Conditions on a *universal_real* operand of a fixed point multiplication or division for which the result shall be in the perfect result set. See G.2.3(22)."

The result is only defined to be in the perfect result set if the result can be computed by a single scaling operation involving a scale factor representable in 64-bits.

* "The result of a fixed point arithmetic operation in overflow situations, when the *Machine_Overflows* attribute of the result type is *False*. See G.2.3(27)."

Not relevant, *Machine_Overflows* is *True* for fixed-point types.

* "The result of an elementary function reference in overflow situations, when the *Machine_Overflows* attribute of the result type is *False*. See G.2.4(4)."

IEEE infinite and Nan values are produced as appropriate.

* "The value of the angle threshold, within which certain elementary functions, complex arithmetic operations, and complex elementary functions yield results conforming to a maximum relative error bound. See G.2.4(10)."

Information on this subject is not yet available.

* "The accuracy of certain elementary functions for parameters beyond the angle threshold. See G.2.4(10)."

Information on this subject is not yet available.

* "The result of a complex arithmetic operation or complex elementary function reference in overflow situations, when the *Machine_Overflows* attribute of the corresponding real type is *False*. See G.2.6(5)."

IEEE infinite and Nan values are produced as appropriate.

* "The accuracy of certain complex arithmetic operations and certain complex elementary functions for parameters (or components thereof) beyond the angle threshold. See G.2.6(8)."

Information on those subjects is not yet available.

* "Information regarding bounded errors and erroneous execution. See H.2(1)."

Information on this subject is not yet available.

* "Implementation-defined aspects of pragma *Inspection_Point*. See H.3.2(8)."

Pragma *Inspection_Point* ensures that the variable is live and can be examined by the debugger at the inspection point.

* "Implementation-defined aspects of pragma *Restrictions*. See H.4(25)."

There are no implementation-defined aspects of pragma *Restrictions*. The use of pragma *Restrictions [No_Exceptions]* has no effect on the generated code. Checks must suppressed by use of pragma *Suppress*.

* "Any restrictions on pragma *Restrictions*. See H.4(27)."

There are no restrictions on pragma *Restrictions*.

8 Intrinsic Subprograms

GNAT allows a user application program to write the declaration:

```
pragma Import (Intrinsic, name);
```

providing that the name corresponds to one of the implemented intrinsic subprograms in GNAT, and that the parameter profile of the referenced subprogram meets the requirements. This chapter describes the set of implemented intrinsic subprograms, and the requirements on parameter profiles. Note that no body is supplied; as with other uses of pragma Import, the body is supplied elsewhere (in this case by the compiler itself). Note that any use of this feature is potentially non-portable, since the Ada standard does not require Ada compilers to implement this feature.

8.1 Intrinsic Operators

All the predefined numeric operators in package Standard in *pragma Import (Intrinsic,..)* declarations. In the binary operator case, the operands must have the same size. The operand or operands must also be appropriate for the operator. For example, for addition, the operands must both be floating-point or both be fixed-point, and the right operand for "**" must have a root type of *Standard.Integer'Base*. You can use an intrinsic operator declaration as in the following example:

```
type Int1 is new Integer;
type Int2 is new Integer;

function "+" (X1 : Int1; X2 : Int2) return Int1;
function "+" (X1 : Int1; X2 : Int2) return Int2;
pragma Import (Intrinsic, "+");
```

This declaration would permit 'mixed mode' arithmetic on items of the differing types *Int1* and *Int2*. It is also possible to specify such operators for private types, if the full views are appropriate arithmetic types.

8.2 Compilation_Date

This intrinsic subprogram is used in the implementation of the library package *GNAT.Source_Info*. The only useful use of the intrinsic import in this case is the one in this unit, so an application program should simply call the function *GNAT.Source_Info.Compilation_Date* to obtain the date of the current compilation (in local time format MMM DD YYYY).

8.3 Compilation_Time

This intrinsic subprogram is used in the implementation of the library package *GNAT.Source_Info*. The only useful use of the intrinsic import in this case is the one in this unit, so an application program should simply call the function *GNAT.Source_Info.Compilation_Time* to obtain the time of the current compilation (in local time format HH:MM:SS).

8.4 Enclosing_Entity

This intrinsic subprogram is used in the implementation of the library package *GNAT.Source_Info*. The only useful use of the intrinsic import in this case is the one in this unit, so an application program should simply call the function *GNAT.Source_Info.Enclosing_Entity* to obtain the name of the current subprogram, package, task, entry, or protected subprogram.

8.5 Exception_Information

This intrinsic subprogram is used in the implementation of the library package *GNAT.Current_Exception*. The only useful use of the intrinsic import in this case is the one in this unit, so an application program should simply call the function *GNAT.Current_Exception.Exception_Information* to obtain the exception information associated with the current exception.

8.6 Exception_Message

This intrinsic subprogram is used in the implementation of the library package *GNAT.Current_Exception*. The only useful use of the intrinsic import in this case is the one in this unit, so an application program should simply call the function *GNAT.Current_Exception.Exception_Message* to obtain the message associated with the current exception.

8.7 Exception_Name

This intrinsic subprogram is used in the implementation of the library package *GNAT.Current_Exception*. The only useful use of the intrinsic import in this case is the one in this unit, so an application program should simply call the function *GNAT.Current_Exception.Exception_Name* to obtain the name of the current exception.

8.8 File

This intrinsic subprogram is used in the implementation of the library package *GNAT.Source_Info*. The only useful use of the intrinsic import in this case is the one in this unit, so an application program should simply call the function *GNAT.Source_Info.File* to obtain the name of the current file.

8.9 Line

This intrinsic subprogram is used in the implementation of the library package *GNAT.Source_Info*. The only useful use of the intrinsic import in this case is the one in this unit, so an application program should simply call the function *GNAT.Source_Info.Line* to obtain the number of the current source line.

8.10 Shifts and Rotates

In standard Ada, the shift and rotate functions are available only for the predefined modular types in package *Interfaces*. However, in GNAT it is possible to define these functions for any integer type (signed or modular), as in this example:

```
function Shift_Left
  (Value  : T;
   Amount : Natural) return T;
```

The function name must be one of Shift_Left, Shift_Right, Shift_Right_Arithmetic, Rotate_Left, or Rotate_Right. T must be an integer type. T'Size must be 8, 16, 32 or 64 bits; if T is modular, the modulus must be 2**8, 2**16, 2**32 or 2**64. The result type must be the same as the type of *Value*. The shift amount must be Natural. The formal parameter names can be anything.

A more convenient way of providing these shift operators is to use the Provide_Shift_Operators pragma, which provides the function declarations and corresponding pragma Import's for all five shift functions.

8.11 Source_Location

This intrinsic subprogram is used in the implementation of the library routine *GNAT.Source_Info.* The only useful use of the intrinsic import in this case is the one in this unit, so an application program should simply call the function *GNAT.Source_Info.Source_Location* to obtain the current source file location.

9 Representation Clauses and Pragmas

This section describes the representation clauses accepted by GNAT, and their effect on the representation of corresponding data objects.

GNAT fully implements Annex C (Systems Programming). This means that all the implementation advice sections in chapter 13 are fully implemented. However, these sections only require a minimal level of support for representation clauses. GNAT provides much more extensive capabilities, and this section describes the additional capabilities provided.

9.1 Alignment Clauses

GNAT requires that all alignment clauses specify a power of 2, and all default alignments are always a power of 2. The default alignment values are as follows:

* *Primitive Types.*

  For primitive types, the alignment is the minimum of the actual size of objects of the type divided by *Storage_Unit*, and the maximum alignment supported by the target. (This maximum alignment is given by the GNAT-specific attribute *Standard'Maximum_Alignment*; see [Attribute Maximum_Alignment], page 114.)

  For example, for type *Long_Float*, the object size is 8 bytes, and the default alignment will be 8 on any target that supports alignments this large, but on some targets, the maximum alignment may be smaller than 8, in which case objects of type *Long_Float* will be maximally aligned.

* *Arrays.*

  For arrays, the alignment is equal to the alignment of the component type for the normal case where no packing or component size is given. If the array is packed, and the packing is effective (see separate section on packed arrays), then the alignment will be one for long packed arrays, or arrays whose length is not known at compile time. For short packed arrays, which are handled internally as modular types, the alignment will be as described for primitive types, e.g., a packed array of length 31 bits will have an object size of four bytes, and an alignment of 4.

* *Records.*

  For the normal non-packed case, the alignment of a record is equal to the maximum alignment of any of its components. For tagged records, this includes the implicit access type used for the tag. If a pragma *Pack* is used and all components are packable (see separate section on pragma *Pack*), then the resulting alignment is 1, unless the layout of the record makes it profitable to increase it.

  A special case is when:

  * the size of the record is given explicitly, or a full record representation clause is given, and
  * the size of the record is 2, 4, or 8 bytes.

  In this case, an alignment is chosen to match the size of the record. For example, if we have:

  ```
  type Small is record
     A, B : Character;
  ```

```
end record;
for Small'Size use 16;
```

then the default alignment of the record type *Small* is 2, not 1. This leads to more efficient code when the record is treated as a unit, and also allows the type to specified as *Atomic* on architectures requiring strict alignment.

An alignment clause may specify a larger alignment than the default value up to some maximum value dependent on the target (obtainable by using the attribute reference *Standard'Maximum_Alignment*). It may also specify a smaller alignment than the default value for enumeration, integer and fixed point types, as well as for record types, for example

```
type V is record
   A : Integer;
end record;

for V'alignment use 1;
```

The default alignment for the type *V* is 4, as a result of the Integer field in the record, but it is permissible, as shown, to override the default alignment of the record with a smaller value.

Note that according to the Ada standard, an alignment clause applies only to the first named subtype. If additional subtypes are declared, then the compiler is allowed to choose any alignment it likes, and there is no way to control this choice. Consider:

```
type R is range 1 .. 10_000;
for R'Alignment use 1;
subtype RS is R range 1 .. 1000;
```

The alignment clause specifies an alignment of 1 for the first named subtype *R* but this does not necessarily apply to *RS*. When writing portable Ada code, you should avoid writing code that explicitly or implicitly relies on the alignment of such subtypes.

For the GNAT compiler, if an explicit alignment clause is given, this value is also used for any subsequent subtypes. So for GNAT, in the above example, you can count on the alignment of *RS* being 1. But this assumption is non-portable, and other compilers may choose different alignments for the subtype *RS*.

9.2 Size Clauses

The default size for a type *T* is obtainable through the language-defined attribute *T'Size* and also through the equivalent GNAT-defined attribute *T'Value_Size*. For objects of type *T*, GNAT will generally increase the type size so that the object size (obtainable through the GNAT-defined attribute *T'Object_Size*) is a multiple of *T'Alignment* * *Storage_Unit*.

For example:

```
type Smallint is range 1 .. 6;

type Rec is record
   Y1 : integer;
   Y2 : boolean;
end record;
```

In this example, *Smallint'Size* = *Smallint'Value_Size* = 3, as specified by the RM rules, but objects of this type will have a size of 8 (*Smallint'Object_Size* = 8), since objects by default occupy an integral number of storage units. On some targets, notably older versions of the Digital Alpha, the size of stand alone objects of this type may be 32, reflecting the inability of the hardware to do byte load/stores.

Similarly, the size of type *Rec* is 40 bits (*Rec'Size* = *Rec'Value_Size* = 40), but the alignment is 4, so objects of this type will have their size increased to 64 bits so that it is a multiple of the alignment (in bits). This decision is in accordance with the specific Implementation Advice in RM 13.3(43):

> "A *Size* clause should be supported for an object if the specified *Size* is at least as large as its subtype's *Size*, and corresponds to a size in storage elements that is a multiple of the object's *Alignment* (if the *Alignment* is nonzero)."

An explicit size clause may be used to override the default size by increasing it. For example, if we have:

```
type My_Boolean is new Boolean;
for My_Boolean'Size use 32;
```

then values of this type will always be 32 bits long. In the case of discrete types, the size can be increased up to 64 bits, with the effect that the entire specified field is used to hold the value, sign- or zero-extended as appropriate. If more than 64 bits is specified, then padding space is allocated after the value, and a warning is issued that there are unused bits.

Similarly the size of records and arrays may be increased, and the effect is to add padding bits after the value. This also causes a warning message to be generated.

The largest Size value permitted in GNAT is 2**31-1. Since this is a Size in bits, this corresponds to an object of size 256 megabytes (minus one). This limitation is true on all targets. The reason for this limitation is that it improves the quality of the code in many cases if it is known that a Size value can be accommodated in an object of type Integer.

9.3 Storage_Size Clauses

For tasks, the *Storage_Size* clause specifies the amount of space to be allocated for the task stack. This cannot be extended, and if the stack is exhausted, then *Storage_Error* will be raised (if stack checking is enabled). Use a *Storage_Size* attribute definition clause, or a *Storage_Size* pragma in the task definition to set the appropriate required size. A useful technique is to include in every task definition a pragma of the form:

```
pragma Storage_Size (Default_Stack_Size);
```

Then *Default_Stack_Size* can be defined in a global package, and modified as required. Any tasks requiring stack sizes different from the default can have an appropriate alternative reference in the pragma.

You can also use the *-d* binder switch to modify the default stack size.

For access types, the *Storage_Size* clause specifies the maximum space available for allocation of objects of the type. If this space is exceeded then *Storage_Error* will be raised by an allocation attempt. In the case where the access type is declared local to a subprogram, the use of a *Storage_Size* clause triggers automatic use of a special predefined storage pool

(*System.Pool_Size*) that ensures that all space for the pool is automatically reclaimed on exit from the scope in which the type is declared.

A special case recognized by the compiler is the specification of a *Storage_Size* of zero for an access type. This means that no items can be allocated from the pool, and this is recognized at compile time, and all the overhead normally associated with maintaining a fixed size storage pool is eliminated. Consider the following example:

```
procedure p is
   type R is array (Natural) of Character;
   type P is access all R;
   for P'Storage_Size use 0;
   --  Above access type intended only for interfacing purposes

   y : P;

   procedure g (m : P);
   pragma Import (C, g);

   --  ...

begin
   --  ...
   y := new R;
end;
```

As indicated in this example, these dummy storage pools are often useful in connection with interfacing where no object will ever be allocated. If you compile the above example, you get the warning:

```
p.adb:16:09: warning: allocation from empty storage pool
p.adb:16:09: warning: Storage_Error will be raised at run time
```

Of course in practice, there will not be any explicit allocators in the case of such an access declaration.

9.4 Size of Variant Record Objects

In the case of variant record objects, there is a question whether Size gives information about a particular variant, or the maximum size required for any variant. Consider the following program

```
with Text_IO; use Text_IO;
procedure q is
   type R1 (A : Boolean := False) is record
     case A is
       when True  => X : Character;
       when False => null;
     end case;
   end record;

   V1 : R1 (False);
```

```
   V2 : R1;

begin
   Put_Line (Integer'Image (V1'Size));
   Put_Line (Integer'Image (V2'Size));
end q;
```

Here we are dealing with a variant record, where the True variant requires 16 bits, and the False variant requires 8 bits. In the above example, both V1 and V2 contain the False variant, which is only 8 bits long. However, the result of running the program is:

```
8
16
```

The reason for the difference here is that the discriminant value of V1 is fixed, and will always be False. It is not possible to assign a True variant value to V1, therefore 8 bits is sufficient. On the other hand, in the case of V2, the initial discriminant value is False (from the default), but it is possible to assign a True variant value to V2, therefore 16 bits must be allocated for V2 in the general case, even fewer bits may be needed at any particular point during the program execution.

As can be seen from the output of this program, the *'Size* attribute applied to such an object in GNAT gives the actual allocated size of the variable, which is the largest size of any of the variants. The Ada Reference Manual is not completely clear on what choice should be made here, but the GNAT behavior seems most consistent with the language in the RM.

In some cases, it may be desirable to obtain the size of the current variant, rather than the size of the largest variant. This can be achieved in GNAT by making use of the fact that in the case of a subprogram parameter, GNAT does indeed return the size of the current variant (because a subprogram has no way of knowing how much space is actually allocated for the actual).

Consider the following modified version of the above program:

```
with Text_IO; use Text_IO;
procedure q is
   type R1 (A : Boolean := False) is record
     case A is
       when True  => X : Character;
       when False => null;
     end case;
   end record;

   V2 : R1;

   function Size (V : R1) return Integer is
   begin
      return V'Size;
   end Size;

begin
```

```
      Put_Line (Integer'Image (V2'Size));
      Put_Line (Integer'Image (Size (V2)));
      V2 := (True, 'x');
      Put_Line (Integer'Image (V2'Size));
      Put_Line (Integer'Image (Size (V2)));
   end q;
```

The output from this program is

```
16
8
16
16
```

Here we see that while the *'Size* attribute always returns the maximum size, regardless of the current variant value, the *Size* function does indeed return the size of the current variant value.

9.5 Biased Representation

In the case of scalars with a range starting at other than zero, it is possible in some cases to specify a size smaller than the default minimum value, and in such cases, GNAT uses an unsigned biased representation, in which zero is used to represent the lower bound, and successive values represent successive values of the type.

For example, suppose we have the declaration:

```
type Small is range -7 .. -4;
for Small'Size use 2;
```

Although the default size of type *Small* is 4, the *Size* clause is accepted by GNAT and results in the following representation scheme:

```
-7 is represented as 2#00#
-6 is represented as 2#01#
-5 is represented as 2#10#
-4 is represented as 2#11#
```

Biased representation is only used if the specified *Size* clause cannot be accepted in any other manner. These reduced sizes that force biased representation can be used for all discrete types except for enumeration types for which a representation clause is given.

9.6 Value_Size and Object_Size Clauses

In Ada 95 and Ada 2005, *T'Size* for a type *T* is the minimum number of bits required to hold values of type *T*. Although this interpretation was allowed in Ada 83, it was not required, and this requirement in practice can cause some significant difficulties. For example, in most Ada 83 compilers, *Natural'Size* was 32. However, in Ada 95 and Ada 2005, *Natural'Size* is typically 31. This means that code may change in behavior when moving from Ada 83 to Ada 95 or Ada 2005. For example, consider:

```
type Rec is record;
   A : Natural;
   B : Natural;
end record;
```

```
for Rec use record
   at 0  range 0 .. Natural'Size - 1;
   at 0  range Natural'Size .. 2 * Natural'Size - 1;
end record;
```

In the above code, since the typical size of *Natural* objects is 32 bits and *Natural'Size* is 31, the above code can cause unexpected inefficient packing in Ada 95 and Ada 2005, and in general there are cases where the fact that the object size can exceed the size of the type causes surprises.

To help get around this problem GNAT provides two implementation defined attributes, *Value_Size* and *Object_Size*. When applied to a type, these attributes yield the size of the type (corresponding to the RM defined size attribute), and the size of objects of the type respectively.

The *Object_Size* is used for determining the default size of objects and components. This size value can be referred to using the *Object_Size* attribute. The phrase 'is used' here means that it is the basis of the determination of the size. The backend is free to pad this up if necessary for efficiency, e.g., an 8-bit stand-alone character might be stored in 32 bits on a machine with no efficient byte access instructions such as the Alpha.

The default rules for the value of *Object_Size* for discrete types are as follows:

* The *Object_Size* for base subtypes reflect the natural hardware size in bits (run the compiler with *-gnatS* to find those values for numeric types). Enumeration types and fixed-point base subtypes have 8, 16, 32 or 64 bits for this size, depending on the range of values to be stored.
* The *Object_Size* of a subtype is the same as the *Object_Size* of the type from which it is obtained.
* The *Object_Size* of a derived base type is copied from the parent base type, and the *Object_Size* of a derived first subtype is copied from the parent first subtype.

The *Value_Size* attribute is the (minimum) number of bits required to store a value of the type. This value is used to determine how tightly to pack records or arrays with components of this type, and also affects the semantics of unchecked conversion (unchecked conversions where the *Value_Size* values differ generate a warning, and are potentially target dependent).

The default rules for the value of *Value_Size* are as follows:

* The *Value_Size* for a base subtype is the minimum number of bits required to store all values of the type (including the sign bit only if negative values are possible).
* If a subtype statically matches the first subtype of a given type, then it has by default the same *Value_Size* as the first subtype. This is a consequence of RM 13.1(14): "if two subtypes statically match, then their subtype-specific aspects are the same".)
* All other subtypes have a *Value_Size* corresponding to the minimum number of bits required to store all values of the subtype. For dynamic bounds, it is assumed that the value can range down or up to the corresponding bound of the ancestor

The RM defined attribute *Size* corresponds to the *Value_Size* attribute.

The *Size* attribute may be defined for a first-named subtype. This sets the *Value_Size* of the first-named subtype to the given value, and the *Object_Size* of this first-named subtype to the given value padded up to an appropriate boundary. It is a consequence of the default rules above that this *Object_Size* will apply to all further subtypes. On the other hand, *Value_Size* is affected only for the first subtype, any dynamic subtypes obtained from it directly, and any statically matching subtypes. The *Value_Size* of any other static subtypes is not affected.

Value_Size and *Object_Size* may be explicitly set for any subtype using an attribute definition clause. Note that the use of these attributes can cause the RM 13.1(14) rule to be violated. If two access types reference aliased objects whose subtypes have differing *Object_Size* values as a result of explicit attribute definition clauses, then it is illegal to convert from one access subtype to the other. For a more complete description of this additional legality rule, see the description of the *Object_Size* attribute.

To get a feel for the difference, consider the following examples (note that in each case the base is *Short_Short_Integer* with a size of 8):

Type or subtype declaration	**Object_Size**	**Value_Size**
`type x1 is range 0 .. 5;`	8	3
`type x2 is range 0 .. 5; for x2'size use 12;`	16	12
`subtype x3 is x2 range 0 .. 3;`	16	2
`subtype x4 is x2'base range 0 .. 10;`	8	4
`dynamic : x2'Base range -64 .. +63;`		
`subtype x5 is x2 range 0 .. dynamic;`	16	3*
`subtype x6 is x2'base range 0 .. dynamic;`	8	7*

Note: the entries marked '*' are not actually specified by the Ada Reference Manual, which has nothing to say about size in the dynamic case. What GNAT does is to allocate sufficient bits to accomodate any possible dynamic values for the bounds at run-time.

So far, so good, but GNAT has to obey the RM rules, so the question is under what conditions must the RM *Size* be used. The following is a list of the occasions on which the RM *Size* must be used:

* Component size for packed arrays or records
* Value of the attribute *Size* for a type
* Warning about sizes not matching for unchecked conversion

For record types, the *Object_Size* is always a multiple of the alignment of the type (this is true for all types). In some cases the *Value_Size* can be smaller. Consider:

```
type R is record
  X : Integer;
  Y : Character;
end record;
```

On a typical 32-bit architecture, the X component will be four bytes, and require four-byte alignment, and the Y component will be one byte. In this case *R'Value_Size* will be 40 (bits) since this is the minimum size required to store a value of this type, and for example, it is permissible to have a component of type R in an outer array whose component size is specified to be 48 bits. However, *R'Object_Size* will be 64 (bits), since it must be rounded up so that this value is a multiple of the alignment (4 bytes = 32 bits).

For all other types, the *Object_Size* and *Value_Size* are the same (and equivalent to the RM attribute *Size*). Only *Size* may be specified for such types.

Note that *Value_Size* can be used to force biased representation for a particular subtype. Consider this example:

```
type R is (A, B, C, D, E, F);
subtype RAB is R range A .. B;
subtype REF is R range E .. F;
```

By default, *RAB* has a size of 1 (sufficient to accommodate the representation of *A* and *B*, 0 and 1), and *REF* has a size of 3 (sufficient to accommodate the representation of *E* and *F*, 4 and 5). But if we add the following *Value_Size* attribute definition clause:

```
for REF'Value_Size use 1;
```

then biased representation is forced for *REF*, and 0 will represent *E* and 1 will represent *F*. A warning is issued when a *Value_Size* attribute definition clause forces biased representation. This warning can be turned off using *-gnatw.B*.

9.7 Component_Size Clauses

Normally, the value specified in a component size clause must be consistent with the subtype of the array component with regard to size and alignment. In other words, the value specified must be at least equal to the size of this subtype, and must be a multiple of the alignment value.

In addition, component size clauses are allowed which cause the array to be packed, by specifying a smaller value. A first case is for component size values in the range 1 through 63. The value specified must not be smaller than the Size of the subtype. GNAT will accurately honor all packing requests in this range. For example, if we have:

```
type r is array (1 .. 8) of Natural;
for r'Component_Size use 31;
```

then the resulting array has a length of 31 bytes (248 bits = 8 * 31). Of course access to the components of such an array is considerably less efficient than if the natural component size of 32 is used. A second case is when the subtype of the component is a record type padded because of its default alignment. For example, if we have:

```
type r is record
  i : Integer;
  j : Integer;
  b : Boolean;
end record;

type a is array (1 .. 8) of r;
for a'Component_Size use 72;
```

then the resulting array has a length of 72 bytes, instead of 96 bytes if the alignment of the record (4) was obeyed.

Note that there is no point in giving both a component size clause and a pragma Pack for the same array type. if such duplicate clauses are given, the pragma Pack will be ignored.

9.8 Bit_Order Clauses

For record subtypes, GNAT permits the specification of the *Bit_Order* attribute. The specification may either correspond to the default bit order for the target, in which case the specification has no effect and places no additional restrictions, or it may be for the non-standard setting (that is the opposite of the default).

In the case where the non-standard value is specified, the effect is to renumber bits within each byte, but the ordering of bytes is not affected. There are certain restrictions placed on component clauses as follows:

* Components fitting within a single storage unit.

  These are unrestricted, and the effect is merely to renumber bits. For example if we are on a little-endian machine with *Low_Order_First* being the default, then the following two declarations have exactly the same effect:

  ```
  type R1 is record
     A : Boolean;
     B : Integer range 1 .. 120;
  end record;

  for R1 use record
     A at 0 range 0 .. 0;
     B at 0 range 1 .. 7;
  end record;

  type R2 is record
     A : Boolean;
     B : Integer range 1 .. 120;
  end record;

  for R2'Bit_Order use High_Order_First;

  for R2 use record
     A at 0 range 7 .. 7;
     B at 0 range 0 .. 6;
  end record;
  ```

  The useful application here is to write the second declaration with the *Bit_Order* attribute definition clause, and know that it will be treated the same, regardless of whether the target is little-endian or big-endian.

* Components occupying an integral number of bytes.

  These are components that exactly fit in two or more bytes. Such component declarations are allowed, but have no effect, since it is important to realize that the *Bit_Order* specification does not affect the ordering of bytes. In particular, the following attempt at getting an endian-independent integer does not work:

```
type R2 is record
   A : Integer;
end record;

for R2'Bit_Order use High_Order_First;

for R2 use record
   A at 0 range 0 .. 31;
end record;
```

This declaration will result in a little-endian integer on a little-endian machine, and a big-endian integer on a big-endian machine. If byte flipping is required for interoperability between big- and little-endian machines, this must be explicitly programmed. This capability is not provided by *Bit_Order*.

* Components that are positioned across byte boundaries

  but do not occupy an integral number of bytes. Given that bytes are not reordered, such fields would occupy a non-contiguous sequence of bits in memory, requiring non-trivial code to reassemble. They are for this reason not permitted, and any component clause specifying such a layout will be flagged as illegal by GNAT.

Since the misconception that Bit_Order automatically deals with all endian-related incompatibilities is a common one, the specification of a component field that is an integral number of bytes will always generate a warning. This warning may be suppressed using *pragma Warnings (Off)* if desired. The following section contains additional details regarding the issue of byte ordering.

9.9 Effect of Bit_Order on Byte Ordering

In this section we will review the effect of the *Bit_Order* attribute definition clause on byte ordering. Briefly, it has no effect at all, but a detailed example will be helpful. Before giving this example, let us review the precise definition of the effect of defining *Bit_Order*. The effect of a non-standard bit order is described in section 13.5.3 of the Ada Reference Manual:

> "2 A bit ordering is a method of interpreting the meaning of the storage place attributes."

To understand the precise definition of storage place attributes in this context, we visit section 13.5.1 of the manual:

> "13 A record_representation_clause (without the mod_clause) specifies the layout. The storage place attributes (see 13.5.2) are taken from the values of the position, first_bit, and last_bit expressions after normalizing those values so that first_bit is less than Storage_Unit."

The critical point here is that storage places are taken from the values after normalization, not before. So the *Bit_Order* interpretation applies to normalized values. The interpretation is described in the later part of the 13.5.3 paragraph:

> "2 A bit ordering is a method of interpreting the meaning of the storage place attributes. High_Order_First (known in the vernacular as 'big endian') means that the first bit of a storage element (bit 0) is the most significant bit (interpreting the sequence of bits that represent a component as an unsigned integer value). Low_Order_First (known in the vernacular as 'little endian') means the opposite: the first bit is the least significant."

Note that the numbering is with respect to the bits of a storage unit. In other words, the specification affects only the numbering of bits within a single storage unit.

We can make the effect clearer by giving an example.

Suppose that we have an external device which presents two bytes, the first byte presented, which is the first (low addressed byte) of the two byte record is called Master, and the second byte is called Slave.

The left most (most significant bit is called Control for each byte, and the remaining 7 bits are called V1, V2, ... V7, where V7 is the rightmost (least significant) bit.

On a big-endian machine, we can write the following representation clause

```
type Data is record
   Master_Control : Bit;
   Master_V1      : Bit;
   Master_V2      : Bit;
   Master_V3      : Bit;
   Master_V4      : Bit;
   Master_V5      : Bit;
   Master_V6      : Bit;
   Master_V7      : Bit;
   Slave_Control  : Bit;
   Slave_V1       : Bit;
   Slave_V2       : Bit;
   Slave_V3       : Bit;
   Slave_V4       : Bit;
   Slave_V5       : Bit;
   Slave_V6       : Bit;
   Slave_V7       : Bit;
end record;

for Data use record
   Master_Control at 0 range 0 .. 0;
   Master_V1      at 0 range 1 .. 1;
   Master_V2      at 0 range 2 .. 2;
   Master_V3      at 0 range 3 .. 3;
   Master_V4      at 0 range 4 .. 4;
   Master_V5      at 0 range 5 .. 5;
   Master_V6      at 0 range 6 .. 6;
   Master_V7      at 0 range 7 .. 7;
   Slave_Control  at 1 range 0 .. 0;
```

```
      Slave_V1       at 1 range 1 .. 1;
      Slave_V2       at 1 range 2 .. 2;
      Slave_V3       at 1 range 3 .. 3;
      Slave_V4       at 1 range 4 .. 4;
      Slave_V5       at 1 range 5 .. 5;
      Slave_V6       at 1 range 6 .. 6;
      Slave_V7       at 1 range 7 .. 7;
   end record;
```

Now if we move this to a little endian machine, then the bit ordering within the byte is backwards, so we have to rewrite the record rep clause as:

```
   for Data use record
      Master_Control at 0 range 7 .. 7;
      Master_V1      at 0 range 6 .. 6;
      Master_V2      at 0 range 5 .. 5;
      Master_V3      at 0 range 4 .. 4;
      Master_V4      at 0 range 3 .. 3;
      Master_V5      at 0 range 2 .. 2;
      Master_V6      at 0 range 1 .. 1;
      Master_V7      at 0 range 0 .. 0;
      Slave_Control  at 1 range 7 .. 7;
      Slave_V1       at 1 range 6 .. 6;
      Slave_V2       at 1 range 5 .. 5;
      Slave_V3       at 1 range 4 .. 4;
      Slave_V4       at 1 range 3 .. 3;
      Slave_V5       at 1 range 2 .. 2;
      Slave_V6       at 1 range 1 .. 1;
      Slave_V7       at 1 range 0 .. 0;
   end record;
```

It is a nuisance to have to rewrite the clause, especially if the code has to be maintained on both machines. However, this is a case that we can handle with the *Bit_Order* attribute if it is implemented. Note that the implementation is not required on byte addressed machines, but it is indeed implemented in GNAT. This means that we can simply use the first record clause, together with the declaration

```
   for Data'Bit_Order use High_Order_First;
```

and the effect is what is desired, namely the layout is exactly the same, independent of whether the code is compiled on a big-endian or little-endian machine.

The important point to understand is that byte ordering is not affected. A *Bit_Order* attribute definition never affects which byte a field ends up in, only where it ends up in that byte. To make this clear, let us rewrite the record rep clause of the previous example as:

```
   for Data'Bit_Order use High_Order_First;
   for Data use record
      Master_Control at 0 range  0 .. 0;
      Master_V1      at 0 range  1 .. 1;
      Master_V2      at 0 range  2 .. 2;
      Master_V3      at 0 range  3 .. 3;
```

```
      Master_V4      at 0 range  4 ..  4;
      Master_V5      at 0 range  5 ..  5;
      Master_V6      at 0 range  6 ..  6;
      Master_V7      at 0 range  7 ..  7;
      Slave_Control  at 0 range  8 ..  8;
      Slave_V1       at 0 range  9 ..  9;
      Slave_V2       at 0 range 10 .. 10;
      Slave_V3       at 0 range 11 .. 11;
      Slave_V4       at 0 range 12 .. 12;
      Slave_V5       at 0 range 13 .. 13;
      Slave_V6       at 0 range 14 .. 14;
      Slave_V7       at 0 range 15 .. 15;
   end record;
```

This is exactly equivalent to saying (a repeat of the first example):

```
   for Data'Bit_Order use High_Order_First;
   for Data use record
      Master_Control at 0 range 0 .. 0;
      Master_V1      at 0 range 1 .. 1;
      Master_V2      at 0 range 2 .. 2;
      Master_V3      at 0 range 3 .. 3;
      Master_V4      at 0 range 4 .. 4;
      Master_V5      at 0 range 5 .. 5;
      Master_V6      at 0 range 6 .. 6;
      Master_V7      at 0 range 7 .. 7;
      Slave_Control  at 1 range 0 .. 0;
      Slave_V1       at 1 range 1 .. 1;
      Slave_V2       at 1 range 2 .. 2;
      Slave_V3       at 1 range 3 .. 3;
      Slave_V4       at 1 range 4 .. 4;
      Slave_V5       at 1 range 5 .. 5;
      Slave_V6       at 1 range 6 .. 6;
      Slave_V7       at 1 range 7 .. 7;
   end record;
```

Why are they equivalent? Well take a specific field, the *Slave_V2* field. The storage place attributes are obtained by normalizing the values given so that the *First_Bit* value is less than 8. After normalizing the values (0,10,10) we get (1,2,2) which is exactly what we specified in the other case.

Now one might expect that the *Bit_Order* attribute might affect bit numbering within the entire record component (two bytes in this case, thus affecting which byte fields end up in), but that is not the way this feature is defined, it only affects numbering of bits, not which byte they end up in.

Consequently it never makes sense to specify a starting bit number greater than 7 (for a byte addressable field) if an attribute definition for *Bit_Order* has been given, and indeed it may be actively confusing to specify such a value, so the compiler generates a warning for such usage.

If you do need to control byte ordering then appropriate conditional values must be used. If in our example, the slave byte came first on some machines we might write:

```
Master_Byte_First constant Boolean := ...;

Master_Byte : constant Natural :=
                1 - Boolean'Pos (Master_Byte_First);
Slave_Byte  : constant Natural :=
                Boolean'Pos (Master_Byte_First);

for Data'Bit_Order use High_Order_First;
for Data use record
   Master_Control at Master_Byte range 0 .. 0;
   Master_V1      at Master_Byte range 1 .. 1;
   Master_V2      at Master_Byte range 2 .. 2;
   Master_V3      at Master_Byte range 3 .. 3;
   Master_V4      at Master_Byte range 4 .. 4;
   Master_V5      at Master_Byte range 5 .. 5;
   Master_V6      at Master_Byte range 6 .. 6;
   Master_V7      at Master_Byte range 7 .. 7;
   Slave_Control  at Slave_Byte  range 0 .. 0;
   Slave_V1       at Slave_Byte  range 1 .. 1;
   Slave_V2       at Slave_Byte  range 2 .. 2;
   Slave_V3       at Slave_Byte  range 3 .. 3;
   Slave_V4       at Slave_Byte  range 4 .. 4;
   Slave_V5       at Slave_Byte  range 5 .. 5;
   Slave_V6       at Slave_Byte  range 6 .. 6;
   Slave_V7       at Slave_Byte  range 7 .. 7;
end record;
```

Now to switch between machines, all that is necessary is to set the boolean constant *Master_Byte_First* in an appropriate manner.

9.10 Pragma Pack for Arrays

Pragma *Pack* applied to an array has no effect unless the component type is packable. For a component type to be packable, it must be one of the following cases:

* Any scalar type
* Any type whose size is specified with a size clause
* Any packed array type with a static size
* Any record type padded because of its default alignment

For all these cases, if the component subtype size is in the range 1 through 63, then the effect of the pragma *Pack* is exactly as though a component size were specified giving the component subtype size. For example if we have:

```
type r is range 0 .. 17;

type ar is array (1 .. 8) of r;
```

```
pragma Pack (ar);
```

Then the component size of *ar* will be set to 5 (i.e., to *r'size*, and the size of the array *ar* will be exactly 40 bits.

Note that in some cases this rather fierce approach to packing can produce unexpected effects. For example, in Ada 95 and Ada 2005, subtype *Natural* typically has a size of 31, meaning that if you pack an array of *Natural*, you get 31-bit close packing, which saves a few bits, but results in far less efficient access. Since many other Ada compilers will ignore such a packing request, GNAT will generate a warning on some uses of pragma *Pack* that it guesses might not be what is intended. You can easily remove this warning by using an explicit *Component_Size* setting instead, which never generates a warning, since the intention of the programmer is clear in this case.

GNAT treats packed arrays in one of two ways. If the size of the array is known at compile time and is less than 64 bits, then internally the array is represented as a single modular type, of exactly the appropriate number of bits. If the length is greater than 63 bits, or is not known at compile time, then the packed array is represented as an array of bytes, and the length is always a multiple of 8 bits.

Note that to represent a packed array as a modular type, the alignment must be suitable for the modular type involved. For example, on typical machines a 32-bit packed array will be represented by a 32-bit modular integer with an alignment of four bytes. If you explicitly override the default alignment with an alignment clause that is too small, the modular representation cannot be used. For example, consider the following set of declarations:

```
type R is range 1 .. 3;
type S is array (1 .. 31) of R;
for S'Component_Size use 2;
for S'Size use 62;
for S'Alignment use 1;
```

If the alignment clause were not present, then a 62-bit modular representation would be chosen (typically with an alignment of 4 or 8 bytes depending on the target). But the default alignment is overridden with the explicit alignment clause. This means that the modular representation cannot be used, and instead the array of bytes representation must be used, meaning that the length must be a multiple of 8. Thus the above set of declarations will result in a diagnostic rejecting the size clause and noting that the minimum size allowed is 64.

One special case that is worth noting occurs when the base type of the component size is 8/16/32 and the subtype is one bit less. Notably this occurs with subtype *Natural*. Consider:

```
type Arr is array (1 .. 32) of Natural;
pragma Pack (Arr);
```

In all commonly used Ada 83 compilers, this pragma Pack would be ignored, since typically *Natural'Size* is 32 in Ada 83, and in any case most Ada 83 compilers did not attempt 31 bit packing.

In Ada 95 and Ada 2005, *Natural'Size* is required to be 31. Furthermore, GNAT really does pack 31-bit subtype to 31 bits. This may result in a substantial unintended performance penalty when porting legacy Ada 83 code. To help prevent this, GNAT generates a warning in such cases. If you really want 31 bit packing in a case like this, you can set the component size explicitly:

```
type Arr is array (1 .. 32) of Natural;
for Arr'Component_Size use 31;
```

Here 31-bit packing is achieved as required, and no warning is generated, since in this case the programmer intention is clear.

9.11 Pragma Pack for Records

Pragma *Pack* applied to a record will pack the components to reduce wasted space from alignment gaps and by reducing the amount of space taken by components. We distinguish between *packable* components and *non-packable* components. Components of the following types are considered packable:

* Components of a primitive type are packable unless they are aliased or of an atomic type.
* Small packed arrays, whose size does not exceed 64 bits, and where the size is statically known at compile time, are represented internally as modular integers, and so they are also packable.

All packable components occupy the exact number of bits corresponding to their *Size* value, and are packed with no padding bits, i.e., they can start on an arbitrary bit boundary.

All other types are non-packable, they occupy an integral number of storage units, and are placed at a boundary corresponding to their alignment requirements.

For example, consider the record

```
type Rb1 is array (1 .. 13) of Boolean;
pragma Pack (Rb1);

type Rb2 is array (1 .. 65) of Boolean;
pragma Pack (Rb2);

type AF is new Float with Atomic;

type X2 is record
   L1 : Boolean;
   L2 : Duration;
   L3 : AF;
   L4 : Boolean;
   L5 : Rb1;
   L6 : Rb2;
end record;
pragma Pack (X2);
```

The representation for the record X2 is as follows:

```
for X2'Size use 224;
for X2 use record
   L1 at  0 range  0 .. 0;
   L2 at  0 range  1 .. 64;
```

```
      L3 at 12 range  0 .. 31;
      L4 at 16 range  0 .. 0;
      L5 at 16 range  1 .. 13;
      L6 at 18 range  0 .. 71;
   end record;
```

Studying this example, we see that the packable fields *L1* and *L2* are of length equal to their sizes, and placed at specific bit boundaries (and not byte boundaries) to eliminate padding. But *L3* is of a non-packable float type (because it is aliased), so it is on the next appropriate alignment boundary.

The next two fields are fully packable, so *L4* and *L5* are minimally packed with no gaps. However, type *Rb2* is a packed array that is longer than 64 bits, so it is itself non-packable. Thus the *L6* field is aligned to the next byte boundary, and takes an integral number of bytes, i.e., 72 bits.

9.12 Record Representation Clauses

Record representation clauses may be given for all record types, including types obtained by record extension. Component clauses are allowed for any static component. The restrictions on component clauses depend on the type of the component.

For all components of an elementary type, the only restriction on component clauses is that the size must be at least the 'Size value of the type (actually the Value_Size). There are no restrictions due to alignment, and such components may freely cross storage boundaries.

Packed arrays with a size up to and including 64 bits are represented internally using a modular type with the appropriate number of bits, and thus the same lack of restriction applies. For example, if you declare:

```
   type R is array (1 .. 49) of Boolean;
   pragma Pack (R);
   for R'Size use 49;
```

then a component clause for a component of type R may start on any specified bit boundary, and may specify a value of 49 bits or greater.

For packed bit arrays that are longer than 64 bits, there are two cases. If the component size is a power of 2 (1,2,4,8,16,32 bits), including the important case of single bits or boolean values, then there are no limitations on placement of such components, and they may start and end at arbitrary bit boundaries.

If the component size is not a power of 2 (e.g., 3 or 5), then an array of this type longer than 64 bits must always be placed on on a storage unit (byte) boundary and occupy an integral number of storage units (bytes). Any component clause that does not meet this requirement will be rejected.

Any aliased component, or component of an aliased type, must have its normal alignment and size. A component clause that does not meet this requirement will be rejected.

The tag field of a tagged type always occupies an address sized field at the start of the record. No component clause may attempt to overlay this tag. When a tagged type appears as a component, the tag field must have proper alignment

In the case of a record extension T1, of a type T, no component clause applied to the type T1 can specify a storage location that would overlap the first T'Size bytes of the record.

For all other component types, including non-bit-packed arrays, the component can be placed at an arbitrary bit boundary, so for example, the following is permitted:

```
type R is array (1 .. 10) of Boolean;
for R'Size use 80;

type Q is record
   G, H : Boolean;
   L, M : R;
end record;

for Q use record
   G at 0 range  0 ..   0;
   H at 0 range  1 ..   1;
   L at 0 range  2 ..  81;
   R at 0 range 82 .. 161;
end record;
```

Note: the above rules apply to recent releases of GNAT 5. In GNAT 3, there are more severe restrictions on larger components. For non-primitive types, including packed arrays with a size greater than 64 bits, component clauses must respect the alignment requirement of the type, in particular, always starting on a byte boundary, and the length must be a multiple of the storage unit.

9.13 Handling of Records with Holes

As a result of alignment considerations, records may contain "holes" or gaps which do not correspond to the data bits of any of the components. Record representation clauses can also result in holes in records.

GNAT does not attempt to clear these holes, so in record objects, they should be considered to hold undefined rubbish. The generated equality routine just tests components so does not access these undefined bits, and assignment and copy operations may or may not preserve the contents of these holes (for assignments, the holes in the target will in practice contain either the bits that are present in the holes in the source, or the bits that were present in the target before the assignment).

If it is necessary to ensure that holes in records have all zero bits, then record objects for which this initialization is desired should be explicitly set to all zero values using Unchecked_Conversion or address overlays. For example

```
type HRec is record
   C : Character;
   I : Integer;
end record;
```

On typical machines, integers need to be aligned on a four-byte boundary, resulting in three bytes of undefined rubbish following the 8-bit field for C. To ensure that the hole in a variable of type HRec is set to all zero bits, you could for example do:

```
type Base is record
   Dummy1, Dummy2 : Integer := 0;
end record;
```

```
BaseVar : Base;
RealVar : Hrec;
for RealVar'Address use BaseVar'Address;
```

Now the 8-bytes of the value of RealVar start out containing all zero bits. A safer approach is to just define dummy fields, avoiding the holes, as in:

```
type HRec is record
   C      : Character;
   Dummy1 : Short_Short_Integer := 0;
   Dummy2 : Short_Short_Integer := 0;
   Dummy3 : Short_Short_Integer := 0;
   I      : Integer;
end record;
```

And to make absolutely sure that the intent of this is followed, you can use representation clauses:

```
for Hrec use record
   C      at 0 range 0 .. 7;
   Dummy1 at 1 range 0 .. 7;
   Dummy2 at 2 range 0 .. 7;
   Dummy3 at 3 range 0 .. 7;
   I      at 4 range 0 .. 31;
end record;
for Hrec'Size use 64;
```

9.14 Enumeration Clauses

The only restriction on enumeration clauses is that the range of values must be representable. For the signed case, if one or more of the representation values are negative, all values must be in the range:

```
System.Min_Int .. System.Max_Int
```

For the unsigned case, where all values are nonnegative, the values must be in the range:

```
0 .. System.Max_Binary_Modulus;
```

A *confirming* representation clause is one in which the values range from 0 in sequence, i.e., a clause that confirms the default representation for an enumeration type. Such a confirming representation is permitted by these rules, and is specially recognized by the compiler so that no extra overhead results from the use of such a clause.

If an array has an index type which is an enumeration type to which an enumeration clause has been applied, then the array is stored in a compact manner. Consider the declarations:

```
type r is (A, B, C);
for r use (A => 1, B => 5, C => 10);
type t is array (r) of Character;
```

The array type t corresponds to a vector with exactly three elements and has a default size equal to *3*Character'Size*. This ensures efficient use of space, but means that accesses to elements of the array will incur the overhead of converting representation values to the corresponding positional values, (i.e., the value delivered by the *Pos* attribute).

9.15 Address Clauses

The reference manual allows a general restriction on representation clauses, as found in RM 13.1(22):

> "An implementation need not support representation items containing nonstatic expressions, except that an implementation should support a representation item for a given entity if each nonstatic expression in the representation item is a name that statically denotes a constant declared before the entity."

In practice this is applicable only to address clauses, since this is the only case in which a nonstatic expression is permitted by the syntax. As the AARM notes in sections 13.1 (22.a-22.h):

> 22.a Reason: This is to avoid the following sort of thing:
>
> 22.b X : Integer := F(...); Y : Address := G(...); for X'Address use Y;
>
> 22.c In the above, we have to evaluate the initialization expression for X before we know where to put the result. This seems like an unreasonable implementation burden.
>
> 22.d The above code should instead be written like this:
>
> 22.e Y : constant Address := G(...); X : Integer := F(...); for X'Address use Y;
>
> 22.f This allows the expression 'Y' to be safely evaluated before X is created.
>
> 22.g The constant could be a formal parameter of mode in.
>
> 22.h An implementation can support other nonstatic expressions if it wants to. Expressions of type Address are hardly ever static, but their value might be known at compile time anyway in many cases.

GNAT does indeed permit many additional cases of nonstatic expressions. In particular, if the type involved is elementary there are no restrictions (since in this case, holding a temporary copy of the initialization value, if one is present, is inexpensive). In addition, if there is no implicit or explicit initialization, then there are no restrictions. GNAT will reject only the case where all three of these conditions hold:

* The type of the item is non-elementary (e.g., a record or array).
* There is explicit or implicit initialization required for the object. Note that access values are always implicitly initialized.
* The address value is nonstatic. Here GNAT is more permissive than the RM, and allows the address value to be the address of a previously declared stand-alone variable, as long as it does not itself have an address clause.

  ```
  Anchor  : Some_Initialized_Type;
  Overlay : Some_Initialized_Type;
  for Overlay'Address use Anchor'Address;
  ```

  However, the prefix of the address clause cannot be an array component, or a component of a discriminated record.

As noted above in section 22.h, address values are typically nonstatic. In particular the To_Address function, even if applied to a literal value, is a nonstatic function call. To avoid this minor annoyance, GNAT provides the implementation defined attribute 'To_Address. The following two expressions have identical values:

```
To_Address (16#1234_0000#)
System'To_Address (16#1234_0000#);
```

except that the second form is considered to be a static expression, and thus when used as an address clause value is always permitted.

Additionally, GNAT treats as static an address clause that is an unchecked_conversion of a static integer value. This simplifies the porting of legacy code, and provides a portable equivalent to the GNAT attribute *To_Address*.

Another issue with address clauses is the interaction with alignment requirements. When an address clause is given for an object, the address value must be consistent with the alignment of the object (which is usually the same as the alignment of the type of the object). If an address clause is given that specifies an inappropriately aligned address value, then the program execution is erroneous.

Since this source of erroneous behavior can have unfortunate effects on machines with strict alignment requirements, GNAT checks (at compile time if possible, generating a warning, or at execution time with a run-time check) that the alignment is appropriate. If the run-time check fails, then *Program_Error* is raised. This run-time check is suppressed if range checks are suppressed, or if the special GNAT check Alignment_Check is suppressed, or if *pragma Restrictions (No_Elaboration_Code)* is in effect. It is also suppressed by default on non-strict alignment machines (such as the x86).

Finally, GNAT does not permit overlaying of objects of controlled types or composite types containing a controlled component. In most cases, the compiler can detect an attempt at such overlays and will generate a warning at compile time and a Program_Error exception at run time.

An address clause cannot be given for an exported object. More understandably the real restriction is that objects with an address clause cannot be exported. This is because such variables are not defined by the Ada program, so there is no external object to export.

It is permissible to give an address clause and a pragma Import for the same object. In this case, the variable is not really defined by the Ada program, so there is no external symbol to be linked. The link name and the external name are ignored in this case. The reason that we allow this combination is that it provides a useful idiom to avoid unwanted initializations on objects with address clauses.

When an address clause is given for an object that has implicit or explicit initialization, then by default initialization takes place. This means that the effect of the object declaration is to overwrite the memory at the specified address. This is almost always not what the programmer wants, so GNAT will output a warning:

```
with System;
package G is
   type R is record
      M : Integer := 0;
   end record;

   Ext : R;
   for Ext'Address use System'To_Address (16#1234_1234#);
```

```
    |
>>> warning: implicit initialization of "Ext" may
    modify overlaid storage
>>> warning: use pragma Import for "Ext" to suppress
    initialization (RM B(24))

end G;
```

As indicated by the warning message, the solution is to use a (dummy) pragma Import to suppress this initialization. The pragma tell the compiler that the object is declared and initialized elsewhere. The following package compiles without warnings (and the initialization is suppressed):

```
with System;
package G is
   type R is record
      M : Integer := 0;
   end record;

   Ext : R;
   for Ext'Address use System'To_Address (16#1234_1234#);
   pragma Import (Ada, Ext);
end G;
```

A final issue with address clauses involves their use for overlaying variables, as in the following example:

```
A : Integer;
B : Integer;
for B'Address use A'Address;
```

or alternatively, using the form recommended by the RM:

```
A    : Integer;
Addr : constant Address := A'Address;
B    : Integer;
for B'Address use Addr;
```

In both of these cases, *A* and *B* become aliased to one another via the address clause. This use of address clauses to overlay variables, achieving an effect similar to unchecked conversion was erroneous in Ada 83, but in Ada 95 and Ada 2005 the effect is implementation defined. Furthermore, the Ada RM specifically recommends that in a situation like this, *B* should be subject to the following implementation advice (RM 13.3(19)):

> "19 If the Address of an object is specified, or it is imported or exported, then the implementation should not perform optimizations based on assumptions of no aliases."

GNAT follows this recommendation, and goes further by also applying this recommendation to the overlaid variable (*A* in the above example) in this case. This means that the overlay works "as expected", in that a modification to one of the variables will affect the value of the other.

More generally, GNAT interprets this recommendation conservatively for address clauses: in the cases other than overlays, it considers that the object is effectively subject to pragma *Volatile* and implements the associated semantics.

Note that when address clause overlays are used in this way, there is an issue of unintentional initialization, as shown by this example:

```
package Overwrite_Record is
   type R is record
      A : Character := 'C';
      B : Character := 'A';
   end record;
   X : Short_Integer := 3;
   Y : R;
   for Y'Address use X'Address;
       |
>>> warning: default initialization of "Y" may
    modify "X", use pragma Import for "Y" to
    suppress initialization (RM B.1(24))

end Overwrite_Record;
```

Here the default initialization of *Y* will clobber the value of *X*, which justifies the warning. The warning notes that this effect can be eliminated by adding a *pragma Import* which suppresses the initialization:

```
package Overwrite_Record is
   type R is record
      A : Character := 'C';
      B : Character := 'A';
   end record;
   X : Short_Integer := 3;
   Y : R;
   for Y'Address use X'Address;
   pragma Import (Ada, Y);
end Overwrite_Record;
```

Note that the use of *pragma Initialize_Scalars* may cause variables to be initialized when they would not otherwise have been in the absence of the use of this pragma. This may cause an overlay to have this unintended clobbering effect. The compiler avoids this for scalar types, but not for composite objects (where in general the effect of *Initialize_Scalars* is part of the initialization routine for the composite object:

```
pragma Initialize_Scalars;
with Ada.Text_IO;  use Ada.Text_IO;
procedure Overwrite_Array is
   type Arr is array (1 .. 5) of Integer;
   X : Arr := (others => 1);
   A : Arr;
   for A'Address use X'Address;
       |
```

```
>>> warning: default initialization of "A" may
    modify "X", use pragma Import for "A" to
    suppress initialization (RM B.1(24))

begin
   if X /= Arr'(others => 1) then
      Put_Line ("X was clobbered");
   else
      Put_Line ("X was not clobbered");
   end if;
end Overwrite_Array;
```

The above program generates the warning as shown, and at execution time, prints *X was clobbered*. If the *pragma Import* is added as suggested:

```
pragma Initialize_Scalars;
with Ada.Text_IO;  use Ada.Text_IO;
procedure Overwrite_Array is
   type Arr is array (1 .. 5) of Integer;
   X : Arr := (others => 1);
   A : Arr;
   for A'Address use X'Address;
   pragma Import (Ada, A);
begin
   if X /= Arr'(others => 1) then
      Put_Line ("X was clobbered");
   else
      Put_Line ("X was not clobbered");
   end if;
end Overwrite_Array;
```

then the program compiles without the warning and when run will generate the output *X was not clobbered*.

9.16 Use of Address Clauses for Memory-Mapped I/O

A common pattern is to use an address clause to map an atomic variable to a location in memory that corresponds to a memory-mapped I/O operation or operations, for example:

```
type Mem_Word is record
   A,B,C,D : Byte;
end record;
pragma Atomic (Mem_Word);
for Mem_Word_Size use 32;

Mem : Mem_Word;
for Mem'Address use some-address;
...
Temp := Mem;
Temp.A := 32;
```

```
Mem := Temp;
```

For a full access (reference or modification) of the variable (Mem) in this case, as in the above examples, GNAT guarantees that the entire atomic word will be accessed, in accordance with the RM C.6(15) clause.

A problem arises with a component access such as:

```
Mem.A := 32;
```

Note that the component A is not declared as atomic. This means that it is not clear what this assignment means. It could correspond to full word read and write as given in the first example, or on architectures that supported such an operation it might be a single byte store instruction. The RM does not have anything to say in this situation, and GNAT does not make any guarantee. The code generated may vary from target to target. GNAT will issue a warning in such a case:

```
Mem.A := 32;
|
>>> warning: access to non-atomic component of atomic array,
    may cause unexpected accesses to atomic object
```

It is best to be explicit in this situation, by either declaring the components to be atomic if you want the byte store, or explicitly writing the full word access sequence if that is what the hardware requires. Alternatively, if the full word access sequence is required, GNAT also provides the pragma *Volatile_Full_Access* which can be used in lieu of pragma *Atomic* and will give the additional guarantee.

9.17 Effect of Convention on Representation

Normally the specification of a foreign language convention for a type or an object has no effect on the chosen representation. In particular, the representation chosen for data in GNAT generally meets the standard system conventions, and for example records are laid out in a manner that is consistent with C. This means that specifying convention C (for example) has no effect.

There are four exceptions to this general rule:

* *Convention Fortran and array subtypes.*

  If pragma Convention Fortran is specified for an array subtype, then in accordance with the implementation advice in section 3.6.2(11) of the Ada Reference Manual, the array will be stored in a Fortran-compatible column-major manner, instead of the normal default row-major order.

* *Convention C and enumeration types*

  GNAT normally stores enumeration types in 8, 16, or 32 bits as required to accommodate all values of the type. For example, for the enumeration type declared by:

  ```
  type Color is (Red, Green, Blue);
  ```

  8 bits is sufficient to store all values of the type, so by default, objects of type *Color* will be represented using 8 bits. However, normal C convention is to use 32 bits for all enum values in C, since enum values are essentially of type int. If pragma *Convention C* is specified for an Ada enumeration type, then the size is modified as necessary (usually to 32 bits) to be consistent with the C convention for enum values.

Note that this treatment applies only to types. If Convention C is given for an enumeration object, where the enumeration type is not Convention C, then Object_Size bits are allocated. For example, for a normal enumeration type, with less than 256 elements, only 8 bits will be allocated for the object. Since this may be a surprise in terms of what C expects, GNAT will issue a warning in this situation. The warning can be suppressed by giving an explicit size clause specifying the desired size.

* *Convention C/Fortran and Boolean types*

  In C, the usual convention for boolean values, that is values used for conditions, is that zero represents false, and nonzero values represent true. In Ada, the normal convention is that two specific values, typically 0/1, are used to represent false/true respectively.

  Fortran has a similar convention for *LOGICAL* values (any nonzero value represents true).

  To accommodate the Fortran and C conventions, if a pragma Convention specifies C or Fortran convention for a derived Boolean, as in the following example:

```
type C_Switch is new Boolean;
pragma Convention (C, C_Switch);
```

  then the GNAT generated code will treat any nonzero value as true. For truth values generated by GNAT, the conventional value 1 will be used for True, but when one of these values is read, any nonzero value is treated as True.

9.18 Conventions and Anonymous Access Types

The RM is not entirely clear on convention handling in a number of cases, and in particular, it is not clear on the convention to be given to anonymous access types in general, and in particular what is to be done for the case of anonymous access-to-subprogram.

In GNAT, we decide that if an explicit Convention is applied to an object or component, and its type is such an anonymous type, then the convention will apply to this anonymous type as well. This seems to make sense since it is anomolous in any case to have a different convention for an object and its type, and there is clearly no way to explicitly specify a convention for an anonymous type, since it doesn't have a name to specify!

Furthermore, we decide that if a convention is applied to a record type, then this convention is inherited by any of its components that are of an anonymous access type which do not have an explicitly specified convention.

The following program shows these conventions in action:

```
package ConvComp is
   type Foo is range 1 .. 10;
   type T1 is record
      A : access function (X : Foo) return Integer;
      B : Integer;
   end record;
   pragma Convention (C, T1);

   type T2 is record
      A : access function (X : Foo) return Integer;
      pragma Convention  (C, A);
```

```
      B : Integer;
   end record;
   pragma Convention (COBOL, T2);

   type T3 is record
      A : access function (X : Foo) return Integer;
      pragma Convention  (COBOL, A);
      B : Integer;
   end record;
   pragma Convention (C, T3);

   type T4 is record
      A : access function (X : Foo) return Integer;
      B : Integer;
   end record;
   pragma Convention (COBOL, T4);

   function F (X : Foo) return Integer;
   pragma Convention (C, F);

   function F (X : Foo) return Integer is (13);

   TV1 : T1 := (F'Access, 12);  -- OK
   TV2 : T2 := (F'Access, 13);  -- OK

   TV3 : T3 := (F'Access, 13);  -- ERROR
                |
>>> subprogram "F" has wrong convention
>>> does not match access to subprogram declared at line 17
     38.    TV4 : T4 := (F'Access, 13);  -- ERROR
                |
>>> subprogram "F" has wrong convention
>>> does not match access to subprogram declared at line 24
     39. end ConvComp;
```

9.19 Determining the Representations chosen by GNAT

Although the descriptions in this section are intended to be complete, it is often easier to simply experiment to see what GNAT accepts and what the effect is on the layout of types and objects.

As required by the Ada RM, if a representation clause is not accepted, then it must be rejected as illegal by the compiler. However, when a representation clause or pragma is accepted, there can still be questions of what the compiler actually does. For example, if a partial record representation clause specifies the location of some components and not others, then where are the non-specified components placed? Or if pragma *Pack* is used on a record, then exactly where are the resulting fields placed? The section on pragma *Pack* in this chapter can be used to answer the second question, but it is often easier to just see what the compiler does.

For this purpose, GNAT provides the option *-gnatR*. If you compile with this option, then the compiler will output information on the actual representations chosen, in a format similar to source representation clauses. For example, if we compile the package:

```
package q is
   type r (x : boolean) is tagged record
      case x is
         when True => S : String (1 .. 100);
         when False => null;
      end case;
   end record;

   type r2 is new r (false) with record
      y2 : integer;
   end record;

   for r2 use record
      y2 at 16 range 0 .. 31;
   end record;

   type x is record
      y : character;
   end record;

   type x1 is array (1 .. 10) of x;
   for x1'component_size use 11;

   type ia is access integer;

   type Rb1 is array (1 .. 13) of Boolean;
   pragma Pack (rb1);

   type Rb2 is array (1 .. 65) of Boolean;
   pragma Pack (rb2);

   type x2 is record
      l1 : Boolean;
      l2 : Duration;
      l3 : Float;
      l4 : Boolean;
      l5 : Rb1;
      l6 : Rb2;
   end record;
   pragma Pack (x2);
end q;
```

using the switch *-gnatR* we obtain the following output:

```
Representation information for unit q
-------------------------------------

for r'Size use ??;
for r'Alignment use 4;
for r use record
   x    at 4 range  0 .. 7;
   _tag at 0 range  0 .. 31;
   s    at 5 range  0 .. 799;
end record;

for r2'Size use 160;
for r2'Alignment use 4;
for r2 use record
   x       at  4 range  0 .. 7;
   _tag    at  0 range  0 .. 31;
   _parent at  0 range  0 .. 63;
   y2      at 16 range  0 .. 31;
end record;

for x'Size use 8;
for x'Alignment use 1;
for x use record
   y at 0 range  0 .. 7;
end record;

for x1'Size use 112;
for x1'Alignment use 1;
for x1'Component_Size use 11;

for rb1'Size use 13;
for rb1'Alignment use 2;
for rb1'Component_Size use 1;

for rb2'Size use 72;
for rb2'Alignment use 1;
for rb2'Component_Size use 1;

for x2'Size use 224;
for x2'Alignment use 4;
for x2 use record
   l1 at  0 range  0 .. 0;
   l2 at  0 range  1 .. 64;
   l3 at 12 range  0 .. 31;
   l4 at 16 range  0 .. 0;
```

```
      15 at 16 range  1 .. 13;
      16 at 18 range  0 .. 71;
   end record;
```

The Size values are actually the Object_Size, i.e., the default size that will be allocated for objects of the type. The ?? size for type r indicates that we have a variant record, and the actual size of objects will depend on the discriminant value.

The Alignment values show the actual alignment chosen by the compiler for each record or array type.

The record representation clause for type r shows where all fields are placed, including the compiler generated tag field (whose location cannot be controlled by the programmer).

The record representation clause for the type extension r2 shows all the fields present, including the parent field, which is a copy of the fields of the parent type of r2, i.e., r1.

The component size and size clauses for types rb1 and rb2 show the exact effect of pragma *Pack* on these arrays, and the record representation clause for type x2 shows how pragma *Pack* affects this record type.

In some cases, it may be useful to cut and paste the representation clauses generated by the compiler into the original source to fix and guarantee the actual representation to be used.

10 Standard Library Routines

The Ada Reference Manual contains in Annex A a full description of an extensive set of standard library routines that can be used in any Ada program, and which must be provided by all Ada compilers. They are analogous to the standard C library used by C programs.

GNAT implements all of the facilities described in annex A, and for most purposes the description in the Ada Reference Manual, or appropriate Ada text book, will be sufficient for making use of these facilities.

In the case of the input-output facilities, [The Implementation of Standard I/O], page 226, gives details on exactly how GNAT interfaces to the file system. For the remaining packages, the Ada Reference Manual should be sufficient. The following is a list of the packages included, together with a brief description of the functionality that is provided.

For completeness, references are included to other predefined library routines defined in other sections of the Ada Reference Manual (these are cross-indexed from Annex A). For further details see the relevant package declarations in the run-time library. In particular, a few units are not implemented, as marked by the presence of pragma Unimplemented_Unit, and in this case the package declaration contains comments explaining why the unit is not implemented.

`Ada` *(A.2)*
: This is a parent package for all the standard library packages. It is usually included implicitly in your program, and itself contains no useful data or routines.

`Ada.Assertions` *(11.4.2)*
: *Assertions* provides the *Assert* subprograms, and also the declaration of the *Assertion_Error* exception.

`Ada.Asynchronous_Task_Control` *(D.11)*
: *Asynchronous_Task_Control* provides low level facilities for task synchronization. It is typically not implemented. See package spec for details.

`Ada.Calendar` *(9.6)*
: *Calendar* provides time of day access, and routines for manipulating times and durations.

`Ada.Calendar.Arithmetic` *(9.6.1)*
: This package provides additional arithmetic operations for *Calendar*.

`Ada.Calendar.Formatting` *(9.6.1)*
: This package provides formatting operations for *Calendar*.

`Ada.Calendar.Time_Zones` *(9.6.1)*
: This package provides additional *Calendar* facilities for handling time zones.

`Ada.Characters` *(A.3.1)*
: This is a dummy parent package that contains no useful entities

`Ada.Characters.Conversions` *(A.3.2)*
: This package provides character conversion functions.

`Ada.Characters.Handling` *(A.3.2)*
This package provides some basic character handling capabilities, including classification functions for classes of characters (e.g., test for letters, or digits).

`Ada.Characters.Latin_1` *(A.3.3)*
This package includes a complete set of definitions of the characters that appear in type CHARACTER. It is useful for writing programs that will run in international environments. For example, if you want an upper case E with an acute accent in a string, it is often better to use the definition of *UC_E_Acute* in this package. Then your program will print in an understandable manner even if your environment does not support these extended characters.

`Ada.Command_Line` *(A.15)*
This package provides access to the command line parameters and the name of the current program (analogous to the use of *argc* and *argv* in C), and also allows the exit status for the program to be set in a system-independent manner.

`Ada.Complex_Text_IO` *(G.1.3)*
This package provides text input and output of complex numbers.

`Ada.Containers` *(A.18.1)*
A top level package providing a few basic definitions used by all the following specific child packages that provide specific kinds of containers.

`Ada.Containers.Bounded_Priority_Queues` *(A.18.31)*

`Ada.Containers.Bounded_Synchronized_Queues` *(A.18.29)*

`Ada.Containers.Doubly_Linked_Lists` *(A.18.3)*

`Ada.Containers.Generic_Array_Sort` *(A.18.26)*

`Ada.Containers.Generic_Constrained_Array_Sort` *(A.18.26)*

`Ada.Containers.Generic_Sort` *(A.18.26)*

`Ada.Containers.Hashed_Maps` *(A.18.5)*

`Ada.Containers.Hashed_Sets` *(A.18.8)*

`Ada.Containers.Indefinite_Doubly_Linked_Lists` *(A.18.12)*

`Ada.Containers.Indefinite_Hashed_Maps` *(A.18.13)*

`Ada.Containers.Indefinite_Hashed_Sets` *(A.18.15)*

`Ada.Containers.Indefinite_Holders` *(A.18.18)*

`Ada.Containers.Indefinite_Multiway_Trees` *(A.18.17)*

`Ada.Containers.Indefinite_Ordered_Maps` *(A.18.14)*

`Ada.Containers.Indefinite_Ordered_Sets` *(A.18.16)*

`Ada.Containers.Indefinite_Vectors` *(A.18.11)*

`Ada.Containers.Multiway_Trees` *(A.18.10)*

`Ada.Containers.Ordered_Maps` *(A.18.6)*

`Ada.Containers.Ordered_Sets` *(A.18.9)*

`Ada.Containers.Synchronized_Queue_Interfaces` *(A.18.27)*

`Ada.Containers.Unbounded_Priority_Queues` *(A.18.30)*

`Ada.Containers.Unbounded_Synchronized_Queues` *(A.18.28)*

`Ada.Containers.Vectors` *(A.18.2)*

`Ada.Directories` *(A.16)*
: This package provides operations on directories.

`Ada.Directories.Hierarchical_File_Names` *(A.16.1)*
: This package provides additional directory operations handling hiearchical file names.

`Ada.Directories.Information` *(A.16)*
: This is an implementation defined package for additional directory operations, which is not implemented in GNAT.

`Ada.Decimal` *(F.2)*
: This package provides constants describing the range of decimal numbers implemented, and also a decimal divide routine (analogous to the COBOL verb DIVIDE ... GIVING ... REMAINDER ...)

`Ada.Direct_IO` *(A.8.4)*
: This package provides input-output using a model of a set of records of fixed-length, containing an arbitrary definite Ada type, indexed by an integer record number.

`Ada.Dispatching` *(D.2.1)*
: A parent package containing definitions for task dispatching operations.

`Ada.Dispatching.EDF` *(D.2.6)*
: Not implemented in GNAT.

`Ada.Dispatching.Non_Preemptive` *(D.2.4)*
: Not implemented in GNAT.

`Ada.Dispatching.Round_Robin` *(D.2.5)*
: Not implemented in GNAT.

`Ada.Dynamic_Priorities` *(D.5)*
: This package allows the priorities of a task to be adjusted dynamically as the task is running.

`Ada.Environment_Variables` *(A.17)*
: This package provides facilities for accessing environment variables.

`Ada.Exceptions` *(11.4.1)*
: This package provides additional information on exceptions, and also contains facilities for treating exceptions as data objects, and raising exceptions with associated messages.

`Ada.Execution_Time` *(D.14)*
: Not implemented in GNAT.

`Ada.Execution_Time.Group_Budgets` *(D.14.2)*
: Not implemented in GNAT.

`Ada.Execution_Time.Timers` *(D.14.1)'*
: Not implemented in GNAT.

`Ada.Finalization` *(7.6)*
: This package contains the declarations and subprograms to support the use of controlled types, providing for automatic initialization and finalization (analogous to the constructors and destructors of C++).

`Ada.Float_Text_IO` *(A.10.9)*
: A library level instantiation of Text_IO.Float_IO for type Float.

`Ada.Float_Wide_Text_IO` *(A.10.9)*
: A library level instantiation of Wide_Text_IO.Float_IO for type Float.

`Ada.Float_Wide_Wide_Text_IO` *(A.10.9)*
: A library level instantiation of Wide_Wide_Text_IO.Float_IO for type Float.

`Ada.Integer_Text_IO` *(A.10.9)*
: A library level instantiation of Text_IO.Integer_IO for type Integer.

`Ada.Integer_Wide_Text_IO` *(A.10.9)*
: A library level instantiation of Wide_Text_IO.Integer_IO for type Integer.

`Ada.Integer_Wide_Wide_Text_IO` *(A.10.9)*
: A library level instantiation of Wide_Wide_Text_IO.Integer_IO for type Integer.

`Ada.Interrupts` *(C.3.2)*
: This package provides facilities for interfacing to interrupts, which includes the set of signals or conditions that can be raised and recognized as interrupts.

`Ada.Interrupts.Names` *(C.3.2)*
: This package provides the set of interrupt names (actually signal or condition names) that can be handled by GNAT.

`Ada.IO_Exceptions` *(A.13)*
: This package defines the set of exceptions that can be raised by use of the standard IO packages.

`Ada.Iterator_Interfaces` *(5.5.1)*
: This package provides a generic interface to generalized iterators.

`Ada.Locales` *(A.19)*
: This package provides declarations providing information (Language and Country) about the current locale.

`Ada.Numerics`
: This package contains some standard constants and exceptions used throughout the numerics packages. Note that the constants pi and e are defined here, and it is better to use these definitions than rolling your own.

`Ada.Numerics.Complex_Arrays` *(G.3.2)*
: Provides operations on arrays of complex numbers.

`Ada.Numerics.Complex_Elementary_Functions`
: Provides the implementation of standard elementary functions (such as log and trigonometric functions) operating on complex numbers using the standard *Float* and the *Complex* and *Imaginary* types created by the package *Numerics.Complex_Types*.

`Ada.Numerics.Complex_Types`
: This is a predefined instantiation of *Numerics.Generic_Complex_Types* using *Standard.Float* to build the type *Complex* and *Imaginary*.

`Ada.Numerics.Discrete_Random`
: This generic package provides a random number generator suitable for generating uniformly distributed values of a specified discrete subtype.

`Ada.Numerics.Float_Random`
: This package provides a random number generator suitable for generating uniformly distributed floating point values in the unit interval.

`Ada.Numerics.Generic_Complex_Elementary_Functions`
: This is a generic version of the package that provides the implementation of standard elementary functions (such as log and trigonometric functions) for an arbitrary complex type.

The following predefined instantiations of this package are provided:

* `Short_Float`

  Ada.Numerics.Short_Complex_Elementary_Functions

* `Float`

  Ada.Numerics.Complex_Elementary_Functions

* `Long_Float`

  Ada.Numerics.Long_Complex_Elementary_Functions

`Ada.Numerics.Generic_Complex_Types`
: This is a generic package that allows the creation of complex types, with associated complex arithmetic operations.

The following predefined instantiations of this package exist

* `Short_Float`

  Ada.Numerics.Short_Complex_Complex_Types

* `Float`

  Ada.Numerics.Complex_Complex_Types

* `Long_Float`

  Ada.Numerics.Long_Complex_Complex_Types

`Ada.Numerics.Generic_Elementary_Functions`
: This is a generic package that provides the implementation of standard elementary functions (such as log an trigonometric functions) for an arbitrary float type.

The following predefined instantiations of this package exist

* `Short_Float`

  Ada.Numerics.Short_Elementary_Functions

* `Float`

  Ada.Numerics.Elementary_Functions

* `Long_Float`

  Ada.Numerics.Long_Elementary_Functions

`Ada.Numerics.Generic_Real_Arrays` *(G.3.1)*
Generic operations on arrays of reals

`Ada.Numerics.Real_Arrays` *(G.3.1)*
Preinstantiation of Ada.Numerics.Generic_Real_Arrays (Float).

`Ada.Real_Time` *(D.8)*
This package provides facilities similar to those of *Calendar*, but operating with a finer clock suitable for real time control. Note that annex D requires that there be no backward clock jumps, and GNAT generally guarantees this behavior, but of course if the external clock on which the GNAT runtime depends is deliberately reset by some external event, then such a backward jump may occur.

`Ada.Real_Time.Timing_Events` *(D.15)*
Not implemented in GNAT.

`Ada.Sequential_IO` *(A.8.1)*
This package provides input-output facilities for sequential files, which can contain a sequence of values of a single type, which can be any Ada type, including indefinite (unconstrained) types.

`Ada.Storage_IO` *(A.9)*
This package provides a facility for mapping arbitrary Ada types to and from a storage buffer. It is primarily intended for the creation of new IO packages.

`Ada.Streams` *(13.13.1)*
This is a generic package that provides the basic support for the concept of streams as used by the stream attributes (*Input*, *Output*, *Read* and *Write*).

`Ada.Streams.Stream_IO` *(A.12.1)*
This package is a specialization of the type *Streams* defined in package *Streams* together with a set of operations providing Stream_IO capability. The Stream_IO model permits both random and sequential access to a file which can contain an arbitrary set of values of one or more Ada types.

`Ada.Strings` *(A.4.1)*
This package provides some basic constants used by the string handling packages.

`Ada.Strings.Bounded` *(A.4.4)*
This package provides facilities for handling variable length strings. The bounded model requires a maximum length. It is thus somewhat more limited than the unbounded model, but avoids the use of dynamic allocation or finalization.

`Ada.Strings.Bounded.Equal_Case_Insensitive` *(A.4.10)*
Provides case-insensitive comparisons of bounded strings

`Ada.Strings.Bounded.Hash` *(A.4.9)*
This package provides a generic hash function for bounded strings

`Ada.Strings.Bounded.Hash_Case_Insensitive` *(A.4.9)*
This package provides a generic hash function for bounded strings that converts the string to be hashed to lower case.

`Ada.Strings.Bounded.Less_Case_Insensitive` *(A.4.10)*
: This package provides a comparison function for bounded strings that works in a case insensitive manner by converting to lower case before the comparison.

`Ada.Strings.Fixed` *(A.4.3)*
: This package provides facilities for handling fixed length strings.

`Ada.Strings.Fixed.Equal_Case_Insensitive` *(A.4.10)*
: This package provides an equality function for fixed strings that compares the strings after converting both to lower case.

`Ada.Strings.Fixed.Hash_Case_Insensitive` *(A.4.9)*
: This package provides a case insensitive hash function for fixed strings that converts the string to lower case before computing the hash.

`Ada.Strings.Fixed.Less_Case_Insensitive` *(A.4.10)*
: This package provides a comparison function for fixed strings that works in a case insensitive manner by converting to lower case before the comparison.

`Ada.Strings.Hash` *(A.4.9)*
: This package provides a hash function for strings.

`Ada.Strings.Hash_Case_Insensitive` *(A.4.9)*
: This package provides a hash function for strings that is case insensitive. The string is converted to lower case before computing the hash.

`Ada.Strings.Less_Case_Insensitive` *(A.4.10)*
: This package provides a comparison function for\strings that works in a case insensitive manner by converting to lower case before the comparison.

`Ada.Strings.Maps` *(A.4.2)*
: This package provides facilities for handling character mappings and arbitrarily defined subsets of characters. For instance it is useful in defining specialized translation tables.

`Ada.Strings.Maps.Constants` *(A.4.6)*
: This package provides a standard set of predefined mappings and predefined character sets. For example, the standard upper to lower case conversion table is found in this package. Note that upper to lower case conversion is non-trivial if you want to take the entire set of characters, including extended characters like E with an acute accent, into account. You should use the mappings in this package (rather than adding 32 yourself) to do case mappings.

`Ada.Strings.Unbounded` *(A.4.5)*
: This package provides facilities for handling variable length strings. The unbounded model allows arbitrary length strings, but requires the use of dynamic allocation and finalization.

`Ada.Strings.Unbounded.Equal_Case_Insensitive` *(A.4.10)*
: Provides case-insensitive comparisons of unbounded strings

`Ada.Strings.Unbounded.Hash` *(A.4.9)*
: This package provides a generic hash function for unbounded strings

`Ada.Strings.Unbounded.Hash_Case_Insensitive` *(A.4.9)*
: This package provides a generic hash function for unbounded strings that converts the string to be hashed to lower case.

`Ada.Strings.Unbounded.Less_Case_Insensitive` *(A.4.10)*
: This package provides a comparison function for unbounded strings that works in a case insensitive manner by converting to lower case before the comparison.

`Ada.Strings.UTF_Encoding` *(A.4.11)*
: This package provides basic definitions for dealing with UTF-encoded strings.

`Ada.Strings.UTF_Encoding.Conversions` *(A.4.11)*
: This package provides conversion functions for UTF-encoded strings.

`Ada.Strings.UTF_Encoding.Strings` *(A.4.11)*

`Ada.Strings.UTF_Encoding.Wide_Strings` *(A.4.11)*

`Ada.Strings.UTF_Encoding.Wide_Wide_Strings` *(A.4.11)*
: These packages provide facilities for handling UTF encodings for Strings, Wide_Strings and Wide_Wide_Strings.

`Ada.Strings.Wide_Bounded` *(A.4.7)*

`Ada.Strings.Wide_Fixed` *(A.4.7)*

`Ada.Strings.Wide_Maps` *(A.4.7)*

`Ada.Strings.Wide_Unbounded` *(A.4.7)*
: These packages provide analogous capabilities to the corresponding packages without `Wide_` in the name, but operate with the types *Wide_String* and *Wide_Character* instead of *String* and *Character*. Versions of all the child packages are available.

`Ada.Strings.Wide_Wide_Bounded` *(A.4.7)*

`Ada.Strings.Wide_Wide_Fixed` *(A.4.7)*

`Ada.Strings.Wide_Wide_Maps` *(A.4.7)*

`Ada.Strings.Wide_Wide_Unbounded` *(A.4.7)*
: These packages provide analogous capabilities to the corresponding packages without `Wide_` in the name, but operate with the types *Wide_Wide_String* and *Wide_Wide_Character* instead of *String* and *Character*.

`Ada.Synchronous_Barriers` *(D.10.1)*
: This package provides facilities for synchronizing tasks at a low level with barriers.

`Ada.Synchronous_Task_Control` *(D.10)*
: This package provides some standard facilities for controlling task communication in a synchronous manner.

`Ada.Synchronous_Task_Control.EDF` *(D.10)*
: Not implemented in GNAT.

`Ada.Tags`
: This package contains definitions for manipulation of the tags of tagged values.

`Ada.Tags.Generic_Dispatching_Constructor` *(3.9)*
This package provides a way of constructing tagged class-wide values given only the tag value.

`Ada.Task_Attributes` *(C.7.2)*
This package provides the capability of associating arbitrary task-specific data with separate tasks.

`Ada.Task_Identifification` *(C.7.1)*
This package provides capabilities for task identification.

`Ada.Task_Termination` *(C.7.3)*
This package provides control over task termination.

`Ada.Text_IO`
This package provides basic text input-output capabilities for character, string and numeric data. The subpackages of this package are listed next. Note that although these are defined as subpackages in the RM, they are actually transparently implemented as child packages in GNAT, meaning that they are only loaded if needed.

`Ada.Text_IO.Decimal_IO`
Provides input-output facilities for decimal fixed-point types

`Ada.Text_IO.Enumeration_IO`
Provides input-output facilities for enumeration types.

`Ada.Text_IO.Fixed_IO`
Provides input-output facilities for ordinary fixed-point types.

`Ada.Text_IO.Float_IO`
Provides input-output facilities for float types. The following predefined instantiations of this generic package are available:

* `Short_Float`
  Short_Float_Text_IO
* `Float`
  Float_Text_IO
* `Long_Float`
  Long_Float_Text_IO

`Ada.Text_IO.Integer_IO`
Provides input-output facilities for integer types. The following predefined instantiations of this generic package are available:

* `Short_Short_Integer`
  Ada.Short_Short_Integer_Text_IO
* `Short_Integer`
  Ada.Short_Integer_Text_IO
* `Integer`
  Ada.Integer_Text_IO

* `Long_Integer`
  Ada.Long_Integer_Text_IO
* `Long_Long_Integer`
  Ada.Long_Long_Integer_Text_IO

`Ada.Text_IO.Modular_IO`
: Provides input-output facilities for modular (unsigned) types.

`Ada.Text_IO.Bounded_IO (A.10.11)`
: Provides input-output facilities for bounded strings.

`Ada.Text_IO.Complex_IO (G.1.3)`
: This package provides basic text input-output capabilities for complex data.

`Ada.Text_IO.Editing (F.3.3)`
: This package contains routines for edited output, analogous to the use of pictures in COBOL. The picture formats used by this package are a close copy of the facility in COBOL.

`Ada.Text_IO.Text_Streams (A.12.2)`
: This package provides a facility that allows Text_IO files to be treated as streams, so that the stream attributes can be used for writing arbitrary data, including binary data, to Text_IO files.

`Ada.Text_IO.Unbounded_IO (A.10.12)`
: This package provides input-output facilities for unbounded strings.

`Ada.Unchecked_Conversion (13.9)`
: This generic package allows arbitrary conversion from one type to another of the same size, providing for breaking the type safety in special circumstances.

  If the types have the same Size (more accurately the same Value_Size), then the effect is simply to transfer the bits from the source to the target type without any modification. This usage is well defined, and for simple types whose representation is typically the same across all implementations, gives a portable method of performing such conversions.

  If the types do not have the same size, then the result is implementation defined, and thus may be non-portable. The following describes how GNAT handles such unchecked conversion cases.

  If the types are of different sizes, and are both discrete types, then the effect is of a normal type conversion without any constraint checking. In particular if the result type has a larger size, the result will be zero or sign extended. If the result type has a smaller size, the result will be truncated by ignoring high order bits.

  If the types are of different sizes, and are not both discrete types, then the conversion works as though pointers were created to the source and target, and the pointer value is converted. The effect is that bits are copied from successive low order storage units and bits of the source up to the length of the target type.

A warning is issued if the lengths differ, since the effect in this case is implementation dependent, and the above behavior may not match that of some other compiler.

A pointer to one type may be converted to a pointer to another type using unchecked conversion. The only case in which the effect is undefined is when one or both pointers are pointers to unconstrained array types. In this case, the bounds information may get incorrectly transferred, and in particular, GNAT uses double size pointers for such types, and it is meaningless to convert between such pointer types. GNAT will issue a warning if the alignment of the target designated type is more strict than the alignment of the source designated type (since the result may be unaligned in this case).

A pointer other than a pointer to an unconstrained array type may be converted to and from System.Address. Such usage is common in Ada 83 programs, but note that Ada.Address_To_Access_Conversions is the preferred method of performing such conversions in Ada 95 and Ada 2005. Neither unchecked conversion nor Ada.Address_To_Access_Conversions should be used in conjunction with pointers to unconstrained objects, since the bounds information cannot be handled correctly in this case.

`Ada.Unchecked_Deallocation` *(13.11.2)*
This generic package allows explicit freeing of storage previously allocated by use of an allocator.

`Ada.Wide_Text_IO` *(A.11)*
This package is similar to *Ada.Text_IO*, except that the external file supports wide character representations, and the internal types are *Wide_Character* and *Wide_String* instead of *Character* and *String*. The corresponding set of nested packages and child packages are defined.

`Ada.Wide_Wide_Text_IO` *(A.11)*
This package is similar to *Ada.Text_IO*, except that the external file supports wide character representations, and the internal types are *Wide_Character* and *Wide_String* instead of *Character* and *String*. The corresponding set of nested packages and child packages are defined.

For packages in Interfaces and System, all the RM defined packages are available in GNAT, see the Ada 2012 RM for full details.

11 The Implementation of Standard I/O

GNAT implements all the required input-output facilities described in A.6 through A.14. These sections of the Ada Reference Manual describe the required behavior of these packages from the Ada point of view, and if you are writing a portable Ada program that does not need to know the exact manner in which Ada maps to the outside world when it comes to reading or writing external files, then you do not need to read this chapter. As long as your files are all regular files (not pipes or devices), and as long as you write and read the files only from Ada, the description in the Ada Reference Manual is sufficient.

However, if you want to do input-output to pipes or other devices, such as the keyboard or screen, or if the files you are dealing with are either generated by some other language, or to be read by some other language, then you need to know more about the details of how the GNAT implementation of these input-output facilities behaves.

In this chapter we give a detailed description of exactly how GNAT interfaces to the file system. As always, the sources of the system are available to you for answering questions at an even more detailed level, but for most purposes the information in this chapter will suffice.

Another reason that you may need to know more about how input-output is implemented arises when you have a program written in mixed languages where, for example, files are shared between the C and Ada sections of the same program. GNAT provides some additional facilities, in the form of additional child library packages, that facilitate this sharing, and these additional facilities are also described in this chapter.

11.1 Standard I/O Packages

The Standard I/O packages described in Annex A for

* Ada.Text_IO
* Ada.Text_IO.Complex_IO
* Ada.Text_IO.Text_Streams
* Ada.Wide_Text_IO
* Ada.Wide_Text_IO.Complex_IO
* Ada.Wide_Text_IO.Text_Streams
* Ada.Wide_Wide_Text_IO
* Ada.Wide_Wide_Text_IO.Complex_IO
* Ada.Wide_Wide_Text_IO.Text_Streams
* Ada.Stream_IO
* Ada.Sequential_IO
* Ada.Direct_IO

are implemented using the C library streams facility; where

* All files are opened using *fopen*.
* All input/output operations use *fread*/*fwrite*.

There is no internal buffering of any kind at the Ada library level. The only buffering is that provided at the system level in the implementation of the library routines that support streams. This facilitates shared use of these streams by mixed language programs. Note though that system level buffering is explicitly enabled at elaboration of the standard I/O packages and that can have an impact on mixed language programs, in particular those using I/O before calling the Ada elaboration routine (e.g., adainit). It is recommended to call the Ada elaboration routine before performing any I/O or when impractical, flush the common I/O streams and in particular Standard_Output before elaborating the Ada code.

11.2 FORM Strings

The format of a FORM string in GNAT is:

```
"keyword=value,keyword=value,...,keyword=value"
```

where letters may be in upper or lower case, and there are no spaces between values. The order of the entries is not important. Currently the following keywords defined.

```
TEXT_TRANSLATION=[YES|NO|TEXT|BINARY|U8TEXT|WTEXT|U16TEXT]
SHARED=[YES|NO]
WCEM=[n|h|u|s|e|8|b]
ENCODING=[UTF8|8BITS]
```

The use of these parameters is described later in this section. If an unrecognized keyword appears in a form string, it is silently ignored and not considered invalid.

11.3 Direct_IO

Direct_IO can only be instantiated for definite types. This is a restriction of the Ada language, which means that the records are fixed length (the length being determined by `type'Size`, rounded up to the next storage unit boundary if necessary).

The records of a Direct_IO file are simply written to the file in index sequence, with the first record starting at offset zero, and subsequent records following. There is no control information of any kind. For example, if 32-bit integers are being written, each record takes 4-bytes, so the record at index K starts at offset (K-1)*4.

There is no limit on the size of Direct_IO files, they are expanded as necessary to accommodate whatever records are written to the file.

11.4 Sequential_IO

Sequential_IO may be instantiated with either a definite (constrained) or indefinite (unconstrained) type.

For the definite type case, the elements written to the file are simply the memory images of the data values with no control information of any kind. The resulting file should be read using the same type, no validity checking is performed on input.

For the indefinite type case, the elements written consist of two parts. First is the size of the data item, written as the memory image of a *Interfaces.C.size_t* value, followed by the memory image of the data value. The resulting file can only be read using the same (unconstrained) type. Normal assignment checks are performed on these read operations, and if these checks fail, *Data_Error* is raised. In particular, in the array case, the lengths must match, and in the variant record case, if the variable for a particular read operation is constrained, the discriminants must match.

Note that it is not possible to use Sequential_IO to write variable length array items, and then read the data back into different length arrays. For example, the following will raise *Data_Error*:

```
package IO is new Sequential_IO (String);
F : IO.File_Type;
S : String (1..4);
...
IO.Create (F)
IO.Write (F, "hello!")
IO.Reset (F, Mode=>In_File);
IO.Read (F, S);
Put_Line (S);
```

On some Ada implementations, this will print *hell*, but the program is clearly incorrect, since there is only one element in the file, and that element is the string *hello!*.

In Ada 95 and Ada 2005, this kind of behavior can be legitimately achieved using Stream_IO, and this is the preferred mechanism. In particular, the above program fragment rewritten to use Stream_IO will work correctly.

11.5 Text_IO

Text_IO files consist of a stream of characters containing the following special control characters:

```
LF (line feed, 16#0A#) Line Mark
FF (form feed, 16#0C#) Page Mark
```

A canonical Text_IO file is defined as one in which the following conditions are met:

* The character *LF* is used only as a line mark, i.e., to mark the end of the line.
* The character *FF* is used only as a page mark, i.e., to mark the end of a page and consequently can appear only immediately following a *LF* (line mark) character.
* The file ends with either *LF* (line mark) or *LF-FF* (line mark, page mark). In the former case, the page mark is implicitly assumed to be present.

A file written using Text_IO will be in canonical form provided that no explicit *LF* or *FF* characters are written using *Put* or *Put_Line*. There will be no *FF* character at the end of the file unless an explicit *New_Page* operation was performed before closing the file.

A canonical Text_IO file that is a regular file (i.e., not a device or a pipe) can be read using any of the routines in Text_IO. The semantics in this case will be exactly as defined in the Ada Reference Manual, and all the routines in Text_IO are fully implemented.

A text file that does not meet the requirements for a canonical Text_IO file has one of the following:

* The file contains *FF* characters not immediately following a *LF* character.
* The file contains *LF* or *FF* characters written by *Put* or *Put_Line*, which are not logically considered to be line marks or page marks.

* The file ends in a character other than *LF* or *FF*, i.e., there is no explicit line mark or page mark at the end of the file.

Text_IO can be used to read such non-standard text files but subprograms to do with line or page numbers do not have defined meanings. In particular, a *FF* character that does not follow a *LF* character may or may not be treated as a page mark from the point of view of page and line numbering. Every *LF* character is considered to end a line, and there is an implied *LF* character at the end of the file.

11.5.1 Stream Pointer Positioning

Ada.Text_IO has a definition of current position for a file that is being read. No internal buffering occurs in Text_IO, and usually the physical position in the stream used to implement the file corresponds to this logical position defined by Text_IO. There are two exceptions:

* After a call to *End_Of_Page* that returns *True*, the stream is positioned past the *LF* (line mark) that precedes the page mark. Text_IO maintains an internal flag so that subsequent read operations properly handle the logical position which is unchanged by the *End_Of_Page* call.
* After a call to *End_Of_File* that returns *True*, if the Text_IO file was positioned before the line mark at the end of file before the call, then the logical position is unchanged, but the stream is physically positioned right at the end of file (past the line mark, and past a possible page mark following the line mark. Again Text_IO maintains internal flags so that subsequent read operations properly handle the logical position.

These discrepancies have no effect on the observable behavior of Text_IO, but if a single Ada stream is shared between a C program and Ada program, or shared (using `shared=yes` in the form string) between two Ada files, then the difference may be observable in some situations.

11.5.2 Reading and Writing Non-Regular Files

A non-regular file is a device (such as a keyboard), or a pipe. Text_IO can be used for reading and writing. Writing is not affected and the sequence of characters output is identical to the normal file case, but for reading, the behavior of Text_IO is modified to avoid undesirable look-ahead as follows:

An input file that is not a regular file is considered to have no page marks. Any *Ascii.FF* characters (the character normally used for a page mark) appearing in the file are considered to be data characters. In particular:

* *Get_Line* and *Skip_Line* do not test for a page mark following a line mark. If a page mark appears, it will be treated as a data character.
* This avoids the need to wait for an extra character to be typed or entered from the pipe to complete one of these operations.
* *End_Of_Page* always returns *False*
* *End_Of_File* will return *False* if there is a page mark at the end of the file.

Output to non-regular files is the same as for regular files. Page marks may be written to non-regular files using *New_Page*, but as noted above they will not be treated as page marks on input if the output is piped to another Ada program.

Another important discrepancy when reading non-regular files is that the end of file indication is not 'sticky'. If an end of file is entered, e.g., by pressing the `EOT` key, then end of file is signaled once (i.e., the test *End_Of_File* will yield *True*, or a read will raise *End_Error*), but then reading can resume to read data past that end of file indication, until another end of file indication is entered.

11.5.3 Get_Immediate

Get_Immediate returns the next character (including control characters) from the input file. In particular, Get_Immediate will return LF or FF characters used as line marks or page marks. Such operations leave the file positioned past the control character, and it is thus not treated as having its normal function. This means that page, line and column counts after this kind of Get_Immediate call are set as though the mark did not occur. In the case where a Get_Immediate leaves the file positioned between the line mark and page mark (which is not normally possible), it is undefined whether the FF character will be treated as a page mark.

11.5.4 Treating Text_IO Files as Streams

The package *Text_IO.Streams* allows a Text_IO file to be treated as a stream. Data written to a Text_IO file in this stream mode is binary data. If this binary data contains bytes 16#0A# (*LF*) or 16#0C# (*FF*), the resulting file may have non-standard format. Similarly if read operations are used to read from a Text_IO file treated as a stream, then *LF* and *FF* characters may be skipped and the effect is similar to that described above for *Get_Immediate*.

11.5.5 Text_IO Extensions

A package GNAT.IO_Aux in the GNAT library provides some useful extensions to the standard *Text_IO* package:

* function File_Exists (Name : String) return Boolean; Determines if a file of the given name exists.
* function Get_Line return String; Reads a string from the standard input file. The value returned is exactly the length of the line that was read.
* function Get_Line (File : Ada.Text_IO.File_Type) return String; Similar, except that the parameter File specifies the file from which the string is to be read.

11.5.6 Text_IO Facilities for Unbounded Strings

The package *Ada.Strings.Unbounded.Text_IO* in library files *a-suteio.ads/adb* contains some GNAT-specific subprograms useful for Text_IO operations on unbounded strings:

* function Get_Line (File : File_Type) return Unbounded_String; Reads a line from the specified file and returns the result as an unbounded string.
* procedure Put (File : File_Type; U : Unbounded_String); Writes the value of the given unbounded string to the specified file Similar to the effect of *Put (To_String (U))* except that an extra copy is avoided.
* procedure Put_Line (File : File_Type; U : Unbounded_String); Writes the value of the given unbounded string to the specified file, followed by a *New_Line*. Similar to the effect of *Put_Line (To_String (U))* except that an extra copy is avoided.

In the above procedures, *File* is of type *Ada.Text_IO.File_Type* and is optional. If the parameter is omitted, then the standard input or output file is referenced as appropriate.

The package *Ada.Strings.Wide_Unbounded.Wide_Text_IO* in library files `a-swuwti.ads` and `a-swuwti.adb` provides similar extended *Wide_Text_IO* functionality for unbounded wide strings.

The package *Ada.Strings.Wide_Wide_Unbounded.Wide_Wide_Text_IO* in library files `a-szuzti.ads` and `a-szuzti.adb` provides similar extended *Wide_Wide_Text_IO* functionality for unbounded wide wide strings.

11.6 Wide_Text_IO

Wide_Text_IO is similar in most respects to Text_IO, except that both input and output files may contain special sequences that represent wide character values. The encoding scheme for a given file may be specified using a FORM parameter:

```
WCEM='x'
```

as part of the FORM string (WCEM = wide character encoding method), where *x* is one of the following characters

Character	**Encoding**
h	Hex ESC encoding
u	Upper half encoding
s	Shift-JIS encoding
e	EUC Encoding
8	UTF-8 encoding
b	Brackets encoding

The encoding methods match those that can be used in a source program, but there is no requirement that the encoding method used for the source program be the same as the encoding method used for files, and different files may use different encoding methods.

The default encoding method for the standard files, and for opened files for which no WCEM parameter is given in the FORM string matches the wide character encoding specified for the main program (the default being brackets encoding if no coding method was specified with -gnatW).

Hex Coding

In this encoding, a wide character is represented by a five character sequence:

```
ESC a b c d
```

where a, *b*, *c*, *d* are the four hexadecimal characters (using upper case letters) of the wide character code. For example, ESC A345 is used to represent the wide character with code 16#A345#. This scheme is compatible with use of the full *Wide_Character* set.

Upper Half Coding

The wide character with encoding 16#abcd#, where the upper bit is on (i.e., a is in the range 8-F) is represented as two bytes 16#ab# and 16#cd#. The second byte may never be a format control character, but is not required to be in the upper half. This method can be also used for shift-JIS or EUC where the internal coding matches the external coding.

Shift JIS Coding

A wide character is represented by a two character sequence 16#ab# and 16#cd#, with the restrictions described for upper half encoding as described above. The internal character code is the corresponding JIS character according to the standard algorithm for Shift-JIS conversion. Only characters defined in the JIS code set table can be used with this encoding method.

EUC Coding

A wide character is represented by a two character sequence 16#ab# and 16#cd#, with both characters being in the upper half. The internal character code is the corresponding JIS character according to the EUC encoding algorithm. Only characters defined in the JIS code set table can be used with this encoding method.

UTF-8 Coding

A wide character is represented using UCS Transformation Format 8 (UTF-8) as defined in Annex R of ISO 10646-1/Am.2. Depending on the character value, the representation is a one, two, or three byte sequence:

```
16#0000#-16#007f#: 2#0xxxxxxx#
16#0080#-16#07ff#: 2#110xxxxx# 2#10xxxxxx#
16#0800#-16#ffff#: 2#1110xxxx# 2#10xxxxxx# 2#10xxxxxx#
```

where the xxx bits correspond to the left-padded bits of the 16-bit character value. Note that all lower half ASCII characters are represented as ASCII bytes and all upper half characters and other wide characters are represented as sequences of upper-half (The full UTF-8 scheme allows for encoding 31-bit characters as 6-byte sequences, but in this implementation, all UTF-8 sequences of four or more bytes length will raise a Constraint_Error, as will all invalid UTF-8 sequences.)

Brackets Coding

In this encoding, a wide character is represented by the following eight character sequence:

```
[ " a b c d " ]
```

where *a*, *b*, *c*, *d* are the four hexadecimal characters (using uppercase letters) of the wide character code. For example, *["A345"]* is used to represent the wide character with code *16#A345#*. This scheme is compatible with use of the full Wide_Character set. On input, brackets coding can also be used for upper half characters, e.g., *["C1"]* for lower case a. However, on output, brackets notation is only used for wide characters with a code greater than *16#FF#*.

Note that brackets coding is not normally used in the context of Wide_Text_IO or Wide_Wide_Text_IO, since it is really just designed as a portable way of encoding source files. In the context of Wide_Text_IO or Wide_Wide_Text_IO, it can only be used if the file does not contain any instance of the left bracket character other than to encode wide character values using the brackets encoding method. In practice it is expected that some standard wide character encoding method such as UTF-8 will be used for text input output.

If brackets notation is used, then any occurrence of a left bracket in the input file which is not the start of a valid wide character sequence will cause Constraint_Error to be raised. It is possible to encode a left bracket as ["5B"] and Wide_Text_IO and Wide_Wide_Text_IO input will interpret this as a left bracket.

However, when a left bracket is output, it will be output as a left bracket and not as ["5B"]. We make this decision because for normal use of Wide_Text_IO for outputting messages, it is unpleasant to clobber left brackets. For example, if we write:

```
Put_Line ("Start of output [first run]");
```

we really do not want to have the left bracket in this message clobbered so that the output reads:

```
Start of output ["5B"]first run]
```

In practice brackets encoding is reasonably useful for normal Put_Line use since we won't get confused between left brackets and wide character sequences in the output. But for input, or when files are written out and read back in, it really makes better sense to use one of the standard encoding methods such as UTF-8.

For the coding schemes other than UTF-8, Hex, or Brackets encoding, not all wide character values can be represented. An attempt to output a character that cannot be represented using the encoding scheme for the file causes Constraint_Error to be raised. An invalid wide character sequence on input also causes Constraint_Error to be raised.

11.6.1 Stream Pointer Positioning

Ada.Wide_Text_IO is similar to *Ada.Text_IO* in its handling of stream pointer positioning ([Text_IO], page 229). There is one additional case:

If *Ada.Wide_Text_IO.Look_Ahead* reads a character outside the normal lower ASCII set (i.e., a character in the range:

```
Wide_Character'Val (16#0080#) .. Wide_Character'Val (16#FFFF#)
```

then although the logical position of the file pointer is unchanged by the *Look_Ahead* call, the stream is physically positioned past the wide character sequence. Again this is to avoid the need for buffering or backup, and all *Wide_Text_IO* routines check the internal indication that this situation has occurred so that this is not visible to a normal program using *Wide_Text_IO*. However, this discrepancy can be observed if the wide text file shares a stream with another file.

11.6.2 Reading and Writing Non-Regular Files

As in the case of Text_IO, when a non-regular file is read, it is assumed that the file contains no page marks (any form characters are treated as data characters), and *End_Of_Page* always returns *False*. Similarly, the end of file indication is not sticky, so it is possible to read beyond an end of file.

11.7 Wide_Wide_Text_IO

Wide_Wide_Text_IO is similar in most respects to Text_IO, except that both input and output files may contain special sequences that represent wide wide character values. The encoding scheme for a given file may be specified using a FORM parameter:

```
WCEM='x'
```

as part of the FORM string (WCEM = wide character encoding method), where *x* is one of the following characters

Character	**Encoding**
h	Hex ESC encoding
u	Upper half encoding
s	Shift-JIS encoding
e	EUC Encoding
8	UTF-8 encoding
b	Brackets encoding

The encoding methods match those that can be used in a source program, but there is no requirement that the encoding method used for the source program be the same as the encoding method used for files, and different files may use different encoding methods.

The default encoding method for the standard files, and for opened files for which no WCEM parameter is given in the FORM string matches the wide character encoding specified for the main program (the default being brackets encoding if no coding method was specified with -gnatW).

UTF-8 Coding

A wide character is represented using UCS Transformation Format 8 (UTF-8) as defined in Annex R of ISO 10646-1/Am.2. Depending on the character value, the representation is a one, two, three, or four byte sequence:

```
16#000000#-16#00007f#: 2#0xxxxxxx#
16#000080#-16#0007ff#: 2#110xxxxx# 2#10xxxxxx#
16#000800#-16#00ffff#: 2#1110xxxx# 2#10xxxxxx# 2#10xxxxxx#
16#010000#-16#10ffff#: 2#11110xxx# 2#10xxxxxx# 2#10xxxxxx# 2#10xxxxxx#
```

where the xxx bits correspond to the left-padded bits of the 21-bit character value. Note that all lower half ASCII characters are represented as ASCII bytes and all upper half characters and other wide characters are represented as sequences of upper-half characters.

Brackets Coding

In this encoding, a wide wide character is represented by the following eight character sequence if is in wide character range

```
[ " a b c d " ]
```

and by the following ten character sequence if not

```
[ " a b c d e f " ]
```

where *a*, *b*, *c*, *d*, *e*, and *f* are the four or six hexadecimal characters (using uppercase letters) of the wide wide character code. For example, *["01A345"]* is used to represent the wide wide character with code *16#01A345#*.

This scheme is compatible with use of the full Wide_Wide_Character set. On input, brackets coding can also be used for upper half characters, e.g., *["C1"]* for lower case a. However, on output, brackets notation is only used for wide characters with a code greater than *16#FF#*.

If is also possible to use the other Wide_Character encoding methods, such as Shift-JIS, but the other schemes cannot support the full range of wide wide characters. An attempt to output a character that cannot be represented using the encoding scheme for the file causes Constraint_Error to be raised. An invalid wide character sequence on input also causes Constraint_Error to be raised.

11.7.1 Stream Pointer Positioning

Ada.Wide_Wide_Text_IO is similar to *Ada.Text_IO* in its handling of stream pointer positioning ([Text_IO], page 229). There is one additional case:

If *Ada.Wide_Wide_Text_IO.Look_Ahead* reads a character outside the normal lower ASCII set (i.e., a character in the range:

```
Wide_Wide_Character'Val (16#0080#) .. Wide_Wide_Character'Val (16#10FFFF#)
```

then although the logical position of the file pointer is unchanged by the *Look_Ahead* call, the stream is physically positioned past the wide character sequence. Again this is to avoid the need for buffering or backup, and all *Wide_Wide_Text_IO* routines check the internal indication that this situation has occurred so that this is not visible to a normal program using *Wide_Wide_Text_IO*. However, this discrepancy can be observed if the wide text file shares a stream with another file.

11.7.2 Reading and Writing Non-Regular Files

As in the case of Text_IO, when a non-regular file is read, it is assumed that the file contains no page marks (any form characters are treated as data characters), and *End_Of_Page* always returns *False*. Similarly, the end of file indication is not sticky, so it is possible to read beyond an end of file.

11.8 Stream_IO

A stream file is a sequence of bytes, where individual elements are written to the file as described in the Ada Reference Manual. The type *Stream_Element* is simply a byte. There are two ways to read or write a stream file.

* The operations *Read* and *Write* directly read or write a sequence of stream elements with no control information.
* The stream attributes applied to a stream file transfer data in the manner described for stream attributes.

11.9 Text Translation

`Text_Translation=xxx` may be used as the Form parameter passed to Text_IO.Create and Text_IO.Open. `Text_Translation=xxx` has no effect on Unix systems. Possible values are:

* `Yes` or `Text` is the default, which means to translate LF to/from CR/LF on Windows systems.

  `No` disables this translation; i.e. it uses binary mode. For output files, `Text_Translation=No` may be used to create Unix-style files on Windows.
* `wtext` translation enabled in Unicode mode. (corresponds to _O_WTEXT).
* `u8text` translation enabled in Unicode UTF-8 mode. (corresponds to O_U8TEXT).
* `u16text` translation enabled in Unicode UTF-16 mode. (corresponds to_O_U16TEXT).

11.10 Shared Files

Section A.14 of the Ada Reference Manual allows implementations to provide a wide variety of behavior if an attempt is made to access the same external file with two or more internal files.

To provide a full range of functionality, while at the same time minimizing the problems of portability caused by this implementation dependence, GNAT handles file sharing as follows:

* In the absence of a `shared=xxx` form parameter, an attempt to open two or more files with the same full name is considered an error and is not supported. The exception *Use_Error* will be raised. Note that a file that is not explicitly closed by the program remains open until the program terminates.
* If the form parameter `shared=no` appears in the form string, the file can be opened or created with its own separate stream identifier, regardless of whether other files sharing the same external file are opened. The exact effect depends on how the C stream routines handle multiple accesses to the same external files using separate streams.
* If the form parameter `shared=yes` appears in the form string for each of two or more files opened using the same full name, the same stream is shared between these files, and the semantics are as described in Ada Reference Manual, Section A.14.

When a program that opens multiple files with the same name is ported from another Ada compiler to GNAT, the effect will be that *Use_Error* is raised.

The documentation of the original compiler and the documentation of the program should then be examined to determine if file sharing was expected, and `shared=xxx` parameters added to *Open* and *Create* calls as required.

When a program is ported from GNAT to some other Ada compiler, no special attention is required unless the `shared=xxx` form parameter is used in the program. In this case, you must examine the documentation of the new compiler to see if it supports the required file sharing semantics, and form strings modified appropriately. Of course it may be the case that the program cannot be ported if the target compiler does not support the required functionality. The best approach in writing portable code is to avoid file sharing (and hence the use of the `shared=xxx` parameter in the form string) completely.

One common use of file sharing in Ada 83 is the use of instantiations of Sequential_IO on the same file with different types, to achieve heterogeneous input-output. Although this approach will work in GNAT if `shared=yes` is specified, it is preferable in Ada to use Stream_IO for this purpose (using the stream attributes)

11.11 Filenames encoding

An encoding form parameter can be used to specify the filename encoding `encoding=xxx`.

* If the form parameter `encoding=utf8` appears in the form string, the filename must be encoded in UTF-8.
* If the form parameter `encoding=8bits` appears in the form string, the filename must be a standard 8bits string.

In the absence of a `encoding=xxx` form parameter, the encoding is controlled by the `GNAT_CODE_PAGE` environment variable. And if not set `utf8` is assumed.

CP_ACP

The current system Windows ANSI code page.

CP_UTF8

UTF-8 encoding

This encoding form parameter is only supported on the Windows platform. On the other Operating Systems the run-time is supporting UTF-8 natively.

11.12 File content encoding

For text files it is possible to specify the encoding to use. This is controlled by the by the `GNAT_CCS_ENCODING` environment variable. And if not set `TEXT` is assumed.

The possible values are those supported on Windows:

TEXT

Translated text mode

WTEXT

Translated unicode encoding

U16TEXT

Unicode 16-bit encoding

U8TEXT

Unicode 8-bit encoding

This encoding is only supported on the Windows platform.

11.13 Open Modes

Open and *Create* calls result in a call to *fopen* using the mode shown in the following table:

Open **and** *Create* **Call Modes**

	OPEN	**CREATE**
Append_File	"r+"	"w+"
In_File	"r"	"w+"
Out_File (Direct_IO)	"r+"	"w"
Out_File (all other cases)	"w"	"w"
Inout_File	"r+"	"w+"

If text file translation is required, then either `b` or `t` is added to the mode, depending on the setting of Text. Text file translation refers to the mapping of CR/LF sequences in an external file to LF characters internally. This mapping only occurs in DOS and DOS-like systems, and is not relevant to other systems.

A special case occurs with Stream_IO. As shown in the above table, the file is initially opened in `r` or `w` mode for the *In_File* and *Out_File* cases. If a *Set_Mode* operation subsequently requires switching from reading to writing or vice-versa, then the file is reopened in `r+` mode to permit the required operation.

11.14 Operations on C Streams

The package *Interfaces.C_Streams* provides an Ada program with direct access to the C library functions for operations on C streams:

```
package Interfaces.C_Streams is
  -- Note: the reason we do not use the types that are in
  -- Interfaces.C is that we want to avoid dragging in the
  -- code in this unit if possible.
  subtype chars is System.Address;
  -- Pointer to null-terminated array of characters
  subtype FILEs is System.Address;
  -- Corresponds to the C type FILE*
  subtype voids is System.Address;
  -- Corresponds to the C type void*
  subtype int is Integer;
  subtype long is Long_Integer;
  -- Note: the above types are subtypes deliberately, and it
  -- is part of this spec that the above correspondences are
  -- guaranteed.  This means that it is legitimate to, for
  -- example, use Integer instead of int.  We provide these
```

```
-- synonyms for clarity, but in some cases it may be
-- convenient to use the underlying types (for example to
-- avoid an unnecessary dependency of a spec on the spec
-- of this unit).
type size_t is mod 2 ** Standard'Address_Size;
NULL_Stream : constant FILEs;
-- Value returned (NULL in C) to indicate an
-- fdopen/fopen/tmpfile error
----------------------------------
-- Constants Defined in stdio.h --
----------------------------------
EOF : constant int;
-- Used by a number of routines to indicate error or
-- end of file
IOFBF : constant int;
IOLBF : constant int;
IONBF : constant int;
-- Used to indicate buffering mode for setvbuf call
SEEK_CUR : constant int;
SEEK_END : constant int;
SEEK_SET : constant int;
-- Used to indicate origin for fseek call
function stdin return FILEs;
function stdout return FILEs;
function stderr return FILEs;
-- Streams associated with standard files
--------------------------
-- Standard C functions --
--------------------------
-- The functions selected below are ones that are
-- available in UNIX (but not necessarily in ANSI C).
-- These are very thin interfaces
-- which copy exactly the C headers.  For more
-- documentation on these functions, see the Microsoft C
-- "Run-Time Library Reference" (Microsoft Press, 1990,
-- ISBN 1-55615-225-6), which includes useful information
-- on system compatibility.
procedure clearerr (stream : FILEs);
function fclose (stream : FILEs) return int;
function fdopen (handle : int; mode : chars) return FILEs;
function feof (stream : FILEs) return int;
function ferror (stream : FILEs) return int;
function fflush (stream : FILEs) return int;
function fgetc (stream : FILEs) return int;
function fgets (strng : chars; n : int; stream : FILEs)
    return chars;
function fileno (stream : FILEs) return int;
```

```
function fopen (filename : chars; Mode : chars)
    return FILEs;
-- Note: to maintain target independence, use
-- text_translation_required, a boolean variable defined in
-- a-sysdep.c to deal with the target dependent text
-- translation requirement.  If this variable is set,
-- then  b/t should be appended to the standard mode
-- argument to set the text translation mode off or on
-- as required.
function fputc (C : int; stream : FILEs) return int;
function fputs (Strng : chars; Stream : FILEs) return int;
function fread
   (buffer : voids;
    size : size_t;
    count : size_t;
    stream : FILEs)
    return size_t;
function freopen
   (filename : chars;
    mode : chars;
    stream : FILEs)
    return FILEs;
function fseek
   (stream : FILEs;
    offset : long;
    origin : int)
    return int;
function ftell (stream : FILEs) return long;
function fwrite
   (buffer : voids;
    size : size_t;
    count : size_t;
    stream : FILEs)
    return size_t;
function isatty (handle : int) return int;
procedure mktemp (template : chars);
-- The return value (which is just a pointer to template)
-- is discarded
procedure rewind (stream : FILEs);
function rmtmp return int;
function setvbuf
   (stream : FILEs;
    buffer : chars;
    mode : int;
    size : size_t)
    return int;
```

```
   function tmpfile return FILEs;
   function ungetc (c : int; stream : FILEs) return int;
   function unlink (filename : chars) return int;
   ---------------------
   -- Extra functions --
   ---------------------
   -- These functions supply slightly thicker bindings than
   -- those above.  They are derived from functions in the
   -- C Run-Time Library, but may do a bit more work than
   -- just directly calling one of the Library functions.
   function is_regular_file (handle : int) return int;
   -- Tests if given handle is for a regular file (result 1)
   -- or for a non-regular file (pipe or device, result 0).
   ---------------------------------
   -- Control of Text/Binary Mode --
   ---------------------------------
   -- If text_translation_required is true, then the following
   -- functions may be used to dynamically switch a file from
   -- binary to text mode or vice versa.  These functions have
   -- no effect if text_translation_required is false (i.e., in
   -- normal UNIX mode).  Use fileno to get a stream handle.
   procedure set_binary_mode (handle : int);
   procedure set_text_mode (handle : int);
   ----------------------------
   -- Full Path Name support --
   ----------------------------
   procedure full_name (nam : chars; buffer : chars);
   -- Given a NUL terminated string representing a file
   -- name, returns in buffer a NUL terminated string
   -- representing the full path name for the file name.
   -- On systems where it is relevant the   drive is also
   -- part of the full path name.  It is the responsibility
   -- of the caller to pass an actual parameter for buffer
   -- that is big enough for any full path name.  Use
   -- max_path_len given below as the size of buffer.
   max_path_len : integer;
   -- Maximum length of an allowable full path name on the
   -- system, including a terminating NUL character.
end Interfaces.C_Streams;
```

11.15 Interfacing to C Streams

The packages in this section permit interfacing Ada files to C Stream operations.

```
with Interfaces.C_Streams;
package Ada.Sequential_IO.C_Streams is
   function C_Stream (F : File_Type)
      return Interfaces.C_Streams.FILEs;
```

```
   procedure Open
     (File : in out File_Type;
      Mode : in File_Mode;
      C_Stream : in Interfaces.C_Streams.FILEs;
      Form : in String := "");
end Ada.Sequential_IO.C_Streams;

with Interfaces.C_Streams;
package Ada.Direct_IO.C_Streams is
   function C_Stream (F : File_Type)
      return Interfaces.C_Streams.FILEs;
   procedure Open
     (File : in out File_Type;
      Mode : in File_Mode;
      C_Stream : in Interfaces.C_Streams.FILEs;
      Form : in String := "");
end Ada.Direct_IO.C_Streams;

with Interfaces.C_Streams;
package Ada.Text_IO.C_Streams is
   function C_Stream (F : File_Type)
      return Interfaces.C_Streams.FILEs;
   procedure Open
     (File : in out File_Type;
      Mode : in File_Mode;
      C_Stream : in Interfaces.C_Streams.FILEs;
      Form : in String := "");
end Ada.Text_IO.C_Streams;

with Interfaces.C_Streams;
package Ada.Wide_Text_IO.C_Streams is
   function C_Stream (F : File_Type)
      return Interfaces.C_Streams.FILEs;
   procedure Open
     (File : in out File_Type;
      Mode : in File_Mode;
      C_Stream : in Interfaces.C_Streams.FILEs;
      Form : in String := "");
end Ada.Wide_Text_IO.C_Streams;

with Interfaces.C_Streams;
package Ada.Wide_Wide_Text_IO.C_Streams is
   function C_Stream (F : File_Type)
      return Interfaces.C_Streams.FILEs;
   procedure Open
     (File : in out File_Type;
      Mode : in File_Mode;
```

```
        C_Stream : in Interfaces.C_Streams.FILEs;
        Form : in String := "");
end Ada.Wide_Wide_Text_IO.C_Streams;

with Interfaces.C_Streams;
package Ada.Stream_IO.C_Streams is
   function C_Stream (F : File_Type)
      return Interfaces.C_Streams.FILEs;
   procedure Open
     (File : in out File_Type;
      Mode : in File_Mode;
      C_Stream : in Interfaces.C_Streams.FILEs;
      Form : in String := "");
end Ada.Stream_IO.C_Streams;
```

In each of these six packages, the *C_Stream* function obtains the *FILE* pointer from a currently opened Ada file. It is then possible to use the *Interfaces.C_Streams* package to operate on this stream, or the stream can be passed to a C program which can operate on it directly. Of course the program is responsible for ensuring that only appropriate sequences of operations are executed.

One particular use of relevance to an Ada program is that the *setvbuf* function can be used to control the buffering of the stream used by an Ada file. In the absence of such a call the standard default buffering is used.

The *Open* procedures in these packages open a file giving an existing C Stream instead of a file name. Typically this stream is imported from a C program, allowing an Ada file to operate on an existing C file.

12 The GNAT Library

The GNAT library contains a number of general and special purpose packages. It represents functionality that the GNAT developers have found useful, and which is made available to GNAT users. The packages described here are fully supported, and upwards compatibility will be maintained in future releases, so you can use these facilities with the confidence that the same functionality will be available in future releases.

The chapter here simply gives a brief summary of the facilities available. The full documentation is found in the spec file for the package. The full sources of these library packages, including both spec and body, are provided with all GNAT releases. For example, to find out the full specifications of the SPITBOL pattern matching capability, including a full tutorial and extensive examples, look in the `g-spipat.ads` file in the library.

For each entry here, the package name (as it would appear in a *with* clause) is given, followed by the name of the corresponding spec file in parentheses. The packages are children in four hierarchies, *Ada*, *Interfaces*, *System*, and *GNAT*, the latter being a GNAT-specific hierarchy.

Note that an application program should only use packages in one of these four hierarchies if the package is defined in the Ada Reference Manual, or is listed in this section of the GNAT Programmers Reference Manual. All other units should be considered internal implementation units and should not be directly *with*'ed by application code. The use of a *with* statement that references one of these internal implementation units makes an application potentially dependent on changes in versions of GNAT, and will generate a warning message.

12.1 *Ada.Characters.Latin_9* (`a-chlat9.ads`)

This child of *Ada.Characters* provides a set of definitions corresponding to those in the RM-defined package *Ada.Characters.Latin_1* but with the few modifications required for *Latin-9* The provision of such a package is specifically authorized by the Ada Reference Manual (RM A.3.3(27)).

12.2 *Ada.Characters.Wide_Latin_1* (`a-cwila1.ads`)

This child of *Ada.Characters* provides a set of definitions corresponding to those in the RM-defined package *Ada.Characters.Latin_1* but with the types of the constants being *Wide_Character* instead of *Character*. The provision of such a package is specifically authorized by the Ada Reference Manual (RM A.3.3(27)).

12.3 *Ada.Characters.Wide_Latin_9* (`a-cwila1.ads`)

This child of *Ada.Characters* provides a set of definitions corresponding to those in the GNAT defined package *Ada.Characters.Latin_9* but with the types of the constants being *Wide_Character* instead of *Character*. The provision of such a package is specifically authorized by the Ada Reference Manual (RM A.3.3(27)).

12.4 *Ada.Characters.Wide_Wide_Latin_1* (a-chzla1.ads)

This child of *Ada.Characters* provides a set of definitions corresponding to those in the RM-defined package *Ada.Characters.Latin_1* but with the types of the constants being *Wide_Wide_Character* instead of *Character*. The provision of such a package is specifically authorized by the Ada Reference Manual (RM A.3.3(27)).

12.5 *Ada.Characters.Wide_Wide_Latin_9* (a-chzla9.ads)

This child of *Ada.Characters* provides a set of definitions corresponding to those in the GNAT defined package *Ada.Characters.Latin_9* but with the types of the constants being *Wide_Wide_Character* instead of *Character*. The provision of such a package is specifically authorized by the Ada Reference Manual (RM A.3.3(27)).

12.6 *Ada.Containers.Formal_Doubly_Linked_Lists* (a-cfdlli.ads)

This child of *Ada.Containers* defines a modified version of the Ada 2005 container for doubly linked lists, meant to facilitate formal verification of code using such containers. The specification of this unit is compatible with SPARK 2014.

Note that although this container was designed with formal verification in mind, it may well be generally useful in that it is a simplified more efficient version than the one defined in the standard. In particular it does not have the complex overhead required to detect cursor tampering.

12.7 *Ada.Containers.Formal_Hashed_Maps* (a-cfhama.ads)

This child of *Ada.Containers* defines a modified version of the Ada 2005 container for hashed maps, meant to facilitate formal verification of code using such containers. The specification of this unit is compatible with SPARK 2014.

Note that although this container was designed with formal verification in mind, it may well be generally useful in that it is a simplified more efficient version than the one defined in the standard. In particular it does not have the complex overhead required to detect cursor tampering.

12.8 *Ada.Containers.Formal_Hashed_Sets* (a-cfhase.ads)

This child of *Ada.Containers* defines a modified version of the Ada 2005 container for hashed sets, meant to facilitate formal verification of code using such containers. The specification of this unit is compatible with SPARK 2014.

Note that although this container was designed with formal verification in mind, it may well be generally useful in that it is a simplified more efficient version than the one defined in the standard. In particular it does not have the complex overhead required to detect cursor tampering.

12.9 *Ada.Containers.Formal_Ordered_Maps* (`a-cforma.ads`)

This child of *Ada.Containers* defines a modified version of the Ada 2005 container for ordered maps, meant to facilitate formal verification of code using such containers. The specification of this unit is compatible with SPARK 2014.

Note that although this container was designed with formal verification in mind, it may well be generally useful in that it is a simplified more efficient version than the one defined in the standard. In particular it does not have the complex overhead required to detect cursor tampering.

12.10 *Ada.Containers.Formal_Ordered_Sets* (`a-cforse.ads`)

This child of *Ada.Containers* defines a modified version of the Ada 2005 container for ordered sets, meant to facilitate formal verification of code using such containers. The specification of this unit is compatible with SPARK 2014.

Note that although this container was designed with formal verification in mind, it may well be generally useful in that it is a simplified more efficient version than the one defined in the standard. In particular it does not have the complex overhead required to detect cursor tampering.

12.11 *Ada.Containers.Formal_Vectors* (`a-cofove.ads`)

This child of *Ada.Containers* defines a modified version of the Ada 2005 container for vectors, meant to facilitate formal verification of code using such containers. The specification of this unit is compatible with SPARK 2014.

Note that although this container was designed with formal verification in mind, it may well be generally useful in that it is a simplified more efficient version than the one defined in the standard. In particular it does not have the complex overhead required to detect cursor tampering.

12.12 *Ada.Containers.Formal_Indefinite_Vectors* (`a-cfinve.ads`)

This child of *Ada.Containers* defines a modified version of the Ada 2005 container for vectors of indefinite elements, meant to facilitate formal verification of code using such containers. The specification of this unit is compatible with SPARK 2014.

Note that although this container was designed with formal verification in mind, it may well be generally useful in that it is a simplified more efficient version than the one defined in the standard. In particular it does not have the complex overhead required to detect cursor tampering.

12.13 *Ada.Containers.Bounded_Holders* (`a-coboho.ads`)

This child of *Ada.Containers* defines a modified version of Indefinite_Holders that avoids heap allocation.

12.14 *Ada.Command_Line.Environment* (`a-colien.ads`)

This child of *Ada.Command_Line* provides a mechanism for obtaining environment values on systems where this concept makes sense.

12.15 *Ada.Command_Line.Remove* (`a-colire.ads`)

This child of *Ada.Command_Line* provides a mechanism for logically removing arguments from the argument list. Once removed, an argument is not visible to further calls on the subprograms in *Ada.Command_Line* will not see the removed argument.

12.16 *Ada.Command_Line.Response_File* (`a-clrefi.ads`)

This child of *Ada.Command_Line* provides a mechanism facilities for getting command line arguments from a text file, called a "response file". Using a response file allow passing a set of arguments to an executable longer than the maximum allowed by the system on the command line.

12.17 *Ada.Direct_IO.C_Streams* (`a-diocst.ads`)

This package provides subprograms that allow interfacing between C streams and *Direct_IO*. The stream identifier can be extracted from a file opened on the Ada side, and an Ada file can be constructed from a stream opened on the C side.

12.18 *Ada.Exceptions.Is_Null_Occurrence* (`a-einuoc.ads`)

This child subprogram provides a way of testing for the null exception occurrence (*Null_Occurrence*) without raising an exception.

12.19 *Ada.Exceptions.Last_Chance_Handler* (`a-elchha.ads`)

This child subprogram is used for handling otherwise unhandled exceptions (hence the name last chance), and perform clean ups before terminating the program. Note that this subprogram never returns.

12.20 *Ada.Exceptions.Traceback* (`a-exctra.ads`)

This child package provides the subprogram (*Tracebacks*) to give a traceback array of addresses based on an exception occurrence.

12.21 *Ada.Sequential_IO.C_Streams* (`a-siocst.ads`)

This package provides subprograms that allow interfacing between C streams and *Sequential_IO*. The stream identifier can be extracted from a file opened on the Ada side, and an Ada file can be constructed from a stream opened on the C side.

12.22 *Ada.Streams.Stream_IO.C_Streams* (`a-ssicst.ads`)

This package provides subprograms that allow interfacing between C streams and *Stream_IO*. The stream identifier can be extracted from a file opened on the Ada side, and an Ada file can be constructed from a stream opened on the C side.

12.23 *Ada.Strings.Unbounded.Text_IO* (a-suteio.ads)

This package provides subprograms for Text_IO for unbounded strings, avoiding the necessity for an intermediate operation with ordinary strings.

12.24 *Ada.Strings.Wide_Unbounded.Wide_Text_IO* (a-swuwti.ads)

This package provides subprograms for Text_IO for unbounded wide strings, avoiding the necessity for an intermediate operation with ordinary wide strings.

12.25 *Ada.Strings.Wide_Wide_Unbounded.Wide_Wide_Text_IO* (a-szuzti.ads)

This package provides subprograms for Text_IO for unbounded wide wide strings, avoiding the necessity for an intermediate operation with ordinary wide wide strings.

12.26 *Ada.Text_IO.C_Streams* (a-tiocst.ads)

This package provides subprograms that allow interfacing between C streams and *Text_IO*. The stream identifier can be extracted from a file opened on the Ada side, and an Ada file can be constructed from a stream opened on the C side.

12.27 *Ada.Text_IO.Reset_Standard_Files* (a-tirsfi.ads)

This procedure is used to reset the status of the standard files used by Ada.Text_IO. This is useful in a situation (such as a restart in an embedded application) where the status of the files may change during execution (for example a standard input file may be redefined to be interactive).

12.28 *Ada.Wide_Characters.Unicode* (a-wichun.ads)

This package provides subprograms that allow categorization of Wide_Character values according to Unicode categories.

12.29 *Ada.Wide_Text_IO.C_Streams* (a-wtcstr.ads)

This package provides subprograms that allow interfacing between C streams and *Wide_Text_IO*. The stream identifier can be extracted from a file opened on the Ada side, and an Ada file can be constructed from a stream opened on the C side.

12.30 *Ada.Wide_Text_IO.Reset_Standard_Files* (a-wrstfi.ads)

This procedure is used to reset the status of the standard files used by Ada.Wide_Text_IO. This is useful in a situation (such as a restart in an embedded application) where the status of the files may change during execution (for example a standard input file may be redefined to be interactive).

12.31 *Ada.Wide_Wide_Characters.Unicode* (`a-zchuni.ads`)

This package provides subprograms that allow categorization of Wide_Wide_Character values according to Unicode categories.

12.32 *Ada.Wide_Wide_Text_IO.C_Streams* (`a-ztcstr.ads`)

This package provides subprograms that allow interfacing between C streams and *Wide_Wide_Text_IO*. The stream identifier can be extracted from a file opened on the Ada side, and an Ada file can be constructed from a stream opened on the C side.

12.33 *Ada.Wide_Wide_Text_IO.Reset_Standard_Files* (`a-zrstfi.ads`)

This procedure is used to reset the status of the standard files used by Ada.Wide_Wide_Text_IO. This is useful in a situation (such as a restart in an embedded application) where the status of the files may change during execution (for example a standard input file may be redefined to be interactive).

12.34 *GNAT.Altivec* (`g-altive.ads`)

This is the root package of the GNAT AltiVec binding. It provides definitions of constants and types common to all the versions of the binding.

12.35 *GNAT.Altivec.Conversions* (`g-altcon.ads`)

This package provides the Vector/View conversion routines.

12.36 *GNAT.Altivec.Vector_Operations* (`g-alveop.ads`)

This package exposes the Ada interface to the AltiVec operations on vector objects. A soft emulation is included by default in the GNAT library. The hard binding is provided as a separate package. This unit is common to both bindings.

12.37 *GNAT.Altivec.Vector_Types* (`g-alvety.ads`)

This package exposes the various vector types part of the Ada binding to AltiVec facilities.

12.38 *GNAT.Altivec.Vector_Views* (`g-alvevi.ads`)

This package provides public 'View' data types from/to which private vector representations can be converted via GNAT.Altivec.Conversions. This allows convenient access to individual vector elements and provides a simple way to initialize vector objects.

12.39 *GNAT.Array_Split* (`g-arrspl.ads`)

Useful array-manipulation routines: given a set of separators, split an array wherever the separators appear, and provide direct access to the resulting slices.

12.40 *GNAT.AWK* (`g-awk.ads`)

Provides AWK-like parsing functions, with an easy interface for parsing one or more files containing formatted data. The file is viewed as a database where each record is a line and a field is a data element in this line.

12.41 *GNAT.Bind_Environment* (`g-binenv.ads`)

Provides access to key=value associations captured at bind time. These associations can be specified using the *-V* binder command line switch.

12.42 *GNAT.Bounded_Buffers* (`g-boubuf.ads`)

Provides a concurrent generic bounded buffer abstraction. Instances are useful directly or as parts of the implementations of other abstractions, such as mailboxes.

12.43 *GNAT.Bounded_Mailboxes* (`g-boumai.ads`)

Provides a thread-safe asynchronous intertask mailbox communication facility.

12.44 *GNAT.Bubble_Sort* (`g-bubsor.ads`)

Provides a general implementation of bubble sort usable for sorting arbitrary data items. Exchange and comparison procedures are provided by passing access-to-procedure values.

12.45 *GNAT.Bubble_Sort_A* (`g-busora.ads`)

Provides a general implementation of bubble sort usable for sorting arbitrary data items. Move and comparison procedures are provided by passing access-to-procedure values. This is an older version, retained for compatibility. Usually *GNAT.Bubble_Sort* will be preferable.

12.46 *GNAT.Bubble_Sort_G* (`g-busorg.ads`)

Similar to *Bubble_Sort_A* except that the move and sorting procedures are provided as generic parameters, this improves efficiency, especially if the procedures can be inlined, at the expense of duplicating code for multiple instantiations.

12.47 *GNAT.Byte_Order_Mark* (`g-byorma.ads`)

Provides a routine which given a string, reads the start of the string to see whether it is one of the standard byte order marks (BOM's) which signal the encoding of the string. The routine includes detection of special XML sequences for various UCS input formats.

12.48 *GNAT.Byte_Swapping* (`g-bytswa.ads`)

General routines for swapping the bytes in 2-, 4-, and 8-byte quantities. Machine-specific implementations are available in some cases.

12.49 *GNAT.Calendar* (`g-calend.ads`)

Extends the facilities provided by *Ada.Calendar* to include handling of days of the week, an extended *Split* and *Time_Of* capability. Also provides conversion of *Ada.Calendar.Time* values to and from the C *timeval* format.

12.50 *GNAT.Calendar.Time_IO* (`g-catiio.ads`)

12.51 *GNAT.CRC32* (`g-crc32.ads`)

This package implements the CRC-32 algorithm. For a full description of this algorithm see *Computation of Cyclic Redundancy Checks via Table Look-Up*, *Communications of the ACM*, Vol. 31 No. 8, pp. 1008-1013, Aug. 1988. Sarwate, D.V.

12.52 *GNAT.Case_Util* (`g-casuti.ads`)

A set of simple routines for handling upper and lower casing of strings without the overhead of the full casing tables in *Ada.Characters.Handling*.

12.53 *GNAT.CGI* (`g-cgi.ads`)

This is a package for interfacing a GNAT program with a Web server via the Common Gateway Interface (CGI). Basically this package parses the CGI parameters, which are a set of key/value pairs sent by the Web server. It builds a table whose index is the key and provides some services to deal with this table.

12.54 *GNAT.CGI.Cookie* (`g-cgicoo.ads`)

This is a package to interface a GNAT program with a Web server via the Common Gateway Interface (CGI). It exports services to deal with Web cookies (piece of information kept in the Web client software).

12.55 *GNAT.CGI.Debug* (`g-cgideb.ads`)

This is a package to help debugging CGI (Common Gateway Interface) programs written in Ada.

12.56 *GNAT.Command_Line* (`g-comlin.ads`)

Provides a high level interface to *Ada.Command_Line* facilities, including the ability to scan for named switches with optional parameters and expand file names using wild card notations.

12.57 *GNAT.Compiler_Version* (`g-comver.ads`)

Provides a routine for obtaining the version of the compiler used to compile the program. More accurately this is the version of the binder used to bind the program (this will normally be the same as the version of the compiler if a consistent tool set is used to compile all units of a partition).

12.58 *GNAT.Ctrl_C* (g-ctrl_c.ads)

Provides a simple interface to handle Ctrl-C keyboard events.

12.59 *GNAT.Current_Exception* (g-curexc.ads)

Provides access to information on the current exception that has been raised without the need for using the Ada 95 / Ada 2005 exception choice parameter specification syntax. This is particularly useful in simulating typical facilities for obtaining information about exceptions provided by Ada 83 compilers.

12.60 *GNAT.Debug_Pools* (g-debpoo.ads)

Provide a debugging storage pools that helps tracking memory corruption problems. See *The GNAT Debug_Pool Facility* section in the *GNAT User's Guide*.

12.61 *GNAT.Debug_Utilities* (g-debuti.ads)

Provides a few useful utilities for debugging purposes, including conversion to and from string images of address values. Supports both C and Ada formats for hexadecimal literals.

12.62 *GNAT.Decode_String* (g-decstr.ads)

A generic package providing routines for decoding wide character and wide wide character strings encoded as sequences of 8-bit characters using a specified encoding method. Includes validation routines, and also routines for stepping to next or previous encoded character in an encoded string. Useful in conjunction with Unicode character coding. Note there is a preinstantiation for UTF-8. See next entry.

12.63 *GNAT.Decode_UTF8_String* (g-deutst.ads)

A preinstantiation of GNAT.Decode_Strings for UTF-8 encoding.

12.64 *GNAT.Directory_Operations* (g-dirope.ads)

Provides a set of routines for manipulating directories, including changing the current directory, making new directories, and scanning the files in a directory.

12.65 *GNAT.Directory_Operations.Iteration* (g-diopit.ads)

A child unit of GNAT.Directory_Operations providing additional operations for iterating through directories.

12.66 *GNAT.Dynamic_HTables* (g-dynhta.ads)

A generic implementation of hash tables that can be used to hash arbitrary data. Provided in two forms, a simple form with built in hash functions, and a more complex form in which the hash function is supplied.

This package provides a facility similar to that of *GNAT.HTable*, except that this package declares a type that can be used to define dynamic instances of the hash table, while an instantiation of *GNAT.HTable* creates a single instance of the hash table.

12.67 *GNAT.Dynamic_Tables* (`g-dyntab.ads`)

A generic package providing a single dimension array abstraction where the length of the array can be dynamically modified.

This package provides a facility similar to that of *GNAT.Table*, except that this package declares a type that can be used to define dynamic instances of the table, while an instantiation of *GNAT.Table* creates a single instance of the table type.

12.68 *GNAT.Encode_String* (`g-encstr.ads`)

A generic package providing routines for encoding wide character and wide wide character strings as sequences of 8-bit characters using a specified encoding method. Useful in conjunction with Unicode character coding. Note there is a preinstantiation for UTF-8. See next entry.

12.69 *GNAT.Encode_UTF8_String* (`g-enutst.ads`)

A preinstantiation of GNAT.Encode_Strings for UTF-8 encoding.

12.70 *GNAT.Exception_Actions* (`g-excact.ads`)

Provides callbacks when an exception is raised. Callbacks can be registered for specific exceptions, or when any exception is raised. This can be used for instance to force a core dump to ease debugging.

12.71 *GNAT.Exception_Traces* (`g-exctra.ads`)

Provides an interface allowing to control automatic output upon exception occurrences.

12.72 *GNAT.Exceptions* (`g-expect.ads`)

Normally it is not possible to raise an exception with a message from a subprogram in a pure package, since the necessary types and subprograms are in *Ada.Exceptions* which is not a pure unit. *GNAT.Exceptions* provides a facility for getting around this limitation for a few predefined exceptions, and for example allow raising *Constraint_Error* with a message from a pure subprogram.

12.73 *GNAT.Expect* (`g-expect.ads`)

Provides a set of subprograms similar to what is available with the standard Tcl Expect tool. It allows you to easily spawn and communicate with an external process. You can send commands or inputs to the process, and compare the output with some expected regular expression. Currently *GNAT.Expect* is implemented on all native GNAT ports. It is not implemented for cross ports, and in particular is not implemented for VxWorks or LynxOS.

12.74 *GNAT.Expect.TTY* (`g-exptty.ads`)

As GNAT.Expect but using pseudo-terminal. Currently *GNAT.Expect.TTY* is implemented on all native GNAT ports. It is not implemented for cross ports, and in particular is not implemented for VxWorks or LynxOS.

12.75 *GNAT.Float_Control* (`g-flocon.ads`)

Provides an interface for resetting the floating-point processor into the mode required for correct semantic operation in Ada. Some third party library calls may cause this mode to be modified, and the Reset procedure in this package can be used to reestablish the required mode.

12.76 *GNAT.Formatted_String* (`g-forstr.ads`)

Provides support for C/C++ printf() formatted strings. The format is copied from the printf() routine and should therefore gives identical output. Some generic routines are provided to be able to use types derived from Integer, Float or enumerations as values for the formatted string.

12.77 *GNAT.Heap_Sort* (`g-heasor.ads`)

Provides a general implementation of heap sort usable for sorting arbitrary data items. Exchange and comparison procedures are provided by passing access-to-procedure values. The algorithm used is a modified heap sort that performs approximately N*log(N) comparisons in the worst case.

12.78 *GNAT.Heap_Sort_A* (`g-hesora.ads`)

Provides a general implementation of heap sort usable for sorting arbitrary data items. Move and comparison procedures are provided by passing access-to-procedure values. The algorithm used is a modified heap sort that performs approximately N*log(N) comparisons in the worst case. This differs from *GNAT.Heap_Sort* in having a less convenient interface, but may be slightly more efficient.

12.79 *GNAT.Heap_Sort_G* (`g-hesorg.ads`)

Similar to *Heap_Sort_A* except that the move and sorting procedures are provided as generic parameters, this improves efficiency, especially if the procedures can be inlined, at the expense of duplicating code for multiple instantiations.

12.80 *GNAT.HTable* (`g-htable.ads`)

A generic implementation of hash tables that can be used to hash arbitrary data. Provides two approaches, one a simple static approach, and the other allowing arbitrary dynamic hash tables.

12.81 *GNAT.IO* (`g-io.ads`)

A simple preelaborable input-output package that provides a subset of simple Text_IO functions for reading characters and strings from Standard_Input, and writing characters, strings and integers to either Standard_Output or Standard_Error.

12.82 *GNAT.IO_Aux* (`g-io_aux.ads`)

Provides some auxiliary functions for use with Text_IO, including a test for whether a file exists, and functions for reading a line of text.

12.83 *GNAT.Lock_Files* (g-locfil.ads)

Provides a general interface for using files as locks. Can be used for providing program level synchronization.

12.84 *GNAT.MBBS_Discrete_Random* (g-mbdira.ads)

The original implementation of *Ada.Numerics.Discrete_Random*. Uses a modified version of the Blum-Blum-Shub generator.

12.85 *GNAT.MBBS_Float_Random* (g-mbflra.ads)

The original implementation of *Ada.Numerics.Float_Random*. Uses a modified version of the Blum-Blum-Shub generator.

12.86 *GNAT.MD5* (g-md5.ads)

Implements the MD5 Message-Digest Algorithm as described in RFC 1321, and the HMAC-MD5 message authentication function as described in RFC 2104 and FIPS PUB 198.

12.87 *GNAT.Memory_Dump* (g-memdum.ads)

Provides a convenient routine for dumping raw memory to either the standard output or standard error files. Uses GNAT.IO for actual output.

12.88 *GNAT.Most_Recent_Exception* (g-moreex.ads)

Provides access to the most recently raised exception. Can be used for various logging purposes, including duplicating functionality of some Ada 83 implementation dependent extensions.

12.89 *GNAT.OS_Lib* (g-os_lib.ads)

Provides a range of target independent operating system interface functions, including time/date management, file operations, subprocess management, including a portable spawn procedure, and access to environment variables and error return codes.

12.90 *GNAT.Perfect_Hash_Generators* (g-pehage.ads)

Provides a generator of static minimal perfect hash functions. No collisions occur and each item can be retrieved from the table in one probe (perfect property). The hash table size corresponds to the exact size of the key set and no larger (minimal property). The key set has to be know in advance (static property). The hash functions are also order preserving. If w2 is inserted after w1 in the generator, their hashcode are in the same order. These hashing functions are very convenient for use with realtime applications.

12.91 *GNAT.Random_Numbers* (g-rannum.ads)

Provides random number capabilities which extend those available in the standard Ada library and are more convenient to use.

12.92 *GNAT.Regexp* (`g-regexp.ads`)

A simple implementation of regular expressions, using a subset of regular expression syntax copied from familiar Unix style utilities. This is the simplest of the three pattern matching packages provided, and is particularly suitable for 'file globbing' applications.

12.93 *GNAT.Registry* (`g-regist.ads`)

This is a high level binding to the Windows registry. It is possible to do simple things like reading a key value, creating a new key. For full registry API, but at a lower level of abstraction, refer to the Win32.Winreg package provided with the Win32Ada binding

12.94 *GNAT.Regpat* (`g-regpat.ads`)

A complete implementation of Unix-style regular expression matching, copied from the original V7 style regular expression library written in C by Henry Spencer (and binary compatible with this C library).

12.95 *GNAT.Rewrite_Data* (`g-rewdat.ads`)

A unit to rewrite on-the-fly string occurrences in a stream of data. The implementation has a very minimal memory footprint as the full content to be processed is not loaded into memory all at once. This makes this interface usable for large files or socket streams.

12.96 *GNAT.Secondary_Stack_Info* (`g-sestin.ads`)

Provide the capability to query the high water mark of the current task's secondary stack.

12.97 *GNAT.Semaphores* (`g-semaph.ads`)

Provides classic counting and binary semaphores using protected types.

12.98 *GNAT.Serial_Communications* (`g-sercom.ads`)

Provides a simple interface to send and receive data over a serial port. This is only supported on GNU/Linux and Windows.

12.99 *GNAT.SHA1* (`g-sha1.ads`)

Implements the SHA-1 Secure Hash Algorithm as described in FIPS PUB 180-3 and RFC 3174, and the HMAC-SHA1 message authentication function as described in RFC 2104 and FIPS PUB 198.

12.100 *GNAT.SHA224* (`g-sha224.ads`)

Implements the SHA-224 Secure Hash Algorithm as described in FIPS PUB 180-3, and the HMAC-SHA224 message authentication function as described in RFC 2104 and FIPS PUB 198.

12.101 *GNAT.SHA256* (g-sha256.ads)

Implements the SHA-256 Secure Hash Algorithm as described in FIPS PUB 180-3, and the HMAC-SHA256 message authentication function as described in RFC 2104 and FIPS PUB 198.

12.102 *GNAT.SHA384* (g-sha384.ads)

Implements the SHA-384 Secure Hash Algorithm as described in FIPS PUB 180-3, and the HMAC-SHA384 message authentication function as described in RFC 2104 and FIPS PUB 198.

12.103 *GNAT.SHA512* (g-sha512.ads)

Implements the SHA-512 Secure Hash Algorithm as described in FIPS PUB 180-3, and the HMAC-SHA512 message authentication function as described in RFC 2104 and FIPS PUB 198.

12.104 *GNAT.Signals* (g-signal.ads)

Provides the ability to manipulate the blocked status of signals on supported targets.

12.105 *GNAT.Sockets* (g-socket.ads)

A high level and portable interface to develop sockets based applications. This package is based on the sockets thin binding found in *GNAT.Sockets.Thin*. Currently *GNAT.Sockets* is implemented on all native GNAT ports and on VxWorks cross prots. It is not implemented for the LynxOS cross port.

12.106 *GNAT.Source_Info* (g-souinf.ads)

Provides subprograms that give access to source code information known at compile time, such as the current file name and line number. Also provides subprograms yielding the date and time of the current compilation (like the C macros *__DATE__* and *__TIME__*)

12.107 *GNAT.Spelling_Checker* (g-speche.ads)

Provides a function for determining whether one string is a plausible near misspelling of another string.

12.108 *GNAT.Spelling_Checker_Generic* (g-spchge.ads)

Provides a generic function that can be instantiated with a string type for determining whether one string is a plausible near misspelling of another string.

12.109 *GNAT.Spitbol.Patterns* (g-spipat.ads)

A complete implementation of SNOBOL4 style pattern matching. This is the most elaborate of the pattern matching packages provided. It fully duplicates the SNOBOL4 dynamic pattern construction and matching capabilities, using the efficient algorithm developed by Robert Dewar for the SPITBOL system.

12.110 *GNAT.Spitbol* (g-spitbo.ads)

The top level package of the collection of SPITBOL-style functionality, this package provides basic SNOBOL4 string manipulation functions, such as Pad, Reverse, Trim, Substr capability, as well as a generic table function useful for constructing arbitrary mappings from strings in the style of the SNOBOL4 TABLE function.

12.111 *GNAT.Spitbol.Table_Boolean* (g-sptabo.ads)

A library level of instantiation of *GNAT.Spitbol.Patterns.Table* for type *Standard.Boolean*, giving an implementation of sets of string values.

12.112 *GNAT.Spitbol.Table_Integer* (g-sptain.ads)

A library level of instantiation of *GNAT.Spitbol.Patterns.Table* for type *Standard.Integer*, giving an implementation of maps from string to integer values.

12.113 *GNAT.Spitbol.Table_VString* (g-sptavs.ads)

A library level of instantiation of *GNAT.Spitbol.Patterns.Table* for a variable length string type, giving an implementation of general maps from strings to strings.

12.114 *GNAT.SSE* (g-sse.ads)

Root of a set of units aimed at offering Ada bindings to a subset of the Intel(r) Streaming SIMD Extensions with GNAT on the x86 family of targets. It exposes vector component types together with a general introduction to the binding contents and use.

12.115 *GNAT.SSE.Vector_Types* (g-ssvety.ads)

SSE vector types for use with SSE related intrinsics.

12.116 *GNAT.Strings* (g-string.ads)

Common String access types and related subprograms. Basically it defines a string access and an array of string access types.

12.117 *GNAT.String_Split* (g-strspl.ads)

Useful string manipulation routines: given a set of separators, split a string wherever the separators appear, and provide direct access to the resulting slices. This package is instantiated from *GNAT.Array_Split*.

12.118 *GNAT.Table* (g-table.ads)

A generic package providing a single dimension array abstraction where the length of the array can be dynamically modified.

This package provides a facility similar to that of *GNAT.Dynamic_Tables*, except that this package declares a single instance of the table type, while an instantiation of *GNAT.Dynamic_Tables* creates a type that can be used to define dynamic instances of the table.

12.119 *GNAT.Task_Lock* (g-tasloc.ads)

A very simple facility for locking and unlocking sections of code using a single global task lock. Appropriate for use in situations where contention between tasks is very rarely expected.

12.120 *GNAT.Time_Stamp* (g-timsta.ads)

Provides a simple function that returns a string YYYY-MM-DD HH:MM:SS.SS that represents the current date and time in ISO 8601 format. This is a very simple routine with minimal code and there are no dependencies on any other unit.

12.121 *GNAT.Threads* (g-thread.ads)

Provides facilities for dealing with foreign threads which need to be known by the GNAT run-time system. Consult the documentation of this package for further details if your program has threads that are created by a non-Ada environment which then accesses Ada code.

12.122 *GNAT.Traceback* (g-traceb.ads)

Provides a facility for obtaining non-symbolic traceback information, useful in various debugging situations.

12.123 *GNAT.Traceback.Symbolic* (g-trasym.ads)

12.124 *GNAT.UTF_32* (g-table.ads)

This is a package intended to be used in conjunction with the *Wide_Character* type in Ada 95 and the *Wide_Wide_Character* type in Ada 2005 (available in *GNAT* in Ada 2005 mode). This package contains Unicode categorization routines, as well as lexical categorization routines corresponding to the Ada 2005 lexical rules for identifiers and strings, and also a lower case to upper case fold routine corresponding to the Ada 2005 rules for identifier equivalence.

12.125 *GNAT.Wide_Spelling_Checker* (g-u3spch.ads)

Provides a function for determining whether one wide wide string is a plausible near misspelling of another wide wide string, where the strings are represented using the UTF_32_String type defined in System.Wch_Cnv.

12.126 *GNAT.Wide_Spelling_Checker* (g-wispch.ads)

Provides a function for determining whether one wide string is a plausible near misspelling of another wide string.

12.127 *GNAT.Wide_String_Split* (g-wistsp.ads)

Useful wide string manipulation routines: given a set of separators, split a wide string wherever the separators appear, and provide direct access to the resulting slices. This package is instantiated from *GNAT.Array_Split*.

12.128 *GNAT.Wide_Wide_Spelling_Checker* (g-zspche.ads)

Provides a function for determining whether one wide wide string is a plausible near misspelling of another wide wide string.

12.129 *GNAT.Wide_Wide_String_Split* (g-zistsp.ads)

Useful wide wide string manipulation routines: given a set of separators, split a wide wide string wherever the separators appear, and provide direct access to the resulting slices. This package is instantiated from *GNAT.Array_Split*.

12.130 *Interfaces.C.Extensions* (i-cexten.ads)

This package contains additional C-related definitions, intended for use with either manually or automatically generated bindings to C libraries.

12.131 *Interfaces.C.Streams* (i-cstrea.ads)

This package is a binding for the most commonly used operations on C streams.

12.132 *Interfaces.Packed_Decimal* (i-pacdec.ads)

This package provides a set of routines for conversions to and from a packed decimal format compatible with that used on IBM mainframes.

12.133 *Interfaces.VxWorks* (i-vxwork.ads)

This package provides a limited binding to the VxWorks API. In particular, it interfaces with the VxWorks hardware interrupt facilities.

12.134 *Interfaces.VxWorks.IO* (i-vxwoio.ads)

This package provides a binding to the ioctl (IO/Control) function of VxWorks, defining a set of option values and function codes. A particular use of this package is to enable the use of Get_Immediate under VxWorks.

12.135 *System.Address_Image* (s-addima.ads)

This function provides a useful debugging function that gives an (implementation dependent) string which identifies an address.

12.136 *System.Assertions* (s-assert.ads)

This package provides the declaration of the exception raised by an run-time assertion failure, as well as the routine that is used internally to raise this assertion.

12.137 *System.Atomic_Counters* (s-atocou.ads)

This package provides the declaration of an atomic counter type, together with efficient routines (using hardware synchronization primitives) for incrementing, decrementing, and testing of these counters. This package is implemented on most targets, including all Alpha, ia64, PowerPC, SPARC V9, x86, and x86_64 platforms.

12.138 *System.Memory* (`s-memory.ads`)

This package provides the interface to the low level routines used by the generated code for allocation and freeing storage for the default storage pool (analogous to the C routines malloc and free. It also provides a reallocation interface analogous to the C routine realloc. The body of this unit may be modified to provide alternative allocation mechanisms for the default pool, and in addition, direct calls to this unit may be made for low level allocation uses (for example see the body of *GNAT.Tables*).

12.139 *System.Multiprocessors* (`s-multip.ads`)

This is an Ada 2012 unit defined in the Ada 2012 Reference Manual, but in GNAT we also make it available in Ada 95 and Ada 2005 (where it is technically an implementation-defined addition).

12.140 *System.Multiprocessors.Dispatching_Domains* (`s-mudido.ads`)

This is an Ada 2012 unit defined in the Ada 2012 Reference Manual, but in GNAT we also make it available in Ada 95 and Ada 2005 (where it is technically an implementation-defined addition).

12.141 *System.Partition_Interface* (`s-parint.ads`)

This package provides facilities for partition interfacing. It is used primarily in a distribution context when using Annex E with *GLADE*.

12.142 *System.Pool_Global* (`s-pooglo.ads`)

This package provides a storage pool that is equivalent to the default storage pool used for access types for which no pool is specifically declared. It uses malloc/free to allocate/free and does not attempt to do any automatic reclamation.

12.143 *System.Pool_Local* (`s-pooloc.ads`)

This package provides a storage pool that is intended for use with locally defined access types. It uses malloc/free for allocate/free, and maintains a list of allocated blocks, so that all storage allocated for the pool can be freed automatically when the pool is finalized.

12.144 *System.Restrictions* (`s-restri.ads`)

This package provides facilities for accessing at run time the status of restrictions specified at compile time for the partition. Information is available both with regard to actual restrictions specified, and with regard to compiler determined information on which restrictions are violated by one or more packages in the partition.

12.145 *System.Rident* (`s-rident.ads`)

This package provides definitions of the restrictions identifiers supported by GNAT, and also the format of the restrictions provided in package System.Restrictions. It is not normally necessary to *with* this generic package since the necessary instantiation is included in package System.Restrictions.

12.146 *System.Strings.Stream_Ops* (`s-ststop.ads`)

This package provides a set of stream subprograms for standard string types. It is intended primarily to support implicit use of such subprograms when stream attributes are applied to string types, but the subprograms in this package can be used directly by application programs.

12.147 *System.Unsigned_Types* (`s-unstyp.ads`)

This package contains definitions of standard unsigned types that correspond in size to the standard signed types declared in Standard, and (unlike the types in Interfaces) have corresponding names. It also contains some related definitions for other specialized types used by the compiler in connection with packed array types.

12.148 *System.Wch_Cnv* (`s-wchcnv.ads`)

This package provides routines for converting between wide and wide wide characters and a representation as a value of type *Standard.String*, using a specified wide character encoding method. It uses definitions in package *System.Wch_Con*.

12.149 *System.Wch_Con* (`s-wchcon.ads`)

This package provides definitions and descriptions of the various methods used for encoding wide characters in ordinary strings. These definitions are used by the package *System.Wch_Cnv*.

13 Interfacing to Other Languages

The facilities in Annex B of the Ada Reference Manual are fully implemented in GNAT, and in addition, a full interface to C++ is provided.

13.1 Interfacing to C

Interfacing to C with GNAT can use one of two approaches:

* The types in the package *Interfaces.C* may be used.
* Standard Ada types may be used directly. This may be less portable to other compilers, but will work on all GNAT compilers, which guarantee correspondence between the C and Ada types.

Pragma *Convention C* may be applied to Ada types, but mostly has no effect, since this is the default. The following table shows the correspondence between Ada scalar types and the corresponding C types.

Ada Type	**C Type**
`Integer`	`int`
`Short_Integer`	`short`
`Short_Short_Integer`	`signed char`
`Long_Integer`	`long`
`Long_Long_Integer`	`long long`
`Short_Float`	`float`
`Float`	`float`
`Long_Float`	`double`
`Long_Long_Float`	This is the longest floating-point type supported by the hardware.

Additionally, there are the following general correspondences between Ada and C types:

* Ada enumeration types map to C enumeration types directly if pragma *Convention C* is specified, which causes them to have int length. Without pragma *Convention C*, Ada enumeration types map to 8, 16, or 32 bits (i.e., C types *signed char*, *short*, *int*, respectively) depending on the number of values passed. This is the only case in which pragma *Convention C* affects the representation of an Ada type.
* Ada access types map to C pointers, except for the case of pointers to unconstrained types in Ada, which have no direct C equivalent.
* Ada arrays map directly to C arrays.

* Ada records map directly to C structures.
* Packed Ada records map to C structures where all members are bit fields of the length corresponding to the `type'Size` value in Ada.

13.2 Interfacing to C++

The interface to C++ makes use of the following pragmas, which are primarily intended to be constructed automatically using a binding generator tool, although it is possible to construct them by hand.

Using these pragmas it is possible to achieve complete inter-operability between Ada tagged types and C++ class definitions. See [Implementation Defined Pragmas], page 4, for more details.

pragma CPP_Class ([Entity =>] 'LOCAL_NAME')

The argument denotes an entity in the current declarative region that is declared as a tagged or untagged record type. It indicates that the type corresponds to an externally declared C++ class type, and is to be laid out the same way that C++ would lay out the type.

Note: Pragma *CPP_Class* is currently obsolete. It is supported for backward compatibility but its functionality is available using pragma *Import* with *Convention = CPP*.

pragma CPP_Constructor ([Entity =>] 'LOCAL_NAME')

This pragma identifies an imported function (imported in the usual way with pragma *Import*) as corresponding to a C++ constructor.

A few restrictions are placed on the use of the *Access* attribute in conjunction with subprograms subject to convention *CPP*: the attribute may be used neither on primitive operations of a tagged record type with convention *CPP*, imported or not, nor on subprograms imported with pragma *CPP_Constructor*.

In addition, C++ exceptions are propagated and can be handled in an *others* choice of an exception handler. The corresponding Ada occurrence has no message, and the simple name of the exception identity contains `Foreign_Exception`. Finalization and awaiting dependent tasks works properly when such foreign exceptions are propagated.

It is also possible to import a C++ exception using the following syntax:

```
LOCAL_NAME : exception;
pragma Import (Cpp,
  [Entity =>] LOCAL_NAME,
  [External_Name =>] static_string_EXPRESSION);
```

The *External_Name* is the name of the C++ RTTI symbol. You can then cover a specific C++ exception in an exception handler.

13.3 Interfacing to COBOL

Interfacing to COBOL is achieved as described in section B.4 of the Ada Reference Manual.

13.4 Interfacing to Fortran

Interfacing to Fortran is achieved as described in section B.5 of the Ada Reference Manual. The pragma *Convention Fortran*, applied to a multi-dimensional array causes the array to be stored in column-major order as required for convenient interface to Fortran.

13.5 Interfacing to non-GNAT Ada code

It is possible to specify the convention *Ada* in a pragma *Import* or pragma *Export*. However this refers to the calling conventions used by GNAT, which may or may not be similar enough to those used by some other Ada 83 / Ada 95 / Ada 2005 compiler to allow interoperation.

If arguments types are kept simple, and if the foreign compiler generally follows system calling conventions, then it may be possible to integrate files compiled by other Ada compilers, provided that the elaboration issues are adequately addressed (for example by eliminating the need for any load time elaboration).

In particular, GNAT running on VMS is designed to be highly compatible with the DEC Ada 83 compiler, so this is one case in which it is possible to import foreign units of this type, provided that the data items passed are restricted to simple scalar values or simple record types without variants, or simple array types with fixed bounds.

14 Specialized Needs Annexes

Ada 95, Ada 2005, and Ada 2012 define a number of Specialized Needs Annexes, which are not required in all implementations. However, as described in this chapter, GNAT implements all of these annexes:

Systems Programming (Annex C)
The Systems Programming Annex is fully implemented.

Real-Time Systems (Annex D)
The Real-Time Systems Annex is fully implemented.

Distributed Systems (Annex E)
Stub generation is fully implemented in the GNAT compiler. In addition, a complete compatible PCS is available as part of the GLADE system, a separate product. When the two products are used in conjunction, this annex is fully implemented.

Information Systems (Annex F)
The Information Systems annex is fully implemented.

Numerics (Annex G)
The Numerics Annex is fully implemented.

Safety and Security / High-Integrity Systems (Annex H)
The Safety and Security Annex (termed the High-Integrity Systems Annex in Ada 2005) is fully implemented.

15 Implementation of Specific Ada Features

This chapter describes the GNAT implementation of several Ada language facilities.

15.1 Machine Code Insertions

Package *Machine_Code* provides machine code support as described in the Ada Reference Manual in two separate forms:

* Machine code statements, consisting of qualified expressions that fit the requirements of RM section 13.8.
* An intrinsic callable procedure, providing an alternative mechanism of including machine instructions in a subprogram.

The two features are similar, and both are closely related to the mechanism provided by the asm instruction in the GNU C compiler. Full understanding and use of the facilities in this package requires understanding the asm instruction, see the section on Extended Asm in *Using_the_GNU_Compiler_Collection_(GCC)*.

Calls to the function *Asm* and the procedure *Asm* have identical semantic restrictions and effects as described below. Both are provided so that the procedure call can be used as a statement, and the function call can be used to form a code_statement.

Consider this C *asm* instruction:

```
asm ("fsinx %1 %0" : "=f" (result) : "f" (angle));
```

The equivalent can be written for GNAT as:

```
Asm ("fsinx %1 %0",
     My_Float'Asm_Output ("=f", result),
     My_Float'Asm_Input  ("f",  angle));
```

The first argument to *Asm* is the assembler template, and is identical to what is used in GNU C. This string must be a static expression. The second argument is the output operand list. It is either a single *Asm_Output* attribute reference, or a list of such references enclosed in parentheses (technically an array aggregate of such references).

The *Asm_Output* attribute denotes a function that takes two parameters. The first is a string, the second is the name of a variable of the type designated by the attribute prefix. The first (string) argument is required to be a static expression and designates the constraint (see the section on Constraints in *Using_the_GNU_Compiler_Collection_(GCC)*) for the parameter; e.g., what kind of register is required. The second argument is the variable to be written or updated with the result. The possible values for constraint are the same as those used in the RTL, and are dependent on the configuration file used to build the GCC back end. If there are no output operands, then this argument may either be omitted, or explicitly given as *No_Output_Operands*. No support is provided for GNU C's symbolic names for output parameters.

The second argument of `my_float'Asm_Output` functions as though it were an *out* parameter, which is a little curious, but all names have the form of expressions, so there is no syntactic irregularity, even though normally functions would not be permitted *out* parameters. The third argument is the list of input operands. It is either a single *Asm_Input* attribute reference, or a list of such references enclosed in parentheses (technically an array aggregate of such references).

The *Asm_Input* attribute denotes a function that takes two parameters. The first is a string, the second is an expression of the type designated by the prefix. The first (string) argument is required to be a static expression, and is the constraint for the parameter, (e.g., what kind of register is required). The second argument is the value to be used as the input argument. The possible values for the constraint are the same as those used in the RTL, and are dependent on the configuration file used to built the GCC back end. No support is provided for GNU C's symbolic names for input parameters.

If there are no input operands, this argument may either be omitted, or explicitly given as *No_Input_Operands*. The fourth argument, not present in the above example, is a list of register names, called the *clobber* argument. This argument, if given, must be a static string expression, and is a space or comma separated list of names of registers that must be considered destroyed as a result of the *Asm* call. If this argument is the null string (the default value), then the code generator assumes that no additional registers are destroyed. In addition to registers, the special clobbers *memory* and *cc* as described in the GNU C docs are both supported.

The fifth argument, not present in the above example, called the *volatile* argument, is by default *False*. It can be set to the literal value *True* to indicate to the code generator that all optimizations with respect to the instruction specified should be suppressed, and in particular an instruction that has outputs will still be generated, even if none of the outputs are used. See *Using_the_GNU_Compiler_Collection_(GCC)* for the full description. Generally it is strongly advisable to use Volatile for any ASM statement that is missing either input or output operands or to avoid unwanted optimizations. A warning is generated if this advice is not followed.

No support is provided for GNU C's *asm goto* feature.

The *Asm* subprograms may be used in two ways. First the procedure forms can be used anywhere a procedure call would be valid, and correspond to what the RM calls 'intrinsic' routines. Such calls can be used to intersperse machine instructions with other Ada statements. Second, the function forms, which return a dummy value of the limited private type *Asm_Insn*, can be used in code statements, and indeed this is the only context where such calls are allowed. Code statements appear as aggregates of the form:

```
Asm_Insn'(Asm (...));
Asm_Insn'(Asm_Volatile (...));
```

In accordance with RM rules, such code statements are allowed only within subprograms whose entire body consists of such statements. It is not permissible to intermix such statements with other Ada statements.

Typically the form using intrinsic procedure calls is more convenient and more flexible. The code statement form is provided to meet the RM suggestion that such a facility should be made available. The following is the exact syntax of the call to *Asm*. As usual, if named notation is used, the arguments may be given in arbitrary order, following the normal rules for use of positional and named arguments:

```
ASM_CALL ::= Asm (
                 [Template =>] static_string_EXPRESSION
               [,[Outputs  =>] OUTPUT_OPERAND_LIST       ]
               [,[Inputs   =>] INPUT_OPERAND_LIST        ]
               [,[Clobber  =>] static_string_EXPRESSION ]
```

```
                    [,[Volatile =>] static_boolean_EXPRESSION] )

OUTPUT_OPERAND_LIST ::=
  [PREFIX.]No_Output_Operands
| OUTPUT_OPERAND_ATTRIBUTE
| (OUTPUT_OPERAND_ATTRIBUTE {,OUTPUT_OPERAND_ATTRIBUTE})

OUTPUT_OPERAND_ATTRIBUTE ::=
  SUBTYPE_MARK'Asm_Output (static_string_EXPRESSION, NAME)

INPUT_OPERAND_LIST ::=
  [PREFIX.]No_Input_Operands
| INPUT_OPERAND_ATTRIBUTE
| (INPUT_OPERAND_ATTRIBUTE {,INPUT_OPERAND_ATTRIBUTE})

INPUT_OPERAND_ATTRIBUTE ::=
  SUBTYPE_MARK'Asm_Input (static_string_EXPRESSION, EXPRESSION)
```

The identifiers *No_Input_Operands* and *No_Output_Operands* are declared in the package *Machine_Code* and must be referenced according to normal visibility rules. In particular if there is no *use* clause for this package, then appropriate package name qualification is required.

15.2 GNAT Implementation of Tasking

This chapter outlines the basic GNAT approach to tasking (in particular, a multi-layered library for portability) and discusses issues related to compliance with the Real-Time Systems Annex.

15.2.1 Mapping Ada Tasks onto the Underlying Kernel Threads

GNAT's run-time support comprises two layers:

* GNARL (GNAT Run-time Layer)
* GNULL (GNAT Low-level Library)

In GNAT, Ada's tasking services rely on a platform and OS independent layer known as GNARL. This code is responsible for implementing the correct semantics of Ada's task creation, rendezvous, protected operations etc.

GNARL decomposes Ada's tasking semantics into simpler lower level operations such as create a thread, set the priority of a thread, yield, create a lock, lock/unlock, etc. The spec for these low-level operations constitutes GNULLI, the GNULL Interface. This interface is directly inspired from the POSIX real-time API.

If the underlying executive or OS implements the POSIX standard faithfully, the GNULL Interface maps as is to the services offered by the underlying kernel. Otherwise, some target dependent glue code maps the services offered by the underlying kernel to the semantics expected by GNARL.

Whatever the underlying OS (VxWorks, UNIX, Windows, etc.) the key point is that each Ada task is mapped on a thread in the underlying kernel. For example, in the case of VxWorks, one Ada task = one VxWorks task.

In addition Ada task priorities map onto the underlying thread priorities. Mapping Ada tasks onto the underlying kernel threads has several advantages:

* The underlying scheduler is used to schedule the Ada tasks. This makes Ada tasks as efficient as kernel threads from a scheduling standpoint.
* Interaction with code written in C containing threads is eased since at the lowest level Ada tasks and C threads map onto the same underlying kernel concept.
* When an Ada task is blocked during I/O the remaining Ada tasks are able to proceed.
* On multiprocessor systems Ada tasks can execute in parallel.

Some threads libraries offer a mechanism to fork a new process, with the child process duplicating the threads from the parent. GNAT does not support this functionality when the parent contains more than one task.

15.2.2 Ensuring Compliance with the Real-Time Annex

Although mapping Ada tasks onto the underlying threads has significant advantages, it does create some complications when it comes to respecting the scheduling semantics specified in the real-time annex (Annex D).

For instance the Annex D requirement for the *FIFO_Within_Priorities* scheduling policy states:

> *When the active priority of a ready task that is not running changes, or the setting of its base priority takes effect, the task is removed from the ready queue for its old active priority and is added at the tail of the ready queue for its new active priority, except in the case where the active priority is lowered due to the loss of inherited priority, in which case the task is added at the head of the ready queue for its new active priority.*

While most kernels do put tasks at the end of the priority queue when a task changes its priority, (which respects the main FIFO_Within_Priorities requirement), almost none keep a thread at the beginning of its priority queue when its priority drops from the loss of inherited priority.

As a result most vendors have provided incomplete Annex D implementations.

The GNAT run-time, has a nice cooperative solution to this problem which ensures that accurate FIFO_Within_Priorities semantics are respected.

The principle is as follows. When an Ada task T is about to start running, it checks whether some other Ada task R with the same priority as T has been suspended due to the loss of priority inheritance. If this is the case, T yields and is placed at the end of its priority queue. When R arrives at the front of the queue it executes.

Note that this simple scheme preserves the relative order of the tasks that were ready to execute in the priority queue where R has been placed at the end.

15.3 GNAT Implementation of Shared Passive Packages

GNAT fully implements the pragma *Shared_Passive* for the purpose of designating shared passive packages. This allows the use of passive partitions in the context described in the Ada Reference Manual; i.e., for communication between separate partitions of a distributed application using the features in Annex E.

However, the implementation approach used by GNAT provides for more extensive usage as follows:

Communication between separate programs
This allows separate programs to access the data in passive partitions, using protected objects for synchronization where needed. The only requirement is that the two programs have a common shared file system. It is even possible for programs running on different machines with different architectures (e.g., different endianness) to communicate via the data in a passive partition.

Persistence between program runs
The data in a passive package can persist from one run of a program to another, so that a later program sees the final values stored by a previous run of the same program.

The implementation approach used is to store the data in files. A separate stream file is created for each object in the package, and an access to an object causes the corresponding file to be read or written.

The environment variable *SHARED_MEMORY_DIRECTORY* should be set to the directory to be used for these files. The files in this directory have names that correspond to their fully qualified names. For example, if we have the package

```
package X is
  pragma Shared_Passive (X);
  Y : Integer;
  Z : Float;
end X;
```

and the environment variable is set to */stemp/*, then the files created will have the names:

```
/stemp/x.y
/stemp/x.z
```

These files are created when a value is initially written to the object, and the files are retained until manually deleted. This provides the persistence semantics. If no file exists, it means that no partition has assigned a value to the variable; in this case the initial value declared in the package will be used. This model ensures that there are no issues in synchronizing the elaboration process, since elaboration of passive packages elaborates the initial values, but does not create the files.

The files are written using normal *Stream_IO* access. If you want to be able to communicate between programs or partitions running on different architectures, then you should use the XDR versions of the stream attribute routines, since these are architecture independent.

If active synchronization is required for access to the variables in the shared passive package, then as described in the Ada Reference Manual, the package may contain protected objects used for this purpose. In this case a lock file (whose name is `___lock` (three underscores) is created in the shared memory directory.

This is used to provide the required locking semantics for proper protected object synchronization.

GNAT supports shared passive packages on all platforms except for OpenVMS.

15.4 Code Generation for Array Aggregates

Aggregates have a rich syntax and allow the user to specify the values of complex data structures by means of a single construct. As a result, the code generated for aggregates can be quite complex and involve loops, case statements and multiple assignments. In the simplest cases, however, the compiler will recognize aggregates whose components and constraints are fully static, and in those cases the compiler will generate little or no executable code. The following is an outline of the code that GNAT generates for various aggregate constructs. For further details, you will find it useful to examine the output produced by the -gnatG flag to see the expanded source that is input to the code generator. You may also want to examine the assembly code generated at various levels of optimization.

The code generated for aggregates depends on the context, the component values, and the type. In the context of an object declaration the code generated is generally simpler than in the case of an assignment. As a general rule, static component values and static subtypes also lead to simpler code.

15.4.1 Static constant aggregates with static bounds

For the declarations:

```
type One_Dim is array (1..10) of integer;
ar0 : constant One_Dim := (1, 2, 3, 4, 5, 6, 7, 8, 9, 0);
```

GNAT generates no executable code: the constant ar0 is placed in static memory. The same is true for constant aggregates with named associations:

```
Cr1 : constant One_Dim := (4 => 16, 2 => 4, 3 => 9, 1 => 1, 5 .. 10 => 0);
Cr3 : constant One_Dim := (others => 7777);
```

The same is true for multidimensional constant arrays such as:

```
type two_dim is array (1..3, 1..3) of integer;
Unit : constant two_dim := ( (1,0,0), (0,1,0), (0,0,1));
```

The same is true for arrays of one-dimensional arrays: the following are static:

```
type ar1b  is array (1..3) of boolean;
type ar_ar is array (1..3) of ar1b;
None  : constant ar1b := (others => false);     --  fully static
None2 : constant ar_ar := (1..3 => None);       --  fully static
```

However, for multidimensional aggregates with named associations, GNAT will generate assignments and loops, even if all associations are static. The following two declarations generate a loop for the first dimension, and individual component assignments for the second dimension:

```
Zero1: constant two_dim := (1..3 => (1..3 => 0));
Zero2: constant two_dim := (others => (others => 0));
```

15.4.2 Constant aggregates with unconstrained nominal types

In such cases the aggregate itself establishes the subtype, so that associations with *others* cannot be used. GNAT determines the bounds for the actual subtype of the aggregate, and allocates the aggregate statically as well. No code is generated for the following:

```
type One_Unc is array (natural range <>) of integer;
Cr_Unc : constant One_Unc := (12,24,36);
```

15.4.3 Aggregates with static bounds

In all previous examples the aggregate was the initial (and immutable) value of a constant. If the aggregate initializes a variable, then code is generated for it as a combination of individual assignments and loops over the target object. The declarations

```
Cr_Var1 : One_Dim := (2, 5, 7, 11, 0, 0, 0, 0, 0, 0);
Cr_Var2 : One_Dim := (others > -1);
```

generate the equivalent of

```
Cr_Var1 (1) := 2;
Cr_Var1 (2) := 3;
Cr_Var1 (3) := 5;
Cr_Var1 (4) := 11;

for I in Cr_Var2'range loop
   Cr_Var2 (I) := -1;
end loop;
```

15.4.4 Aggregates with nonstatic bounds

If the bounds of the aggregate are not statically compatible with the bounds of the nominal subtype of the target, then constraint checks have to be generated on the bounds. For a multidimensional array, constraint checks may have to be applied to sub-arrays individually, if they do not have statically compatible subtypes.

15.4.5 Aggregates in assignment statements

In general, aggregate assignment requires the construction of a temporary, and a copy from the temporary to the target of the assignment. This is because it is not always possible to convert the assignment into a series of individual component assignments. For example, consider the simple case:

```
A := (A(2), A(1));
```

This cannot be converted into:

```
A(1) := A(2);
A(2) := A(1);
```

So the aggregate has to be built first in a separate location, and then copied into the target. GNAT recognizes simple cases where this intermediate step is not required, and the assignments can be performed in place, directly into the target. The following sufficient criteria are applied:

* The bounds of the aggregate are static, and the associations are static.
* The components of the aggregate are static constants, names of simple variables that are not renamings, or expressions not involving indexed components whose operands obey these rules.

If any of these conditions are violated, the aggregate will be built in a temporary (created either by the front-end or the code generator) and then that temporary will be copied onto the target.

15.5 The Size of Discriminated Records with Default Discriminants

If a discriminated type *T* has discriminants with default values, it is possible to declare an object of this type without providing an explicit constraint:

```
type Size is range 1..100;

type Rec (D : Size := 15) is record
   Name : String (1..D);
end T;

Word : Rec;
```

Such an object is said to be *unconstrained.* The discriminant of the object can be modified by a full assignment to the object, as long as it preserves the relation between the value of the discriminant, and the value of the components that depend on it:

```
Word := (3, "yes");

Word := (5, "maybe");

Word := (5, "no"); -- raises Constraint_Error
```

In order to support this behavior efficiently, an unconstrained object is given the maximum size that any value of the type requires. In the case above, *Word* has storage for the discriminant and for a *String* of length 100. It is important to note that unconstrained objects do not require dynamic allocation. It would be an improper implementation to place on the heap those components whose size depends on discriminants. (This improper implementation was used by some Ada83 compilers, where the *Name* component above would have been stored as a pointer to a dynamic string). Following the principle that dynamic storage management should never be introduced implicitly, an Ada compiler should reserve the full size for an unconstrained declared object, and place it on the stack.

This maximum size approach has been a source of surprise to some users, who expect the default values of the discriminants to determine the size reserved for an unconstrained object: "If the default is 15, why should the object occupy a larger size?" The answer, of course, is that the discriminant may be later modified, and its full range of values must be taken into account. This is why the declaration:

```
type Rec (D : Positive := 15) is record
   Name : String (1..D);
end record;

Too_Large : Rec;
```

is flagged by the compiler with a warning: an attempt to create *Too_Large* will raise *Storage_Error*, because the required size includes *Positive'Last* bytes. As the first example indicates, the proper approach is to declare an index type of 'reasonable' range so that unconstrained objects are not too large.

One final wrinkle: if the object is declared to be *aliased*, or if it is created in the heap by means of an allocator, then it is *not* unconstrained: it is constrained by the default values of the discriminants, and those values cannot be modified by full assignment. This is because in the presence of aliasing all views of the object (which may be manipulated by different tasks, say) must be consistent, so it is imperative that the object, once created, remain invariant.

15.6 Strict Conformance to the Ada Reference Manual

The dynamic semantics defined by the Ada Reference Manual impose a set of run-time checks to be generated. By default, the GNAT compiler will insert many run-time checks into the compiled code, including most of those required by the Ada Reference Manual. However, there are two checks that are not enabled in the default mode for efficiency reasons: checks for access before elaboration on subprogram calls, and stack overflow checking (most operating systems do not perform this check by default).

Strict conformance to the Ada Reference Manual can be achieved by adding two compiler options for dynamic checks for access-before-elaboration on subprogram calls and generic instantiations (*-gnatE*), and stack overflow checking (*-fstack-check*).

Note that the result of a floating point arithmetic operation in overflow and invalid situations, when the *Machine_Overflows* attribute of the result type is *False*, is to generate IEEE NaN and infinite values. This is the case for machines compliant with the IEEE floating-point standard, but on machines that are not fully compliant with this standard, such as Alpha, the *-mieee* compiler flag must be used for achieving IEEE confirming behavior (although at the cost of a significant performance penalty), so infinite and NaN values are properly generated.

16 Implementation of Ada 2012 Features

This chapter contains a complete list of Ada 2012 features that have been implemented. Generally, these features are only available if the *-gnat12* (Ada 2012 features enabled) option is set, which is the default behavior, or if the configuration pragma *Ada_2012* is used.

However, new pragmas, attributes, and restrictions are unconditionally available, since the Ada 95 standard allows the addition of new pragmas, attributes, and restrictions (there are exceptions, which are documented in the individual descriptions), and also certain packages were made available in earlier versions of Ada.

An ISO date (YYYY-MM-DD) appears in parentheses on the description line. This date shows the implementation date of the feature. Any wavefront subsequent to this date will contain the indicated feature, as will any subsequent releases. A date of 0000-00-00 means that GNAT has always implemented the feature, or implemented it as soon as it appeared as a binding interpretation.

Each feature corresponds to an Ada Issue ('AI') approved by the Ada standardization group (ISO/IEC JTC1/SC22/WG9) for inclusion in Ada 2012. The features are ordered based on the relevant sections of the Ada Reference Manual ("RM"). When a given AI relates to multiple points in the RM, the earliest is used.

A complete description of the AIs may be found in `http://www.ada-auth.org/ai05-summary.html`.

* *AI-0176 Quantified expressions (2010-09-29)*

  Both universally and existentially quantified expressions are implemented. They use the new syntax for iterators proposed in AI05-139-2, as well as the standard Ada loop syntax.

  RM References: 1.01.04 (12) 2.09 (2/2) 4.04 (7) 4.05.09 (0)

* *AI-0079 Allow other_format characters in source (2010-07-10)*

  Wide characters in the unicode category *other_format* are now allowed in source programs between tokens, but not within a token such as an identifier.

  RM References: 2.01 (4/2) 2.02 (7)

* *AI-0091 Do not allow other_format in identifiers (0000-00-00)*

  Wide characters in the unicode category *other_format* are not permitted within an identifier, since this can be a security problem. The error message for this case has been improved to be more specific, but GNAT has never allowed such characters to appear in identifiers.

  RM References: 2.03 (3.1/2) 2.03 (4/2) 2.03 (5/2) 2.03 (5.1/2) 2.03 (5.2/2) 2.03 (5.3/2) 2.09 (2/2)

* *AI-0100 Placement of pragmas (2010-07-01)*

  This AI is an earlier version of AI-163. It simplifies the rules for legal placement of pragmas. In the case of lists that allow pragmas, if the list may have no elements, then the list may consist solely of pragmas.

  RM References: 2.08 (7)

* *AI-0163 Pragmas in place of null (2010-07-01)*

  A statement sequence may be composed entirely of pragmas. It is no longer necessary to add a dummy *null* statement to make the sequence legal.

RM References: 2.08 (7) 2.08 (16)

* *AI-0080 'View of' not needed if clear from context (0000-00-00)*

  This is an editorial change only, described as non-testable in the AI.

  RM References: 3.01 (7)

* *AI-0183 Aspect specifications (2010-08-16)*

  Aspect specifications have been fully implemented except for pre and post- conditions, and type invariants, which have their own separate AI's. All forms of declarations listed in the AI are supported. The following is a list of the aspects supported (with GNAT implementation aspects marked)

Supported Aspect	**Source**
Ada_2005	– GNAT
Ada_2012	– GNAT
Address	
Alignment	
Atomic	
Atomic_Components	
Bit_Order	
Component_Size	
Contract_Cases	– GNAT
Discard_Names	
External_Tag	
Favor_Top_Level	– GNAT
Inline	
Inline_Always	– GNAT
Invariant	– GNAT
Machine_Radix	
No_Return	

Object_Size – GNAT

Pack

Persistent_BSS – GNAT

Post

Pre

Predicate

Preelaborable_Initialization

Pure_Function – GNAT

Remote_Access_Type – GNAT

Shared – GNAT

Size

Storage_Pool

Storage_Size

Stream_Size

Suppress

Suppress_Debug_Info – GNAT

Test_Case – GNAT

Thread_Local_Storage – GNAT

Type_Invariant

Unchecked_Union

Universal_Aliasing – GNAT

Unmodified – GNAT

Unreferenced – GNAT

Unreferenced_Objects – GNAT

Unsuppress

Value_Size – GNAT

Volatile

Volatile_Components

Warnings – GNAT

Note that for aspects with an expression, e.g. *Size*, the expression is treated like a default expression (visibility is analyzed at the point of occurrence of the aspect, but evaluation of the expression occurs at the freeze point of the entity involved).

RM References: 3.02.01 (3) 3.02.02 (2) 3.03.01 (2/2) 3.08 (6) 3.09.03 (1.1/2) 6.01 (2/2) 6.07 (2/2) 9.05.02 (2/2) 7.01 (3) 7.03 (2) 7.03 (3) 9.01 (2/2) 9.01 (3/2) 9.04 (2/2) 9.04 (3/2) 9.05.02 (2/2) 11.01 (2) 12.01 (3) 12.03 (2/2) 12.04 (2/2) 12.05 (2) 12.06 (2.1/2) 12.06 (2.2/2) 12.07 (2) 13.01 (0.1/2) 13.03 (5/1) 13.03.01 (0)

* *AI-0128 Inequality is a primitive operation (0000-00-00)*

  If an equality operator ("=") is declared for a type, then the implicitly declared inequality operator ("/=") is a primitive operation of the type. This is the only reasonable interpretation, and is the one always implemented by GNAT, but the RM was not entirely clear in making this point.

  RM References: 3.02.03 (6) 6.06 (6)

* *AI-0003 Qualified expressions as names (2010-07-11)*

  In Ada 2012, a qualified expression is considered to be syntactically a name, meaning that constructs such as *A'(F(X)).B* are now legal. This is useful in disambiguating some cases of overloading.

  RM References: 3.03 (11) 3.03 (21) 4.01 (2) 4.04 (7) 4.07 (3) 5.04 (7)

* *AI-0120 Constant instance of protected object (0000-00-00)*

  This is an RM editorial change only. The section that lists objects that are constant failed to include the current instance of a protected object within a protected function. This has always been treated as a constant in GNAT.

  RM References: 3.03 (21)

* *AI-0008 General access to constrained objects (0000-00-00)*

  The wording in the RM implied that if you have a general access to a constrained object, it could be used to modify the discriminants. This was obviously not intended. *Constraint_Error* should be raised, and GNAT has always done so in this situation.

  RM References: 3.03 (23) 3.10.02 (26/2) 4.01 (9) 6.04.01 (17) 8.05.01 (5/2)

* *AI-0093 Additional rules use immutably limited (0000-00-00)*

  This is an editorial change only, to make more widespread use of the Ada 2012 'immutably limited'.

  RM References: 3.03 (23.4/3)

* *AI-0096 Deriving from formal private types (2010-07-20)*

  In general it is illegal for a type derived from a formal limited type to be nonlimited. This AI makes an exception to this rule: derivation is legal if it appears in the private part of the generic, and the formal type is not tagged. If the type is tagged, the legality check must be applied to the private part of the package.

  RM References: 3.04 (5.1/2) 6.02 (7)

* *AI-0181 Soft hyphen is a non-graphic character (2010-07-23)*

  From Ada 2005 on, soft hyphen is considered a non-graphic character, which means that it has a special name (*SOFT_HYPHEN*) in conjunction with the *Image* and *Value* attributes for the character types. Strictly speaking this is an inconsistency with Ada 95, but in practice the use of these attributes is so obscure that it will not cause problems.

  RM References: 3.05.02 (2/2) A.01 (35/2) A.03.03 (21)

* *AI-0182 Additional forms for 'Character'Value* (0000-00-00)'

  This AI allows *Character'Value* to accept the string *'?'* where *?* is any character including non-graphic control characters. GNAT has always accepted such strings. It also allows strings such as *HEX_00000041* to be accepted, but GNAT does not take advantage of this permission and raises *Constraint_Error*, as is certainly still permitted.

  RM References: 3.05 (56/2)

* *AI-0214 Defaulted discriminants for limited tagged (2010-10-01)*

  Ada 2012 relaxes the restriction that forbids discriminants of tagged types to have default expressions by allowing them when the type is limited. It is often useful to define a default value for a discriminant even though it can't be changed by assignment.

  RM References: 3.07 (9.1/2) 3.07.02 (3)

* *AI-0102 Some implicit conversions are illegal (0000-00-00)*

  It is illegal to assign an anonymous access constant to an anonymous access variable. The RM did not have a clear rule to prevent this, but GNAT has always generated an error for this usage.

  RM References: 3.07 (16) 3.07.01 (9) 6.04.01 (6) 8.06 (27/2)

* *AI-0158 Generalizing membership tests (2010-09-16)*

  This AI extends the syntax of membership tests to simplify complex conditions that can be expressed as membership in a subset of values of any type. It introduces syntax for a list of expressions that may be used in loop contexts as well.

  RM References: 3.08.01 (5) 4.04 (3) 4.05.02 (3) 4.05.02 (5) 4.05.02 (27)

* *AI-0173 Testing if tags represent abstract types (2010-07-03)*

  The function *Ada.Tags.Type_Is_Abstract* returns *True* if invoked with the tag of an abstract type, and *False* otherwise.

  RM References: 3.09 (7.4/2) 3.09 (12.4/2)

* *AI-0076 function with controlling result (0000-00-00)*

  This is an editorial change only. The RM defines calls with controlling results, but uses the term 'function with controlling result' without an explicit definition.

  RM References: 3.09.02 (2/2)

* *AI-0126 Dispatching with no declared operation (0000-00-00)*

  This AI clarifies dispatching rules, and simply confirms that dispatching executes the operation of the parent type when there is no explicitly or implicitly declared operation for the descendant type. This has always been the case in all versions of GNAT.

  RM References: 3.09.02 (20/2) 3.09.02 (20.1/2) 3.09.02 (20.2/2)

* *AI-0097 Treatment of abstract null extension (2010-07-19)*

  The RM as written implied that in some cases it was possible to create an object of an abstract type, by having an abstract extension inherit a non- abstract constructor from its parent type. This mistake has been corrected in GNAT and in the RM, and this construct is now illegal.

  RM References: 3.09.03 (4/2)

* *AI-0203 Extended return cannot be abstract (0000-00-00)*

  A return_subtype_indication cannot denote an abstract subtype. GNAT has never permitted such usage.

  RM References: 3.09.03 (8/3)

* *AI-0198 Inheriting abstract operators (0000-00-00)*

  This AI resolves a conflict between two rules involving inherited abstract operations and predefined operators. If a derived numeric type inherits an abstract operator, it overrides the predefined one. This interpretation was always the one implemented in GNAT.

  RM References: 3.09.03 (4/3)

* *AI-0073 Functions returning abstract types (2010-07-10)*

  This AI covers a number of issues regarding returning abstract types. In particular generic functions cannot have abstract result types or access result types designated an abstract type. There are some other cases which are detailed in the AI. Note that this binding interpretation has not been retrofitted to operate before Ada 2012 mode, since it caused a significant number of regressions.

  RM References: 3.09.03 (8) 3.09.03 (10) 6.05 (8/2)

* *AI-0070 Elaboration of interface types (0000-00-00)*

  This is an editorial change only, there are no testable consequences short of checking for the absence of generated code for an interface declaration.

  RM References: 3.09.04 (18/2)

* *AI-0208 Characteristics of incomplete views (0000-00-00)*

  The wording in the Ada 2005 RM concerning characteristics of incomplete views was incorrect and implied that some programs intended to be legal were now illegal. GNAT had never considered such programs illegal, so it has always implemented the intent of this AI.

  RM References: 3.10.01 (2.4/2) 3.10.01 (2.6/2)

* *AI-0162 Incomplete type completed by partial view (2010-09-15)*

  Incomplete types are made more useful by allowing them to be completed by private types and private extensions.

  RM References: 3.10.01 (2.5/2) 3.10.01 (2.6/2) 3.10.01 (3) 3.10.01 (4/2)

* *AI-0098 Anonymous subprogram access restrictions (0000-00-00)*

  An unintentional omission in the RM implied some inconsistent restrictions on the use of anonymous access to subprogram values. These restrictions were not intentional, and have never been enforced by GNAT.

  RM References: 3.10.01 (6) 3.10.01 (9.2/2)

* *AI-0199 Aggregate with anonymous access components (2010-07-14)*

  A choice list in a record aggregate can include several components of (distinct) anonymous access types as long as they have matching designated subtypes.

  RM References: 4.03.01 (16)

* *AI-0220 Needed components for aggregates (0000-00-00)*

  This AI addresses a wording problem in the RM that appears to permit some complex cases of aggregates with nonstatic discriminants. GNAT has always implemented the intended semantics.

  RM References: 4.03.01 (17)

* *AI-0147 Conditional expressions (2009-03-29)*

  Conditional expressions are permitted. The form of such an expression is:

  ```
  (if expr then expr {elsif expr then expr} [else expr])
  ```

  The parentheses can be omitted in contexts where parentheses are present anyway, such as subprogram arguments and pragma arguments. If the **else** clause is omitted, **else** *True* is assumed; thus `(if A then B)` is a way to conveniently represent *(A implies B)* in standard logic.

  RM References: 4.03.03 (15) 4.04 (1) 4.04 (7) 4.05.07 (0) 4.07 (2) 4.07 (3) 4.09 (12) 4.09 (33) 5.03 (3) 5.03 (4) 7.05 (2.1/2)

* *AI-0037 Out-of-range box associations in aggregate (0000-00-00)*

  This AI confirms that an association of the form *Indx* => <> in an array aggregate must raise *Constraint_Error* if *Indx* is out of range. The RM specified a range check on other associations, but not when the value of the association was defaulted. GNAT has always inserted a constraint check on the index value.

  RM References: 4.03.03 (29)

* *AI-0123 Composability of equality (2010-04-13)*

  Equality of untagged record composes, so that the predefined equality for a composite type that includes a component of some untagged record type *R* uses the equality operation of *R* (which may be user-defined or predefined). This makes the behavior of untagged records identical to that of tagged types in this respect.

  This change is an incompatibility with previous versions of Ada, but it corrects a non-uniformity that was often a source of confusion. Analysis of a large number of industrial programs indicates that in those rare cases where a composite type had an untagged record component with a user-defined equality, either there was no use of the composite equality, or else the code expected the same composability as for tagged types, and thus had a bug that would be fixed by this change.

RM References: 4.05.02 (9.7/2) 4.05.02 (14) 4.05.02 (15) 4.05.02 (24) 8.05.04 (8)

* *AI-0088 The value of exponentiation (0000-00-00)*

  This AI clarifies the equivalence rule given for the dynamic semantics of exponentiation: the value of the operation can be obtained by repeated multiplication, but the operation can be implemented otherwise (for example using the familiar divide-by-two-and-square algorithm, even if this is less accurate), and does not imply repeated reads of a volatile base.

  RM References: 4.05.06 (11)

* *AI-0188 Case expressions (2010-01-09)*

  Case expressions are permitted. This allows use of constructs such as:

  ```
  X := (case Y is when 1 => 2, when 2 => 3, when others => 31)
  ```

  RM References: 4.05.07 (0) 4.05.08 (0) 4.09 (12) 4.09 (33)

* *AI-0104 Null exclusion and uninitialized allocator (2010-07-15)*

  The assignment `Ptr := new not null Some_Ptr;` will raise `Constraint_Error` because the default value of the allocated object is **null**. This useless construct is illegal in Ada 2012.

  RM References: 4.08 (2)

* *AI-0157 Allocation/Deallocation from empty pool (2010-07-11)*

  Allocation and Deallocation from an empty storage pool (i.e. allocation or deallocation of a pointer for which a static storage size clause of zero has been given) is now illegal and is detected as such. GNAT previously gave a warning but not an error.

  RM References: 4.08 (5.3/2) 13.11.02 (4) 13.11.02 (17)

* *AI-0179 Statement not required after label (2010-04-10)*

  It is not necessary to have a statement following a label, so a label can appear at the end of a statement sequence without the need for putting a null statement afterwards, but it is not allowable to have only labels and no real statements in a statement sequence.

  RM References: 5.01 (2)

* *AI-0139-2 Syntactic sugar for iterators (2010-09-29)*

  The new syntax for iterating over arrays and containers is now implemented. Iteration over containers is for now limited to read-only iterators. Only default iterators are supported, with the syntax: *for Elem of C*.

  RM References: 5.05

* *AI-0134 Profiles must match for full conformance (0000-00-00)*

  For full conformance, the profiles of anonymous-access-to-subprogram parameters must match. GNAT has always enforced this rule.

  RM References: 6.03.01 (18)

* *AI-0207 Mode conformance and access constant (0000-00-00)*

  This AI confirms that access_to_constant indication must match for mode conformance. This was implemented in GNAT when the qualifier was originally introduced in Ada 2005.

RM References: 6.03.01 (16/2)

* *AI-0046 Null exclusion match for full conformance (2010-07-17)*

  For full conformance, in the case of access parameters, the null exclusion must match (either both or neither must have `not null`).

  RM References: 6.03.02 (18)

* *AI-0118 The association of parameter associations (0000-00-00)*

  This AI clarifies the rules for named associations in subprogram calls and generic instantiations. The rules have been in place since Ada 83.

  RM References: 6.04.01 (2) 12.03 (9)

* *AI-0196 Null exclusion tests for out parameters (0000-00-00)*

  Null exclusion checks are not made for ***out*** parameters when evaluating the actual parameters. GNAT has never generated these checks.

  RM References: 6.04.01 (13)

* *AI-0015 Constant return objects (0000-00-00)*

  The return object declared in an *extended_return_statement* may be declared constant. This was always intended, and GNAT has always allowed it.

  RM References: 6.05 (2.1/2) 3.03 (10/2) 3.03 (21) 6.05 (5/2) 6.05 (5.7/2)

* *AI-0032 Extended return for class-wide functions (0000-00-00)*

  If a function returns a class-wide type, the object of an extended return statement can be declared with a specific type that is covered by the class- wide type. This has been implemented in GNAT since the introduction of extended returns. Note AI-0103 complements this AI by imposing matching rules for constrained return types.

  RM References: 6.05 (5.2/2) 6.05 (5.3/2) 6.05 (5.6/2) 6.05 (5.8/2) 6.05 (8/2)

* *AI-0103 Static matching for extended return (2010-07-23)*

  If the return subtype of a function is an elementary type or a constrained type, the subtype indication in an extended return statement must match statically this return subtype.

  RM References: 6.05 (5.2/2)

* *AI-0058 Abnormal completion of an extended return (0000-00-00)*

  The RM had some incorrect wording implying wrong treatment of abnormal completion in an extended return. GNAT has always implemented the intended correct semantics as described by this AI.

  RM References: 6.05 (22/2)

* *AI-0050 Raising Constraint_Error early for function call (0000-00-00)*

  The implementation permissions for raising *Constraint_Error* early on a function call when it was clear an exception would be raised were over-permissive and allowed mishandling of discriminants in some cases. GNAT did not take advantage of these incorrect permissions in any case.

  RM References: 6.05 (24/2)

* *AI-0125 Nonoverridable operations of an ancestor (2010-09-28)*

  In Ada 2012, the declaration of a primitive operation of a type extension or private extension can also override an inherited primitive that is not visible at the point of this declaration.

RM References: 7.03.01 (6) 8.03 (23) 8.03.01 (5/2) 8.03.01 (6/2)

* *AI-0062 Null exclusions and deferred constants (0000-00-00)*

  A full constant may have a null exclusion even if its associated deferred constant does not. GNAT has always allowed this.

  RM References: 7.04 (6/2) 7.04 (7.1/2)

* *AI-0178 Incomplete views are limited (0000-00-00)*

  This AI clarifies the role of incomplete views and plugs an omission in the RM. GNAT always correctly restricted the use of incomplete views and types.

  RM References: 7.05 (3/2) 7.05 (6/2)

* *AI-0087 Actual for formal nonlimited derived type (2010-07-15)*

  The actual for a formal nonlimited derived type cannot be limited. In particular, a formal derived type that extends a limited interface but which is not explicitly limited cannot be instantiated with a limited type.

  RM References: 7.05 (5/2) 12.05.01 (5.1/2)

* *AI-0099 Tag determines whether finalization needed (0000-00-00)*

  This AI clarifies that 'needs finalization' is part of dynamic semantics, and therefore depends on the run-time characteristics of an object (i.e. its tag) and not on its nominal type. As the AI indicates: "we do not expect this to affect any implementation''.

  RM References: 7.06.01 (6) 7.06.01 (7) 7.06.01 (8) 7.06.01 (9/2)

* *AI-0064 Redundant finalization rule (0000-00-00)*

  This is an editorial change only. The intended behavior is already checked by an existing ACATS test, which GNAT has always executed correctly.

  RM References: 7.06.01 (17.1/1)

* *AI-0026 Missing rules for Unchecked_Union (2010-07-07)*

  Record representation clauses concerning Unchecked_Union types cannot mention the discriminant of the type. The type of a component declared in the variant part of an Unchecked_Union cannot be controlled, have controlled components, nor have protected or task parts. If an Unchecked_Union type is declared within the body of a generic unit or its descendants, then the type of a component declared in the variant part cannot be a formal private type or a formal private extension declared within the same generic unit.

  RM References: 7.06 (9.4/2) B.03.03 (9/2) B.03.03 (10/2)

* *AI-0205 Extended return declares visible name (0000-00-00)*

  This AI corrects a simple omission in the RM. Return objects have always been visible within an extended return statement.

  RM References: 8.03 (17)

* *AI-0042 Overriding versus implemented-by (0000-00-00)*

  This AI fixes a wording gap in the RM. An operation of a synchronized interface can be implemented by a protected or task entry, but the abstract operation is not being overridden in the usual sense, and it must be stated separately that this implementation is legal. This has always been the case in GNAT.

  RM References: 9.01 (9.2/2) 9.04 (11.1/2)

* *AI-0030 Requeue on synchronized interfaces (2010-07-19)*

  Requeue is permitted to a protected, synchronized or task interface primitive providing it is known that the overriding operation is an entry. Otherwise the requeue statement has the same effect as a procedure call. Use of pragma *Implemented* provides a way to impose a static requirement on the overriding operation by adhering to one of the implementation kinds: entry, protected procedure or any of the above.

  RM References: 9.05 (9) 9.05.04 (2) 9.05.04 (3) 9.05.04 (5) 9.05.04 (6) 9.05.04 (7) 9.05.04 (12)

* *AI-0201 Independence of atomic object components (2010-07-22)*

  If an Atomic object has a pragma *Pack* or a *Component_Size* attribute, then individual components may not be addressable by independent tasks. However, if the representation clause has no effect (is confirming), then independence is not compromised. Furthermore, in GNAT, specification of other appropriately addressable component sizes (e.g. 16 for 8-bit characters) also preserves independence. GNAT now gives very clear warnings both for the declaration of such a type, and for any assignment to its components.

  RM References: 9.10 (1/3) C.06 (22/2) C.06 (23/2)

* *AI-0009 Pragma Independent[_Components] (2010-07-23)*

  This AI introduces the new pragmas *Independent* and *Independent_Components*, which control guaranteeing independence of access to objects and components. The AI also requires independence not unaffected by confirming rep clauses.

  RM References: 9.10 (1) 13.01 (15/1) 13.02 (9) 13.03 (13) C.06 (2) C.06 (4) C.06 (6) C.06 (9) C.06 (13) C.06 (14)

* *AI-0072 Task signalling using 'Terminated (0000-00-00)*

  This AI clarifies that task signalling for reading *'Terminated* only occurs if the result is True. GNAT semantics has always been consistent with this notion of task signalling.

  RM References: 9.10 (6.1/1)

* *AI-0108 Limited incomplete view and discriminants (0000-00-00)*

  This AI confirms that an incomplete type from a limited view does not have discriminants. This has always been the case in GNAT.

  RM References: 10.01.01 (12.3/2)

* *AI-0129 Limited views and incomplete types (0000-00-00)*

  This AI clarifies the description of limited views: a limited view of a package includes only one view of a type that has an incomplete declaration and a full declaration (there is no possible ambiguity in a client package). This AI also fixes an omission: a nested package in the private part has no limited view. GNAT always implemented this correctly.

  RM References: 10.01.01 (12.2/2) 10.01.01 (12.3/2)

* *AI-0077 Limited withs and scope of declarations (0000-00-00)*

  This AI clarifies that a declaration does not include a context clause, and confirms that it is illegal to have a context in which both a limited and a nonlimited view of a package are accessible. Such double visibility was always rejected by GNAT.

  RM References: 10.01.02 (12/2) 10.01.02 (21/2) 10.01.02 (22/2)

* *AI-0122 Private with and children of generics (0000-00-00)*

  This AI clarifies the visibility of private children of generic units within instantiations of a parent. GNAT has always handled this correctly.

  RM References: 10.01.02 (12/2)

* *AI-0040 Limited with clauses on descendant (0000-00-00)*

  This AI confirms that a limited with clause in a child unit cannot name an ancestor of the unit. This has always been checked in GNAT.

  RM References: 10.01.02 (20/2)

* *AI-0132 Placement of library unit pragmas (0000-00-00)*

  This AI fills a gap in the description of library unit pragmas. The pragma clearly must apply to a library unit, even if it does not carry the name of the enclosing unit. GNAT has always enforced the required check.

  RM References: 10.01.05 (7)

* *AI-0034 Categorization of limited views (0000-00-00)*

  The RM makes certain limited with clauses illegal because of categorization considerations, when the corresponding normal with would be legal. This is not intended, and GNAT has always implemented the recommended behavior.

  RM References: 10.02.01 (11/1) 10.02.01 (17/2)

* *AI-0035 Inconsistencies with Pure units (0000-00-00)*

  This AI remedies some inconsistencies in the legality rules for Pure units. Derived access types are legal in a pure unit (on the assumption that the rule for a zero storage pool size has been enforced on the ancestor type). The rules are enforced in generic instances and in subunits. GNAT has always implemented the recommended behavior.

  RM References: 10.02.01 (15.1/2) 10.02.01 (15.4/2) 10.02.01 (15.5/2) 10.02.01 (17/2)

* *AI-0219 Pure permissions and limited parameters (2010-05-25)*

  This AI refines the rules for the cases with limited parameters which do not allow the implementations to omit 'redundant'. GNAT now properly conforms to the requirements of this binding interpretation.

  RM References: 10.02.01 (18/2)

* *AI-0043 Rules about raising exceptions (0000-00-00)*

  This AI covers various omissions in the RM regarding the raising of exceptions. GNAT has always implemented the intended semantics.

  RM References: 11.04.01 (10.1/2) 11 (2)

* *AI-0200 Mismatches in formal package declarations (0000-00-00)*

  This AI plugs a gap in the RM which appeared to allow some obviously intended illegal instantiations. GNAT has never allowed these instantiations.

  RM References: 12.07 (16)

* *AI-0112 Detection of duplicate pragmas (2010-07-24)*

  This AI concerns giving names to various representation aspects, but the practical effect is simply to make the use of duplicate *Atomic[_Components]*, *Volatile[_Components]*, and *Independent[_Components]* pragmas illegal, and GNAT now performs this required check.

RM References: 13.01 (8)

* *AI-0106 No representation pragmas on generic formals (0000-00-00)*

  The RM appeared to allow representation pragmas on generic formal parameters, but this was not intended, and GNAT has never permitted this usage.

  RM References: 13.01 (9.1/1)

* *AI-0012 Pack/Component_Size for aliased/atomic (2010-07-15)*

  It is now illegal to give an inappropriate component size or a pragma *Pack* that attempts to change the component size in the case of atomic or aliased components. Previously GNAT ignored such an attempt with a warning.

  RM References: 13.02 (6.1/2) 13.02 (7) C.06 (10) C.06 (11) C.06 (21)

* *AI-0039 Stream attributes cannot be dynamic (0000-00-00)*

  The RM permitted the use of dynamic expressions (such as `ptr.all`)' for stream attributes, but these were never useful and are now illegal. GNAT has always regarded such expressions as illegal.

  RM References: 13.03 (4) 13.03 (6) 13.13.02 (38/2)

* *AI-0095 Address of intrinsic subprograms (0000-00-00)*

  The prefix of *'Address* cannot statically denote a subprogram with convention *Intrinsic.* The use of the *Address* attribute raises *Program_Error* if the prefix denotes a subprogram with convention *Intrinsic.*

  RM References: 13.03 (11/1)

* *AI-0116 Alignment of class-wide objects (0000-00-00)*

  This AI requires that the alignment of a class-wide object be no greater than the alignment of any type in the class. GNAT has always followed this recommendation.

  RM References: 13.03 (29) 13.11 (16)

* *AI-0146 Type invariants (2009-09-21)*

  Type invariants may be specified for private types using the aspect notation. Aspect *Type_Invariant* may be specified for any private type, *Type_Invariant'Class* can only be specified for tagged types, and is inherited by any descendent of the tagged types. The invariant is a boolean expression that is tested for being true in the following situations: conversions to the private type, object declarations for the private type that are default initialized, and [**in**] **out** parameters and returned result on return from any primitive operation for the type that is visible to a client. GNAT defines the synonyms *Invariant* for *Type_Invariant* and *Invariant'Class* for *Type_Invariant'Class.*

  RM References: 13.03.03 (00)

* *AI-0078 Relax Unchecked_Conversion alignment rules (0000-00-00)*

  In Ada 2012, compilers are required to support unchecked conversion where the target alignment is a multiple of the source alignment. GNAT always supported this case (and indeed all cases of differing alignments, doing copies where required if the alignment was reduced).

  RM References: 13.09 (7)

* *AI-0195 Invalid value handling is implementation defined (2010-07-03)*

  The handling of invalid values is now designated to be implementation defined. This is a documentation change only, requiring Annex M in the GNAT Reference Manual to document this handling. In GNAT, checks for invalid values are made only when necessary to avoid erroneous behavior. Operations like assignments which cannot cause erroneous behavior ignore the possibility of invalid values and do not do a check. The date given above applies only to the documentation change, this behavior has always been implemented by GNAT.

RM References: 13.09.01 (10)

* *AI-0193 Alignment of allocators (2010-09-16)*

  This AI introduces a new attribute *Max_Alignment_For_Allocation*, analogous to *Max_Size_In_Storage_Elements*, but for alignment instead of size.

  RM References: 13.11 (16) 13.11 (21) 13.11.01 (0) 13.11.01 (1) 13.11.01 (2) 13.11.01 (3)

* *AI-0177 Parameterized expressions (2010-07-10)*

  The new Ada 2012 notion of parameterized expressions is implemented. The form is:

  ```
  function-specification is (expression)
  ```

  This is exactly equivalent to the corresponding function body that returns the expression, but it can appear in a package spec. Note that the expression must be parenthesized.

  RM References: 13.11.01 (3/2)

* *AI-0033 Attach/Interrupt_Handler in generic (2010-07-24)*

  Neither of these two pragmas may appear within a generic template, because the generic might be instantiated at other than the library level.

  RM References: 13.11.02 (16) C.03.01 (7/2) C.03.01 (8/2)

* *AI-0161 Restriction No_Default_Stream_Attributes (2010-09-11)*

  A new restriction *No_Default_Stream_Attributes* prevents the use of any of the default stream attributes for elementary types. If this restriction is in force, then it is necessary to provide explicit subprograms for any stream attributes used.

  RM References: 13.12.01 (4/2) 13.13.02 (40/2) 13.13.02 (52/2)

* *AI-0194 Value of Stream_Size attribute (0000-00-00)*

  The *Stream_Size* attribute returns the default number of bits in the stream representation of the given type. This value is not affected by the presence of stream subprogram attributes for the type. GNAT has always implemented this interpretation.

  RM References: 13.13.02 (1.2/2)

* *AI-0109 Redundant check in S'Class'Input (0000-00-00)*

  This AI is an editorial change only. It removes the need for a tag check that can never fail.

  RM References: 13.13.02 (34/2)

* *AI-0007 Stream read and private scalar types (0000-00-00)*

  The RM as written appeared to limit the possibilities of declaring read attribute procedures for private scalar types. This limitation was not intended, and has never been enforced by GNAT.

  RM References: 13.13.02 (50/2) 13.13.02 (51/2)

* *AI-0065 Remote access types and external streaming (0000-00-00)*

  This AI clarifies the fact that all remote access types support external streaming. This fixes an obvious oversight in the definition of the language, and GNAT always implemented the intended correct rules.

  RM References: 13.13.02 (52/2)

* *AI-0019 Freezing of primitives for tagged types (0000-00-00)*

  The RM suggests that primitive subprograms of a specific tagged type are frozen when the tagged type is frozen. This would be an incompatible change and is not intended. GNAT has never attempted this kind of freezing and its behavior is consistent with the recommendation of this AI.

  RM References: 13.14 (2) 13.14 (3/1) 13.14 (8.1/1) 13.14 (10) 13.14 (14) 13.14 (15.1/2)

* *AI-0017 Freezing and incomplete types (0000-00-00)*

  So-called 'Taft-amendment types' (i.e., types that are completed in package bodies) are not frozen by the occurrence of bodies in the enclosing declarative part. GNAT always implemented this properly.

  RM References: 13.14 (3/1)

* *AI-0060 Extended definition of remote access types (0000-00-00)*

  This AI extends the definition of remote access types to include access to limited, synchronized, protected or task class-wide interface types. GNAT already implemented this extension.

  RM References: A (4) E.02.02 (9/1) E.02.02 (9.2/1) E.02.02 (14/2) E.02.02 (18)

* *AI-0114 Classification of letters (0000-00-00)*

  The code points 170 (*FEMININE ORDINAL INDICATOR*), 181 (*MICRO SIGN*), and 186 (*MASCULINE ORDINAL INDICATOR*) are technically considered lower case letters by Unicode. However, they are not allowed in identifiers, and they return *False* to *Ada.Characters.Handling.Is_Letter/Is_Lower*. This behavior is consistent with that defined in Ada 95.

  RM References: A.03.02 (59) A.04.06 (7)

* *AI-0185 Ada.Wide_[Wide_]Characters.Handling (2010-07-06)*

  Two new packages *Ada.Wide_[Wide_]Characters.Handling* provide classification functions for *Wide_Character* and *Wide_Wide_Character*, as well as providing case folding routines for *Wide_[Wide_]Character* and *Wide_[Wide_]String*.

  RM References: A.03.05 (0) A.03.06 (0)

* *AI-0031 Add From parameter to Find_Token (2010-07-25)*

  A new version of *Find_Token* is added to all relevant string packages, with an extra parameter *From*. Instead of starting at the first character of the string, the search for a matching Token starts at the character indexed by the value of *From*. These procedures are available in all versions of Ada but if used in versions earlier than Ada 2012 they will generate a warning that an Ada 2012 subprogram is being used.

  RM References: A.04.03 (16) A.04.03 (67) A.04.03 (68/1) A.04.04 (51) A.04.05 (46)

* *AI-0056 Index on null string returns zero (0000-00-00)*

  The wording in the Ada 2005 RM implied an incompatible handling of the *Index* functions, resulting in raising an exception instead of returning zero in some situations.

This was not intended and has been corrected. GNAT always returned zero, and is thus consistent with this AI.

RM References: A.04.03 (56.2/2) A.04.03 (58.5/2)

* *AI-0137 String encoding package (2010-03-25)*

  The packages *Ada.Strings.UTF_Encoding*, together with its child packages, *Conversions*, *Strings*, *Wide_Strings*, and *Wide_Wide_Strings* have been implemented. These packages (whose documentation can be found in the spec files `a-stuten.ads`, `a-suenco.ads`, `a-suenst.ads`, `a-suewst.ads`, `a-suezst.ads`) allow encoding and decoding of *String*, *Wide_String*, and *Wide_Wide_String* values using UTF coding schemes (including UTF-8, UTF-16LE, UTF-16BE, and UTF-16), as well as conversions between the different UTF encodings. With the exception of *Wide_Wide_Strings*, these packages are available in Ada 95 and Ada 2005 mode as well as Ada 2012 mode. The *Wide_Wide_Strings package* is available in Ada 2005 mode as well as Ada 2012 mode (but not in Ada 95 mode since it uses *Wide_Wide_Character*).

  RM References: A.04.11

* *AI-0038 Minor errors in Text_IO (0000-00-00)*

  These are minor errors in the description on three points. The intent on all these points has always been clear, and GNAT has always implemented the correct intended semantics.

  RM References: A.10.05 (37) A.10.07 (8/1) A.10.07 (10) A.10.07 (12) A.10.08 (10) A.10.08 (24)

* *AI-0044 Restrictions on container instantiations (0000-00-00)*

  This AI places restrictions on allowed instantiations of generic containers. These restrictions are not checked by the compiler, so there is nothing to change in the implementation. This affects only the RM documentation.

  RM References: A.18 (4/2) A.18.02 (231/2) A.18.03 (145/2) A.18.06 (56/2) A.18.08 (66/2) A.18.09 (79/2) A.18.26 (5/2) A.18.26 (9/2)

* *AI-0127 Adding Locale Capabilities (2010-09-29)*

  This package provides an interface for identifying the current locale.

  RM References: A.19 A.19.01 A.19.02 A.19.03 A.19.05 A.19.06 A.19.07 A.19.08 A.19.09 A.19.10 A.19.11 A.19.12 A.19.13

* *AI-0002 Export C with unconstrained arrays (0000-00-00)*

  The compiler is not required to support exporting an Ada subprogram with convention C if there are parameters or a return type of an unconstrained array type (such as *String*). GNAT allows such declarations but generates warnings. It is possible, but complicated, to write the corresponding C code and certainly such code would be specific to GNAT and non-portable.

  RM References: B.01 (17) B.03 (62) B.03 (71.1/2)

* *AI-0216 No_Task_Hierarchy forbids local tasks (0000-00-00)*

  It is clearly the intention that *No_Task_Hierarchy* is intended to forbid tasks declared locally within subprograms, or functions returning task objects, and that is the implementation that GNAT has always provided. However the language in the RM was not sufficiently clear on this point. Thus this is a documentation change in the RM only.

RM References: D.07 (3/3)

* *AI-0211 No_Relative_Delays forbids Set_Handler use (2010-07-09)*

  The restriction *No_Relative_Delays* forbids any calls to the subprogram *Ada.Real_Time.Timing_Events.Set_Handler*.

  RM References: D.07 (5) D.07 (10/2) D.07 (10.4/2) D.07 (10.7/2)

* *AI-0190 pragma Default_Storage_Pool (2010-09-15)*

  This AI introduces a new pragma *Default_Storage_Pool*, which can be used to control storage pools globally. In particular, you can force every access type that is used for allocation (**new**) to have an explicit storage pool, or you can declare a pool globally to be used for all access types that lack an explicit one.

  RM References: D.07 (8)

* *AI-0189 No_Allocators_After_Elaboration (2010-01-23)*

  This AI introduces a new restriction *No_Allocators_After_Elaboration*, which says that no dynamic allocation will occur once elaboration is completed. In general this requires a run-time check, which is not required, and which GNAT does not attempt. But the static cases of allocators in a task body or in the body of the main program are detected and flagged at compile or bind time.

  RM References: D.07 (19.1/2) H.04 (23.3/2)

* *AI-0171 Pragma CPU and Ravenscar Profile (2010-09-24)*

  A new package *System.Multiprocessors* is added, together with the definition of pragma *CPU* for controlling task affinity. A new no dependence restriction, on *System.Multiprocessors.Dispatching_Domains*, is added to the Ravenscar profile.

  RM References: D.13.01 (4/2) D.16

* *AI-0210 Correct Timing_Events metric (0000-00-00)*

  This is a documentation only issue regarding wording of metric requirements, that does not affect the implementation of the compiler.

  RM References: D.15 (24/2)

* *AI-0206 Remote types packages and preelaborate (2010-07-24)*

  Remote types packages are now allowed to depend on preelaborated packages. This was formerly considered illegal.

  RM References: E.02.02 (6)

* *AI-0152 Restriction No_Anonymous_Allocators (2010-09-08)*

  Restriction *No_Anonymous_Allocators* prevents the use of allocators where the type of the returned value is an anonymous access type.

  RM References: H.04 (8/1)

17 Obsolescent Features

This chapter describes features that are provided by GNAT, but are considered obsolescent since there are preferred ways of achieving the same effect. These features are provided solely for historical compatibility purposes.

17.1 pragma No_Run_Time

The pragma *No_Run_Time* is used to achieve an affect similar to the use of the "Zero Foot Print" configurable run time, but without requiring a specially configured run time. The result of using this pragma, which must be used for all units in a partition, is to restrict the use of any language features requiring run-time support code. The preferred usage is to use an appropriately configured run-time that includes just those features that are to be made accessible.

17.2 pragma Ravenscar

The pragma *Ravenscar* has exactly the same effect as pragma *Profile (Ravenscar)*. The latter usage is preferred since it is part of the new Ada 2005 standard.

17.3 pragma Restricted_Run_Time

The pragma *Restricted_Run_Time* has exactly the same effect as pragma *Profile (Restricted)*. The latter usage is preferred since the Ada 2005 pragma *Profile* is intended for this kind of implementation dependent addition.

17.4 pragma Task_Info

The functionality provided by pragma *Task_Info* is now part of the Ada language. The *CPU* aspect and the package *System.Multiprocessors* offer a less system-dependent way to specify task affinity or to query the number of processsors.

Syntax

```
pragma Task_Info (EXPRESSION);
```

This pragma appears within a task definition (like pragma *Priority*) and applies to the task in which it appears. The argument must be of type *System.Task_Info.Task_Info_Type*. The *Task_Info* pragma provides system dependent control over aspects of tasking implementation, for example, the ability to map tasks to specific processors. For details on the facilities available for the version of GNAT that you are using, see the documentation in the spec of package System.Task_Info in the runtime library.

17.5 package System.Task_Info (`s-tasinf.ads`)

This package provides target dependent functionality that is used to support the *Task_Info* pragma. The predefined Ada package *System.Multiprocessors* and the *CPU* aspect now provide a standard replacement for GNAT's *Task_Info* functionality.

18 Compatibility and Porting Guide

This chapter presents some guidelines for developing portable Ada code, describes the compatibility issues that may arise between GNAT and other Ada compilation systems (including those for Ada 83), and shows how GNAT can expedite porting applications developed in other Ada environments.

18.1 Writing Portable Fixed-Point Declarations

The Ada Reference Manual gives an implementation freedom to choose bounds that are narrower by *Small* from the given bounds. For example, if we write

```
type F1 is delta 1.0 range -128.0 .. +128.0;
```

then the implementation is allowed to choose -128.0 .. +127.0 if it likes, but is not required to do so.

This leads to possible portability problems, so let's have a closer look at this, and figure out how to avoid these problems.

First, why does this freedom exist, and why would an implementation take advantage of it? To answer this, take a closer look at the type declaration for *F1* above. If the compiler uses the given bounds, it would need 9 bits to hold the largest positive value (and typically that means 16 bits on all machines). But if the implementation chooses the +127.0 bound then it can fit values of the type in 8 bits.

Why not make the user write +127.0 if that's what is wanted? The rationale is that if you are thinking of fixed point as a kind of 'poor man's floating-point', then you don't want to be thinking about the scaled integers that are used in its representation. Let's take another example:

```
type F2 is delta 2.0**(-15) range -1.0 .. +1.0;
```

Looking at this declaration, it seems casually as though it should fit in 16 bits, but again that extra positive value +1.0 has the scaled integer equivalent of 2**15 which is one too big for signed 16 bits. The implementation can treat this as:

```
type F2 is delta 2.0**(-15) range -1.0 .. +1.0-(2.0**(-15));
```

and the Ada language design team felt that this was too annoying to require. We don't need to debate this decision at this point, since it is well established (the rule about narrowing the ranges dates to Ada 83).

But the important point is that an implementation is not required to do this narrowing, so we have a potential portability problem. We could imagine three types of implementation:

a. those that narrow the range automatically if they can figure out that the narrower range will allow storage in a smaller machine unit,
b. those that will narrow only if forced to by a *'Size* clause, and
c. those that will never narrow.

Now if we are language theoreticians, we can imagine a fourth approach: to narrow all the time, e.g. to treat

```
type F3 is delta 1.0 range -10.0 .. +23.0;
```

as though it had been written:

```
type F3 is delta 1.0 range -9.0 .. +22.0;
```

But although technically allowed, such a behavior would be hostile and silly, and no real compiler would do this. All real compilers will fall into one of the categories (a), (b) or (c) above.

So, how do you get the compiler to do what you want? The answer is give the actual bounds you want, and then use a *'Small* clause and a *'Size* clause to absolutely pin down what the compiler does. E.g., for *F2* above, we will write:

```
My_Small : constant := 2.0**(-15);
My_First : constant := -1.0;
My_Last  : constant := +1.0 - My_Small;

type F2 is delta My_Small range My_First .. My_Last;
```

and then add

```
for F2'Small use my_Small;
for F2'Size  use 16;
```

In practice all compilers will do the same thing here and will give you what you want, so the above declarations are fully portable. If you really want to play language lawyer and guard against ludicrous behavior by the compiler you could add

```
Test1 : constant := 1 / Boolean'Pos (F2'First = My_First);
Test2 : constant := 1 / Boolean'Pos (F2'Last  = My_Last);
```

One or other or both are allowed to be illegal if the compiler is behaving in a silly manner, but at least the silly compiler will not get away with silently messing with your (very clear) intentions.

If you follow this scheme you will be guaranteed that your fixed-point types will be portable.

18.2 Compatibility with Ada 83

Ada 95 and the subsequent revisions Ada 2005 and Ada 2012 are highly upwards compatible with Ada 83. In particular, the design intention was that the difficulties associated with moving from Ada 83 to later versions of the standard should be no greater than those that occur when moving from one Ada 83 system to another.

However, there are a number of points at which there are minor incompatibilities. The *Ada 95 Annotated Reference Manual* contains full details of these issues as they relate to Ada 95, and should be consulted for a complete treatment. In practice the following subsections treat the most likely issues to be encountered.

18.2.1 Legal Ada 83 programs that are illegal in Ada 95

Some legal Ada 83 programs are illegal (i.e., they will fail to compile) in Ada 95 and later versions of the standard:

* *Character literals*

  Some uses of character literals are ambiguous. Since Ada 95 has introduced *Wide_Character* as a new predefined character type, some uses of character literals that were legal in Ada 83 are illegal in Ada 95. For example:

```
for Char in 'A' .. 'Z' loop ... end loop;
```

The problem is that 'A' and 'Z' could be from either *Character* or *Wide_Character*. The simplest correction is to make the type explicit; e.g.:

```
for Char in Character range 'A' .. 'Z' loop ... end loop;
```

* *New reserved words*

  The identifiers *abstract*, *aliased*, *protected*, *requeue*, *tagged*, and *until* are reserved in Ada 95. Existing Ada 83 code using any of these identifiers must be edited to use some alternative name.

* *Freezing rules*

  The rules in Ada 95 are slightly different with regard to the point at which entities are frozen, and representation pragmas and clauses are not permitted past the freeze point. This shows up most typically in the form of an error message complaining that a representation item appears too late, and the appropriate corrective action is to move the item nearer to the declaration of the entity to which it refers.

  A particular case is that representation pragmas cannot be applied to a subprogram body. If necessary, a separate subprogram declaration must be introduced to which the pragma can be applied.

* *Optional bodies for library packages*

  In Ada 83, a package that did not require a package body was nevertheless allowed to have one. This lead to certain surprises in compiling large systems (situations in which the body could be unexpectedly ignored by the binder). In Ada 95, if a package does not require a body then it is not permitted to have a body. To fix this problem, simply remove a redundant body if it is empty, or, if it is non-empty, introduce a dummy declaration into the spec that makes the body required. One approach is to add a private part to the package declaration (if necessary), and define a parameterless procedure called *Requires_Body*, which must then be given a dummy procedure body in the package body, which then becomes required. Another approach (assuming that this does not introduce elaboration circularities) is to add an *Elaborate_Body* pragma to the package spec, since one effect of this pragma is to require the presence of a package body.

* *Numeric_Error is the same exception as Constraint_Error*

  In Ada 95, the exception *Numeric_Error* is a renaming of *Constraint_Error*. This means that it is illegal to have separate exception handlers for the two exceptions. The fix is simply to remove the handler for the *Numeric_Error* case (since even in Ada 83, a compiler was free to raise *Constraint_Error* in place of *Numeric_Error* in all cases).

* *Indefinite subtypes in generics*

  In Ada 83, it was permissible to pass an indefinite type (e.g, *String*) as the actual for a generic formal private type, but then the instantiation would be illegal if there were any instances of declarations of variables of this type in the generic body. In Ada 95, to avoid this clear violation of the methodological principle known as the 'contract model', the generic declaration explicitly indicates whether or not such instantiations are permitted. If a generic formal parameter has explicit unknown discriminants, indicated by using *(<>)* after the subtype name, then it can be instantiated with indefinite types, but no stand-alone variables can be declared of this type. Any attempt to declare such a variable will result in an illegality at the time the generic is declared. If the *(<>)* notation is not used, then it is illegal to instantiate the generic with an indefinite type. This is the potential incompatibility issue when porting Ada 83 code to Ada 95. It will show up as a compile time error, and the fix is usually simply to add the *(<>)* to the generic declaration.

18.2.2 More deterministic semantics

* *Conversions*

  Conversions from real types to integer types round away from 0. In Ada 83 the conversion Integer(2.5) could deliver either 2 or 3 as its value. This implementation freedom was intended to support unbiased rounding in statistical applications, but in practice it interfered with portability. In Ada 95 the conversion semantics are unambiguous, and rounding away from 0 is required. Numeric code may be affected by this change in semantics. Note, though, that this issue is no worse than already existed in Ada 83 when porting code from one vendor to another.

* *Tasking*

  The Real-Time Annex introduces a set of policies that define the behavior of features that were implementation dependent in Ada 83, such as the order in which open select branches are executed.

18.2.3 Changed semantics

The worst kind of incompatibility is one where a program that is legal in Ada 83 is also legal in Ada 95 but can have an effect in Ada 95 that was not possible in Ada 83. Fortunately this is extremely rare, but the one situation that you should be alert to is the change in the predefined type *Character* from 7-bit ASCII to 8-bit Latin-1.

* *Range of type 'Character'*

  The range of *Standard.Character* is now the full 256 characters of Latin-1, whereas in most Ada 83 implementations it was restricted to 128 characters. Although some of the effects of this change will be manifest in compile-time rejection of legal Ada 83 programs it is possible for a working Ada 83 program to have a different effect in Ada 95, one that was not permitted in Ada 83. As an example, the expression *Character'Pos(Character'Last)* returned *127* in Ada 83 and now delivers *255* as its value. In general, you should look at the logic of any character-processing Ada 83 program and see whether it needs to be adapted to work correctly with Latin-1. Note that the predefined Ada 95 API has a character handling package that may be relevant if code needs to be adapted to account for the additional Latin-1 elements. The desirable fix is to modify the program to accommodate the full character set, but in some cases it may be convenient to define a subtype or derived type of Character that covers only the restricted range.

18.2.4 Other language compatibility issues

* *-gnat83* switch

  All implementations of GNAT provide a switch that causes GNAT to operate in Ada 83 mode. In this mode, some but not all compatibility problems of the type described above are handled automatically. For example, the new reserved words introduced in Ada 95 and Ada 2005 are treated simply as identifiers as in Ada 83. However, in practice, it is usually advisable to make the necessary modifications to the program to remove the need for using this switch. See the *Compiling Different Versions of Ada* section in the *GNAT User's Guide.*

* Support for removed Ada 83 pragmas and attributes

  A number of pragmas and attributes from Ada 83 were removed from Ada 95, generally because they were replaced by other mechanisms. Ada 95 and Ada 2005 compilers are allowed, but not required, to implement these missing elements. In contrast with some other compilers, GNAT implements all such pragmas and attributes, eliminating this compatibility concern. These include *pragma Interface* and the floating point type attributes (*Emax*, *Mantissa*, etc.), among other items.

18.3 Compatibility between Ada 95 and Ada 2005

Although Ada 2005 was designed to be upwards compatible with Ada 95, there are a number of incompatibilities. Several are enumerated below; for a complete description please see the *Annotated Ada 2005 Reference Manual*, or section 9.1.1 in *Rationale for Ada 2005.*

* *New reserved words.*

  The words *interface*, *overriding* and *synchronized* are reserved in Ada 2005. A pre-Ada 2005 program that uses any of these as an identifier will be illegal.

* *New declarations in predefined packages.*

  A number of packages in the predefined environment contain new declarations: *Ada.Exceptions*, *Ada.Real_Time*, *Ada.Strings*, *Ada.Strings.Fixed*, *Ada.Strings.Bounded*, *Ada.Strings.Unbounded*, *Ada.Strings.Wide_Fixed*, *Ada.Strings.Wide_Bounded*, *Ada.Strings.Wide_Unbounded*, *Ada.Tags*, *Ada.Text_IO*, and *Interfaces.C*. If an Ada 95 program does a *with* and *use* of any of these packages, the new declarations may cause name clashes.

* *Access parameters.*

  A nondispatching subprogram with an access parameter cannot be renamed as a dispatching operation. This was permitted in Ada 95.

* *Access types, discriminants, and constraints.*

  Rule changes in this area have led to some incompatibilities; for example, constrained subtypes of some access types are not permitted in Ada 2005.

* *Aggregates for limited types.*

  The allowance of aggregates for limited types in Ada 2005 raises the possibility of ambiguities in legal Ada 95 programs, since additional types now need to be considered in expression resolution.

* *Fixed-point multiplication and division.*

  Certain expressions involving '*' or '/' for a fixed-point type, which were legal in Ada 95 and invoked the predefined versions of these operations, are now ambiguous. The ambiguity may be resolved either by applying a type conversion to the expression, or by explicitly invoking the operation from package *Standard*.

* *Return-by-reference types.*

  The Ada 95 return-by-reference mechanism has been removed. Instead, the user can declare a function returning a value from an anonymous access type.

18.4 Implementation-dependent characteristics

Although the Ada language defines the semantics of each construct as precisely as practical, in some situations (for example for reasons of efficiency, or where the effect is heavily dependent on the host or target platform) the implementation is allowed some freedom. In porting Ada 83 code to GNAT, you need to be aware of whether / how the existing code exercised such implementation dependencies. Such characteristics fall into several categories, and GNAT offers specific support in assisting the transition from certain Ada 83 compilers.

18.4.1 Implementation-defined pragmas

Ada compilers are allowed to supplement the language-defined pragmas, and these are a potential source of non-portability. All GNAT-defined pragmas are described in the *Implementation Defined Pragmas* chapter of the *GNAT Reference Manual*, and these include several that are specifically intended to correspond to other vendors' Ada 83 pragmas. For migrating from VADS, the pragma *Use_VADS_Size* may be useful. For compatibility with HP Ada 83, GNAT supplies the pragmas *Extend_System*, *Ident*, *Inline_Generic*, *Interface_Name*, *Passive*, *Suppress_All*, and *Volatile*. Other relevant pragmas include *External* and *Link_With*. Some vendor-specific Ada 83 pragmas (*Share_Generic*, *Subtitle*, and *Title*) are recognized, thus avoiding compiler rejection of units that contain such pragmas; they are not relevant in a GNAT context and hence are not otherwise implemented.

18.4.2 Implementation-defined attributes

Analogous to pragmas, the set of attributes may be extended by an implementation. All GNAT-defined attributes are described in *Implementation Defined Attributes* section of the *GNAT Reference Manual*, and these include several that are specifically intended to correspond to other vendors' Ada 83 attributes. For migrating from VADS, the attribute *VADS_Size* may be useful. For compatibility with HP Ada 83, GNAT supplies the attributes *Bit*, *Machine_Size* and *Type_Class*.

18.4.3 Libraries

Vendors may supply libraries to supplement the standard Ada API. If Ada 83 code uses vendor-specific libraries then there are several ways to manage this in Ada 95 and later versions of the standard:

* If the source code for the libraries (specs and bodies) are available, then the libraries can be migrated in the same way as the application.
* If the source code for the specs but not the bodies are available, then you can reimplement the bodies.
* Some features introduced by Ada 95 obviate the need for library support. For example most Ada 83 vendors supplied a package for unsigned integers. The Ada 95 modular type feature is the preferred way to handle this need, so instead of migrating or reimplementing the unsigned integer package it may be preferable to retrofit the application using modular types.

18.4.4 Elaboration order

The implementation can choose any elaboration order consistent with the unit dependency relationship. This freedom means that some orders can result in Program_Error being raised due to an 'Access Before Elaboration': an attempt to invoke a subprogram before its body has been elaborated, or to instantiate a generic before the generic body has been elaborated. By default GNAT attempts to choose a safe order (one that will not encounter access before elaboration problems) by implicitly inserting *Elaborate* or *Elaborate_All* pragmas where needed. However, this can lead to the creation of elaboration circularities and a resulting rejection of the program by gnatbind. This issue is thoroughly described in the *Elaboration Order Handling in GNAT* appendix in the *GNAT User's Guide*. In brief, there are several ways to deal with this situation:

* Modify the program to eliminate the circularities, e.g., by moving elaboration-time code into explicitly-invoked procedures
* Constrain the elaboration order by including explicit *Elaborate_Body* or *Elaborate* pragmas, and then inhibit the generation of implicit *Elaborate_All* pragmas either globally (as an effect of the *-gnatE* switch) or locally (by selectively suppressing elaboration checks via pragma *Suppress(Elaboration_Check)* when it is safe to do so).

18.4.5 Target-specific aspects

Low-level applications need to deal with machine addresses, data representations, interfacing with assembler code, and similar issues. If such an Ada 83 application is being ported to different target hardware (for example where the byte endianness has changed) then you will need to carefully examine the program logic; the porting effort will heavily depend on the robustness of the original design. Moreover, Ada 95 (and thus Ada 2005 and Ada 2012) are sometimes incompatible with typical Ada 83 compiler practices regarding implicit packing, the meaning of the Size attribute, and the size of access values. GNAT's approach to these issues is described in [Representation Clauses], page 302.

18.5 Compatibility with Other Ada Systems

If programs avoid the use of implementation dependent and implementation defined features, as documented in the *Ada Reference Manual*, there should be a high degree of portability between GNAT and other Ada systems. The following are specific items which have proved troublesome in moving Ada 95 programs from GNAT to other Ada 95 compilers, but do not affect porting code to GNAT. (As of January 2007, GNAT is the only compiler available for Ada 2005; the following issues may or may not arise for Ada 2005 programs when other compilers appear.)

* *Ada 83 Pragmas and Attributes*

  Ada 95 compilers are allowed, but not required, to implement the missing Ada 83 pragmas and attributes that are no longer defined in Ada 95. GNAT implements all such pragmas and attributes, eliminating this as a compatibility concern, but some other Ada 95 compilers reject these pragmas and attributes.

* *Specialized Needs Annexes*

  GNAT implements the full set of special needs annexes. At the current time, it is the only Ada 95 compiler to do so. This means that programs making use of these features may not be portable to other Ada 95 compilation systems.

* *Representation Clauses*

Some other Ada 95 compilers implement only the minimal set of representation clauses required by the Ada 95 reference manual. GNAT goes far beyond this minimal set, as described in the next section.

18.6 Representation Clauses

The Ada 83 reference manual was quite vague in describing both the minimal required implementation of representation clauses, and also their precise effects. Ada 95 (and thus also Ada 2005) are much more explicit, but the minimal set of capabilities required is still quite limited.

GNAT implements the full required set of capabilities in Ada 95 and Ada 2005, but also goes much further, and in particular an effort has been made to be compatible with existing Ada 83 usage to the greatest extent possible.

A few cases exist in which Ada 83 compiler behavior is incompatible with the requirements in Ada 95 (and thus also Ada 2005). These are instances of intentional or accidental dependence on specific implementation dependent characteristics of these Ada 83 compilers. The following is a list of the cases most likely to arise in existing Ada 83 code.

* *Implicit Packing*

  Some Ada 83 compilers allowed a Size specification to cause implicit packing of an array or record. This could cause expensive implicit conversions for change of representation in the presence of derived types, and the Ada design intends to avoid this possibility. Subsequent AI's were issued to make it clear that such implicit change of representation in response to a Size clause is inadvisable, and this recommendation is represented explicitly in the Ada 95 (and Ada 2005) Reference Manuals as implementation advice that is followed by GNAT. The problem will show up as an error message rejecting the size clause. The fix is simply to provide the explicit pragma *Pack*, or for more fine tuned control, provide a Component_Size clause.

* *Meaning of Size Attribute*

  The Size attribute in Ada 95 (and Ada 2005) for discrete types is defined as the minimal number of bits required to hold values of the type. For example, on a 32-bit machine, the size of *Natural* will typically be 31 and not 32 (since no sign bit is required). Some Ada 83 compilers gave 31, and some 32 in this situation. This problem will usually show up as a compile time error, but not always. It is a good idea to check all uses of the 'Size attribute when porting Ada 83 code. The GNAT specific attribute Object_Size can provide a useful way of duplicating the behavior of some Ada 83 compiler systems.

* *Size of Access Types*

  A common assumption in Ada 83 code is that an access type is in fact a pointer, and that therefore it will be the same size as a System.Address value. This assumption is true for GNAT in most cases with one exception. For the case of a pointer to an unconstrained array type (where the bounds may vary from one value of the access type to another), the default is to use a 'fat pointer', which is represented as two separate pointers, one to the bounds, and one to the array. This representation has a number of advantages, including improved efficiency. However, it may cause some difficulties in porting existing Ada 83 code which makes the assumption that, for example, pointers fit in 32 bits on a machine with 32-bit addressing.

To get around this problem, GNAT also permits the use of 'thin pointers' for access types in this case (where the designated type is an unconstrained array type). These thin pointers are indeed the same size as a System.Address value. To specify a thin pointer, use a size clause for the type, for example:

```
type X is access all String;
for X'Size use Standard'Address_Size;
```

which will cause the type X to be represented using a single pointer. When using this representation, the bounds are right behind the array. This representation is slightly less efficient, and does not allow quite such flexibility in the use of foreign pointers or in using the Unrestricted_Access attribute to create pointers to non-aliased objects. But for any standard portable use of the access type it will work in a functionally correct manner and allow porting of existing code. Note that another way of forcing a thin pointer representation is to use a component size clause for the element size in an array, or a record representation clause for an access field in a record.

See the documentation of Unrestricted_Access in the GNAT RM for a full discussion of possible problems using this attribute in conjunction with thin pointers.

18.7 Compatibility with HP Ada 83

All the HP Ada 83 pragmas and attributes are recognized, although only a subset of them can sensibly be implemented. The description of pragmas in [Implementation Defined Pragmas], page 4 indicates whether or not they are applicable to GNAT.

* *Default floating-point representation*

  In GNAT, the default floating-point format is IEEE, whereas in HP Ada 83, it is VMS format.

* *System*

  the package System in GNAT exactly corresponds to the definition in the Ada 95 reference manual, which means that it excludes many of the HP Ada 83 extensions. However, a separate package Aux_DEC is provided that contains the additional definitions, and a special pragma, Extend_System allows this package to be treated transparently as an extension of package System.

19 GNU Free Documentation License

Preamble

The purpose of this License is to make a manual, textbook, or other functional and useful document "free" in the sense of freedom: to assure everyone the effective freedom to copy and redistribute it, with or without modifying it, either commercially or noncommercially. Secondarily, this License preserves for the author and publisher a way to get credit for their work, while not being considered responsible for modifications made by others.

This License is a kind of "copyleft", which means that derivative works of the document must themselves be free in the same sense. It complements the GNU General Public License, which is a copyleft license designed for free software.

We have designed this License in order to use it for manuals for free software, because free software needs free documentation: a free program should come with manuals providing the same freedoms that the software does. But this License is not limited to software manuals; it can be used for any textual work, regardless of subject matter or whether it is published as a printed book. We recommend this License principally for works whose purpose is instruction or reference.

1. APPLICABILITY AND DEFINITIONS

This License applies to any manual or other work, in any medium, that contains a notice placed by the copyright holder saying it can be distributed under the terms of this License. Such a notice grants a world-wide, royalty-free license, unlimited in duration, to use that work under the conditions stated herein. The **Document**, below, refers to any such manual or work. Any member of the public is a licensee, and is addressed as "**you**". You accept the license if you copy, modify or distribute the work in a way requiring permission under copyright law.

A "**Modified Version**" of the Document means any work containing the Document or a portion of it, either copied verbatim, or with modifications and/or translated into another language.

A "**Secondary Section**" is a named appendix or a front-matter section of the Document that deals exclusively with the relationship of the publishers or authors of the Document to the Document's overall subject (or to related matters) and contains nothing that could fall directly within that overall subject. (Thus, if the Document is in part a textbook of mathematics, a Secondary Section may not explain any mathematics.) The relationship could be a matter of historical connection with the subject or with related matters, or of legal, commercial, philosophical, ethical or political position regarding them.

The "**Invariant Sections**" are certain Secondary Sections whose titles are designated, as being those of Invariant Sections, in the notice that says that the Document is released under this License. If a section does not fit the above definition of Secondary then it is not allowed to be designated as Invariant. The Document may contain zero Invariant Sections. If the Document does not identify any Invariant Sections then there are none.

The "**Cover Texts**" are certain short passages of text that are listed, as Front-Cover Texts or Back-Cover Texts, in the notice that says that the Document is released under this License. A Front-Cover Text may be at most 5 words, and a Back-Cover Text may be at most 25 words.

A "**Transparent**" copy of the Document means a machine-readable copy, represented in a format whose specification is available to the general public, that is suitable for revising the document straightforwardly with generic text editors or (for images composed of pixels) generic paint programs or (for drawings) some widely available drawing editor, and that is suitable for input to text formatters or for automatic translation to a variety of formats suitable for input to text formatters. A copy made in an otherwise Transparent file format whose markup, or absence of markup, has been arranged to thwart or discourage subsequent modification by readers is not Transparent. An image format is not Transparent if used for any substantial amount of text. A copy that is not "Transparent" is called **Opaque**.

Examples of suitable formats for Transparent copies include plain ASCII without markup, Texinfo input format, LaTeX input format, SGML or XML using a publicly available DTD, and standard-conforming simple HTML, PostScript or PDF designed for human modification. Examples of transparent image formats include PNG, XCF and JPG. Opaque formats include proprietary formats that can be read and edited only by proprietary word processors, SGML or XML for which the DTD and/or processing tools are not generally available, and the machine-generated HTML, PostScript or PDF produced by some word processors for output purposes only.

The "**Title Page**" means, for a printed book, the title page itself, plus such following pages as are needed to hold, legibly, the material this License requires to appear in the title page. For works in formats which do not have any title page as such, "Title Page" means the text near the most prominent appearance of the work's title, preceding the beginning of the body of the text.

The "**publisher**" means any person or entity that distributes copies of the Document to the public.

A section "**Entitled XYZ**" means a named subunit of the Document whose title either is precisely XYZ or contains XYZ in parentheses following text that translates XYZ in another language. (Here XYZ stands for a specific section name mentioned below, such as "**Acknowledgements**", "**Dedications**", "**Endorsements**", or "**History**".) To "**Preserve the Title**" of such a section when you modify the Document means that it remains a section "Entitled XYZ" according to this definition.

The Document may include Warranty Disclaimers next to the notice which states that this License applies to the Document. These Warranty Disclaimers are considered to be included by reference in this License, but only as regards disclaiming warranties: any other implication that these Warranty Disclaimers may have is void and has no effect on the meaning of this License.

2. VERBATIM COPYING

You may copy and distribute the Document in any medium, either commercially or noncommercially, provided that this License, the copyright notices, and the license notice saying this License applies to the Document are reproduced in all copies, and that you add no other conditions whatsoever to those of this License. You may not use technical measures to obstruct or control the reading or further copying of the copies you make or distribute.

However, you may accept compensation in exchange for copies. If you distribute a large enough number of copies you must also follow the conditions in section 3.

You may also lend copies, under the same conditions stated above, and you may publicly display copies.

3. COPYING IN QUANTITY

If you publish printed copies (or copies in media that commonly have printed covers) of the Document, numbering more than 100, and the Document's license notice requires Cover Texts, you must enclose the copies in covers that carry, clearly and legibly, all these Cover Texts: Front-Cover Texts on the front cover, and Back-Cover Texts on the back cover. Both covers must also clearly and legibly identify you as the publisher of these copies. The front cover must present the full title with all words of the title equally prominent and visible. You may add other material on the covers in addition. Copying with changes limited to the covers, as long as they preserve the title of the Document and satisfy these conditions, can be treated as verbatim copying in other respects.

If the required texts for either cover are too voluminous to fit legibly, you should put the first ones listed (as many as fit reasonably) on the actual cover, and continue the rest onto adjacent pages.

If you publish or distribute Opaque copies of the Document numbering more than 100, you must either include a machine-readable Transparent copy along with each Opaque copy, or state in or with each Opaque copy a computer-network location from which the general network-using public has access to download using public-standard network protocols a complete Transparent copy of the Document, free of added material. If you use the latter option, you must take reasonably prudent steps, when you begin distribution of Opaque copies in quantity, to ensure that this Transparent copy will remain thus accessible at the stated location until at least one year after the last time you distribute an Opaque copy (directly or through your agents or retailers) of that edition to the public.

It is requested, but not required, that you contact the authors of the Document well before redistributing any large number of copies, to give them a chance to provide you with an updated version of the Document.

4. MODIFICATIONS

You may copy and distribute a Modified Version of the Document under the conditions of sections 2 and 3 above, provided that you release the Modified Version under precisely this License, with the Modified Version filling the role of the Document, thus licensing distribution and modification of the Modified Version to whoever possesses a copy of it. In addition, you must do these things in the Modified Version:

A. Use in the Title Page (and on the covers, if any) a title distinct from that of the Document, and from those of previous versions (which should, if there were any, be listed in the History section of the Document). You may use the same title as a previous version if the original publisher of that version gives permission.

B. List on the Title Page, as authors, one or more persons or entities responsible for authorship of the modifications in the Modified Version, together with at least five of the principal authors of the Document (all of its principal authors, if it has fewer than five), unless they release you from this requirement.

C. State on the Title page the name of the publisher of the Modified Version, as the publisher.

D. Preserve all the copyright notices of the Document.
E. Add an appropriate copyright notice for your modifications adjacent to the other copyright notices.
F. Include, immediately after the copyright notices, a license notice giving the public permission to use the Modified Version under the terms of this License, in the form shown in the Addendum below.
G. Preserve in that license notice the full lists of Invariant Sections and required Cover Texts given in the Document's license notice.
H. Include an unaltered copy of this License.
I. Preserve the section Entitled "History", Preserve its Title, and add to it an item stating at least the title, year, new authors, and publisher of the Modified Version as given on the Title Page. If there is no section Entitled "History" in the Document, create one stating the title, year, authors, and publisher of the Document as given on its Title Page, then add an item describing the Modified Version as stated in the previous sentence.
J. Preserve the network location, if any, given in the Document for public access to a Transparent copy of the Document, and likewise the network locations given in the Document for previous versions it was based on. These may be placed in the "History" section. You may omit a network location for a work that was published at least four years before the Document itself, or if the original publisher of the version it refers to gives permission.
K. For any section Entitled "Acknowledgements" or "Dedications", Preserve the Title of the section, and preserve in the section all the substance and tone of each of the contributor acknowledgements and/or dedications given therein.
L. Preserve all the Invariant Sections of the Document, unaltered in their text and in their titles. Section numbers or the equivalent are not considered part of the section titles.
M. Delete any section Entitled "Endorsements". Such a section may not be included in the Modified Version.
N. Do not retitle any existing section to be Entitled "Endorsements" or to conflict in title with any Invariant Section.
O. Preserve any Warranty Disclaimers.

If the Modified Version includes new front-matter sections or appendices that qualify as Secondary Sections and contain no material copied from the Document, you may at your option designate some or all of these sections as invariant. To do this, add their titles to the list of Invariant Sections in the Modified Version's license notice. These titles must be distinct from any other section titles.

You may add a section Entitled "Endorsements", provided it contains nothing but endorsements of your Modified Version by various parties—for example, statements of peer review or that the text has been approved by an organization as the authoritative definition of a standard.

You may add a passage of up to five words as a Front-Cover Text, and a passage of up to 25 words as a Back-Cover Text, to the end of the list of Cover Texts in the Modified Version. Only one passage of Front-Cover Text and one of Back-Cover Text may be added by (or through arrangements made by) any one entity. If the Document already includes a cover text for the same cover, previously added by you or by arrangement made by the same entity you are acting on behalf of, you may not add another; but you may replace the old one, on explicit permission from the previous publisher that added the old one.

The author(s) and publisher(s) of the Document do not by this License give permission to use their names for publicity for or to assert or imply endorsement of any Modified Version.

5. COMBINING DOCUMENTS

You may combine the Document with other documents released under this License, under the terms defined in section 4 above for modified versions, provided that you include in the combination all of the Invariant Sections of all of the original documents, unmodified, and list them all as Invariant Sections of your combined work in its license notice, and that you preserve all their Warranty Disclaimers.

The combined work need only contain one copy of this License, and multiple identical Invariant Sections may be replaced with a single copy. If there are multiple Invariant Sections with the same name but different contents, make the title of each such section unique by adding at the end of it, in parentheses, the name of the original author or publisher of that section if known, or else a unique number. Make the same adjustment to the section titles in the list of Invariant Sections in the license notice of the combined work.

In the combination, you must combine any sections Entitled "History" in the various original documents, forming one section Entitled "History"; likewise combine any sections Entitled "Acknowledgements", and any sections Entitled "Dedications". You must delete all sections Entitled "Endorsements".

6. COLLECTIONS OF DOCUMENTS

You may make a collection consisting of the Document and other documents released under this License, and replace the individual copies of this License in the various documents with a single copy that is included in the collection, provided that you follow the rules of this License for verbatim copying of each of the documents in all other respects.

You may extract a single document from such a collection, and distribute it individually under this License, provided you insert a copy of this License into the extracted document, and follow this License in all other respects regarding verbatim copying of that document.

7. AGGREGATION WITH INDEPENDENT WORKS

A compilation of the Document or its derivatives with other separate and independent documents or works, in or on a volume of a storage or distribution medium, is called an "aggregate" if the copyright resulting from the compilation is not used to limit the legal rights of the compilation's users beyond what the individual works permit. When the Document is included in an aggregate, this License does not apply to the other works in the aggregate which are not themselves derivative works of the Document.

If the Cover Text requirement of section 3 is applicable to these copies of the Document, then if the Document is less than one half of the entire aggregate, the Document's Cover Texts may be placed on covers that bracket the Document within the aggregate, or the electronic equivalent of covers if the Document is in electronic form. Otherwise they must appear on printed covers that bracket the whole aggregate.

8. TRANSLATION

Translation is considered a kind of modification, so you may distribute translations of the Document under the terms of section 4. Replacing Invariant Sections with translations requires special permission from their copyright holders, but you may include translations of some or all Invariant Sections in addition to the original versions of these Invariant Sections. You may include a translation of this License, and all the license notices in the Document, and any Warranty Disclaimers, provided that you also include the original English version of this License and the original versions of those notices and disclaimers. In case of a disagreement between the translation and the original version of this License or a notice or disclaimer, the original version will prevail.

If a section in the Document is Entitled "Acknowledgements", "Dedications", or "History", the requirement (section 4) to Preserve its Title (section 1) will typically require changing the actual title.

9. TERMINATION

You may not copy, modify, sublicense, or distribute the Document except as expressly provided under this License. Any attempt otherwise to copy, modify, sublicense, or distribute it is void, and will automatically terminate your rights under this License.

However, if you cease all violation of this License, then your license from a particular copyright holder is reinstated (a) provisionally, unless and until the copyright holder explicitly and finally terminates your license, and (b) permanently, if the copyright holder fails to notify you of the violation by some reasonable means prior to 60 days after the cessation.

Moreover, your license from a particular copyright holder is reinstated permanently if the copyright holder notifies you of the violation by some reasonable means, this is the first time you have received notice of violation of this License (for any work) from that copyright holder, and you cure the violation prior to 30 days after your receipt of the notice.

Termination of your rights under this section does not terminate the licenses of parties who have received copies or rights from you under this License. If your rights have been terminated and not permanently reinstated, receipt of a copy of some or all of the same material does not give you any rights to use it.

10. FUTURE REVISIONS OF THIS LICENSE

The Free Software Foundation may publish new, revised versions of the GNU Free Documentation License from time to time. Such new versions will be similar in spirit to the present version, but may differ in detail to address new problems or concerns. See `http://www.gnu.org/copyleft/`.

Each version of the License is given a distinguishing version number. If the Document specifies that a particular numbered version of this License "or any later version" applies to it, you have the option of following the terms and conditions either of that specified version or of any later version that has been published (not as a draft) by the Free Software Foundation. If the Document does not specify a version number of this License, you may choose any version ever published (not as a draft) by the Free Software Foundation. If the Document specifies that a proxy can decide which future versions of this License can be used, that proxy's public statement of acceptance of a version permanently authorizes you to choose that version for the Document.

11. RELICENSING

"Massive Multiauthor Collaboration Site" (or "MMC Site") means any World Wide Web server that publishes copyrightable works and also provides prominent facilities for anybody to edit those works. A public wiki that anybody can edit is an example of such a server. A

"Massive Multiauthor Collaboration" (or "MMC") contained in the site means any set of copyrightable works thus published on the MMC site.

"CC-BY-SA" means the Creative Commons Attribution-Share Alike 3.0 license published by Creative Commons Corporation, a not-for-profit corporation with a principal place of business in San Francisco, California, as well as future copyleft versions of that license published by that same organization.

"Incorporate" means to publish or republish a Document, in whole or in part, as part of another Document.

An MMC is "eligible for relicensing" if it is licensed under this License, and if all works that were first published under this License somewhere other than this MMC, and subsequently incorporated in whole or in part into the MMC, (1) had no cover texts or invariant sections, and (2) were thus incorporated prior to November 1, 2008.

The operator of an MMC Site may republish an MMC contained in the site under CC-BY-SA on the same site at any time before August 1, 2009, provided the MMC is eligible for relicensing.

ADDENDUM: How to use this License for your documents

To use this License in a document you have written, include a copy of the License in the document and put the following copyright and license notices just after the title page:

> Copyright © YEAR YOUR NAME. Permission is granted to copy, distribute and/or modify this document under the terms of the GNU Free Documentation License, Version 1.3 or any later version published by the Free Software Foundation; with no Invariant Sections, no Front-Cover Texts, and no Back-Cover Texts. A copy of the license is included in the section entitled "GNU Free Documentation License".

If you have Invariant Sections, Front-Cover Texts and Back-Cover Texts, replace the "with ... Texts." line with this:

> with the Invariant Sections being LIST THEIR TITLES, with the Front-Cover Texts being LIST, and with the Back-Cover Texts being LIST.

If you have Invariant Sections without Cover Texts, or some other combination of the three, merge those two alternatives to suit the situation.

If your document contains nontrivial examples of program code, we recommend releasing these examples in parallel under your choice of free software license, such as the GNU General Public License, to permit their use in free software.

Index

-

-gnat12 option (gcc) 277
-gnatR (gcc) 212

_

___lock file (for shared passive packages) 272

A

Abort_Signal 107
Abstract_State 99
Access 122
Access values 112
Accuracy 164
Accuracy requirements 164
Ada 2005 Language Reference Manual 3
Ada 2012 implementation status 277
Ada 83 attributes 110, 111, 113, 114, 117, 118, 120
Ada 95 Language Reference Manual 3
Ada Extensions 32
Ada.Characters.Handling 155
Ada.Characters.Latin_9 (a-chlat9.ads) 245
Ada.Characters.Wide_Latin_1 (a-cwila1.ads) .. 245
Ada.Characters.Wide_Latin_9 (a-cwila1.ads) .. 245
Ada.Characters.Wide_Wide_Latin_1 (a-chzla1.ads) 246
Ada.Characters.Wide_Wide_Latin_9 (a-chzla9.ads) 246
Ada.Command_Line.Environment (a-colien.ads) 248
Ada.Command_Line.Remove (a-colire.ads) 248
Ada.Command_Line.Response_File (a-clrefi.ads) 248
Ada.Containers.Bounded_Holders (a-coboho.ads) 247
Ada.Containers.Formal_Doubly_Linked_Lists (a-cfdlli.ads) 246
Ada.Containers.Formal_Hashed_Maps (a-cfhama.ads) 246
Ada.Containers.Formal_Hashed_Sets (a-cfhase.ads) 246
Ada.Containers.Formal_Indefinite_Vectors (a-cfinve.ads) 247
Ada.Containers.Formal_Ordered_Maps (a-cforma.ads) 247
Ada.Containers.Formal_Ordered_Sets (a-cforse.ads) 247
Ada.Containers.Formal_Vectors (a-cofove.ads) 247
Ada.Direct_IO.C_Streams (a-diocst.ads) 248
Ada.Exceptions.Is_Null_Occurrence (a-einuoc.ads) 248
Ada.Exceptions.Last_Chance_Handler (a-elchha.ads) 248
Ada.Exceptions.Traceback (a-exctra.ads) 248
Ada.Sequential_IO.C_Streams (a-siocst.ads) ... 248
Ada.Streams.Stream_IO.C_Streams (a-ssicst.ads) 248
Ada.Strings.Unbounded.Text_IO (a-suteio.ads) 249
Ada.Strings.Wide_Unbounded.Wide_Text_IO (a-swuwti.ads) 249
Ada.Strings.Wide_Wide_Unbounded.Wide_Wide_Text_IO (a-szuzti.ads) 249
Ada.Text_IO.C_Streams (a-tiocst.ads) 249
Ada.Text_IO.Reset_Standard_Files (a-tirsfi.ads) 249
Ada.Wide_Characters.Unicode (a-wichun.ads) 249
Ada.Wide_Text_IO.C_Streams (a-wtcstr.ads) 249
Ada.Wide_Text_IO.Reset_Standard_Files (a-wrstfi.ads) 249
Ada.Wide_Wide_Characters.Unicode (a-zchuni.ads) 250
Ada.Wide_Wide_Text_IO.C_Streams (a-ztcstr.ads) 250
Ada.Wide_Wide_Text_IO.Reset_Standard_Files (a-zrstfi.ads) 250
Ada_2012 configuration pragma 277
Address 153
Address Clause 205
Address clauses 150
Address image 261
Address of subprogram code 108
Address_Size 107
AI-0002 (Ada 2012 feature) 292
AI-0003 (Ada 2012 feature) 280
AI-0007 (Ada 2012 feature) 290
AI-0008 (Ada 2012 feature) 280
AI-0009 (Ada 2012 feature) 287
AI-0012 (Ada 2012 feature) 289
AI-0015 (Ada 2012 feature) 285
AI-0017 (Ada 2012 feature) 291
AI-0019 (Ada 2012 feature) 291
AI-0026 (Ada 2012 feature) 286
AI-0030 (Ada 2012 feature) 287
AI-0031 (Ada 2012 feature) 291
AI-0032 (Ada 2012 feature) 285
AI-0033 (Ada 2012 feature) 290
AI-0034 (Ada 2012 feature) 288
AI-0035 (Ada 2012 feature) 288
AI-0037 (Ada 2012 feature) 283
AI-0038 (Ada 2012 feature) 292
AI-0039 (Ada 2012 feature) 289
AI-0040 (Ada 2012 feature) 288
AI-0042 (Ada 2012 feature) 286

AI-0043 (Ada 2012 feature) 288
AI-0044 (Ada 2012 feature) 292
AI-0046 (Ada 2012 feature) 285
AI-0050 (Ada 2012 feature) 285
AI-0056 (Ada 2012 feature) 291
AI-0058 (Ada 2012 feature) 285
AI-0060 (Ada 2012 feature) 291
AI-0062 (Ada 2012 feature) 286
AI-0064 (Ada 2012 feature) 286
AI-0065 (Ada 2012 feature) 291
AI-0070 (Ada 2012 feature) 282
AI-0072 (Ada 2012 feature) 287
AI-0073 (Ada 2012 feature) 282
AI-0076 (Ada 2012 feature) 282
AI-0077 (Ada 2012 feature) 287
AI-0078 (Ada 2012 feature) 289
AI-0079 (Ada 2012 feature) 277
AI-0080 (Ada 2012 feature) 278
AI-0087 (Ada 2012 feature) 286
AI-0088 (Ada 2012 feature) 284
AI-0091 (Ada 2012 feature) 277
AI-0093 (Ada 2012 feature) 281
AI-0095 (Ada 2012 feature) 289
AI-0096 (Ada 2012 feature) 281
AI-0097 (Ada 2012 feature) 282
AI-0098 (Ada 2012 feature) 283
AI-0099 (Ada 2012 feature) 286
AI-0100 (Ada 2012 feature) 277
AI-0102 (Ada 2012 feature) 281
AI-0103 (Ada 2012 feature) 285
AI-0104 (Ada 2012 feature) 284
AI-0106 (Ada 2012 feature) 289
AI-0108 (Ada 2012 feature) 287
AI-0109 (Ada 2012 feature) 290
AI-0112 (Ada 2012 feature) 288
AI-0114 (Ada 2012 feature) 291
AI-0116 (Ada 2012 feature) 289
AI-0118 (Ada 2012 feature) 285
AI-0120 (Ada 2012 feature) 280
AI-0122 (Ada 2012 feature) 288
AI-0123 (Ada 2012 feature) 283
AI-0125 (Ada 2012 feature) 285
AI-0126 (Ada 2012 feature) 282
AI-0127 (Ada 2012 feature) 292
AI-0128 (Ada 2012 feature) 280
AI-0129 (Ada 2012 feature) 287
AI-0132 (Ada 2012 feature) 288
AI-0134 (Ada 2012 feature) 284
AI-0137 (Ada 2012 feature) 292
AI-0139-2 (Ada 2012 feature) 284
AI-0146 (Ada 2012 feature) 289
AI-0147 (Ada 2012 feature) 283
AI-0152 (Ada 2012 feature) 293
AI-0157 (Ada 2012 feature) 284
AI-0158 (Ada 2012 feature) 281
AI-0161 (Ada 2012 feature) 290
AI-0162 (Ada 2012 feature) 283
AI-0163 (Ada 2012 feature) 277
AI-0171 (Ada 2012 feature) 293
AI-0173 (Ada 2012 feature) 281
AI-0176 (Ada 2012 feature) 277
AI-0177 (Ada 2012 feature) 290
AI-0178 (Ada 2012 feature) 286
AI-0179 (Ada 2012 feature) 284
AI-0181 (Ada 2012 feature) 281
AI-0182 (Ada 2012 feature) 281
AI-0183 (Ada 2012 feature) 278
AI-0185 (Ada 2012 feature) 291
AI-0188 (Ada 2012 feature) 284
AI-0189 (Ada 2012 feature) 293
AI-0190 (Ada 2012 feature) 293
AI-0193 (Ada 2012 feature) 290
AI-0194 (Ada 2012 feature) 290
AI-0195 (Ada 2012 feature) 289
AI-0196 (Ada 2012 feature) 285
AI-0198 (Ada 2012 feature) 282
AI-0199 (Ada 2012 feature) 283
AI-0200 (Ada 2012 feature) 288
AI-0201 (Ada 2012 feature) 287
AI-0203 (Ada 2012 feature) 282
AI-0205 (Ada 2012 feature) 286
AI-0206 (Ada 2012 feature) 293
AI-0207 (Ada 2012 feature) 284
AI-0208 (Ada 2012 feature) 282
AI-0210 (Ada 2012 feature) 293
AI-0211 (Ada 2012 feature) 293
AI-0214 (Ada 2012 feature) 281
AI-0219 (Ada 2012 feature) 288
AI-0220 (Ada 2012 feature) 283
AI05-0216 (Ada 2012 feature) 292
Alignment 57, 114, 121, 186
Alignment Clause 185
Alignment clauses 150
Alignments of components 18
allocator 121
Alternative Character Sets 146
AltiVec 250
Annex E 271
Annotate 99
Anonymous access types 211
Argument passing mechanisms 28
argument removal 248
Array packing 37
Array splitter 250
Arrays 147, 254, 259
as private type 153
Asm_Input 107
Asm_Output 107
Assert_Failure 261
Assertions 13, 15, 261
Async_Readers 100
Async_Writers 100
Atomic Synchronization 25, 27
Atomic_Always_Lock_Free 108
Attribute 206
Attribute Loop_Entry 88

Attribute Old ... 88
AWK ... 251

B

Biased representation ... 190
Big endian ... 109
Bind environment ... 251
Bit ... 108
bit ordering ... 194
Bit ordering ... 153
Bit_Order Clause ... 194
Bit_Position ... 108
Boolean_Entry_Barriers ... 138
Bounded Buffers ... 251
Bounded errors ... 145
Bounded-length strings ... 155
Bubble sort ... 251
byte ordering ... 195
Byte swapping ... 251

C

C ... 157
C streams ... 261
C Streams ... 248, 249, 250
Calendar ... 252
casing ... 33
Casing of External names ... 33
Casing utilities ... 252
CGI (Common Gateway Interface) ... 252
CGI (Common Gateway Interface) cookie support ... 252
CGI (Common Gateway Interface) debugging ... 252
Character handling ('GNAT.Case_Util') ... 252
Character Sets ... 146
Check names ... 15
Check pragma control ... 15
Checks ... 62, 64, 65, 67, 148
Child Units ... 145
COBOL ... 158
COBOL support ... 162
Code_Address ... 108
Command line ... 248, 252
Compatibility (between Ada 83 and Ada 95 / Ada 2005 / Ada 2012) ... 296
Compatibility between Ada 95 and Ada 2005 .. 299
Compilation_Date ... 182
Compilation_Time ... 182
Compiler Version ... 252
Compiler_Version ... 109
complex arithmetic ... 164
Complex arithmetic accuracy ... 164
Complex elementary functions ... 163
Complex types ... 162
Component Clause ... 202
Component_Size (in pragma Component_Alignment) ... 18
Component_Size Clause ... 193
Component_Size clauses ... 151
Component_Size_4 (in pragma Component_Alignment) ... 19
configuration pragma Ada_2012 ... 277
Constant_After_Elaboration ... 100
Constrained ... 109
Contract cases ... 19
Contract_Cases ... 100
control ... 15
Controlling assertions ... 15
Convention ... 210
Convention for anonymous access types ... 211
Conventions ... 3, 21
Conversion ... 263
Cookie support in CGI ... 252
CRC32 ... 252
Current exception ... 253
Current time ... 260
Cyclic Redundancy Check ... 252

D

Debug pools ... 253
Debugging ... 253, 254
debugging with Initialize_Scalars ... 41
DEC Ada 83 ... 31
Dec Ada 83 casing compatibility ... 33
Decimal radix support ... 162
Decoding strings ... 253
Decoding UTF-8 strings ... 253
default ... 186
Default (in pragma Component_Alignment) 19
default settings ... 57
Default_Bit_Order ... 109
Default_Initial_Condition ... 100
Default_Scalar_Storage_Order ... 23, 109
Default_Storage_Pool ... 24
Deferring aborts ... 5
defining ... 15
Defining check names ... 15
Depends ... 100
Deref ... 109
Descriptor ... 109
Descriptor_Size ... 109
determination of ... 212
Dimension ... 100
Dimension_System ... 101
Directory operations ... 253
Directory operations iteration ... 253
Disable_Controlled ... 101
Discriminants ... 112
Distribution Systems Annex ... 271
Dope vector ... 109
Dump Memory ... 256
Duration'Small ... 148

E

effect on representation 210
Effective_Reads 102
Effective_Writes 102
Elab_Body 110
Elab_Spec 110
Elab_Subp_Body 110
Elaborated 110
Elaboration control 26
Elimination of unused subprograms 26
Emax 110
Enabled 110
Enclosing_Entity 183
Encoding strings 254
Encoding UTF-8 strings 254
Endianness 118, 251
Entry queuing policies 161
Enum_Rep 111
Enum_Val 111
enumeration 152
Enumeration representation clauses 152
Enumeration values 147
Environment entries 248
Epsilon 111
Error detection 145
exception 66, 261
Exception 256
Exception actions 254
Exception information 148
Exception retrieval 253
Exception traces 254
Exception_Information' 183
Exception_Message 66, 183
Exception_Name 183
exceptions 254
Exceptions 254
Export 156, 206
extendable 254, 259
extending 31
extensions for unbounded strings 249
extensions for unbounded wide strings 249
extensions for unbounded wide wide strings 249
Extensions_Visible 102
External Names 33

F

Fast_Math 111
Favor_Top_Level 102
File 183
File locking 256
Fixed_Value 112
Float types 147
Floating-point overflow 14
Floating-Point Processor 255
foreign 260
Foreign threads 260
Forking a new process 271
Formal container for doubly linked lists 246
Formal container for hashed maps 246
Formal container for hashed sets 246
Formal container for ordered maps 247
Formal container for ordered sets 247
Formal container for vectors 247
Formatted String 255
Fortran 158
From_Any 112

G

Get_Immediate 156, 231, 261
Ghost 102
global 262
Global 102
Global storage pool 262
GNAT Extensions 32
GNAT.Altivec (g-altive.ads) 250
GNAT.Altivec.Conversions (g-altcon.ads) 250
GNAT.Altivec.Vector_Operations (g-alveop.ads) .. 250
GNAT.Altivec.Vector_Types (g-alvety.ads) 250
GNAT.Altivec.Vector_Views (g-alvevi.ads) 250
GNAT.Array_Split (g-arrspl.ads) 250
GNAT.AWK (g-awk.ads) 251
GNAT.Bind_Environment (g-binenv.ads) 251
GNAT.Bounded_Buffers (g-boubuf.ads) 251
GNAT.Bounded_Mailboxes (g-boumai.ads) 251
GNAT.Bubble_Sort (g-bubsor.ads) 251
GNAT.Bubble_Sort_A (g-busora.ads) 251
GNAT.Bubble_Sort_G (g-busorg.ads) 251
GNAT.Byte_Order_Mark (g-byorma.ads) 251
GNAT.Byte_Swapping (g-bytswa.ads) 251
GNAT.Calendar (g-calend.ads) 252
GNAT.Calendar.Time_IO (g-catiio.ads) 252
GNAT.Case_Util (g-casuti.ads) 252
GNAT.CGI (g-cgi.ads) 252
GNAT.CGI.Cookie (g-cgicoo.ads) 252
GNAT.CGI.Debug (g-cgideb.ads) 252
GNAT.Command_Line (g-comlin.ads) 252
GNAT.Compiler_Version (g-comver.ads) 252
GNAT.CRC32 (g-crc32.ads) 252
GNAT.Ctrl_C (g-ctrl_c.ads) 253
GNAT.Current_Exception (g-curexc.ads) 253
GNAT.Debug_Pools (g-debpoo.ads) 253
GNAT.Debug_Utilities (g-debuti.ads) 253
GNAT.Decode_String (g-decstr.ads) 253
GNAT.Decode_UTF8_String (g-deutst.ads) 253
GNAT.Directory_Operations (g-dirope.ads) 253
GNAT.Directory_Operations.Iteration (g-diopit.ads) ... 253
GNAT.Dynamic_HTables (g-dynhta.ads) 253
GNAT.Dynamic_Tables (g-dyntab.ads) 254
GNAT.Encode_String (g-encstr.ads) 254
GNAT.Encode_UTF8_String (g-enutst.ads) 254
GNAT.Exception_Actions (g-excact.ads) 254
GNAT.Exception_Traces (g-exctra.ads) 254

GNAT.Exceptions (g-expect.ads) 254
GNAT.Expect (g-expect.ads) 254
GNAT.Expect.TTY (g-exptty.ads) 254
GNAT.Float_Control (g-flocon.ads) 255
GNAT.Formatted_String (g-forstr.ads) 255
GNAT.Heap_Sort (g-heasor.ads) 255
GNAT.Heap_Sort_A (g-hesora.ads) 255
GNAT.Heap_Sort_G (g-hesorg.ads) 255
GNAT.HTable (g-htable.ads) 255
GNAT.IO (g-io.ads) 255
GNAT.IO_Aux (g-io_aux.ads) 255
GNAT.Lock_Files (g-locfil.ads) 256
GNAT.MBBS_Discrete_Random (g-mbdira.ads) 256
GNAT.MBBS_Float_Random (g-mbflra.ads) .. 256
GNAT.MD5 (g-md5.ads) 256
GNAT.Memory_Dump (g-memdum.ads) 256
GNAT.Most_Recent_Exception (g-moreex.ads) 256
GNAT.OS_Lib (g-os_lib.ads) 256
GNAT.Perfect_Hash_Generators (g-pehage.ads) 256
GNAT.Random_Numbers (g-rannum.ads) 256
GNAT.Regexp (g-regexp.ads) 257
GNAT.Registry (g-regist.ads) 257
GNAT.Regpat (g-regpat.ads) 257
GNAT.Rewrite_Data (g-rewdat.ads) 257
GNAT.Secondary_Stack_Info (g-sestin.ads) 257
GNAT.Semaphores (g-semaph.ads) 257
GNAT.Serial_Communications (g-sercom.ads) 257
GNAT.SHA1 (g-sha1.ads) 257
GNAT.SHA224 (g-sha224.ads) 257
GNAT.SHA256 (g-sha256.ads) 258
GNAT.SHA384 (g-sha384.ads) 258
GNAT.SHA512 (g-sha512.ads) 258
GNAT.Signals (g-signal.ads) 258
GNAT.Sockets (g-socket.ads) 258
GNAT.Source_Info (g-souinf.ads) 258
GNAT.Spelling_Checker (g-speche.ads) 258
GNAT.Spelling_Checker_Generic (g-spchge.ads) 258
GNAT.Spitbol (g-spitbo.ads) 259
GNAT.Spitbol.Patterns (g-spipat.ads) 258
GNAT.Spitbol.Table_Boolean (g-sptabo.ads) .. 259
GNAT.Spitbol.Table_Integer (g-sptain.ads) ... 259
GNAT.Spitbol.Table_VString (g-sptavs.ads) .. 259
GNAT.SSE (g-sse.ads) 259
GNAT.SSE.Vector_Types (g-ssvety.ads) 259
GNAT.String_Split (g-strspl.ads) 259
GNAT.Strings (g-string.ads) 259
GNAT.Table (g-table.ads) 259
GNAT.Task_Lock (g-tasloc.ads) 260
GNAT.Threads (g-thread.ads) 260
GNAT.Time_Stamp (g-timsta.ads) 260
GNAT.Traceback (g-traceb.ads) 260
GNAT.Traceback.Symbolic (g-trasym.ads) 260
GNAT.UTF_32 (g-table.ads) 260
GNAT.Wide_Spelling_Checker (g-u3spch.ads) 260
GNAT.Wide_Spelling_Checker (g-wispch.ads) 260
GNAT.Wide_String_Split (g-wistsp.ads)....... 260
GNAT.Wide_Wide_Spelling_Checker (g-zspche.ads)........................... 261
GNAT.Wide_Wide_String_Split (g-zistsp.ads) 261

H

handling long command lines 248
Handling of Records with Holes............... 203
Has_Access_Values 112
Has_Discriminants............................ 112
Hash functions 256
Hash tables.............................. 253, 255
Heap usage.................................... 154

I

I/O interfacing 261
IBM Packed Format.......................... 261
Image 261
Img 112
Immediate_Reclamation 128
Implementation-dependent features 2
implicit 154
Import 206
Initial_Condition 102
Initialization 84
Initializes 102
Inline_Always 102
Input/Output facilities 255
Integer maps 259
Integer types 147
Integer_Value................................. 113
Interfaces 156
Interfaces.C.Extensions (i-cexten.ads) 261
Interfaces.C.Streams (i-cstrea.ads) 261
Interfaces.Packed_Decimal (i-pacdec.ads)...... 261
Interfaces.VxWorks (i-vxwork.ads) 261
Interfaces.VxWorks.IO (i-vxwoio.ads) 261
interfacing.................................... 261
Interfacing to C++ 22, 70
Interfacing to VxWorks....................... 261
Interfacing to VxWorks' I/O.................. 261
interfacing with......................... 157, 158
Interfacing with 'Text_IO' 249
Interfacing with 'Wide_Text_IO' 249
Interfacing with 'Wide_Wide_Text_IO' 250
Interfacing with C++ 21, 22
Interfacing with Direct_IO 248
Interfacing with Sequential_IO 248
Interfacing with Stream_IO 248
Interrupt 253
Interrupt support............................. 159

Interrupts 160
Intrinsic operator 182
Intrinsic Subprograms 182
Invalid representations 12
Invalid values 12
Invalid_Value 113
Invariant 102
Invariant'Class 102
IO support 249
Iterable 102, 113

L

Large 113
Latin-1 298
Latin_1 constants for Wide_Character 245
Latin_1 constants for Wide_Wide_Character .. 246
Latin_9 constants for Character 245
Latin_9 constants for Wide_Character 245
Latin_9 constants for Wide_Wide_Character .. 246
Library_Level 113
License checking 45
Line 183
Linker_Section 103
Little endian 109
local 262
Local storage pool 262
Lock_Free 103, 113
Locking 260
Locking Policies 161
Locking using files 256
Loop_Entry 114

M

Machine Code insertions 268
Machine operations 158
Machine_Size 114
Mailboxes 251
Mantissa 114
Maps 259
Max_Asynchronous_Select_Nesting 128
Max_Entry_Queue_Depth 128
Max_Entry_Queue_Length 128
Max_Protected_Entries 128
Max_Select_Alternatives 128
Max_Storage_At_Blocking 129
Max_Task_Entries 129
Max_Tasks 129
maximum 114
Maximum_Alignment 114
Maximum_Alignment attribute 185
Mechanism_Code 114
Memory allocation 262
Memory corruption debugging 253
Memory-mapped I/O 209
Message Digest MD5 256
monotonic 161
multidimensional 147
Multidimensional arrays 147
Multiprocessor interface 262

N

Named assertions 13, 15
Named numbers 122
No_Abort_Statements 129
No_Access_Parameter_Allocators 129
No_Access_Subprograms 129
No_Allocators 129
No_Anonymous_Allocators 129
No_Asynchronous_Control 129
No_Calendar 129
No_Coextensions 129
No_Default_Initialization 130
No_Delay 130
No_Dependence 130
No_Direct_Boolean_Operators 130
No_Dispatch 130
No_Dispatching_Calls 130
No_Dynamic_Attachment 131
No_Dynamic_Interrupts 131
No_Dynamic_Priorities 131
No_Dynamic_Sized_Objects 139
No_Elaboration_Code 138
No_Elaboration_Code_All 103
No_Entry_Calls_In_Elaboration_Code 131
No_Entry_Queue 139
No_Enumeration_Maps 132
No_Exception_Handlers 132
No_Exception_Propagation 132
No_Exception_Registration 132
No_Exceptions 132
No_Finalization 132
No_Fixed_Point 133
No_Floating_Point 133
No_Implementation_Aspect_Specifications 139
No_Implementation_Attributes 139
No_Implementation_Identifiers 140
No_Implementation_Pragmas 140
No_Implementation_Restrictions 140
No_Implementation_Units 140
No_Implicit_Aliasing 140
No_Implicit_Conditionals 133
No_Implicit_Dynamic_Code 133
No_Implicit_Heap_Allocations 133
No_Implicit_Loops 134
No_Implicit_Protected_Object_Allocations 134
No_Implicit_Task_Allocations 134
No_Initialize_Scalars 134
No_IO 134
No_Local_Allocators 134
No_Local_Protected_Objects 134
No_Local_Timing_Events 134
No_Long_Long_Integers 134
No_Multiple_Elaboration 134

No_Nested_Finalization 135
No_Obsolescent_Features 140
No_Protected_Type_Allocators 135
No_Protected_Types 135
No_Recursion 135
No_Reentrancy 135
No_Relative_Delay 135
No_Requeue 135
No_Requeue_Statements 135
No_Secondary_Stack 135
No_Select_Statements 135
No_Specific_Termination_Handlers 136
No_Specification_of_Aspect 136
No_Standard_Allocators_After_Elaboration ... 136
No_Standard_Storage_Pools 136
No_Stream_Optimizations 136
No_Streams 136
No_Tagged_Streams 103
No_Task_Allocators 136
No_Task_At_Interrupt_Priority 136
No_Task_Attributes 136
No_Task_Attributes_Package 136
No_Task_Hierarchy 137
No_Task_Termination 137
No_Tasking 137
No_Terminate_Alternatives 137
No_Unchecked_Access 137
No_Unchecked_Conversion 137
No_Unchecked_Deallocation 137
No_Use_Of_Entity 137
No_Wide_Characters 140
Null_Occurrence 248
Null_Parameter 114
Numerics 162

O

Object_Size 103, 115, 190
Obsolsecent 104
obtaining most recent 256
of an address 261
of bits 194
of bytes 195
of compiler 252
of objects 190
Old 116
on 'Address' 153
Operating System interface 256
Operations 153
operations of 153
ordering 194, 195
Overlaying of objects 207

P

Package 'Interrupts' 160
Package Interfaces 156
Package Task_Attributes 160
Packed Decimal 261
Packed types 149
Parameters 114, 116
Parsing 251
Part_Of 104
Partition communication subsystem 162
Partition interfacing functions 262
Passed_By_Reference 116
passing 114
Passing by copy 13
passing mechanism 114
Pattern matching 257, 258
PCS 162
Persistent_BSS 104
Pool_Address 116
Portability 2
Post 62, 64
Postcondition 62
postconditions 62, 64
Pragma 185
pragma Ada_2012 277
Pragma Component_Alignment 18
Pragma Pack (for arrays) 199
Pragma Pack (for records) 201
Pragma Pack (for type Natural) 200
Pragma Pack warning 200
pragma Shared_Passive 271
Pragmas 145
Pre 64
Pre-elaboration requirements 160
Pre_Class 67
preconditions 64, 65, 67
Preconditions 65
Predicate 104
Preemptive abort 161
Prefix_Exception_Messages 66
Protected procedure handlers 160
Pure 254
Pure packages 254
Pure_Barriers 137
Pure_Function 104

R

Random number generation 155, 256
Range_Length 116
Rational compatibility 60
Rational profile 60, 92
Rational Profile 37
Read attribute 155
Real-Time Systems Annex compliance 271
Record Representation Clause 202
Record representation clauses 152
records 152
Refined_Depends 104
Refined_Global 104
Refined_Post 104
Refined_State 104

Regular expressions 257
Remote_Access_Type 104
Removing command line arguments 248
representation 185
Representation 212, 263
Representation Clause 185
Representation clauses 149, 152
Representation Clauses 185
representation of 122
Representation of enums 111
Representation of wide characters 263
Representation Pragma 185
response file 248
Response file for command line 248
Restriction_Set 116
Restrictions 116
Restrictions definitions 262
Result 117
Return values 114
Rewrite data 257
Rotate_Left 183
Rotate_Right 183
Run-time restrictions access 262

S

Safe_Emax 117
Safe_Large 117
Safe_Small 118
Scalar storage order 118
Scalar_Storage_Order 23, 104, 118
Secondary Stack Info 257
Secure Hash Algorithm SHA-1 257
Secure Hash Algorithm SHA-224 257
Secure Hash Algorithm SHA-256 258
Secure Hash Algorithm SHA-384 258
Secure Hash Algorithm SHA-512 258
Semaphores 257
Sequential elaboration policy 164
Serial_Communications 257
Sets of strings 259
setting for not-first subtype 127
Shared 104
Shared passive packages 271
SHARED_MEMORY_DIRECTORY environment variable 272
Shift operators 70
Shift_Left 183
Shift_Right 183
Shift_Right_Arithmetic 183
Signals 258
simple 76, 119
Simple I/O 255
Simple storage pool 76, 119
Simple_Barriers 138
Simple_Storage_Pool 105, 119
Simple_Storage_Pool_Type 105
size 188
Size 92, 115, 127, 188, 190
Size Clause 186
Size clauses 151
Size for biased representation 190
Size of 'Address' 107
Small 120
Sockets 258
Sorting 251, 255
Source Information 258
Source_Location 184
SPARK 140
SPARK_05 140
SPARK_Mode 105
Spawn capability 256
Spell checking 258, 260, 261
SPITBOL interface 259
SPITBOL pattern matching 258
SPITBOL Tables 259
Static_Priorities 138
Static_Storage_Size 138
Storage place attributes 153
Storage pool 76, 119, 262
Storage_Size Clause 187
Storage_Unit 120
Storage_Unit (in pragma Component_Alignment) 19
Stream files 231
Stream operations 263
Stream oriented attributes 154, 155
String decoding 253
String encoding 254
String maps 259
String splitter 259
String stream operations 263
Stub_Type 120
Subprogram address 108
subtypes 186
Suppress_Debug_Info 105
Suppress_Initialization 105
Suppressing external name 29, 30, 31
Suppressing initialization 84
suppression of 84, 148
Suppression of checks 148
synonyms 21
System 31
System.Address_Image (s-addima.ads) 261
System.Assertions (s-assert.ads) 261
System.Atomic_Counters (s-atocou.ads) 261
System.Memory (s-memory.ads) 262
System.Multiprocessors (s-multip.ads) 262
System.Multiprocessors.Dispatching_Domains (s-mudido.ads) 262
System.Partition_Interface (s-parint.ads) 262
System.Pool_Global (s-pooglo.ads) 262
System.Pool_Local (s-pooloc.ads) 262
System.Restrictions (s-restri.ads) 262
System.Rident (s-rident.ads) 262
System.Strings.Stream_Ops (s-ststop.ads) 263

System.Unsigned_Types (s-unstyp.ads) 263
System.Wch_Cnv (s-wchcnv.ads) 263
System.Wch_Con (s-wchcon.ads) 263
System_Allocator_Alignment 121

T

Table implementation 254, 259
Target_Name 121
Task locking 260
Task specific storage 87
Task synchronization 260
Task_Attributes 87, 160
Tasking restrictions 161
Test cases 86
Test_Case 105
testing for 112, 248
Text_IO 249, 255
Text_IO extensions 231
Text_IO for unbounded strings 231
Text_IO operations 231
Text_IO resetting standard files 249
Thread_Local_Storage 105
Threads 260
Time 161, 252
Time stamp 260
TLS (Thread Local Storage) 87
To_Address 121, 206
To_Any 121
Trace back facilities 260
Traceback for Exception Occurrence 248
trampoline 133
Type_Class 121
Type_Key 122
TypeCode 122
typographical 3
Typographical conventions 3

U

Unbounded_String 231, 249
Unbounded_Wide_String 249
Unbounded_Wide_Wide_String 249
Unchecked conversion 153
Unchecked deallocation 154
Unconstrained_Array 122
Unevaluated_Use_Of_Old 88
Unicode 253, 254
Unicode categorization 249, 250
Unions in C 88
Universal_Aliasing 105
Universal_Data 105
Universal_Literal_String 122
unmodified 90
Unmodified 105
unreferenced 90, 91
Unreferenced 105
Unreferenced_Objects 105
unrestricted 122
Unrestricted_Access 122
Update 125
used for objects 115
UTF-8 .... 253, 254
UTF-8 representation 251
UTF-8 string decoding 253
UTF-8 string encoding 254

V

VADS compatibility 92, 127
VADS_Size 127
Valid_Scalars 126
Value_Size 105, 127, 190
variant record objects 188
Variant record objects 188
Version 252
Volatile_Full_Access 106
Volatile_Function 106
VxWorks 261

W

Warnings 90, 91, 106
Wchar_T_Size 127
when passed by reference 116
Wide characte representations 251
Wide Character 263
Wide character codes 260
Wide character decoding 253
Wide character encoding 253, 254
Wide String 263
Wide_Character 249
Wide_String splitter 260
Wide_Text_IO resetting standard files 249
Wide_Wide_Character 250
Wide_Wide_String splitter 261
Wide_Wide_Text_IO resetting standard files .. 250
Windows Registry 257
Word_Size 127
Write attribute 155

X

XDR representation 155

Z

Zero address 114

www.ingramcontent.com/pod-product-compliance
Lightning Source LLC
Chambersburg PA
CBHW062348220526
45472CB00008B/1735
9789888406371